BIBLE AND SWORD

By Barbara W. Tuchman

BIBLE AND SWORD (1956)

THE ZIMMERMANN TELEGRAM (1958)

THE GUNS OF AUGUST (1962)

THE PROUD TOWER (1966)

STILWELL AND THE AMERICAN EXPERIENCE IN CHINA (1971)

NOTES FROM CHINA (1972)

A DISTANT MIRROR (1978)

PRACTICING HISTORY (1981)

THE MARCH OF FOLLY (1984)

THE FIRST SALUTE (1988)

Barbara W. Tuchman

BIBLE AND SWORD

England and Palestine from the

Bronze Age to Balfour

BALLANTINE BOOKS • NEW YORK

Copyright © 1956 by New York University Press. Copyright renewed 1984 by Barbara W. Tuchman

Preface copyright © 1984 by Barbara W. Tuchman

All rights reserved under International and Pan-American Copyright Conventions. Published in the United States by Ballantine Books, a division of Random House, Inc., New York, and simultaneously in Canada by Random House of Canada Limited, Toronto.

Preface originally published in German in *Bibel und Schwert: Palästina und der Westen vom frühen Mittelalter bis zur Balfour-Declaration 1917* by S. Fischer Verlag GmbH, Frankfurt. Copyright © 1983 by S. Fischer Verlag GmbH.

Reprinted from the original edition of 1956

http://www.randomhouse.com

Library of Congress Catalog Card Number: 83-91154

ISBN: 0-345-31427-1

This edition published by arrangement with the author.

Manufactured in the United States of America

First Ballantine Books Trade Edition: March 1984

20 19 18 17 16 15 14

In Memory of my Parents

Alma Morgenthau and

Maurice Wertheim

"No other problem of our time is rooted so deeply in the past." [REPORT OF THE ROYAL PALESTINE COMMISSION OF INQUIRY, 1937]

CONTENTS

PREFACE TO THE 1983–1984 EDITION

Inspired by the re-creation of the state of Israel, work on this book was begun thirty-five years ago in 1948 and it was originally published eight years later in 1956. The prolonged gestation was owed partly to the necessity of dividing my time with three young children, the youngest born in 1948, and partly, after the book was finished, to the reluctance of publishers to take a chance on an unknown author and a rather eccentric subject. The unknown and untried do not commonly find publishers eagerly waiting to invest in their efforts. Eventually, New York University Press decided to make the venture and I am happy to record here my thanks to them for the confidence that resulted in my first published book.

The reestablishment of the state of Israel in the same land with the same people and same language after 1900 years of exile seemed to me a unique historical event. I could not think of anything comparable. The history of the Jews is in any case intensely peculiar in the fact of having given the Western world its concept of origins and monotheism, its ethical traditions, and the founder of its prevailing religion, yet suffering dispersion, statelessness, and ceaseless persecution, and finally in our times nearly successful genocide, dramatically followed by fulfillment of the never-relinquished dream of return to the homeland. Viewing this strange and singular history one cannot escape the impression that it must contain some special significance for the history of mankind, that in some way, whether one believes in divine purpose or inscrutable circumstance, the Jews have been singled out to carry the tale of human fate.

As a person with primary interest in history since childhood, and a belief since childhood that the most glorious accomplishment was to write a book, now I suddenly had my subject. It would not be a history of Zionism, since I was not equipped with the languages and background to tackle that; but the origins of the Balfour Declaration which officially reopened Palestine to the Jews was something I felt I could manage. Being reasonably familiar with British history, and at least initially acquainted with the sources, this aspect of the story was within my scope. That more experienced scholars might hesitate to take on a stretch of time that, as it developed, reached from the Bronze Age to Balfour did not occur to me. I simply plunged in with the fearlessness, as a critic was later to remark, of the autodidact.

What should perhaps be explained is why the narrative was not carried on through the thirty year period of the Mandate to the birth of the state in 1948, and why now, after another thirty year period of turbulent history I have not added a supplement bringing the story up to date. The reason is basic to the function of historian, as I see it. In the writing of history one cannot be cooly objective, for that would be to renounce opinion, feeling, and judgment. But at the least one should be as far as possible detached. As regards the fortunes of the Jews and of Israel, I am not detached but emotionally involved. That may be permissible—or unavoidable—to a journalist who tends to become advocate or adversary on strongly felt issues but it invalidates the work of a historian. I found this out when, at the request of the original publisher, I tried indeed to carry the narrative through the Mandate to 1948. It turned into polemic. The British betrayal of their own impulse in establishing the national home, the White Paper policy, the collusion with the Arabs, the ramming of the Exodus and detention of Jewish refugees from Hitler in new concentration camps on Cyprus, and finally the encouragement of the Arab offensive on the heels of Britain's departure was all impossible to relate without outrage. This is not a suitable condition for a historian. The pages I produced

x

were out of keeping with the rest of the book and would have impaired its value. I tore them up and let the book terminate as originally planned, in 1918.

Since 1948, statehood and territory have accomplished two transformations in the condition of the Jewish people. For the first time since 70 A.D. they are no longer wanderers, exiles, aliens in other peoples' lands. They have their own land and they have sovereignty, and this has made the difference. They are in a position to speak for themselves, to define their own goals and policies, and if not entirely in command of their fate, as no nation now is in this globally interconnected world, they are at least their own masters as they once were from Moses to the Maccabees.

The change is reflected in the position of the Jews of the diaspora, not so much in the attitude of non-Jews toward them as in their attitude toward themselves, which is the important thing. Sovereignty in Israel has imparted dignity, confidence, self-respect and a straighter stature to Jews wherever they live. They cannot be the same convenient butt for persecution as during the vulnerable twenty centuries of statelessness, not because anti-Semitism will disappear—it is too useful a vent when for one reason or another societies become disturbed and vengeful—but because Jews will no longer *feel* like victims. It is the vulnerable and the helpless who invite persecution, but since re-acquiring sovereignty, Jews outside as well as inside Israel have gained the courage and confidence for self-defense.

The second transformation has been negative in that a consequence of nationhood has been to make the Jews like other nations. To sustain and defend their state, they have had to use the world's methods, and to have recourse to force that their neighbors have used against them. The dream of a fruitful, peaceful nation that drew the early Zionists has not been allowed realization. Subjected to attack, Israel has had to make itself stronger and more effective in the use of force than its surrounding enemies. This has aroused cries of moral outrage abroad as if Israel had introduced something new and horrid into the relations of states and into the affairs of men. Israeli settlements in occupied territory have been virtuously denounced by Americans with short memories of how Texas was settled and then annexed when no question of survival was at stake.

Survival has been the strongest Jewish principle since the dispersion of the ten tribes, the first fall of the Temple, the Babylonian exile, the Roman conquest, the second exile, and through the long centuries of Christianity's odium and its injuries. With Israel reconstituted at long last, the principle is not likely to be abandoned now, regardless of the breast-beating of Jacobo Timerman. To become like other nations has been the tragedy of statehood, the price of avoiding the greater tragedy of disappearance.

—BARBARA TUCHMAN
Cos Cob, Connecticut
June 1983

FOREWORD

The origins of Britain's role in the restoration of Israel, which is the subject of the following pages, are to be found in two motives, religious and political. One was a debt of conscience owed to the people of the Bible, the other was the strategy of empire which required possession of their land. In 1917 in the course of battle against the Turks, Britain found herself faced with the most delicate conquest in all imperial history. She could have taken Palestine without bothering about its ancient proprietors. Instead, before Allenby entered Jerusalem, Britain, in an odd gesture known as the Balfour Declaration, declared that the country would be open to resettlement by the Jews. As a voluntary assumption of an obligation by a conqueror to a stateless people, the Declaration was something new in the pattern of protectorates. Although later repudiated by its sponsors, it led to an event unique in history, the recreation of a state after a lapse of sovereignty more than two thousand years long.

Palestine, the Holy Land, the source of the Judaeo-Christian civilization of the Western world, had too much history to be conquered in that fit of absence of mind in which Britain, according to a celebrated epigram, had managed her other conquests. It had been the battleground of Hebrews and Assyrians, Greeks and Persians, Romans and Syrians, Saracens and Franks, Turks and Europeans. More blood has been shed for Palestine than for any other spot on earth. To Protestant England it was not only, as Lord Curzon said, the "holiest space of ground on the face of the globe," the land of the Scriptures, the land of the Crusades, the land "to which all our faces are turned when we are finally laid in our graves in the churchyard." It was also the geographical junction between East and West, the bridge-head between three continents, the focal point in the strategy of empire, the area necessary to the defense of the Suez Canal, the road to India and the oil fields of Mosul.

Obviously Palestine was scheduled for inclusion in the British Empire. But why, when the moment was at hand, did England add on the Balfour Declaration? Reasons of empire do not explain it. But long before Britain was an empire or even a maritime power an attachment to Palestine had been developing for spiritual or sentimental or moral or religious reasons or what might be called collectively cultural reasons. Among these the English Bible and its prophecies was the most important single factor. For the Bible, which was a history of the Hebrews and of the prophet they rejected, came to be adopted, in Thomas Huxley's phrase, as "the national epic of Britain." Thereafter England had, so to speak, one foot in Palestine. The other foot was brought in by the requirements of empire that began to be apparent during the Eastern Crisis of the 1830's and were epitomized by a writer in 1917 as "the insistent logic of the military situation on the banks of the Suez Canal."

This book is an attempt to trace up from its beginnings the development of the twin motives, the cultural and imperial, the moral and material, in short to follow Bible and sword until they lead to the Mandate. The power motive is easy to trace, being based on the hard facts of geography, of dates, battles, treaties, and the stuff of power politics. The other is rooted in spongier ground: myths, legends, traditions, ideas. These are, however, of equal importance in the fabric of history and in motivating the behavior of governments and nations. For, as Professor Turner has pointed out, "history originated as myth" and becomes a "social memory" to which men can appeal, "knowing it will provide justification for their present actions or convictions."

If it were not for the conventions of chronology this book would have been told backwards, like a detective story which starts with the denouement and traces clues back to the original motive. That method would have avoided the possible impression that the circumstances of the early chapters necessarily predicated the outcome. They do not form an inevitable progression. Other lands shared with England many of the same ties with Palestine. France played a greater role in the Crusades, Germany underwent a Reformation and Old Testament indoctrination as profound, Holland had a greater trade with the Levant and sheltered the Jews when there were none in England. To put into one narrative various episodes, strains, and influences in England's history that are connected with Palestine is not to argue that each led inevitably to the next but rather that all played some part in the "social memory" behind the eventual sponsorship of Israel's return. Before 1830 this final outcome was at no time inevitable. Lord Shaftesbury's adventure marks the point when events began leading logically toward the Mandate. Probably Disraeli's acquisition of the Suez Canal and Cyprus, 1874–78, made the physical conquest of Palestine inevitable. This was the point of no return.

And so General Allenby entered Jerusalem in 1918, succeeding where Richard the Lion-Hearted had failed. But for that victory the restoration of Israel might not yet be an accomplished fact. Nor would Allenby have succeeded if Richard had not tried; that is to say, if Christianity had not originally supplied the basis for the attachment to the Holy Land. It is a curious irony that the Jews retrieved their home partly through the operation of the religion they gave the Gentiles.

If in our times Bevin did his best to cancel out Balfour,

that was one of those tragic twists of history that can never be erased. But in view of the ultimate result that the Jews won for themselves they can perhaps afford to apply to Israel Sir Horace Plunkett's dictum on his own country's history: that it was one "for Englishmen to remember and Irishmen to forget."

Historically the occupier of Palestine has always met disaster, beginning with the Jews themselves. The country's political geography has conquered its rulers. But now that the original occupant has returned, perhaps the curse will run its course, and the most famous land in history may some day find peace.

CHAPTER I

ORIGINS:

A Fable Agreed Upon

1. Search for an Ancestor

"Our reason for turning to Palestine is that Palestine is our country. I have used that expression before and I refuse to adopt any other."

The speaker was an Englishman, Dr. William Thomson, Archbishop of York, who was addressing the Palestine Exploration Fund in the year 1875. He went on to explain that Palestine was his country because it had given him the "laws by which I try to live" and the "best knowledge I possess." He was referring of course to the Bible, the book of the Hebrew nation and its prophets that came in time to be, as Thomas Huxley said, the "national epic" of England.

For thousands of years already the English had turned toward Palestine in search of their antecedents as the salmon swims back from the sea to the headwaters of its birth. Long before modern archaeology provided a scientific answer, some dim race memory had drawn their thoughts eastward. Man's earliest instinct has always been to find his ancestor—his Creator first, perhaps, and then his ancestor. He has been speculating about him, creating images of him, spinning tales about him, ever since he first began to think. The ancestor image evolved by the English was a dual personality compounded of Brutus, grandson of the Trojan Aeneas, and Gomer, grandson of Noah. He was, in short, a product of the classical legends of Greece and Rome and the Hebrew legends of Palestine; an emigrant from Asia Minor, the cradle of civilization.

In a sense the image-makers were right without knowing it. Centuries later the image of the first inhabitant of Britain evolved by the anthropologists from the accumulated data of head shapes, hair colorings, and flint fragments turns out, curiously enough, to have come from the same part of the world. Without going into the anthropological reasons for believing so, it may be said that the pre-Celt in Britain is considered to have been of Mediterranean if not actually Middle Eastern origin. This shadowy Stone Age figure whose curled-up skeleton lies so mutely, so nakedly in the unearthed burial chambers is the end product so far in the scientific search for a British ancestor.

But who was he, and where did he come from? Tradition, anticipating archaeology, had traced this British ancestor back to Asia Minor, to that remote, uncertain spot where Noah and his family began the repopulation of the world after the Flood. Tradition is, of course, not scientific fact, but scientific fact is not always available. When the truth—that is, verifiable fact—is unobtainable, then tradition must substitute. One historian, Sir John Morris-Jones, has defined tradition as "a popular account of what once took place." It thus becomes, he adds, "one of our data to be accounted for and interpreted." As such it usually has more influence than actual fact over the behavior of nations. A nation's past history governs its present actions—but only in terms of what its citizens believe their past history to have been. For history, as Napoleon so succinctly put it, "is a fable agreed upon."

Britain's fable, then, begins with the traditions and legends about Brutus and Gomer and their respective grandfathers, Aeneas and Noah. Whether Aeneas really lived in Troy or Noah somewhere in Mesopotamia, who can say? We can say, however, that real migrants from the lands where Aeneas and Noah are supposed to have lived did people the nations of the Western world. Perhaps the pre-Celts who originally settled in the British Isles brought with them memories or legends of an Eastern ancestry. Thus the fable of Brutus-Gomer may have as sound a background as the theories of the archaeologists, who, in any case, arrived at no very different conclusion.

In any event, early in the Anglo-Saxon era, after the second conversion to Christianity in the seventh century, the fable began to take hold. The Roman occupation of Britain during the first three centuries A.D. had brought not only the classical mythology but a new religion from the East, the Judaeo-Christian. It spread widely among the Celts and was firmly enough established to outlast both the Roman withdrawal in 410 A.D. and the subsequent heathen influx of the Anglo-Saxons. Meanwhile the Britons, at least those directly in contact with the Roman administration, learned the Latin tongue and became acquainted with the Bible in the Vulgate. The very earliest surviving essay in England's history (as written by a Briton, not a Roman), the *Epistle* of Gildas, written about the year 550, shows a thorough acquaintance with the Old Testament. Gildas' tale is of the terrible assaults on his countrymen by Saxons, Jutes, and Danes, whom he compares to the scourge of the Assyrians and Philistines upon the Israelites of old. After every battle he cites an Old Testament analogy and on every page quotes from the Pentateuch, the Prophets, or the Psalms.

Two hundred years later the Venerable Bede, the true father of English history, offered certain cautious suppositions about national origins. He traces them back to Scythia, the name used by ancient geographers for the regions around the Black Sea. Here men believed the Ark landed on Mt. Ararat and the races of the world sprang from the progeny of Noah. Bede names the Cymbri, coming from somewhere in this region, as the people who first populated Britain. These Cymbri or Kimbri or Cimmeri or any one of a hundred spellings, migrating from the East, are met with at every turn in the search for the earliest Briton. They were a real tribe who, according to modern anthropologists, appeared in northern Europe along with the Teutonic tribes, some settling in Gaul and some in Britain.

Bede does not deal in fables about Brutus and the sons of Noah. They first appear as Britain's ancestors in the work of a shrouded figure about whom nothing is known save his name, Nennius, and his manuscript, the *Historia Britonum*. Whether he lived in the eighth or the tenth century, in England or Ireland or Wales, whether there were two of him or whether he was someone else altogether has been the subject of learned controversies among the footnotes. Whoever he was, Nennius left an authentic pre-Conquest manuscript, which, as Professor Pollard has said, "makes no critical distinction between the deeds of dragons and those of Anglo-Saxons." One would not expect him to be overcautious about origins and Nennius comes out forthrightly for Brutus who, he says, gave his name to Britain. Brutus was enthusiastically popularized by the twelfth-century chronicler Geoffrey of Monmouth but less exuberant historians preferred to stay under the authority of Scripture and opted for Gomer who is named in Genesis as one of the sons of Japheth among whom the Isles of the Gentiles were divided.

The Reformation fixed Gomer's position as the preferred eldest Briton, rather than Brutus. With the Reformation, the Bible as the revealed word of God became the final authority and Genesis the only acceptable or even thinkable account of man's origin. Embellishments such as Geoffrey's, so popular in medieval times, came to be regarded with suspicion. "If we fynde them mixed with superstycyons," says John Bale, a historian of Henry VIII's time, "we shall measure them by the Scriptures and somewhat beare with the corrupcyon of their tymes." He was followed by the great Elizabethan historian William Camden, who made an attempt to settle the question of origins once and for all. He discarded Brutus and settled for Gomer, who, he says, "gave both original and name to the Gomerians who were afterward called Cimbri or Cimerri. . . . Our Britons, or Cimeri, are the true genuine posterity of Gomer. This is my judgment concerning the original of the Britons; or rather my conjecture." Then, with the caution of the true scientist, Camden warns that the search for first ancestors may never be successful, "for indeed these first planters lie so in the dark hidden depths of antiquity (as it were in some thick grove) that there is very small or no hopes of retrieving by my diligence what hath for so many ages been buried in oblivion."

From Camden on, the ancestor search becomes a process of fusing the Biblical story with the growing body of scientific knowledge about ancient man and his movements. By the time Milton came to write his *History of England*, a century after Camden, Gomer, worked upon by this process, has begun to change from a person to a tribe. Milton calls it an "outlandish figment" that any particular son of Japheth actually settled in Britain, but he carries on without question the tradition that the offspring of Gomer peopled the northern and western lands after the Flood. These offspring were by now generally conceded to be the tribe of Cimerii, whose name scholars derived from Gomer via learned treatises on the permutations of Hebrew, Greek, and Celtic alphabets.

Today anthropologists scorn language as a thread leading back to the past and follow instead the signposts of artifacts and bones. They declare that grammatical structure and not the survival of borrowed words is the criterion of racial affinities. They say the original investigators who followed language rather than bones took the wrong path. But they do not seem to have reached any startlingly different conclusion than that reached by their predecessors who had to fit their conjectures within the confines of Genesis. They have merely replaced an individual Gomer with a tribe from the East as the ancestor of the British Celts.

Bede, living in the very depths of what we are pleased to call the Dark Ages, found the Cimbri, and in the light of modern anthropology the Cimbri are allowed to remain although Gomer has faded out. All of which simply suggests that tradition, the "popular account of what once took place," is not always superseded by science.

2. *The Phoenicians in Albion*

The personified ancestor represented by Gomer or Brutus is a legend. But a real link between ancient Albion and the land of Canaan was established about the time of Moses by peoples who have long since disappeared: the Phoenicians and the pre-Celts. The Phoenicians of Tyre and Sidon were the pre-eminent mariners and merchants of the ancient world. Without compass or sextant they somehow sailed the uncharted seas even into the Atlantic. In the Book of Kings it is told how they piloted King Solomon's triremes as far as Tarshish, the ancient name for Cadiz.

The British hunger for antiquity has seized on these people and variously credited them with having discovered Britain, settled in Britain, or at least traded with Britain. Though not proved beyond all doubt, the Phoenician link is well within the realm of probability, but it is not so much its inherent probability as its association with a known people of antiquity, real figures from the Old Testament, that explains the passionate conviction with which British historians defend it.

The evidence for it centers on the use of tin as a Bronze Age alloy in the East. Tin was mined in Cornwall about that time. Tin appeared as an article of commerce in the markets of Tyre, as we know from the report of the prophet Ezekiel, about 600 B.C. This tin, according to Herodotus, writing in 440 B.C., came from the Isles of the Cassiterides, a name that offers no geographical clue at all, because it simply means "tin" in Greek. However, it came to be identified by all the classical geographers following Herodotus as either the Scilly Isles off Cornwall or as Cornwall itself.

As Camden was the first to put the Gomer-Cimbri-Celt genealogy on a modern footing, so was he the first to bring out the role of the Phoenicians in ancient Britain. With the revival of classical learning in sixteenth-century Europe, English scholars, following Camden, unearthed all the references to the tin trade of the ancients, finding to their delight that through this means Britain's antiquity could be pushed back to equal that of ancient Greece and Troy and the lands of the Bible. One seventeenth-century Cambridge scholar, Aylett Sammes, was so carried away on the wings of this theory that he wrote a book called *The Antiquities of Ancient Britain Derived from the Phoenicians* in which he proved that "the language itself for the most part, as well as the Customs, Religions, Idols, Offices, Dignities of the ancient Britons are all clearly Phoenician."

Another Phoenician monopoly, the famous purple dye derived from shellfish, provided a further clue when pre-Bronze Age shell dumps of the particular kind yielding the purple dye were found on the Cornwall and Devon coasts.

More significant than the tin and shells was the evidence in stone. The mighty and incredible stone monuments at Stonehenge and Avebury, raised, no one knows how, by primitive sun-worshipers in Britain, have an unmistakable affinity with the Canaanite use of sacred stones in the worship of various local Baals. Dr. Borlase, a pioneer Cornish archaeologist, digging among the rich prehistoric mounds of his native Cornwall, thought that the "rude obelisks" found in Britain might have been erected by early Phoenician visitors in honor of their own national deities, "it being the notorious infatuation of Canaanitish nations to pay divine honors to such rude stones." This was written as early as 1769.

Borlase and succeeding scholars believed the Phoenicians discovered Britain about 1400 B.C. Curiously enough, modern archaeologists give 1400 B.C. as the approximate date of Stonehenge and Avebury. They ascribe the stones, of course, not to Phoenicians or Druids, but to the Beaker people, members of the Indo-European family of nations, who, from a starting point in western Mediterranean lands, spread over the Alps and into Britain about 1800 B.C. at the beginning of the Bronze Age. Large-boned muscular people of nomadic culture, depending chiefly on herds but acquainted with agriculture, they had round heads and built round barrows. In Britain they dispossessed the earlier Neolithic population, who (conveniently) had long heads and built long barrows. Archaeologists are immensely fond of the Beaker folk, whose astonishing migrations they trace all over Europe by a trail of Beaker shreds, metal buttons, and belt buckles. But whatever their aptitudes, they are too lately known to compete as forefathers in the imagination of a Bible-reading people. A buried skeleton in a barrow, with no matter how many beakers and buckles, is not so attractive an ancestor as the rulers of ancient Tyre and Sidon* so familiar from the pages of the Old Testament.

The tradition achieved formal embodiment when Lord Leighton, president of the Royal Academy, was commissioned to paint a mural depicting "Ancient Commerce" on the walls of the Royal Exchange in London. Here for all to see are the black-bearded Phoenicians spreading out lengths of purple cloth before avid Britons who offer hides and ingots of tin in exchange.

In the year 146 B.C. the battle between Carthage and Rome for mastery of the Mediterranean world was won

---

*Still the idea persists. In 1924 a book of some scientific pretensions called *The Phoenician Origin of Britons, Scots and Anglo-Saxons* was published by Laurence Waddell. Arguing from the evidence of stone artifacts, the author builds up a good case; but it bothers him that the Phoenicians were Semitic, and he destroys his own claim to be taken seriously by insisting that they were Aryan and that existing pictures of them require "some slight nasal readjustment to the Aryan type."

finally by the Romans. From then on the Phoenicians fade from history, and the temporal power of the East passed to the marching men of Italy. They were soon to be masters of both Palestine and Britain and to provide another link between the two.

3. *Roman Judaea and Roman Britain*

When Britain first emerged out of the fog of prehistory into the pages of Julius Caesar's *Commentaries* the Temple of the Jews was still standing. During the next century or so, between the time of Caesar and the fall of the Temple in 70 A.D., Rome subjugated both Judaea and Britain. Jews and Britons alike became fellow subjects of the Roman Empire, linked by the omnipresent Roman legion.

Pompey entered Jerusalem in 63 B.C. when the feeble heir of the once great Maccabean dynasty called in Roman help against his equally worthless brother. The Romans, of course, stayed. Pompey reduced Judaea to the status of province, and though it later temporarily enjoyed the rank of dependent kingdom under Herod, it remained part of the Roman Empire.

The same pattern of civil strife opening the way to the Roman conqueror was to be played out in Britain. Though Caesar had won an engagement against the Britons, he could not complete the conquest, having his hands full in Gaul and trouble enough at home. But Rome's august shadow now lay on Britain. The opportunity to replace the shadow with the substance came in the fourth decade A.D. when the Emperor Claudius reigned at Rome and Cinoboline or Cymbeline was a king in Britain. Rebellious sons, factious tribes, and questions of tribute had produced civil war in Britain, in the course of which a rebel chieftain went to Rome for aid, revealed the internecine struggles of his countrymen, and came back with the all too willing legions at his heels. The bookish Claudius, though no fighter, was no fool, and he could see a chance for conquest as well as any military man. When the dust had cleared, there stood the Roman as usual. Claudius came to Britain to celebrate his triumph in person and erected a victory arch in honor of the occasion at home.

Parallels between their fortunes continue. The rising of the Celtic tribes under Boadicea and the rising of the Jews in Judaea took place at opposite ends of Nero's empire in the same decade. Both risings were hopeless from the start, both were inspired by fanatic patriotism and maintained by desperate courage, and both failed. In 81 A.D. Boadicea, goaded by Roman brutalities, raised an army whose spiked chariots swept savagely over the Roman settlements in a mighty burst for freedom. It was a valiant stroke that could not be sustained. Roman re-enforcements crossed the channel, crushed the Queen's revolt, massacred her people, and marked the last attempt of Celtic Britain to throw off the Roman yoke. Six years later when Jewish zealots similarly tried to unseat their Roman rulers, they withstood the armies of Vespasian and Titus for three years. But at the last, starved out, Jerusalem was taken by storm, the Temple razed by fire never to rise again, and Jewish statehood canceled.

What mad notion of succeeding against Rome, when every other nation had failed, had driven the Jews to this? the handsome Titus asked, and he reminded them of the recent defeat of the Britons. In the person of this young general, the future emperor and the "darling of the Gods," Palestine and Britain had met, as he himself was aware. As he stood that day on the crumbling ramparts the flames roared and crackled through the sacred Temple that he had tried vainly to preserve against the fanaticism of its last-ditch defenders and the mob anger of his own troops. From inside the walls rose the stench of months of un-buried bodies felled by starvation in the streets. Outside the walls stood a forest of crosses with their rotting burden of civilians caught between starvation and the Romans, captured and crucified by the besiegers as each night they sought to creep out from the doomed city. The walls of the city had only brought its death. Titus, as he looked around, was reminded of another wall that had failed its defenders. "Pray," he asked the prisoners, "what greater obstacle is there than the wall of the ocean which encompasses the Britons and yet they bow down before the arms of the Romans?"

If the coincidence struck Titus, it made an even more profound impression on the English in the Christian era. They believed that the Roman conquest was an expression of the Divine wrath, upon the Britons for being heathen and upon the Jews for rejecting Jesus. The appearance of Vespasian as the instrument of retribution in both instances seemed, in Christian times, clearly an intervention of God. Vespasian himself, a hearty materialist of the reddest Roman vintage, would have been astonished to learn that later generations would refer to him as the divine instrument of a God he had never heard of.

A sense of the romance of history seems almost to insist that, in that moment of time when the fates of Jews and Britons touched briefly, the two rebel peoples must have had some experience of each other. Rome, we know, impressed her subject peoples, including Jews and Britons, into military duty in the auxiliary legions, and these could see service in any part of the Empire. Might there have been any Jewish soldiers in the legions that burned Londinium when it was held by the rebel forces of Boadicea, or any Britons in the legions that stormed the walls of Jerusalem under Titus?

If evidence could be found anywhere, it would be in the records of the two greatest contemporary historians, Tacitus the Roman and Josephus the Jew. Both wrote of events in which they themselves had participated, Josephus in *The Jewish War* and Tacitus in his *Agricola*. But in neither does any evidence turn up of Britons in Judaea or Jews in Britain.

Josephus wrote that there was not a people in the world

who had not some Jews among them; and this can be veri-
fied by references among the ancient writers to Jewish
communities in every province of the Empire from Persia
to Spain, with the one exception of Britain. It is perfectly
possible, indeed probable, that in the wake of the Romans
Jewish merchants or captive slaves from Palestine did
reach this farthest outpost of the Empire. Yet if they did,
they left no traces. A single brick and one Jewish coin dug
up by chance in London two hundred years apart inspired
pages of speculation by enthusiasts, but actually signify
nothing. The brick, found in Mark Lane in 1670, was of
Roman manufacture and bore on its face a bas-relief showing Samson setting fire to the foxes' tails as he drove them
into a field of corn. But this proves little, for others besides
the Jews knew the Old Testament stories, and in any event
the Jews rarely personified their people in pictures. The
coin, minted in Judaea during the bitter few years of independence wrested from Rome by Simon Bar Cochba in
132–35 A.D. equally fails to prove a Jewish habitation in
London, since it might well have been brought by an individual trader or by a Roman soldier who could have picked
it up as a souvenir of battle.

But it calls to mind another curious coincidence. Again
a general from Britain, in this case the Emperor's legate,
Julius Sextus Severus, had to be called to Palestine before
Bar Cochba's furious and fanatic revolt could be quelled.
And, like Titus two generations earlier, he brought a fear-
ful punishment upon the Jews. Thenceforward they were
forbidden to enter Jerusalem, and all but a remnant were
exiled from Palestine.

Despite all these coincidences the historian must come
away empty-handed from the search for evidence of actual
contact between the two peoples at that time. And from
then on their fates diverged. The Jews lost their country,
but somehow retained their sense of nationality in exile.
The Celts of Britain remained in their country, but lost
their nationality under a succession of alien conquerors.

CHAPTER II

APOSTLE TO THE BRITONS:

Joseph of Arimathea

The search for national origins was duplicated in the search for religious origins. National pride demanded for the British church a personified founder, sought him directly in Palestine, and found him in the person of Joseph of Arimathea. Joseph was the rich Jew and secret disciple who sat silent when the Sanhedrin, of which he was a member, voted to hand Jesus over to the civilian arm of Pilate. Later Joseph came forward publicly to claim Jesus' body and give it burial. He was the first person of wealth and influence to join the new sect and was no doubt regarded as a "traitor to his class," for the Galilean gospel was not addressed to the rich and wellborn.

His legend centers in the Abbey of Glastonbury, the oldest in England, which he is credited with having founded. In one of Tennyson's Idylls of the King a monk speaks:

> "From our old books I know
> That Joseph came of old to Glastonbury
> And there the heathen prince, Arviragus,
> Gave him an isle of marsh whereon to build
> A little lonely church in days of yore."

Tennyson of course took Joseph from Malory's *Morte d'Arthur*. In that account Joseph, "by fortune come unto thys lande that at that time was called Grete Bretayne," was able to "disheryt" a "grete felon paynim" who ruled the country, and "after that all the people withturned to the Crystyn feythe."

Malory's work, however, was not the beginning but the end product of centuries of half history, half legend that, with each successive chronicler, increased by what it fed on. By the time medieval chroniclers and romance poets had done with him Joseph emerged not only as the author of Celtic Britain's conversion to Christianity and as bringer of the Grail, but also as the ancestor of Britain's greatest national hero, King Arthur, and the link in some mysterious fashion between Arthur and Israel's national hero, King David.

Why did English tradition settle on the figure of Joseph rather than any other? Perhaps the answer is that he actually did make his way from Palestine to Britain. Other apostles voyaged far from Judaea to carry the gospel, and the Roman ways to Britain were open. At any rate no one can say positively that he did not: one cannot prove a negative, especially when records of the time are so meager. Joseph at least had one important qualification: he was an actor in the events that gave birth to Christianity. From among the Twelve Apostles Rome had chosen Peter, Spain had James, France had Philip, nor could British national pride be satisfied with anyone less immediate to the original scene.

Who first carried Christianity to Britain we do not know, nor are we ever likely to know. In cold fact it probably infiltrated among the inhabitants via the agency of converted Romans, following the pattern that was being played out in other parts of the Roman world. Within two hundred years after the death of Jesus contemporary writers were referring to Christian communities in Britain. By 314 A.D. the Celtic Church in Britain was sufficiently well established to send three bishops as delegates to the Council of Arles. But its shadowy and anonymous beginnings did not satisfy the later church. An ancestor of heroic and antique mold was demanded, and gradually the figure of Joseph came to be accepted as the original apostle to the Britons.

Historical evidence he cannot claim. After a minute survey of all the surviving evidence the indisputable Bishop Stubbs concluded that any reference to apostolic preaching in Britain during the first century A.D. must "rest on guess, mistake or fable." Joseph of Arimathea was the fable agreed upon.

It took such hold that by the end of the Middle Ages Joseph had become officially recognized as the founder of the British church. One can put one's finger on the very moment when it happened. In the year 1431 at the Council of Basle, precedence in seating and other sensitive matters of protocol were determined by the antiquity of the churches of the respective countries. The English cited Joseph as establishing their claim for precedence. In a furious quarrel with the Spanish delegates, carried on for days in resounding Latin rhetoric, the English insisted that Joseph had arrived in Britain before James in Spain, that everyone knew James in fact had been killed before he ever got to Spain, that Glastonbury provided tangible evidence of Joseph's presence in England, and that, regardless of how small a corner of the country he had converted, it was not the quantity but the antiquity of the conversion that was at issue. To buttress their claim the Bishops of London and Rochester who headed the English delegation drew up a memorial stating:

". . . it is certain that in England, as may be ascertained from very ancient books and archives, in particular the archives of the notable abbey of Glastonbury in the diocese of Bath, that Joseph of Arimathea, with twelve companions, was carried to England, escaping either from the persecution of Herod or from that of Roman high officials in Judaea. In that place (England) he preached what he had seen and heard of Christ; and so preaching he converted numberless English people. And from them he acquired many and countless things which were brought to him by those converted to the faith. These things he later left to a church of Christ erected by him at the time when Peter was preaching the faith at Antioch. The church built by Joseph became afterward the seat of a monastery with the rank of abbey, and that noteworthy abbey and monastery has been preserved, praise to Christ Himself, to this day."

In this memorial we have stumbled on that crucial point at which fable is converted into history.

The mainspring of the development of the Joseph legend lay in the ever-present British jealousy of Rome; in the urge to claim for the church in Britain an antiquity antedating that of Rome. In the person of Joseph England's desire to by-pass Rome and to trace the sources of its faith directly to the primary source in the Holy Land could be satisfied. Immediately after the Norman conquest the theory of a personal apostle to the Britons, a witness of, indeed an actor in, the drama of the crucifixion and resurrection, coming direct from Palestine to bring the word, first appears. Now everything Saxon was in its turn contemned by the Norman conquerors, while Celtic culture enjoyed a revival. The Arthurian cycle bursts into full bloom, transmuting the great champion of Celtic Britain and the knights of the Round Table into heroes of the age of chivalry. With it is entwined the legend of the quest for the Holy Grail, and into the leading role steps the onetime member of the Sanhedrin of Jerusalem, Joseph of Arimathea.

As chroniclers and poets from the twelfth to the fifteenth century borrowed, added, and embroidered upon one another's versions, the legend grew in dignity and detail, acquiring tangible evidence along the way, until the whole curious tangle of Gospel, Apocrypha, Celtic folklore, and French romance became an ineradicable part of the national tradition. By 1464 John Hardyng's verse chronicle of Britain's past includes as a matter of fact the statement that "Joseph of Arimathie came unto Britayne with Vespasyan and christened a part of this lande."

During those three centuries the pure conversion legend

became ever more hopelessly entangled in the lore of the Grail, for which the Crusades supplied much of the material. In England the Grail legend was mixed with the Celtic lore of Arthur and his knights and fashioned into pseudohistory by a long succession of chroniclers. Its richest development was in the work of Walter Map, whose *Quete du Saint Graal, Joseph d'Arimathie*, and *Merlin* were written about 1170. His romance of Joseph and the Grail was commissioned, scholars believe, by Henry II, who gave the tale a deliberate push for political reasons. To buttress his claim to head a national church coeval with Rome King Henry seized on the double Joseph-Grail legend, which Map accordingly popularized. Meanwhile the glory and honor of Glastonbury was further enhanced when Henry, with impressive ceremony, caused its churchyard to be dug up and found there, or so he claimed, the true tombs of Arthur and Guinevere. Glastonbury was thus officially confirmed as the burial site of ancient Britain's hero King. Henry's deliberate purpose was to raise Glastonbury above Canterbury, which had uncomfortable memories for him as the scene of Becket's murder and was becoming all too popular as the goal of pilgrimages to Becket's grave.

Joseph's stature now grew rapidly. Not only did he and his descendants figure as keepers of the Grail, but he also came to be considered the ancestor of King Arthur himself. In the later accounts, which, after the fashion of medieval chroniclers, pretend to be true histories, divine intervention directs Joseph to the land of Britain, which is "promised to him and his issue." There he fathers a line, traced down through many "begats" to a lady upon whom Uther Pendragon begat Arthur, "from which it is patent that King Arthur is descended from the stock of Joseph." So says the writer known as John of Glastonbury, who lived about 1400.

Various precious national symbols gradually collect around and attach themselves to the figure of Joseph: not only the Grail, but also the sacred sword that gave Arthur kingship. This sword was originally King David's, "the most marvelous that ever forged was," which is taken out of the Temple and given to Solomon, who sets it to sea in a miraculous ship to find its destined owner, a pure knight "that shalt be the end of my lineage." This person is of course Galahad, who through the alchemy of legend becomes the descendant of both Solomon and Joseph. He also inherits the miraculous white shield with the cross of blood brought from Syria by Joseph. In Malory's *Morte d'Arthur* Joseph on his deathbed bequeathes the shield to Galahad, yet unborn by some 500 years, whom he too calls "the last of my lineage."

David's sword and Solomon's ship are late additions to the legend, dating from fifteenth-century versions. Down the centuries Arthur and his knights had grown in verisimilitude and now appeared in all the chronicles as historical figures who fought Britain's early battles against the Saxon invaders. Perhaps it was inevitable that men should wish to associate them with the Biblical heroes who represented the kingly power of Israel at its height. Or is this association another thread in the skein that carries so many Celtic traditions back to a source in Palestine?

Other Hebraic elements make their appearance. Joseph becomes confused with his Old Testament namesake, Joseph the son of Jacob. In a tremendous fifteenth-century poem by one Henry Lonelich that fills some eight hundred pages, Joseph, upon his arrival in Britain, finds it ruled by a "great felon paynim" called Duke Gaanor and peopled by "Saracens and many other miscreants." This is obviously a medieval version of Pharoah and the Egyptians. Like Pharoah, the Duke has a vision, which his "Saracen" clerks cannot interpret, and Joseph is called upon to give his interpretation, which the Duke acknowledges as the true one. Then, like Nebuchadnezzar when his dream was read by Daniel, he professes himself ready to worship Joseph's God instead of his own and is promptly converted to Christianity.

Another Hebrew symbol appears in the Fisher King, that key figure in all the Joseph-Grain stories, who becomes guardian of the Grail after Joseph dies and survives until Galahad appears. In some versions the Fisher King first appears as King Evalak, a Syrian champion who accompanies Joseph during his wanderings in the East and becomes his first convert. The title Fisher King derives from his having been directed by God to catch a fish, which provides himself and Joseph with sustenance in the wilderness. Like the Leviathan of Jewish tradition that is to provide food for the righteous at the Messiah's coming, and like Leviathan in the Psalms, which God gave "to be meat to the people inhabiting the wilderness," this fish could be partaken of only by the righteous. The Grail itself as a life-giving talisman whose finding restores a waste land to fruitfulness can be found in any number of religious cults. Sometimes it is a dish or cup. Sometimes, as in the *Parzival* of Wolfram von Eschenbach, it is a sacred stone, existing since the Creation. As a stone it has been connected by scholars with Isaiah's "precious corner stone of pure foundation," the stone at the center of the world, the stone that was Jacob's pillow, the cornerstone of the Temple of Solomon. Celtic legend adopts this motif too, for the Stone of Scone, which figures in the crowning of British kings, was believed to have been originally Jacob's pillow brought to Ireland by some forgotten migration of the tribe of Jacob, and thence to Scotland, from where the English conquerors stole it. This is the same stone that made a dramatic reappearance in 1951 when Scottish nationalists hauled it home by automobile.

To construct a theory of Celtic-Jewish connections on the treacherous swamps of the Joseph-Grail legend would be foolhardy indeed. No sooner does the venturesome inquirer put one toe into this quicksand than he is sucked into a morass of romance and folklore, comparative religions, troubadours and minnesingers, pagan and Christian mysteries, oriental and Celtic mythologies where rival scholars struggle hopelessly in a mire of myths and texts. The very subject produces an atmosphere that once to breathe is fatal to clarity, as the deliberate obscurities of T. S. Eliot's *The Waste Land*, the *reductio ad absurdum* of the Grail legend, are proof enough.

But Joseph as apostle to the Britons remained firmly fixed in English tradition for centuries after the Middle Ages. John Leland the sixteenth-century antiquary, assumed the truth of Joseph's apostleship in Britain. So did Sir William Dugdale, whose *Monasticon Anglicanum,* a further inquiry into England's past through the study of old monastery records, appeared about a century later in 1655. At this time the episcopal controversy that rocked England during the tyrannical regime of Archbishop Laud inspired a theologian's plunge into the dim past to clarify the circumstances of English church origins. One of these studies, the *Ecclesiastical Historie of Great Britaine,* by Richard Broughton, has a chapter entitled: "Wherein is proved by all kinds of testimonies and authorities, that for certaine, St. Joseph of Aramathia and divers other holy Associates came to, preached, lyved, dyed and was buryed in Britayne, at the place now called Glastonbury in Summersetshire."

If Broughton was credulous, his contemporary, worthy Tom Fuller, the divine who held his own between Royalists and Puritans and wrote some of the most readable prose of the seventeenth century, was a natural skeptic. Yet in his *Church History of Britain* (1635) he cannot bring himself to deny the substance of the Joseph story, though he admits that "the leaven of monkery hath much swollen and puffed up the circumstance thereof." Acknowledging the lack of verifiable material on the first century, Fuller adds what might be a precept to many less honest historians: "But as I find little so I will feign nothing; the time being better spent in silence than in lying."

Clearly by this time, no matter what evidence pro or con might be added, no one could pry Joseph out of the British tradition. It may even be that he rightfully belongs there, for, as so often happens when modern science goes to work on the stuff of legend, the available facts tend to confirm the legend. Archaeological findings have in fact confirmed the existence of a Stone Age lake village at Glastonbury. It is pictured by the archaeologist Jacquetta Hawkes in terms that fit exactly the story of Joseph and his wattled church in the marsh. "For the security which the times demanded, the founders of the village chose a piece of marshy ground . . . hacked down the growth of alder and willow which cumbered the site and then, with immense labor went on to build up an artificial island on the ground they had cleared. . . . On it stood some sixty round huts with wattled sides, trodden clay floors and roofs thatched with reeds. . . . Inside its protecting wall the village itself is full of life and activity—a compact stronghold of humanity isolated among the swamps."

Perhaps its isolation and protected position accounted for the preservation of Glastonbury's antique traditions. Then at some unknown date a fire apparently destroyed the original community, but in so doing baked hard the clay covering the wattle work and thus made possible its survival. Uncovered after two thousand years, it still carried the impress of the woven reeds or wicker. Examples of stonework typical of the kind found in Syria were also dug up around Glastonbury, suggesting some connection with Joseph's homeland.

As Professor Freeman, an authority on ancient Britain, has said: "We need not believe that the Glastonbury legends are facts but the existence of those legends is a great fact."

CHAPTER III

"WITHIN THY GATES, O JERUSALEM":

The Pilgrim Movement

Pilgrims from Britain first set out on the long journey to Jerusalem back in the murky era between the twilight of the Roman Empire and the pre-dawn hours of the Middle Ages.

The pilgrim movement began in earnest early in the fourth century after the Emperor Constantine declared Christianity the official, or at least the favored, religion of the Roman Empire. His mother, the Empress Helena, having likewise been converted, undertook to locate the exact site of the Gospel's events. On a journey to Palestine in 326 she discovered, after convenient excavations, the True Cross and the Holy Sepulcher. Subsequently her own and her son's activity in dotting Palestine with churches, monuments, and hostels to mark the holy places excited the Christian world and led to a wave of pilgrimages.

Celtic Britain's history during this period lies in shadow. But in Palestine if not in Britain evidence exists of Britons making pilgrimages to the Holy Land, beginning in the fourth century. St. Jerome writing from Bethlehem in 386 remarks: "The Briton no sooner makes progress in religion than he quits his Western sun to go in search of a place of which he knows only through Scripture and common report." This observation is confirmed independently by a contemporary, Palladius Galatea, Bishop of Heliopolis in

Egypt, who lived much of his life in Palestine. In the course of a book of biographical sketches of monks, ascetics, hermits, and other local celebrities Palladius refers to the pilgrims who came from all corners of the world "even from Persia and Britain." Another of Jerome's letters implies that Britons must have been coming in some numbers, though apparently in an insufficiently pious frame of mind to satisfy the writer, for he admonishes prospective pilgrims "that it is as easy to find the way to Heaven in Britain as in Jerusalem."

Who they were we do not know, but how they went we can be sure. They walked. From Edinburgh in the north, Roman roads stretched across Europe, the Balkans, and Asia Minor to Judaea. A pilgrim from Britain could follow them to Dover, cross the straits to Calais, and follow in the legions' footsteps across Gaul, over the Alps, and down into Italy, where he might sail from Brundisium over the Adriatic to Macedonia, plod on across Thrace to Byzantium, and so down through Antioch and Damascus to Jerusalem. Or he might sail from Messina in Sicily across to Carthage and follow the Roman road along the Mediterranean coast to Alexandria, through Egypt and the Sinai desert to his destination.

Perhaps the earliest Britons to go may have been inspired by a sense of kinship with the popularizers of the Holy Land, Helena and Constantine, who had special associations for Britain. According to legend widely believed in the later Middle Ages Helena was of British birth, the daughter of a Welsh king, but whether this was believed by Britons in her lifetime it is impossible to say. Constantine's father, for a fact, was killed at York while leading a Roman campaign against the dreaded Picts and Scots who periodically swooped down on Britain. There Constantine, acclaimed Caesar by his legions, embarked on the career that was to have such great consequences for the world of his time.

From the evidence of St. Jerome it is clear that within

two generations after Constantine's conversion the pilgrimage to Jerusalem had become an established custom; indeed, too much so to suit Jerome, who took a rather jaundiced view of overenthusiastic pilgrims. He complained that "Jerusalem is now made a place of resort from all parts of the world, and there is such a throng of pilgrims of both sexes that all temptation, which in some degree you might avoid elsewhere, is here collected together." Jerome was disapproving by nature, a stern celibate who was forever urging the Roman ladies to abjure baths, second husbands, and other worldly pleasures. His letters, however, and those of his enthusiastic disciple, the Roman matron Paula, show the position Palestine held in the world of his time: "the first of all the nations," as it is called. A man would not choose to learn Greek anywhere but in Athens or Latin anywhere but in Rome, Paula writes; likewise "can we suppose a Christian's education complete who has not visited the Christian Athens? . . . Those who stand first throughout the world are here gathered side by side."

But Jerusalem was gradually yielding to Rome, until, with the definitive establishment of a papal throne under Gregory the Great in 590, the seat of Christian authority was finally transferred to Europe. Jerusalem remained the spiritual home, "the Mother of us all," as the Prior in Ivanhoe put it, and still a goal of pilgrimage. But its temporal history is severed from that of the Roman Empire by the Moslem conquest in 637 A.D. From then on, except for the unedifying episode of the Crusaders' Latin Kingdom of Jerusalem, Palestine remained under one form or another of Moslem rule, through a bewildering succession of Abbasid and Fatimite caliphates, Seljuk and Ottoman Turks, until 1918.

Jerusalem was now adopted as a Holy Place by the Mohammedans. So far it had figured in the new religion only for that fraction of a second between the fall of a cup from Mahomet's bedside table and the catching of it before it reached the ground. It was during this interval that the Prophet had his famous dream of a miraculous midnight journey to Jerusalem astride the winged white steed Al-borak and his ascent thence to heaven. Now, however, Mahomet's followers, late comers to monotheism, were in physical possession of the city that was holy to the two older religions and were able to take advantage of its prestige. With the shrewd opportunism that characterized the founder, they were eager to adopt as much of Jewish and Christian beliefs and practices as could be fitted in between the pages of the Koran. Omar, the conqueror of Jerusalem, paid a visit of respect to the Holy Rock where Abraham had prepared to sacrifice Isaac and where the Temple of Solomon had once stood. Having cleaned it of the filth with which the Christians of that time had defiled it to show their resentment of the Jews, he adopted the site as a Mohammedan place of worship. There the Mosque of Omar was built, and thenceforward Mahomet was supreme where David had reigned and Jesus preached.

Yet the connection between Europe and Palestine was kept alive by the continued flow of pilgrims. Omar established the principle of tolerance for Christians and Jews, whom he respected as fellow monotheists, allowing them to remain as residents of Palestine subject to certain disabilities and permitting them to continue visits to their various shrines on payment of a levy from which he derived a comfortable income. But these privileges depended solely on the personal policy of the reigning sovereign. Pilgrims suffered little danger during the reign of friendly or tolerant caliphs such as Harun al-Rashid, who in 801 signalized his famous long-distance friendship with Charlemagne by sending the Emperor the keys to the Church of the Holy Sepulcher and acknowledging him as Protector of the Christians in the East. But some were rabid anti-Christians like the mad Caliph El-Hakim, a sort of Arab Nero, who in 996 burned down the Church of the Holy Sepulcher and slaughtered thousands of unbelievers. Others, preferring the income to the glory, permitted the Christians' residence and restored the pilgrims' privileges.

From all parts of Europe they took the long road to the Holy Land, drawn partly by devotion, but also by curiosity to visit, to touch, to secure souvenirs of the places and the relics associated with the celebrities of the age. These were of course the saints and churchmen. Religion and its exponents ruled the life of the time. The hardest task today for a person who endeavors to understand the medieval world is to realize the extent to which the doctrines, dogmas, and controversies of the Christian Church enveloped and absorbed all mental activity. Although the Old Testament was known in the imperfect version of the Latin Vulgate, it was predominantly the Gospels and the writings of the early Christian Fathers that established the confines of medieval knowledge. As a result Palestine had almost exclusively Gentile connotations in men's minds. No one thought of Jesus as one of a long line of Hebrew prophets, nor did the earlier prophets or the Mosaic law have the influence that they were to exert later, after the Reformation. To medieval Europeans Palestine meant the soil that their Saviour had trodden, not the land of the Chosen People. Jews of the Middle Ages were exclusively objects of hostility as Christ-killers and usurers. To the earliest Christians, when Christianity was still a sect struggling to establish itself as a Church, the Jews had been the Bourbons of an *ancien régime*. Caiaphas, high priest of the Temple, was to the disciples what George III was to the American colonies. But by the time the Christian Church had become official under Constantine, the Temple had become a ruin and the Jews a homeless sect who, as aliens everywhere, were the more easily contemned. Their thousand years' possession of Palestine hardly entered the mind of the pilgrim, certainly not the pilgrim of the early Middle Ages.

The earliest Briton known to us by name to have reached Palestine was not strictly a pilgrim. He was the British monk Pelagius, expounder of the celebrated heresy named after him, who came to the Holy Land about the year 413. He had been living in Rome until the sack of that city by Alaric the Goth forced him with many other residents to flee to Carthage. Here he came into conflict with St. Augustine, who dominated the Christian scene from his Carthaginian garden. Pelagius, a man of untroubled faith, did not share the awful soul struggles of the Saint of Hippo, nor could he accept Augustine's insistence that salvation was not within man's power to achieve, but was only within the Divine power to bestow. Hoping to find a more sympathetic religious climate, he moved on to Palestine, only to come up against the cantankerous Jerome, who promptly denounced him as an old fool dulled by Scotch porridge. For already his creed, contained in a series of commentaries on St. Paul, which incidentally form the oldest known book to have been written by a Briton, was making enemies for him among the entrenched episcopacy, in proportion as it gained headway in the Christian world.

It was a characteristically British heresy even then; for Pelagius rediscovered Free Will. Repudiating the doctrine of original sin, he suggested instead that sin was a matter of choice rather than an unavoidable inheritance from Adam. This appalling theory filled church officials with horror. For if it were admitted that men were not totally depraved from birth but could achieve righteousness and grace through their own ability, then of what avail was Jesus' atonement on the Cross? If the Redeemer was not a necessity for mankind, no more was the Church. Such subversive ideas could not be allowed by the doctrinaires of the day. Led by Augustine and Jerome, they kept the controversy raging until they had secured the condemnation of Pelagianism as heresy.

Within the lifetime of Pelagius the Roman Empire, pulling in its legions from the provinces in an effort to defend its core against the barbarians, had withdrawn from Britain. The country was left to its own devices against the ever-ready Picts and Scots, soon followed by the Anglo-Saxons. Under the new invaders the heathen pall redescended on the former Romanized settlements, though not on the more remote regions of the North and West. Pushed back by the new barbarians, the Celts retreated to the fringes of the British Isles, and here Celtic Christianity survived. From one of the remarkable Scotch monasteries in the North another figure, the Abbot Andamnan of Iona, emerges to penetrate the cloudy history of that dim era. His connection with Palestine was fortuitous; Andamnan happened to fall host to a French bishop, Arculf, who, sailing home from a nine months' pilgrimage to the Holy Land, was shipwrecked on the stony Scottish coast about the year 690. A storm at sea gave Britain its first in the endless count of English travel books on Palestine.

Warming his guest, no doubt, with the steaming Scotch porridge so despised by Jerome, Andamnan, a man "most learned in the Scriptures," must have listened fascinated to Arculf's first-hand description of the Holy Places. One can imagine the two cowled figures in the bare hall of the monastery, swept by sea wind and Caledonian fog; the traveler telling his tale of far-off places, of sacred shrines and relics, the listener urging him on with eager questions. Andamnan took it down in Latin, the language common to both, and presented the finished work, entitled *De Locis Sanctis*, to the King of Northumbria. From here it came into the hands of a great contemporary and fellow Northumbrian, the Venerable Bede, through whose efforts the book was destined to have a much wider circulation than its remote origin might have warranted. Bede abridged and rewrote *De Locis Sanctis*, including it, though with full credit to Arculf and Andamnan, among his own historical and ecclesiastical works and thus assuring its survival. During the course of the Middle Ages more than one hundred transcripts were made of Bede's condensed version and a score of Andamnan's original. These figures, in the days of painstaking longhand reproduction and scarce parchment, represent a best seller. Setting the pattern from which his innumerable followers never far depart, Arculf visits and describes each place of importance in Jesus' life: Bethlehem, Nazareth, Capernaum, Galilee, the Jordan, and each street, shrine, and stone in Jerusalem, each church, monastery, and hostel sprung up since the Christian era. He records the belief that Jerusalem is the center of the earth, proved, he says, by a "lofty column in the middle of the city which at midday at the summer solstice casts no shadow." He drinks water from the well of Jacob and eats wild locusts, which, boiled in oil, "make a poor sort of food." He sees the last footprints of the Saviour, preserved under a temple on Mt. Olivet, which miraculously remained as before "although the earth is daily carried away by believers." He calculates the exact measurements of the Holy Sepulcher in terms of the width of his palm. The color of the marble, the twelve lamps of the twelve apostles, the niche enshrining the cup, the sponge and the lance used in the crucifixion, every last detail of architecture and furnishings of every edifice, all are remembered by the traveler and written down by the eager reporter.

He notices the natural features of the country, too, remarking on the rich and fruitful plains inland from the coast at Caesarea or noting that at Jericho the Jordan was "about as broad as a man could throw a stone with a sling."

The sites of Old Testament history, chiefly those most easily accessible in and around Jerusalem, which are included in every later tourist itinerary, are also visited: the Patriarchs' tomb at Hebron, the walls of Jericho, the stones of the twelve tribes at Gilgal. Even the task of recounting weird legends about the Dead Sea and swimming in its metallic waters to ascertain if, in truth, one would not sink, is included. It is not clear from the narrative whether Arculf himself visited the Dead Sea, but Andamnan contributes an abundant variety of Dead Sea fantasies. For example, near the awful site where Sodom and Gomorrah were engulfed grow beautiful apples that "excite among spectators a desire to eat them but when plucked they burst and are reduced to ashes and give rise to smoke as if they were still burning."

The narrative describes, for the benefit of future pilgrims, both land approaches to the Holy Land: the southern route by Egypt and Sinai generally used by pilgrims before the Moslem conquest, and the northern one down through Constantinople and Damascus, as well as the direct sea route by Sicily and Cyprus to Jaffa, which became the most popular approach at the height of the pilgrim traffic in the later Middle Ages. Arculf seems to have entered and departed by way of Constantinople, still then, of course, a Christian capital, but he made a side trip by sea to Egypt involving a forty days' sail from Jaffa to Alexandria. Although Arculf does not mention it, there existed at this time a Suez Canal, as we know from a contemporary Latin treatise on geography by an English scholar named Dicuil. This treatise reports a conversation with an English monk, Fidelis, who had actually sailed through the canal from the Nile into the Red Sea while on a pilgrimage to the Holy Land during the first half of the eighth century. In 767 the canal was blocked up by the Caliph Al-Mansur.

Other firsthand reports by Continental pilgrims have survived, but through the accident of his shipwreck and the devoted work of the Scotch abbot Arculf's story belongs to Britain. Launched by the respected Bede, this book contributed to the passion for pilgrimage that soon afterwards seized the Anglo-Saxons. The first of the pilgrims who left an account was St. Willibald of Wessex, the son of a certain Richard who bore the title King, but of what, historians have never been able to decide for certain. Whether Willibald had read *De Locis Sanctis* is not known, but it seems probable that he would have, for he was an intensely pious young man dedicated to the service of the church as a child. In the years after his prolonged pilgrimage Willibald became a renowned bishop carrying on the proselytizing work of his uncle, St. Boniface, among the Teutons.

Two accounts of his life and journeys survive, one anonymous, and one by a nun related to him who took down his reminiscences in after years.

He was described in his old age as "perfect in charity and gentleness"; yet "his look was majestic and terrible to gainsayers." As a youth he must have been equally terrible to less high-minded souls, for at the age of eighteen he managed to persuade his father, brother, and sister, much against their inclination, to undertake the long journey to Jerusalem with him (one wonders how his mother resisted, but the chronicle is silent). When first he urged his father to become a pilgrim and "despise the world" the King refused on the not unnatural ground that it would be "contrary to all humanity" to leave his wife a widow, his children orphans, and his house desolate. But the persistent Willibald maintained that love of Christ prevailed over all natural affections, and the father, "overcome at last by the conversation of his truth-telling son," agreed to go. The decision proved to his sorrow, for the King died on the way, even before the party reached Rome, and was buried at Lucca in Tuscany. In Rome the brother fell ill, but Willibald, leaving him in the care of his sister, pressed on to Palestine in the year 721.

At any given time it is possible to gauge the degree of religious feeling in England by the reaction of the traveler to his first sight of Jerusalem. In the fervent Middle Ages some wept, some prayed, some fell on their knees and kissed the soil. Margery Kempe, a fifteenth-century fanatic, was so overcome at the sight that "she was in point to a fallen offe her asse," but her companions put spices in her mouth to revive her. Indeed, at every place memorable for some incident in the life of Jesus this pilgrim was so much given to "wepyng and sobbyng in lowde voys" that "hir felows wold not latyn hir etyn in their cumpany." Later, after the Reformation, adventurous Elizabethans, seventeenth-century merchants and scholars, cool eighteenth-century skeptics could make the ascent and never notice the bend in the road where Jerusalem first comes into view. Victorians revert to medieval fervor and tend to tears, awe, and solemn thoughts.

Perhaps Willibald set the style for medieval English travelers, for certainly no pilgrim was ever more deeply affected than he. "What spot was there which had witnessed the Lord's miracles," says his chronicle, "on which Willibald, the man of God did not imprint his kisses? What altar was there that he did not bedew with his tears and sighs?"

So ardent were his feelings that he made four sojourns in Jerusalem during his extended stay of several years in the Holy Land. In between he visited all the usual places of religious interest throughout the country and one unusual one, a church on Mt. Tabor consecrated jointly to Jesus, Moses, and Elijah. He drank sour ewe's milk without approval, remarked on the extraordinary native sheep "all one color" (were eighth-century English sheep parti-colored?), and once on a plain thick with olive trees he encountered a lion that roared dreadfully but when approached "hurried off in another direction."

Sometimes he traveled alone, at another time in company with seven unnamed countrymen. On one occasion all eight were arrested on suspicion and imprisoned by the Saracens. "The townsmen used then to come to look at them because they were young and handsome and clad in good garments." When they were brought before the King of the Saracens he asked whence they came and was told: "These men come from the west country where the sun never sets and we know of no land beyond them, but water only." Apparently not regarding such origin as a crime, the King replied: "Why ought we to punish them? They have not sinned against us. Give them leave and let them go."

Each side trip Willibald made required a letter of safe-conduct from the Caliph, a matter of some difficulty, for on one occasion he and his companions could not find the sovereign "because he had fled out of his kingdom." This was the same Emir-al-Mumenin who had earlier released the English party from prison. Perhaps he was too tolerant toward unbelievers to please his subjects.

Tyre and Sidon, Antioch and Damascus, Constantinople and Nicaea were visited before Willibald finally sailed for Sicily and Italy, where he settled for a time at Monte Cassino just ten years after leaving home.

After Willibald there is a long silence, for the times were not friendly to the survival of manuscripts. During the ninth and tenth centuries, while Moslem civilization was at its height both in the arts of peace and in temporal power, Europe was sunk in the darkest period of the Dark Ages. Barbarism, cruelty, moral decrepitude, and cultural lethargy held sway. No light or inspiration came from Rome, where the Church was in the hands of persons described by the great papal historian, Caesar Baronius, as "monstrous men, depraved in life, abandoned in morals, utterly corrupt." Men of the sword, unbridled by established law or strong rulers, left no man's life safe. In England the ravaging Danes burned, destroyed, and slaughtered wherever they passed, with only King Alfred in the southwest offering a valiant resistance. Meeting destruction on every hand, men became disgusted with the world on earth and in a desperate search for security entered monasteries in droves or set off to seek the threshold of heaven in the Holy Land. A period of religious hysteria, in which the year 1000 was expected to bring the end of the world, afflicted all of Western Europe like an epidemic. Hastening to the scene of man's Redemption before the final awful moment of reckoning, "hordes," according to some chroniclers, poured into the Holy Land, of whom a large proportion never returned. Some died of want, some of plague, some were killed by marauding Arabs, some were lost at sea by storms or shipwreck or pirates. Only the lucky or the well provided came back alive.

A highly imaginative account of a mass pilgrimage supposed to have taken place in 1064 is incorporated by the otherwise circumstantial historian, Florence of Worcester, whose chronicle was written in the last quarter of the eleventh century, shortly after the event was supposed to have taken place. He tells of a multitude of 7,000 who accompanied the Archbishop of Mentz (Mainz) and the Bishops of Utrecht, Bamberg, and Ratisbon on a pilgrimage to Jerusalem. They were attacked by the Saracens, who, in search of the gold the Christians were supposed to have swallowed when in fear of capture, pinned as many as they could catch to the earth in the shape of a cross and slit them open from throat to belly. Of the 7,000 a remnant of 2,000 escaped and survived. Although this adventure apparently does not involve people from England, it was included in a chronicle of English history and was probably typical of the atrocity stories circulating at the time, which helped to arouse the fervor for the First Crusade.

Beginning in the eleventh century crowned heads and mitred bishops, fat abbots and helmeted barons joined the simpler people on the road to Jerusalem. Olaf Tryggvason, first Christian king of Norway, made the pilgrimage in 1003, Duke Robert of Normandy, father of William the Conqueror, followed in 1035, and Ealdred, Archbishop of York, who was later to perform the coronation of William the Conqueror, went in 1058 with "such splendour as none other had displayed before him."

In the same decade Earl Sweyn, rascally elder brother of Harold, who was to be King of England, went to Jerusalem in expiation of his many sins and died at Constantinople on his way home about the year 1055. His career seems to have been unusually conscienceless even for the eleventh century. He began by seducing Edviga, the Abbess of Leominster, who he ordered "should be fetched unto him and he had her as long as he listed and afterwards let her fare home." Not so much the act of seduction as its choice of a bride of Christ as victim shocked his countrymen, who thereupon pronounced him an outlaw. He took refuge in

Denmark, but was apparently not a bit chastened, for by some further crime he "ruined himself with the Danes." Allowed to return home to plead for remission of the sentence of outlawry, he promptly murdered his cousin Earl Beorn, who had received part of Sweyn's lands and whom Sweyn had induced to meet him under a truce. Again it was not the murder so much as the violation of the truce that prompted his next punishment. Though he was the eldest son of Earl Godwin, regent of the kingdom, he was pronounced a *nithing,* or man without honor, the lowest form of manhood known to Saxon society. He again took refuge on the Continent, but in the following year, 1050, he was brought home, pardoned, and restored to his earl-dom—a rash act, granted his reputation, though it may have been motivated by some phase in the bewildering rivalries of the Saxon nobles, whose disunity was soon to open the way to William the Conqueror.

The pattern is repeated with monotonous regularity. Sweyn is again outlawed in 1051 for some offense that no chronicler mentions. This time apparently his family has had enough of him, and either to get him out of the country for a long time or to earn him a last chance of forgiveness he is somehow induced to set off for Jerusalem in 1053.

Earl Sweyn as an individual would not warrant much attention were it not that he is the first recorded instance of the type of pilgrim that is to become all too frequent during the Crusades. This is the criminal who joined the pilgrims' ranks to escape imprisonment or execution, as later criminals joined the Foreign Legion. Once having received the blessing of the Church on his journey and the Cross to sew on his cloak, the pilgrim traveled under ecclesiastical protection that put him beyond the reach of the secular arm, just as a fugitive claiming sanctuary inside a church was safe from all pursuers. Moreover the church had a regular table of indulgences that could be won by pilgrimages to holy places. According to one count there were ninety-six holy places in Jerusalem alone, and thirty-three more in the Church of the Holy Sepulcher, not to mention many hundreds in Bethlehem, Nazareth, Galilee, and elsewhere. Neither Rome nor St. James of Compostella, the other two most favored pilgrimages, had anything like this to offer. By adding up partial indulgences granted at each of a number of holy places, five days from one, forty from another, a pilgrim could reduce his expected stay in purgatory to very little, perhaps to nothing. Or if he were a highly placed person or came with an important letter of introduction or made rich gifts to the monastic orders that administered the holy places, he might even secure a plenary indulgence remitting all punishment. Certificates were given to pilgrims testifying to the places they had visited and the devotions performed. On payment of a fee they might even be made Knights of the Sepulcher. Clearly the journey to Palestine provided a convenient out for the man who had made his home too hot to hold him. He could not only place himself beyond the reach of the law and his enemies for a long time, but he could at the same time commute the penalty he might otherwise expect to pay either on earth or in the after life. This system proved so attractive to transgressors that cutthroats and misfits aplenty mingled with the pious, the adventurous, and the purely curious amid the pilgrim multitudes.

Shortly after the pilgrimage of the Saxon Sweyn the sovereignty of England passed to the Norman conquerors, and five years later, in 1071, the sovereignty of Palestine passed from the caliphate of Bagdad to a newer branch of Islam, the Seljuk Turks. The Seljuk conquest provoked the First Crusade; the Norman conquest caused England's participation in what was chiefly a Continental project. During the ensuing two hundred years of intermittent crusades there was of course a constant flow of travelers between England and Palestine, but few English diaries of individual pilgrimages from this period survive. One that has survived is the diary of Saewulf, a prosperous merchant given to fits of piety between periods of indulgence in earthly pleasures. In one of the former he embarked on a pilgrimage to Jerusalem in 1102. Only three years had passed since the taking of Jerusalem by the warriors of the First Crusade, and the Latin kingdom they had established there was in the springtime of its power. For the first time in five hundred years the holy places were in Christian hands. New trade opportunities were opened. Ambitious nobles dreamed of new fiefs that could be carved from the infidel's lands with a battle-ax and a few men-at-arms. Saewulf notes the crowds of travelers going to Palestine, both noble and poor, clergy and lay, true pilgrims and piratical adventurers "embarking with crews of desperate marauders . . . plundering and devastating on their way."

On his arrival Saewulf narrowly escaped death in a terrible storm that wrecked his ship a few hours after he debarked at Jaffa. He has left a harrowing description of the crashing and splintering ships in the harbor, the shrieks of the drowning, the roaring of the wind, the awful sight of a falling mast knocking off a man's head, and in the morning the derelict fragments of twenty-three vessels and the beach strewn with a thousand bodies.

Then comes the hazardous climb up to Jerusalem through the hills where Saracens lie in wait in caves to pounce on unwary travelers and where many unburied corpses lie scattered on the way, "for there is not much earth on the hard rock to dig a grave." This suggests that Palestine already had begun to suffer the soil erosion that during the centuries of Arab cultivation reduced it from the one-time land of milk and honey to a stony goat pasture.

Saewulf spent eight months visiting Jerusalem and the Biblical towns around from Hebron in the south, where Abraham settled and was buried, up through Jericho to Nazareth, Tiberias, and Capernaum in the north. Typical of many medieval travel diaries, Saewulf's narrative passes without a comma from things he actually saw to gossip and popular lore gathered from local guides at each stopping place. To separate out the nuggets of fact is not easy, but his account is valuable less for what it tells of Palestine than for what it tells of the furnishings of the mind of the average twelfth-century tourist. Knowledge of geography and history was not a strong point. When he visited the Mosque of Omar, then in the hands of the Latin monks, Saewulf refers to it as the Temple of Solomon, endows it with an entirely fictitious history according to which it was rebuilt somewhere along the line by Hadrian or Heraclius or "some say it was by Justinian" (Saewulf is not particular), and indicates only the vaguest notion of how and when the Mohammedans entered the picture.

Likewise his description of an enemy fleet encountered on the way home shows how history happening under his eyes was interpreted in terms of ancient history learned from the Bible. "Twenty-six ships of the Saracens suddenly came into sight," he writes. "[They were] the forces of the Admiral of Tyre and Sidon which were carrying an army to Babylonia to assist the Chaldeans in making war on the King of Jerusalem." One would think Saewulf was somehow transported back to the sixth century B.C. when the Chaldean kings of ancient Babylon made war on Jerusalem and took the Israelites into captivity. But of course the king of Jerusalem whom Saewulf is talking about is the crusader king, Baldwin I, and the "Babylonia" he refers to is not the ancient city on the banks of the Euphrates, but Cairo, called Babylon in his time. Saewulf knew well enough where it was, but he peoples it with "Chaldeans" out of confusion with the Biblical city, for to him modern enemies of Jerusalem were the same as the enemy that had come out of the other Babylon to attack it 1,500 years before. Similarly he identified the Christians under King Baldwin of Jerusalem with the city's ancient proprietors, the people of Israel. One finds King Richard in the Third Crusade calling on his troops to "restore the kingdom of

Israel." This self-identification with the ancient though not the contemporary Jews was taken for granted by the Christian powers, who, as the heirs of Christ, regarded themselves as the rightful inheritors of the Holy Land and considered it their duty, in Mandeville's words, to "conquer our right heritage."

The belief that Jerusalem was the geographical center of the world, which Saewulf faithfully repeats, was another concept of his time for which the Bible was responsible.

"For thus saith the Lord, This is Jerusalem, I have set her in the midst of the nations and the countries that are round about." This passage from Ezekiel and other similar ones had by now quite blanketed out the work of the classical geographers, who were not victims of any such confusion. Medieval maps presented an entirely new visualization of the known world, in which Jerusalem is placed in its exact center. Ocean surrounds the circumference of the earth, and beyond the ocean strange animals, sea monsters, and oriental designs adorn the outer rim, representing barbarian lands of which cartographers knew nothing beyond the fact that they existed.

In the same year that Saewulf was in Palestine another pilgrim, Godric, who was to become a saint, also came there. Godric was a combination pirate, shipowner, and merchant whose two journeys to Palestine may have been undertaken in search of adventure and booty rather than salvation, but later came to be remembered as pilgrimages under the influence of the legends that grew up about his name. Godric must have traveled in his own ship, for though he left no personal record a contemporary chronicler reports that "*Gudericus, pirata de regno Angliae,*" took King Baldwin to Jerusalem by sea down the coast from Arsuf to Jaffa after the King's forces met a defeat on the plains of Ramleh and were cut off from Jaffa by land.

In 1106 he made a second journey to the Holy Land, this time on foot, and returned to England to become a venerated hermit, the subject of many saintly adventures, while the legend of his pilgrimages grew yearly, studded with a variety of affecting details. He was said to have vowed never to change clothes or shoes or eat anything but barley bread and water until he should reach Palestine. Once there he bathed in the Jordan and arose cleansed, but threw away his shoes, vowing to walk barefoot ever after in emulation of Jesus, though perhaps the condition of his footgear may have had something to do with his resolve.

Until the Protestant reformation the pilgrim movement was a constant element in the life of the Middle Ages and the pilgrim or palmer a familiar figure to all men of his time. In the two blue-robed figures of the Palmer's Window at Ludlow chapel he has attained the immortality of stained glass. In literature the simile of the pilgrimage to Jerusalem is a familiar one, as in the poignant poem Sir Walter Raleigh wrote on the eve of the scaffold:

> Give me my scallop shell of quiet,
> My Staffe of Faith to walk upon,
> My scrip of joy, Immortal diet,
> My bottle of salvation:
> My gowne of glory, hopes true gage
> And thus Ile take my pilgrimage.

Here are the familiar articles by which everyone recognized the palmer as he trudged along. His particular emblem was the scallop shell, derived probably from the wayfarer's use of it to scoop a drink of water from a stream. The staff lent support to his steps and could in an emergency be used as a weapon. The scrip or leather shoulder bag held what little food or clothing he carried as well as some saint's bones or dust from the Via Dolorosa or splinters from the Cross, bought as souvenirs. The bottle attached to his belt was used to bring home water from the Jordan. Sometimes, too, he carried a bunch of faded palm branches and wore a collection of medallions stuck around the crown of his hat, one for each shrine he had visited.

These were the "signs of Synay" worn by the Palmer in *Piers Plowman*, who boasts that he has visited not only Sinai but also Jerusalem, Bethlehem, Babylon, Alexandria, and Damascus. Indeed, the palmer's journeyings made him a famous fellow of medieval life, a sort of foreign correspondent for the people back home, whom he entertained with tales of far-off lands and strange peoples. Though he acquired a reputation as an inveterate liar, men would always gather eagerly to hear him tell about the Holy City, about the wickedness and splendors of the paynim Saracen, the fabled glories of Byzantium, of wild beasts encountered, brigands and pirates foiled, and great personages met along the way.

Such a one was the Palmer of John Heywood's play "The Four Ps," with whom lying was "comen usage" and who spellbinds his fellow P's—the Pardoner, Poticary, and Pedler—with an account of a barefoot tour of the Holy Places, of how "many a salt tere dyde I swete before thys carkes could come there."

Like the troubadour, the palmer earned alms for his tales, for he was a professional wanderer from shrine to shrine who depended for his livelihood on the free food and lodging that it was customary to offer these wayfarers. A pilgrim, on the other hand, was a settled person who undertook a specific journey for a specific reason at his own expense. Sometimes he went to fulfill a vow, expiate a sin, or perform a mission as did Sir James Douglas, who carried the heart of Robert Bruce in a golden casket to Jerusalem for burial there, since when the Douglases have borne a heart on their coat of arms. Sometimes he went to escape an uncomfortable situation as did a certain Abbot of Ramsay who in the year 1020 was expelled from his monastery when the monks mutinied over his too rigorous insistence on ascetic rules, and who took himself off to Jerusalem in a huff. But most often it was neither piety nor sin, but pure love of travel, that carried the generations of English pilgrims to Palestine. Indeed the English were considered great travelers and from their love of moving about were commonly believed to be under the moon's influence. That lusty epitome of medieval womanhood, Chaucer's Wife of Bath, mentions in passing that she has been to Jerusalem three times, though one wonders when she found the time in between her five wedding trips to the church door.

Sometimes a pilgrim could earn vicarious glory for those who stayed at home if they subscribed to the cost of his journey. It was a practice among the London guilds of the fourteenth century to release a member from his dues if he undertook a pilgrimage, so that his guild brothers, by taking up the cost of his dues, could share in the salvation he earned. In addition each colleague subscribed a penny to the pilgrim destined for Jerusalem (only a halfpenny if his goal was Rome or Compostella) and accompanied him in a body to the outskirts of the town as he set off on his voyage.

From the fourteenth century dates the most popular of all medieval travelogues on Palestine, the *Book of Sir John Mandeville,* knight, who tells us he was "born in England in the town of St. Albans." The unrelenting detection of modern scholars has shown that the author was neither English nor a knight, that his name was not Mandeville, and that his book is a package of borrowings from earlier travelers, geographers, and explorers from Herodotus down to Marco Polo. Yet no other book in that day was so widely read in England or on the Continent. Originally written in Latin and translated by the author himself (if one may believe him) into French and English, the book caught such interest that versions appeared in Italian, Spanish, Dutch, Walloon, Bohemian, German, Danish, and Irish, and some three hundred manuscripts have survived. As soon as printing was invented Mandeville was one of the earliest to be printed, a German edition appearing in 1475 and one in English in 1503. The long-lasting popularity of his book contributed much to the sense of familiarity with Palestine.

Whatever his deficiencies in honesty, Mandeville makes up for them by his enthusiasm for his subject, his inexhaustible supply of information, whether fact or fable, and his exuberance in sharing all of it with his readers. Palestine he says flatly was chosen of God as "the best and most worthy land, and the most virtuous land of all the world, for it is the heart and middle of all the world." He enters by way of Egypt, where he pauses to remark of the pyramids that they were the "granaries of Joseph" which he caused to be built to store grain against bad times. He adds without prejudice that "some men say that they are sepulchers of great lords that were formerly; but this is not true." Twelve days' journeying takes him to Mt. Sinai, and he retells all the adventures of Moses and the children of Israel in the wilderness, including the passage of the Red Sea, "which is not redder than other seas but in some places the gravel is red and therefore they call it the Red Sea." The narrative is liberally laced with an immense variety of nonscriptural miracles and natural wonders such as the annual pilgrimage of "ravens, crows and other fowls of that country" to the monastery of St. Catherine's at the foot of Mt. Sinai, "and each brings a branch of bays or olive in its beak and leaves it there."

From Mt. Sinai another thirteen days takes the traveler across the desert to Gaza, city of Samson and Beersheba, which, says Mandeville, was founded by Bathsheba, "wife of Sir Uriah, the knight." The Dead Sea of course provides him with unexampled profusion of wonders, as that a man can cast iron into it that will float, but a feather will sink. At Hebron, the oldest city of Palestine, the dwelling and burial place of Abraham, Isaac, and Jacob and of their wives and so as sacred to the Moslem sons of Ishmael as to the Jews, Mandeville reports a prophecy associated with a dead oak tree there: "A lord, a prince of the west side of the world, shall win the Land of Promise, that is the Holy Land, with the help of the Christians, and he shall cause mass to be performed under that dying tree and then the tree shall become green and bear both fruit and leaves. And through that miracle many Jews and Saracens shall be converted to the Christian faith." This curious insistence on the convertibility of the Jews will reappear frequently in later chapters, especially in the earnest if misguided efforts of the Evangelical movement. But though the prophecy was forever to remain futile, the first half of it was eventually fulfilled if one can recognize "a prince of the west" in Field Marshal Allenby.

Beginning in the fifteenth century there is a notable change in the tone of Palestine travel diaries, with less of the fabulous and more practical tourist information. By now pilgrimages had become an organized traffic, and a returned pilgrim who tried to awe his listeners with wondrous tales was likely to be tripped up, for too many had been there before him. A regular galley service operated out of Venice, making about five round trips to Jaffa a year, usually going in the spring and early summer. Each of these galleys, privately owned though under the supervision of the Venetian state, could carry as many as a hundred pilgrims, and trading vessels making the voyage to Eastern ports also carried pilgrims for extra profit. The ships, according to an anonymous account, were always "full stuffed with people," so that "the air therein waxeth soon contrarious and groweth alway from evil to worse." The discomforts of the crowded sea voyage, which took four to six weeks, must have been considerable, for the English traveler William Wey advises future pilgrims that a berth on the open upper deck, despite wind and spray, is preferable to the "right smolderynge hote and stynkynge" accommodations in the hold.

The Venetian galleys usually stopped at Cyprus and Rhodes, where the pilgrims could take in the sights, and again at Beirut, the port for Damascus. From there they sailed down the coast to Jaffa, the port for Jerusalem, where the average pilgrim debarked, took a guided three weeks' tour, and returned to Venice on the same ship.

Transportation, for those who could afford it, on mules or camel-back with hired Arab guides was arranged for by the master of the pilgrim galley, who doubled as a tourist agent. Guides were Franciscan monks, sole custodians of the holy places after 1230, who recited the history and traditions associated with each town or monument or site of Biblical events to parties of visitors as they arrived.

More ambitious travelers began their tour in Egypt, sailing from Venice to Alexandria, from where, following the route of the Exodus, they crossed the Sinai desert and entered Palestine from the south. Thomas Swinburne, English mayor of Bordeaux and personage of importance at the court of Richard II, led a party in 1392–93 by this route, covered the length of Palestine, and departed from Damascus and Beirut in the north. A daily itinerary kept by the squire of the party, Thomas Brigg, is stuffed with details of traveling expenses, transportation, guides, fees, imposts, tips, foods, and lodging. Apparently he was kept too busy adding up accounts to record much of what he saw. In the same year the ambitious young cousin of the King, Henry of Bolingbroke, then aged twenty-five, came to Jerusalem on a pilgrimage with one donkey carrying his provisions. Many years later, after he had deposed King Richard and reigned in his stead as Henry IV, the dying King, remembering a prophecy that his life would end in Jerusalem, had himself carried into the "Jerusalem Chamber" at Westminster, where he died.

The fullest record of the average fifteenth-century pilgrimage is the manuscript of William Wey, who went twice to Jerusalem, in 1458 and 1462, and set himself to write a handy travel guide that is touched with the genius of Baedeker. In prose and in rhymed couplets, in English and in Latin, Wey provides the prospective journeyer to Jerusalem with all the information he might need. He gives the rates of exchange in terms of a noble or a ducat along the route he took through Calais, Brabant, Cologne, Lombardy, Venice, Rhodes, and Cyprus to Jaffa, so that his readers may understand the "diversitie of moneys as from England unto Surrey in the holy lande." He advises what kind of contract the traveler should make with the Venetian shipmaster to ensure that it covers food and drink, he suggests extra provisions that the traveler should carry for himself, including "laxitives and restoratives," cooking and eating utensils, and bedding. He tells where a feather bed with a mattress, two pillows, a pair of sheets, and a quilt can be purchased in Venice and resold after use in Palestine for half the purchase price. He cautions the traveler to take only fresh food and drink, only good wine and fresh water, and to keep a careful eye on all his belongings, "for the Sarcenes will go talkyng wyth yow and make good chere, but they wyl stele from yow that ye have and they may."

Wey, who had been appointed one of the original fellows of Eton college on its foundation in 1440, required special permission from the King, Henry VI, to make the journey in order that he might resume his fellowship when he returned. "Wee, having tendre consideration unto his blessed purpose," wrote the King, do license "our well-beloved clerc, Maister William Wey . . . to passe over the see on peregrimage as to Rome, to Jerusalem and to other Holy Places." Possibly Wey was commissioned to undertake the pilgrimage for the very purpose of writing a guidebook, for he certainly took great pains. He provides a table of distances, a glossary of useful words and phrases in transliterated Greek, the spoken language of the Levant, a list of indulgences to be attained at various shrines, an enumeration of all the holy places that can be visited in a thirteen days' tour in and around Jerusalem (ten between Jaffa and Jerusalem, twenty-two in Jerusalem, thirteen in the Church of the Holy Sepulcher, seven in Bethlehem, eight on the Jordan, and so on to a total of one hundred and ten), and a few remarks on the rulers of the country and the laws and regulations affecting Christian travelers. He even supplies ten reasons for undertaking the pilgrimage to begin with, which include the exhortations of St. Jerome, the remission of sins, and the opportunity to acquire relics. Wey's care with dates of arrival and departure gives us an accurate picture of the time required for such a journey in the later Middle Ages. He spent less than three weeks in Palestine on his first trip and less than two on the second, but was away from England altogether nine months each time. The journey from England to Venice took nearly two months the second time because of a detour necessitated by a local war in Germany; otherwise it required a month to six weeks. A month was spent in Venice waiting for a ship, and the sea voyage itself took him one month the first time and nearly seven weeks the second. Comparing this with an itinerary of a pilgrimage made in the last decade of the tenth century by Archbishop Sigeric of Canterbury, we can see that there was little change over a period of five hundred years. It took the Archbishop nearly three months from Rome back to England, the part of the journey covered by the itinerary, but he was slowed by rainy weather. His record shows that a day's march on foot or horseback varied from five to twenty-five miles according to weather, food, and available hostels. A good day's average was fifteen or twenty miles in four or five hours.

By the year in which Wey compiled his careful guidebook the time of the pilgrim was already running out; the end of the Middle Ages was close at hand. Palestine, dominated since the death of Saladin in 1193 by the Mamelukes of Egypt, whose wars with the Crusaders, the Tartars, the Mongols, and various other barbarian hordes had kept the land bloodsoaked for three centuries, now faced a new conqueror. The Ottoman Turks in 1453 had captured Constantinople, with echoes that were heard around the world. Now they were advancing down upon Syria, and by 1517 they had conquered the Mamelukes, absorbed the Egyptian Caliphate into the Turkish Empire, and were masters in Jerusalem and Palestine. Within a few years England

underwent an equally momentous change with the seces-
sion from Roman Catholicism.

Two voyagers of the early sixteenth century have left us
a picture of conditions at the end of the pilgrim era. Sir
Richard Guildford, privy councilor to the first Tudor king,
Henry VII, with his companion John Whitby, Prior of Guis-
borough, left England in April 1506 and arrived at Jaffa in
August. According to an account of Guildford's ill-fated
pilgrimage written by the chaplain who accompanied him,
the party was first detained in the ship for seven days off
Jaffa. Then they were "received by ye Mamelukes and
Saracyns and put into an old cave by name and tale, and
there scryven ever wrytyng oure names man by man as we
entered in the presence of the sayd Lordes and there we
lay in the same grotto or cave Fridaye all day upon bare
stynkynge stable grounde, as well nyght as day, right evyll
intreated by ye Maures." After this ordeal "bothe my mayster and mayster Pryor of Gysborne were sore seke" and
being unable to go on foot to Jerusalem were forced to procure "Camellys with grete dyffyculte and outragyous
coste." The party managed to reach Jerusalem, but there
both Sir Richard and the Prior died of their illness.

A few years later Sir Richard Torkyngton, Rector of
Mulberton in Norfolk, made a pilgrimage. He also com-
plains of maltreatment by the Mamelukes, who put his
party "in great fear which were too long to write." At Jaffa
he found that "now there standeth never an house but only
two towers and certain caves under the ground," but Jerusalem was still "a fair eminent place for it standeth upon
such a grounde that from whence so ever a man cometh,
there he must needs ascend," and from there one can see
"all Arabie." He describes how the city gets its water by
conduits in great plenty from Hebron and Bethlehem, so
that the cisterns are all filled "and much water runneth
now to waste."

On his return journey down from Jerusalem Torkyngton, joined for greater safety with two other English pil-

grims, Robert Crosse, a pewterer of London, and Sir Thomas Toppe, "a priest of the west country." These are among the last names we can group with the devotional pilgrims of the Middle Ages, for within a few years England embraced the Reformation, and the practice of pilgrimage, because of its association with the buying of indulgences and the worship of saints and relics, was sternly disapproved by the reformers. The new tone is typified by Erasmus, who in his satirical dialogues mocks the vanities of pilgrims, "all covered with cockle shells, laden on every side with images of lead and tynne." Wyclif, early herald of the Reformation, had long ago voiced a pronounced distaste for pilgrimages and with some effect for when one of his followers was forced to abjure Lollardy he had to take an oath promising that "I shal neuermore despyse pylgrimage." The road to Jerusalem lies in the heart, the reformers taught. There it was to remain for some time, while the physical Palestine was left to the merchants and diplomats of competing powers.

CHAPTER IV

THE CRUSADES

To be "the sewer of Christendom and drain all the discords out of it" was the primary function of the Crusades, the Reverend Tom Fuller said in his *History of the Holy Warre*, written in 1639. Admittedly a partisan Protestant view, Fuller's dictum can still stand without serious challenge. At the outset the Crusades were set in motion by a thirst for gain, for glory, and for revenge upon the infidel in the name of religion. Exulting in bloodshed, ruthless in cruelty, innocent of geography, strategy, or supply, the first Crusaders plunged headlong eastward with no other plan of campaign than to fall upon Jerusalem and wrest it from the Turks. This in some mad fashion they accomplished only because the enemy was divided against himself. Thereafter mutual dissension defeated them too; even the most elementary loyalty among allies that ought to have been dictated by a sense of self-preservation was lacking. For the next two hundred years the trail of their forked pennons across the heart of the Middle Ages was but a series of vain endeavors to recapture the victories of the first expedition.

Failure seems to have taught them nothing. Like human lemmings each generation of Crusaders flung themselves into the fatal footsteps of their fathers. Palestine itself, the battleground and the prize, became a second country if not a graveyard for half the families of Europe. St. Bernard of Clairvaux, who preached the Second Crusade, boasted that he left but one man in Europe to console every seven widows. But what made the distant land so familiar was not the numbers who went at any one time so much as the fact that they kept on going over and over again to the same place for nearly two centuries, so that often two, three, or four generations in the same family had fought or settled or died in Palestine.

In England the carved stone effigies of four earls of Oxford, each with the crossed legs signifying a participant in the Crusades, lie in the parish church at Hereford. Albericus de Vere, the first Earl, surnamed "the Grim," in full battle dress of chain mail from head to toe, covered by a cloth surplice, sword at his side, spurred feet resting on a lion, lies in stony immortality on a tomb bearing the date 1194. Near him are the second Earl, died 1215, the third Earl, died 1221, and the fifth Earl, died 1295, each with the crossed legs of the Crusader. Similarly in Aldworth church in Berkshire are five cross-legged effigies of the de la Beche family. Such effigies can be found in every country in England, some with feet resting on a boar or stag, some with hand on sword half pulled from its scabbard, some with hands in prayer, some with shields bearing the Templar's cross, some with their ladies also cross-legged lying beside them, their robes fixed forever in straight, stiff folds. The numerous families whose coats of arms bear the scallop shells or George's Cross bespeak the Crusades, and even today inns exist at the sign of the "Saracen's Head."

Yet the Crusades seem not to have penetrated so deeply into the English consciousness as one might expect. They inspired no monument of national history; no one emerged among the nineteenth-century giants to do for the Crusades what Stubbs or Froude or Freeman did for their special fields. All the basic scholarship has been done by the French. Nor was any great literary tradition born of these Eastern adventures, apart from the rather foolish medieval metrical romances celebrating Richard's dining on roasted Saracen or his rescue by Blondel the minstrel. Indeed, the English-speaking people know the Crusades chiefly in the

rose-colored version of Scott's *Talisman,* the only outstand-
ing work of fiction that they inspired in all of English
literature.

Partly this lack is due to the fact that England's real
energies during the crusading epoch were taken up in the
struggles at home between Saxon and Norman, between
nobles and kings, and between Crown and Church.

The figure of Richard alone absorbs most of England's
crusading traditions and glory: yet he was hardly an Englishman, his Queen never set foot in England, and he himself spent no more than seven months of his twelve years'
reign in the country whose crown he wore. It was Palestine
that made him into an English hero. What did England
know of him as king—a towering red-haired, sword-rattling
apparition with the furious temper of the Angevins who
descended upon the country only to be crowned and to
scrape into his treasury every extractable penny to finance
his Crusade? He was gone in such a hurry that England
was hardly aware of him except as a tidal wave of taxation
that poured over them and retreated only to pour over
them again when he had to be ransomed from the prison
of the emperor to whom Leopold of Austria had surrendered him.

Somehow those memories were blotted out by the glorious tale of his prowess in Palestine as he hacked and
slashed his way through the Saracen ranks with sword in
one hand and battle ax in the other. It was in Palestine
that he became Richard the Lion-Hearted and in Palestine
that he was transformed from the quarrelsome, valorous,
conscienceless son of Aquitaine and Anjou into England's
first hero king since Alfred.

He was not, of course, the only king of England to go to
Palestine as either pilgrim or Crusader. Twice the throne
fell empty while its claimant was in the Holy Land. Richard's great-great-uncle, Robert Curthose, Duke of Normandy, eldest son of the Conqueror, lost the English crown
to his younger brother Henry I while away on the First

Crusade. Richard's great-nephew Edward Longshanks had better luck. Though absent in Palestine leading the Seventh Crusade when the king his father died, he was able to succeed to the crown on his return and reigned for twenty years as Edward I, the "English Justinian."

Richard's father Henry II, his brother John, and John's son Henry III all took the vow to go on the Crusades, but the first two were too busy fighting at home and the last too disinclined to fight at all to make good the vow. Others in the royal family substituted. William Longsword, whose father was a bastard brother of Richard the Lion-Heart, cut a great figure in the Crusade of St. Louis; so did Richard, Earl of Cornwall, brother of Henry III. Perhaps the greatest English figure of the thirteenth century, Simon de Montfort, who led the barons' revolt against Henry III, commanded a Crusade to Palestine earlier in his career. Countless others set out with their companies of knights, squires, and foot soldiers, some even with their wives, on the ever-fruitless quest to conquer "our right heritage," "God's land," whose title they had appropriated yet were never able to make good.

It may be that the Bible would never have been able in a later time to take such deep root in the English body had not English blood been shed in the land of the Bible over so many years.

The English share in the First Crusade has commonly been overlooked. Yet, according to the eyewitness chronicler Raymon of Aguelers, an English fleet of thirty vessels manned by English mariners played a vital role by supporting the Crusaders from the sea until they gained their first base with the capture of Antioch. Although William of Malmesbury, writing a generation later, says that "but a faint murmur of Asiatic affairs reached the ears of those who dwelt beyond the British ocean," the murmur must have been louder than he thought. Whether the English naval force was fired by enthusiasm for the Holy War or was simply a group of dispossessed Saxons escaping from

William's conquest, at any rate it was collected in England, sailed under its own leadership, and seized and held Seleucia, the port of Antioch, until the main body of the Crusaders came down from Constantinople by land. Until Antioch was taken the English ships, co-operating with the Genoese, held off attacks by the Saracen fleet and kept open the supply lines to Cyprus. When the Crusaders were ready to march on Jerusalem the English, having by then lost all but nine or ten of their ships, burned the remainder and joined with the land forces, at which point they disappear from history. Perhaps it was their example, though all but ignored in the histories of the time, which determined Richard a hundred years later to go by sea rather than follow the disastrous land march of his predecessors. If so, these nameless men made a contribution, unhonored and unsung, to the development of the sea power that eventually carried England to empire.

Meanwhile Robert Curthose marched with the land army. Though Norman by birth and title, he was, as a member of the newly established royal family, what might be called a first-generation Englishman. In fact, by the time he died William of Malmesbury was speaking of him as "Robert, the Englishman." His followers on the Crusade were chiefly Normans, Bretons, and Angevins. The anonymous "men from England" said to have accompanied him were probably foot soldiers, for among the three hundred and sixty named knights in his train only a handful were defeated Saxon lords or disaffected Anglo-Normans already at odds with the king.

But if the English did not go with Robert, they paid willy-nilly for his share in the Crusade. In order to equip a force he mortgaged the duchy of Normandy to his unpleasant brother William Rufus for five years in return for ten thousand marks. Rufus, to raise this huge sum, imposed heavy taxes on every person in England "so that the whole country groaned."

Yet it was not so bad a bargain, for in Palestine Robert,

a footling fellow at home, pushed around by his father and brothers, turned here, snatched the victory at Antioch from near-defeat, and himself slew the "Red Lion," Kizil-Arslan, the Turkish chief. Though hardly the warrior type, being short, fat, and smiling, yet according to a contemporary account Robert split a Turk in two from head to chest with one stroke of his sword. His valor and his generosity in sharing food, arms, and mounts with other Crusaders in time of famine and penury were acknowledged by all. Indeed, he seems to have been too openhanded and easygoing for those hard-bitten times, for he could not even rule his duchy effectively. "If a weeping criminal was brought to him for justice he would weep with him and set him free." Only in Palestine did Robert's career have its brief moment of glory. He came home only to be victimized again by another of his sterner-purposed family.

Jerusalem was taken by the Crusaders in 1099, and Robert, as the only king's son among them, was the first to be offered the throne. He refused, for he still hoped to wear the crown of England. He left Palestine for home in the year 1100, but while he was still on the way an unknown hand shot the arrow that felled Rufus in the New Forest and rid England of a ruler for whom not one good word has ever been said. Henry I was firmly seated in Rufus' place before Robert could get back. He promptly disposed of his elder brother's claim by shutting the returned Crusader up in prison for the rest of his life and consoled him for the crown, so the chronicles say, by giving him a king's castoff clothes.

One other English group is said to have participated in the first Crusade, though under rather vague circumstances. Odericus Vitalis, whose chronicle is invaluable for this period, states that Edgar Atheling, last of the royal Saxon line, came to Laodicea in Syria, a town under Byzantine rule, at the head "of almost twenty thousand pilgrims . . . from England and other islands of the ocean" and persuaded the populace of the place to name his friend, Duke

Robert, their commander. Who these pilgrims were, what part they played in the further development of the Latin kingdom, and what eventually became of them is nowhere further told.

Poor Robert, always just short of a crown, at least achieved a brief posthumous glory in the only English drama composed on the subject of the Crusades, Thomas Heywood's *Four Prentices of London*. A rampaging fantastical play, it was performed several times about the year 1600 to delighted Elizabethan audiences at the Red Bull. Godfrey of Bouillon and other leading personages of the First Crusade, together with a company of imaginary knights, ladies, bandits, dragons, hermits, and prentices, each generally appearing disguised as someone else, are tossed up in a series of purely fictional events. At the climax before the Holy City "English Robert" speaks words that are as much an anachronism in the mouth of a Crusader as if he had appeared on the stage carrying a gun:

> "Behold the high walls of Jerusalem
> Which Titus and Vespasian once brake down.
> From off these turrets have the ancient Jews
> Seen worlds of people mustering on these plains.
> Oh, princes, which of all your eyes are dry,
> To look upon this temple, now destroyed?
> Yonder did stand the great Jehovah's house. . . .
> There was the Ark, the shewbread, Aaron's rod,
> Sanctum Sanctorum, and the Cherubim.
> Now in that holy place, where God himself
> Was personally present, Pagans dwell,
> False Gods are reared, each temple idols bears
> Oh, who can see this and abstain from tears?"

Here is no mention of the Holy Sepulcher or the Cross. Instead the holy symbols are "Jehovah's house," the Temple, and the Ark; for already, under the influence of the English Bible, Jerusalem was thought of in terms of the Old Testament rather than the New. But Heywood, it is well to remember, was farther away in time from the First Crusade than we are from Heywood.

In fact, so far were the Crusaders from thoughts of Jehovah's house that it was from their throats that there first rang the sinister "Hep, hep!" *(Hierosolayme est perdita)* that became the signal for Jewish pogroms from their day through Hitler's, or such is the Jewish tradition. Though armed with the "sword of the Maccabees," in the words of Pope Urban, the Crusaders struck their first blows at the people of the Maccabees before they ever left Europe. Every Jewish community on their path was put to the sword by the Christian warriors, who could not wait for the end of the journey to bathe their hands in blood. In part these mass massacres were an anticipatory lunge at the infidel in the person of the Jews who were the most convenient victims, the more so as it was rumored that they had devilishly inspired the Turkish persecution of Christians in the Holy Land. Partly also the pogroms were an opportunity for loot, always a powerful motive among the Crusaders.

Popular hatred of the Jews was not a particularly active sentiment until inflamed by the Holy Wars. Medieval man's almost superstitious dread and detestation of the "heretic," the person outside the church, was one component. Another was the common feeling against the person to whom money is owed. Usury, the lending of money at interest, was practiced by the Jews in the Middle Ages because the guild system excluded them from other forms of livelihood, because their own law, while forbidding usury among themselves, permitted it toward non-Jews, and because usury, although Christian law forbade it among Christians, was necessary to the community. Ultimately, when the rise of capitalism and a money economy made it even more necessary, Christian scruples relaxed sufficiently to permit the practice of usury by themselves. But during the Middle Ages it was largely confined to the Jews, and through them it provided the Crown with a lucrative source of revenue. Only practical considerations against milking the cow dry limited the share that the Crown could take from the Jews. In theory they had property rights, but in practice these meant nothing, for the Jew was not allowed to bring a charge against a Christian, and thus his position depended solely on the pleasure and protection of the sovereign.

The more the sovereign encouraged Jewish usury, the more the people hated the Jews. During the crusading era they learned that violence practiced under the banner of the Cross was a simple way to wipe out debt and to seize Jewish gold with impunity. By the time of the Second Crusade in 1146 its preachers were inveighing against the Jewish race in general, and the first recorded accusation of ritual murder was brought in 1144 against the Jews of Oxford. By the time of the Third Crusade in 1190 the association of Crusade and pogrom was automatic, and the killings began immediately on Richard's coronation, though not at his order. Once started, they spread in waves from London to all the cities in which Jews lived, until the final ghastly climax at York, where the only Jews to escape slaughter by the mob were those who slew their wives and children and then died by their own hand. Crusaders preparing for departure and friars who incited the mob against the enemies of Christ were, according to all accounts, the leaders in these attacks, which must have made a deep impression, for the chroniclers describe them at length and with genuine horror. Some of the perpetrators were punished by Richard's ministers, and though there were no further attacks, feeling against the Jews was fed by the episode. Eventually, a century later, another Crusader king, Edward I, preferring to take everything at once instead of continuing to squeeze a source that was drying up, expelled the Jews from England and sequestered to the Crown the property that they were forced to leave behind.

In some way men of the Middle Ages were able utterly

to dissociate in their minds the contemporary Jews from the ancient Hebrews. The archetype of warrior patriot to whom both Richard the Lion-Heart and Robert Bruce were compared by their admirers was Judas Maccabaeus. In fact, it was the great captains and kings among the Hebrews, not their prophets, who particularly appealed to the mailed mentality of the age of "chivalry." Among the "Nine Worthies" of history, "three paynim, three Jews and three Christian men" whose figures so often appear carved over church doors or embroidered in tapestry, the three Jews were represented by Joshua (not Moses), David, and Judas Maccabaeus.

Richard may have been a Maccabee in valor, strength, and strategy, but not in motive. He fought for fun, not for liberty; that is, in Palestine. The rest, perhaps ninety per cent, of his adult life he spent fighting up and down France against his father or the French King or some other feudal rival, but all this is forgotten in the brighter memory of his Crusade. The fable agreed upon as regards Richard is of a sort of second King Arthur, which he was anything but. However, he provided England with a legend and with a feeling for the Holy Land as the locus of his legend, so that for his time and the hundred years that followed many an Englishman could have said: "When I am dead and opened ye shall find Palestine lying in my heart," in paraphrase of what Queen Mary said of Calais.

Of the Second Crusade little need be said. It was an ignominious failure, which, according to a contemporary judgment, "though it did not at all relieve the Holy Land, yet could not be called unfortunate as it served to people heaven with martyrs." Few English joined it, because most of the population were engaged in the seventeen years' oscillating battle between Matilda and Stephen and their partisans. When their successor, Henry of Anjou, succeeded to the throne in 1152 the immediate task of bringing order to the unsettled kingdom absorbed all his energies. He contented himself with placing alms boxes in all the churches for contributions in aid of the Templars, and later he imposed a levy *ad sustentationem Hierosolyem terrae* amounting to twopence in the pound for the first year and a penny in the pound for each of four years thereafter.

After Becket's murder in 1170 Henry himself had to vow a three years' Crusade as the price of absolution for his share of guilt in the century's most celebrated crime. But the greater task of consolidating the sovereignty of England while constantly harassed by dynastic feuds in France caused him to put off his departure from year to year. He took a Crusader's vow, but it is doubtful if he ever seriously intended going, for Henry was a working king whose real interest was at home rather than in dashing off after glory in the East.

The immediate cause of the Third Crusade was Saladin's capture of Jerusalem from the Franks in 1187. A shudder ran through Europe, it is said, when the news was heard that the Holy City had again fallen to the infidel. Pope Urban II, who died shortly after, was popularly supposed to have died of grief. Even Henry felt the event keenly and this time began active preparations to go on the Crusade that the new Pope, Gregory VIII, was preaching. So great was the response that kings, nobles, and knights were taking the vow right and left until, says de Vinsauf, "it was no longer a question of who would take the Cross but who had not yet taken it." He reports, too, that it became the custom to send a distaff and wool, token of a woman's role, to prod reluctant warriors. (De Vinsauf was the supposed author of *Itinerarium Regis Ricardi,* an eyewitness account and, along with Bohadin's history, the most valuable and readable of all the records of the Third Crusade. Since modern scholars have discovered that there was no such person as de Vinsauf, or if there was that he did not write the chronicle, it will be referred to hereafter for the sake of brevity as IRR.)

One outcome of the fate of far-off Jerusalem was Eng-

land's first income tax, devised by Henry II to meet the cost
of the expedition. Crusaders were exempt, but everyone
else had to pay a tenth of all rents and movables. Each
man was to assess himself, but if he were suspected of
under-estimating his income, a jury of his parish was to
decide his true worth. The Saladin Tithe, as it was called,
despite its high purpose was regarded, says Roger of
Wendover, as "a violent extortion which veiled the vice of
rapacity under the name of charity and alarmed the priest-
hood as well as the people." Taxes are never popular.

Despite the urgency, the Crusade was held up by the un-
ending family feuds between Henry, his rebellious sons,
and the French king, Philip Augustus, who were forever
making and breaking combinations with and against one
another. In the midst of these feuds, harried and worn out
at fifty-six, unhorsed on the field of battle by his own son,
Henry died in July 1189. The rampaging Richard was king.
He had taken the Cross two years earlier, within a fortnight
of the news of Jerusalem's fall, and now he could be held
back no longer. Unlike his father, he was unconcerned
with the responsibilities of kingship or with England as a
kingdom, except as it gave him the opportunity to indulge
in grand style his ruling passion for battle, adventure, and
glory. The Crusade offered all these with chivalry's greatest
gage, a renowned and valiant enemy, and salvation for his
soul. He sped to England to be crowned and to organize
some sort of regency for the period of his absence, and
above all to fill his treasury. In an unexampled orgy of taxation and extortion he set about extracting money by every
known method plus some original devices of his own. He
dismissed his father's ministers and put the high offices of
church and state up for public sale. He sold every title that
needed confirming, every castle in dispute, every fief of the
crown that could find a rich enough claimant. "All things
were for sale with him—powers, lordships, earldoms, sher-
iffdoms, castles, towns, manors, and suchlike." From those
who did not want favors or property badly enough to buy

them he collected fines with or without reason, jailed others and forced them to buy their liberty, required payment for security of estates or cash for remission of vows. While Baldwin, Archbishop of Canterbury and his invaluable archdeacon, Giraldus Cambrensis, went up and down England preaching the Crusade and gathering recruits Richard's ministers were even busier raking in fines, bribes, and "presents." When it was put to the King that his methods were questionable he only laughed abruptly and roared: "I would sell London if I could find a buyer."

Within four months, having scraped in every penny that was loose or could be pried loose, he was gone, taking with him the most able and loyal ministers, including Archbishop Baldwin, and his father's prime minister, Ranulf Glanville, both of whom were to die in Palestine, as well as the new justiciar, Hubert Walter. His father, shrewder by far, would have left men he could trust behind to hold things together until his return, but Richard never thought of that. It was a fatal mistake, for if his last year in Palestine had not been punctuated by reports of John's usurpation and his purpose had not been weakened by an agony of indecision whether to go or to stay, he might have taken Jerusalem after all.

Theoretically each knight who joined the ranks was responsible for equipping himself and whatever number of squires and foot soldiers went in his personal train. But Richard, though he may have had no head for governing, was not an irresponsible soldier, and his enormous appetite for money was for the sole purpose of ensuring that he could equip, supply, and maintain an efficient force far from home over the period of a year or more that would win him the victory over Saladin he dreamed of. That he may also have had it in mind to make a greater show of pomp and power than the haughty Philip and Duke Leopold of Austria is not unlikely. But above all he was determined not to repeat the disastrous experience of the earlier overland expeditions, which, by attempting to live off the land, had antagonized the populace along their way and had to fight their way through, losing thousands by battle and starvation before they ever reached Palestine. Richard wanted no taste of the scorched-earth policy of the Turks; but it required vast funds to transport an army by sea, feeding it the while. The Pipe Rolls of the time reveal the methodical planning that went into assembling the fleet. The Sheriff of London, Henry of Cornhill, for example, renders an account of how some five thousand pounds received from the king's constable was spent:

£ 1,126,	13s.,	9½d.	for two parts of thirty-three ships with crews of twenty to twenty-five each provided by the Cinq Ports (the third part representing the share which the Cinq Ports were obligated to furnish to the king)
£ 2,400,	58s.,	4d.	for one year's pay for 790 crewmen
£ 257,	15s.,	8d.	for three ships of Hampton and three ships of Shoreham
£ 529,	5s.		for one year's pay for 174 crewmen
£ 56,	13s.,	4d.	for a ship purchased from Walter the Boatswain's son
£ 185,	10s.,	10d.	for one year's pay for sixty-one sailors and captain of the royal *Esnecche*, the king's ship
£ 10			for repair of same
£ 152,	1s.,	8d.	for pay of fifty sailors and captain of William de Stuteville's two ships
£ 10			for repair of these
£ 9			for repurchase of ship which the king had given to the Hospitallers
£	60s.,	10d.	for pay of one additional sailor in Eustace de Burne's ship

This of course represented only a small part of the whole. Richard also requisitioned "from every city in England two palfreys and two additional sumpter horses [pack animals] and from every manor of the King's own one palfrey and one sumpter horse."

More than a year was spent in France and Sicily recruiting more men and ships and reaching a settlement with Philip out of the two kings' mutual mistrust. It continued to gall the French King that wherever they went Richard dazzled all eyes. Who could but admire the tall figure whom IRR describes, clad in a rose-colored surplice embroidered in solid silver crescents, on his auburn hair a hat of scarlet embroidered with many-colored birds and beasts, at his side a gold-handled sword in a scabbard of woven gold? Indeed, he seemed the very mirror of chivalry as he vaulted astride a faultless Spanish charger wearing a gold bridle, trappings of gold and scarlet spangles, and a saddle chased with two golden lions.

In the spring of 1191 the entire army and fleet was assembled. After requisitioning additional galleys plus two years' supply of wheat, barley, and wine and his sister Queen Joanna's gold plate, Richard was ready for departure in April, Philip having gone on ahead in March. It was an imposing array of two hundred and nineteen ships, the greatest naval force men of that day had ever witnessed, that set sail with banners flying and trumpets sounding across the Mediterranean for Palestine. In the fleet were thirty-nine war galleys, long and slender fighting vessels powered by two tiers of oars; twenty-four huge "busses" or *naves maximae* with three tiers of oars, which carried forty knights, forty foot soldiers, and forty horses with all their equipment and a year's provisions for men and beasts; and one hundred fifty-six smaller vessels carrying half the complement of the busses. They sailed in a wedge formation of eight squadrons with three ships in the front row and sixty in the last, so arranged that a man's shout could be heard from ship to ship and a trumpet's call from squadron to squadron. In the lead sailed Joanna and Berengaria, whom the Queen Mother had brought to Messina for Richard to marry, although he did not get around to celebrating the wedding till they stopped off in Cyprus. The King in his "Esnecche" guarded the rear.

How many sailed with Richard on that grand and tragic venture? Medieval chroniclers have an exasperating disregard for figures and are forever speaking in terms of "multitudes" and "countless" numbers, or asking rhetorically "Who can count them?" or giving up utterly with the all-embracing generalization that there was not a man of influence and renown who was not there. IRR puts ten thousand in Richard's force at the capture of Messina, a figure that fits the known complements of two hundred odd vessels. In addition Archbishop Baldwin sailed independently with a small force of two hundred knights and three hundred foot soldiers, and an unknown number of English mariners joined the fleet of Norsemen and Flemings, totaling twelve thousand according to contemporary records, that had gone to the relief of the Latin kingdom early in 1189, before Richard was king.

No figures exist at all for the population of England at this time. But demographic experts have figured the population at about two million in the decade of Richard's crusade. This would mean, if one assumes that between ten and twenty thousand English took part at some time in the Third Crusade, that approximately one out of a hundred men at the highest or one out of two hundred at the lowest went to Palestine. According to "an owlde Roule . . . of noblemens armes and knights as weare with K. R. I. at ye siege of Acor (Acre)" every county of England supplied men for Richard's ranks, and many came from Wales. A very large proportion never returned. IRR mentions among the casualties of the combined armies during the first two winters in Palestine six archbishops and patriarchs, twelve bishops, forty counts, five hundred noblemen, a "vast" number of clergy, and his usual "innumerable multitude" of others. Most died of illness in the festering camp before Acre. In the fierce battles that followed after Richard took the city and went on to challenge Saladin's might, many were captured and killed by the enemy. A true figure for the combined army is impossible to arrive at, because groups of Crusaders from every part of Europe had been coming ever since the fall of Jerusalem. Some stayed, some died, some went home; and the number mustered from the local Christian forces of Antioch, Tyre, and the other principalities shifted with the intrigues of their leaders.

Perhaps the estimate of Bohadin, Saladin's chronicler, which put the Christian army before Acre at five thousand knights and one hundred thousand foot soldiers is as near the truth as any. Its proportion of one horseman to twenty foot is reasonable, although the higher losses among the foot reduced the proportion at the end more nearly to one in ten or even one in five. Certainly over half the Christian force was lost by the time the Third Crusade was over. At the very last battle before Richard's departure, when he ordered every man who could fight to follow him, he could muster, according to IRR, only five hundred knights and two thousand shieldbearers whose lords had perished. When at last he sailed for home it was in a single galley that could not have carried more than fifty souls, though admittedly others had gone on ahead.

To attempt a guess at what proportion of England's population saw service in Palestine, given the general lack of reliable figures, is foolhardy. All one can say is that fewer than one per cent went, of whom only a fraction ever came home.

When Richard arrived in Palestine in June the Third Crusade was bogged down outside the walls of Acre in a futile siege that had already lasted a year. If the besieged were badly off, so were the besiegers, cut off from the rest of the country, sunk in the squalor and disease of the overcrowded camp, reduced to eating their own horses that had died of starvation or paying fortunes in gold for the carcass of a stray cat. Unable to storm the city or to give up the siege, dulled by debauchery with the hordes of camp followers, the Crusaders had lapsed into a rank and static misery that still seems to smell in the pages of the chroniclers.

Even the arrival in March 1191 of the French under Philip with fresh supplies did not succeed in stimulating the camp to more than half-hearted activity that quickly subsided. Not until the arrival of Richard, who had stopped to conquer and tax Cyprus on the way, was the camp finally galvanized into full-scale action. Richard reached Acre in June, and within four weeks the city, which had withstood nine battles and a hundred skirmishes in nearly three years' siege, capitulated. This is not to say that the victory was Richard's alone, but without his fierce spirit beating them on to the last ounce of effort the Crusaders would never have breached the walls. Though bedridden and shaking from the quartan ague (malaria) almost from the moment of his arrival, Richard directed the battle from his litter, and when the Christians fell back again and again under the hail of darts and arrows from the Turks he had himself carried to the front on a mattress, from which his great voice thundered and goaded the soldiers to a last and successful attempt.

A truce and exchange of prisoners was arranged with Saladin, of which the conditions were to be fulfilled at stated intervals over a three months' period. But when Saladin kept delaying the fulfillment of his part Richard without compunction slaughtered more than two thousand Moslem prisoners. This ruthless act, which appalled even his own army, has provoked shudders of horror and righteous indignation among latter-day historians. Ever since they have discovered that Richard was not entirely the *preux chevalier* of romance and chivalry that his reputation supposed, the pseudo-Strachey school has been at him with open claws, tearing apart what is left of his reputation. The author of IRR, who worshipped the King, said he had the valor of Hector, the magnanimity of Achilles, the liberality of Titus, the eloquence of Nestor, and the prudence of Ulysses; that he was the equal of Alexander and not inferior to Roland. But later historians tend to picture him rather as a remorseless, kindless villain. He was probably not a pleasant or a lovable character; none of the Plantagenets were. But a great soldier and a great commander he certainly was. He possessed that one quality without which nothing else in a commander counts: the determination to win. To this everything else—mercy, moderation, tact—was sacrificed. The avarice that so horrifies his critics was not simple greed: it was a quartermaster's greed for his army. His massacre of the prisoners was not simple cruelty, but a deliberate reminder to Saladin to keep faith with the terms agreed to, which that great opponent understood and respected. The English King was in fact the only Frank Saladin had any respect for, and he once said: "If I should be fated to lose the Holy Land, I had rather lose it to Melec Ric than to any other."

Yet he did not take Jerusalem. Why? The blocked-up cisterns, the heat and diseases, the difficulty of supplying the army, of adapting tactics used on the fertile fields of France to the hostile hills and deserts of Palestine, all these were encountered by the First Crusade. What they did not have to contend with, as Richard did, was a great general in command of the enemy. Saladin was on home ground, he could call on armies from all sides of Palestine, and he was not himself weakened by enemies at his rear. But what really defeated Richard was the divided purpose of his own allies, whose overriding concern was their mutual rivalries. Conrad, Marquis of Tyre, defected to the enemy. The French King pulled out, either because he could not stand being in the shadow of Richard's glory or because he always intended to get home first and grab Richard's French possessions. His defection was not an unmixed loss, for, as Saladin's brother said, "Richard was hindered by the King of France like a cat with a hammer tied to his tail."

The fifteen months from the fall of Acre in July 1191

to Richard's departure in October 1192 was spent in pushing down the coast against repeated enemy raids until Jaffa, the base for the march against Jerusalem, could be reached; in pauses for negotiation; in side campaigns against Ascalon and Darum; and in two fruitless attempts to take the Holy City in the hills.

The southward march from Acre down the old Roman coast road depended on meeting the supply fleet at frequent intervals. Richard planned the march with great care. The army, consisting of five main corps of Templars, Bretons and Angevins, Boitevins, Normans, and English, and lastly Hospitallers, was divided into three longitudinal groups. Furthest inland marched the infantry, to protect the whole against the frequent ambushes of the enemy swooping down from the hills. In the middle were the cavalry; and nearest the sea was the heavy burdened baggage train. The royal standard of England, borne on a covered wagon drawn by four horses, moved in the center, but the King himself generally rode up and down inspecting arrangements and keeping order. Because of the heat he confined the march to the early morning, covering only eight or ten miles a day and resting over a full twenty-four hours every other day. The slow pace was necessitated by the midsummer heat, the weakened condition of the army, and the heavy loss of pack animals sustained at Acre; half the infantry had to carry the baggage and tents on their own backs, changing places with the fighting infantry for relief. For protection against the constant shower of arrows from the enemy the Crusaders wore thick felt cassocks over their mailed shirts, and Bohadin tells of the awe with which the Turks saw the Franks march along unharmed with five or ten arrows apiece sticking out from their backs. Under the burning rays of the sun many dropped dead from the heat, and others fainted and had to be transported by sea. At each evening's halt a designated herald stood up in the midst of the host and cried out *"Sanctum Sepulchrum adjuva!"* (Help us, Holy Sepulchre!) The host took up the cry, repeating it three times, stretching their arms to heaven, weeping copiously, and, according to IRR, deriving relief and refreshment from the ceremony.

As they crept down the coast they knew each day's march brought them closer to the pitched battle that Saladin must launch if he were to stop them from reaching Jaffa. Advance cavalry units of the Turks pricked at the slow phalanx, trying to tease them into battle, it being Saladin's strategy to divide and scatter the Christians over the plains where his rushing horsemen could cut them down. Richard was determined to keep a solid formation that would protect the supply wagons and force the Turks into battle at close quarters. Nerves were strung ever more tensely as they marched, each man sensing in his bones the silent gathering of vast hordes behind the hills. It took Richard's sternest discipline to prevent the overtaut corps commanders from dashing out to engage the enemy prematurely.

At last, eleven miles above Jaffa, at a place called Arsuf the moment came. Unable to contain themselves, the Hospitallers broke ranks and charged the Turks. "King Richard," says IRR, "on seeing his army in motion flew on his horse through the Hospitallers and broke into the Turkish infantry who were astonished at his blows and those of his men and gave way to the right and left." But they regrouped and massed for a charge. "All over the face of the land you could see the well ordered bands of Turks, myriads of banners, of mailed men alone there appeared to be more than twenty thousand. . . . They swept down swifter than eagles, turning the air black with dust raised by their horses, howling their battle cries and sounding the blast of trumpets." The King was wounded by a spear thrust in the left side, but the solid ranks of the infantry withstood the charge, kneeling on one knee with spears advanced while behind them the ballista, a dart-throwing engine on wheels, was brought into action. Although the battle raged all day, the Turks never broke through, and at last they withdrew over ground slippery with blood and strewn with corpses.

Now the armies had met and tested each other's strength in open combat. After this battle Saladin realized that he could not halt the Crusaders' march; but by retreating and playing for time he could outstay them. He withdrew the garrisons from all the fortresses to the south even down to Ascalon, for he had no desire to leave each to be another Acre. Only Darum, the last stronghold on the way to Egypt, was left garrisoned; but Richard took it in a four days' siege.

From this point on, when a united, all-out effort to take Jerusalem might well have succeeded, the Crusade began to fall apart. First the French insisted on remaining in Jaffa to fortify its walls and incidentally enjoy the luxuries of city life after the hardships of the field. When the insistence of the others finally prevailed and an attempt on Jerusalem was made at the New Year, the Duke of Burgundy retreated within sight of the city and ultimately took himself off altogether. Other groups fell away to return to Acre or to join the traitorous Conrad at Tyre. Even the Templars and Hospitallers counseled against taking Jerusalem lest they be left alone afterwards to fight the surrounding Turks. Richard himself, tormented ever since Philips' desertion by the thought of what his rival and his brother John might be doing behind his back, was in a hurry to return to his kingdom lest there be no kingdom left to return to.

This worry and the growing realization that no united effort could probably ever be wrung from the divided army put him in the mood to end the war by a negotiated truce. Through the winter and into the spring of 1192 the conferences dragged on, with proposals and counterproposals concerning the possession of Jerusalem and the various coastal cities and Crusader's castles and even including Richard's absurd and cynical suggestion that his sister Joanna marry Saladin's brother and that they rule Jerusalem between them. The courteous and diplomatic Saladin kept the talks in progress by skilled speechcraft and a constant flow of gifts—a magnificent Spanish horse for Richard, a scarlet tent, fresh fruits or cooling snow brought from the mountains, seven camels richly caparisoned, and a skilled physician to minister to the King.

Meanwhile messengers from England with reports of John's depredations up and down the kingdom implored Richard to return. He decided on a final effort for Jerusalem in June 1192; but again united councils could not be obtained, and bitterly the King gave up. As he turned back from the great goal for which so much effort, blood, and treasure had been vainly spent, a knight turned his steps to a hilltop from which the towers of Jerusalem could be seen. But Richard veiled his face with his cloak, saying: "Blessed Lord God, I pray thee not to let me see thy Holy City that I could not deliver from the hands of thy enemies."

The futility of remaining in Palestine was now obvious. Richard was preparing to sail from Acre when news came that the Saracens had surrounded Jaffa, where a small force of Christians was holding out in imminent danger of death. It was almost as if the fates had taken a hand to amend the bitter humiliation of a brave man. For in the battle of Jaffa Richard performed such feats of arms and won such glory as rang on the tongues of all men. The memory of his exactions was dimmed by the reports of his valor, and when, three years later, Eleanor moved heaven and earth to raise the gigantic ransom demanded by Richard's captor, Englishmen responded with every ounce of treasure, so great was their pride in the Lion-Hearted King.

IRR's account of the relief of Jaffa, written perhaps that very night, seems almost to burst with pride and ecstasy in the battle and in the King's mighty deeds. Richard, he says, interrupted all counsels of caution and exclaimed, "As God lives I will be with them and give them all the aid I can." Already on board ship, he turned the helm southward, ran his galley on the beach at Jaffa, and waded ashore, up to his middle in the waves at the head of a small landing party of but eighty knights and three hundred cross-bowmen.

Himself armed with an arbalest, which he soon exchanged for his "fierce sword," he and his companions dashed forward against the Turks who covered the beach and soon pushed them back. After a terrific battle the town was taken and the Christian garrison saved, but the Turks, ashamed at having been put to rout by so small a number, sent in a new force to take Richard by surprise as he slept in his tent. A last-minute warning shout "To arms! to arms!" awoke the King.

"God of all virtues! Lives there a man who would not be shaken by such a sudden alarm? . . . Oh, who could fully relate the terrible attacks of the infidels? The Turks at first rushed on with horrid yells, hurling their javelins and shooting their arrows. The King ran along the ranks and exhorted every man to be firm and not to flinch. The Turks came on like a whirlwind again and again making the appearance of an attack, that our men might be induced to give way, and when they were close up they swerved their horses off in another direction. The King and his knights who were on horseback perceiving this, put spurs to their horses and charged into the middle of the enemy upsetting them right and left and piercing a large number through the body with their lances. . . . What a terrible combat was then waged! A multitude of Turks . . . rushed towards the royal standard of the lion for they would rather have slain the King than a thousand others. . . . But such was the energy of his courage that it seemed to rejoice at having found an occasion to display itself. His sword which shone like lightning cut down men and horses alike, cleaving them to the middle."

All day he fought, and IRR tells how at times he wielded a sword in one hand and a lance in the other, how he carved a path for himself like a reaper with a sickle, how he inspired such terror in the Turks as to create a panic among them in their rush to get out of his way, how he saw the noble Earl of Leicester fallen from his horse and fighting bravely on foot, how he spurred to him and replaced him on his horse, how he snatched Ralph de Maubon from the enemy and restored him to the army, how Saladin in the midst of battle sent him two fresh horses in honor of his courage, and how the King said he would accept any number of horses from an enemy worse than Saladin, so great was his need of them; how at last "the King, the fierce, the extraordinary King . . . returned safe and unhurt to his friends . . . his person stuck all over with javelins like a deer pierced by the hunters and the trappings of his horse were thickly covered with arrows." And when Saladin asked his crestfallen warriors why they had not taken Melec Ric they answered: "In truth, my lord there never was such a knight since the beginning of the world . . . to engage with him is fatal and his deeds are beyond human nature."

A three years' armistice was now signed, leaving Jerusalem and the hill country to the Saracens but restoring the Church of the Sepulcher and the pilgrims' right of free access to it to the Christians, who also retained the coastal plain and its ports from Tyre to Jaffa. Three parties of Crusaders went up to see the Holy City, but without Richard, who, if he could not go as conqueror, would not go at all. The Lion-Heart sailed away, but the legend of his might remained a byword among the Arabs. If a horse shied at a noise in the bushes, it was believed that the spirit of Melec Ric had frightened him, and a crying child was quieted by the admonition "Hush, England is coming!"

One effect of the Crusades on England was the upheavals in tenure caused by so many knights' mortgaging their lands for cash to outfit themselves. The King was not the only one to go to extremes for money. One John de Camoys sold his wife and all her chattels. A certain Andrew Astley sold his whole state to the abbey of Combe in Warwickshire for three hundred and twenty marks sterling. Others mortgaged their lands, usually to rich abbeys, for three or four or seven years, and if they survived the wars to return home, they were often too impoverished to redeem their property and were forced to spend out their lives as poor brethren in a monastery.

The sixteenth-century researches of Leland and Camden into monastery archives and local parish records turned up many facts about the Crusades. There was one Osborne Gifford who was excommunicated for abducting two nuns (one was apparently not enough) and as the price of absolution had to undertake a three years' crusade in the Holy Land, during which he could wear no shirt or knight's habit, nor could he ever in his life enter a nunnery again. Roger de Mowbray was a rarity who went twice to Palestine in the years of the Second Crusade and survived capture by the Saracens as well. Anyone so favored by fortune was sure to be made the subject of romantic adventures, and Roger was said to have intervened in a mortal combat between a dragon and a lion and, having slain the dragon, so won the gratitude of the lion that it followed him all the way home to England. His son Nigel went with Richard on the Third Crusade. Another made prisoner by the Saracens was Hugh de Hatton, who escaped after seven years' captivity and made his way home in rags. Learning from a shepherd who did not recognize him that he had been given up for dead, Hugh entered his castle, to meet what welcome we do not know. The story leaves him at the threshold, another in the line of long-lost warriors who have been returning home incognito ever since Ulysses came back from Troy.

Banishment was a frequent reason for going off to the Holy Wars. The doughty Fulk Fitzwarin so angered Prince John in a chess game that John hit him over the head with the chessboard, whereupon Fulk retaliated with a blow that almost killed the bad-tempered prince. Promptly banished from court, he set off for Palestine, but was driven by storms to the Barbary coast, where he too was taken prisoner by the Saracens. His captivity appears to have been a pleasant one, for he is reputed to have enjoyed the love of "a noble lady caullid Idonie" during his stay in the Sultan's domain. Eventually he made his way east to join Richard's army at the siege of Acre. In that noble company also was William de Pratelles, famous for saving Richard from capture during a hunting party surprised by an enemy raid. William shouted, "I am the king!" and was carried off a prisoner, but fortunately one of the last things Richard did in Palestine was to exchange ten Turks for his gallant friend.

Even the wicked John, when he was King after Richard's death, took the cross; in the faded ink of Magna Carta it can be read how he promised to adjust all property claims made on him "before we undertook the crusade." But the stern barons, not trusting his intentions, also forced him to promise to make good their claims right away "if perchance we tarry at home and do not make our pilgrimage."

John, of course, did tarry, but his younger son Richard, Earl of Cornwall, was as determined to go as his namesake Richard I had been. As the only responsible man at court, where a pack of French favorites was making a shambles of the government under the complacent eye of his incompetent brother Henry III, Earl Richard felt unable to depart as long as he was heir apparent. But as soon as a son was born to the King he set out for Palestine. Everyone tried to dissuade him, including the Pope, who urged him to buy a remission of his vow. The papal solicitude was no doubt influenced by the fact that Richard, who owned the tin and lead mines of Cornwall and vast timberlands, was reputed the richest prince in Europe. But the Earl would not sell his vow; instead he sold his woods to raise the necessary funds. When he took his leave, says William of Tyre, the people wept, for he was a person wholly minding the public welfare; whereon he told them that even if he had not made his vow he would sooner go than witness the miseries that were coming on the realm. With him went the valiant William Longsword, Earl of Salisbury, later killed in the Crusade in Egypt, seven barons, some fifty or sixty knights, and the usual company of bow- and lance-men. When, however, they landed at Acre in October 1240 they found a truce prevailing between Franks and Moslems, the latter embroiled in the usual war between the Caliphates of Egypt and Syria. As the terms of the truce had not been fulfilled Earl Richard, in the footsteps of his late uncle, marched for Jaffa, but was met by a peace offer from the hard-pressed Sultan of Egypt. A stiff man to deal with, the Earl emerged after long negotiations with the best terms ever won by the Crusaders in treaty: Jerusalem, Nazareth, Bethlehem, and most of the Holy Land were left to the Christians. Earl Richard returned to be hailed on every hand as the deliverer of the Sepulcher.

He had been joined in Palestine by Simon de Montfort, whose recent marriage to the King's sister had raised such a storm that he found it prudent to leave home for Palestine. Simon, who was to be called a second Joshua in battle, had recently, with the Crusader's consistent animus against the Jews, expelled the descendants of Joshua from his borough of Leicester. He had not yet emerged as the great opponent of royal tyranny, perhaps the only man to fight for principle in all the bloody feuds between kings and nobles from the Conquest to the Tudors. Though he left no mark on events in Palestine, his powerful person-ality and abilities must have been recognized by the local Franks, for they offered him the regency of the Latin king-dom during the minority of its boy ruler. But Simon felt greater longings in him and went home to make himself master of England before his ultimate defeat and brutal death.

The end of the crusading era was now drawing near. Palestine had become a battleground for new Islamic hordes. Kharezmians and Kurds were pushed down from the north by the advancing Mongols and were followed soon by the Tartar Khans themselves. Within two years of the Earl of Cornwall's treaty victories, Jerusalem was again lost. Tyre and Acre remained the last toeholds of the Franks in Palestine. Subsequent Crusades were directed at Egypt and the Barbary coast, where the Mameluke dynasty ruled. The last organized efforts of the West were the two fruitless expeditions led by St. Louis of France, that "drum filled with wind" as the Moslem poet called him.

In the second of these, 1269–72, he was joined by Prince Edward of England, who undertook the Crusade in fulfillment of a vow made when he accomplished the overthrow of Simon de Montfort. On his arrival at Tunis with four earls, four barons, and about a thousand men Edward was disgusted to find that Louis and the other princes had signed a treaty with the Sultan. Edward promptly sailed for Acre with his own men, where he raised an army of about seven thousand from the local Franks; but he accomplished nothing more than the conquest of Nazareth in revenge for the Saracens' destruction of Christian shrines in that place. Struck down by an assassin's poisoned dagger, the Prince was near death for months. Finally he too signed a truce, to last for ten years, ten months, and ten days, after which he departed for home, where he found himself king on arrival. He was the last prince of the West to fight in Palestine.

A letter reached Edward in 1281 from Sir Joseph de Cancy, a knight of the Hospital of St. John whom the King had commissioned to keep him informed of "news of events as they befell in the Holy Land." It tells of a battle Sir Joseph witnessed between the Saracens and the Mongol Tartars and goes on to lament: "Never in our remembrance was the Holy Land in such poor estate as it is at this day, wasted by lack of rain, divers pestilences and the paynim. . . . Never have we seen so few soldiers [of the Franks] or so little good counsel in it." He is sure that with able generals and adequate supplies the infidel could be driven out, and he concludes by urging Edward to come back and complete the conquest.

But now the time had run out. Edward was engaged in conquering a nearer kingdom over the border, and he never returned to the East. The later popes had fouled their own cause by the unction with which they persuaded Crusaders to buy back their vows with gold for the Vatican coffers. When the Grand Master of the Templars came to Europe to beg for help against the resurgent Mamelukes he was able to round up no more than a few hundred Italian mercenaries. Palestine was a lost cause. Exactly one hundred years after Richard the Lion-Heart broke the walls of Acre two hundred thousand Mamelukes marched against the Crusaders' last city. In 1291 Acre fell; the same year that Edward expelled the Jews from England the last Christians were driven from Palestine.

CHAPTER V

THE BIBLE IN ENGLISH

In the year 1538 Henry VIII issued a proclamation ordering "one book of the whole Bible of the largest volume in
English" to be placed in every church in England. The
proclamation further ordered the clergy to place the Bible
"in some convenient place . . . whereas your parishioners
may most commodiously resort to the same and read it";
also "that you shall discourage no man from reading or
hearing of the said Bible but you shall expressly stir, provoke and exhort every person to read the same."

With the translation of the Bible into English and its
adoption as the highest authority for an autonomous English Church, the history, traditions, and moral law of the
Hebrew nation became part of the English culture; became
for a period of three centuries the most powerful single influence on that culture. It linked, to repeat Matthew
Arnold's phrase, "the genius and history of us English to
the genius and history of the Hebrew people." This is far
from saying that it made England a Judaeophil nation, but
without the background of the English Bible it is doubtful
that the Balfour Declaration would ever have been issued
in the name of the British government or the Mandate for
Palestine undertaken, even given the strategic factors that
later came into play.

Wherever the Reformation took hold the Bible replaced
the Pope as the final spiritual authority. The Palestinian
origins of Christianity were stressed more and more in
order to reduce the pretensions of Rome. Where the papal
bull had ruled earlier the word of God as revealed in the

Hebrew testaments to Abraham and Moses, to Isaiah, Elijah, and Daniel, to Jesus and Paul now governed instead.

"Consider the great historical fact," said Thomas Huxley, "that this book has been woven into the life of all that is best and noblest in English history, that it has become the national epic of Britain." Here is the curious fact of the family history of one nation becoming the national epic of another. After the publication of the King James version in 1611 the adoption was complete. The Bible was as much England's own as Good Queen Bess or Queen Victoria. Writers on the English Bible habitually use phrases like "this national Bible," "this greatest of English classics"; and one, H. W. Hoare in his *Evolution of the English Bible*, even goes so far as to call it "the most venerable of the national heirlooms," which shows how far enthusiasm can betray a scholar. For the English Bible is not venerable as compared to, for example, Chaucer, nor is it an heirloom except in translation. Its content was and remains a record of the origins, the beliefs, the laws and customs and the history of the Jewish people of Palestine, most of it set down before anyone in England could read or write. And yet no other book penetrated so deeply the bone and the spirit of English life. When the dying Walter Scott asked Lockhart to read aloud to him and Lockhart asked what book, Scott replied: "There is but one."

Whether the innate content of the Bible or the beauty of the King James version was the more responsible for its influences on the English people is a matter of opinion. A library could be assembled of works dealing only with the effect of the Authorized Version on the speech and literature of England. But it is not the literary aspect that concerns us so much as the effect of the Bible in familiarizing, in associating, the English with the Hebraic tradition of Palestine.

Why did this collection of Jewish family history become *the* book in English culture? Why did Milton, setting out to compose an epic of England's beginnings, find himself

turning instead to Biblical themes for *Paradise Lost* and
Samson Agonistes? Why did Bunyan go to the same source
for *Pilgrim's Progress,* which was to become like a second
Bible in most households? Why, asks the Welsh writer
John Cowper Powys, have the English a "mania" for the
Old Testament, and why is it that "our Anglo-Celtic race
has come to find its *individual religion* in Jewish emotion
and Jewish imagination as nowhere else?" He suggests
that "perhaps in the ancient aboriginals of these islands
there was a pre-Celtic strain that was not Aryan at all and
that is stirred in its atavistic depths by this Semitic book?"
The average Englishman would sniff at this Celtic explanation (although it might appeal to the enthusiasts of the
Anglo-Israel movement, who by a tortured interpretation
of stray passages from the Bible have convinced themselves that the English are the true descendants of the ten
lost tribes of Israel). But one need not go so far back as the
atavistic depths of the aboriginal Britons to understand
the appeal of the Old Testament. Basically its appeal was
in the two ideas that made it different from any other
corpus of mythico-religious literature: the idea of the one-
ness of God and the ideal of an orderly society based on
rules of social behavior between man and man and between man and God. The case is put in the solemn tones
of Mr. Gladstone, the archetype of Bible-bred Englishman,
who himself rather resembled one of the ancient prophets.
Christianity owes to the Hebrews, he wrote, the conception
of the Unity of God, and when we ask how this idea, "so
prevailingly denied in ancient times has been kept alive in
the world during the long period of universal darkness and
safely handed down to us, the reply is that it was upheld
and upheld exclusively, as a living article of religious obligation, in one small country, among one small and generally disparaged people and that the country and the
people were those who received this precious truth and
preserved it in and by the Scripture of the Old Testament."
A single God and a chosen people who are the transmit-

ters of His message and who try, however imperfectly, to live by it—in these terms generation after generation of English came to know the Book. Everyone knew it. In many homes it was the only book in the house and, being so, was read over and over until its words and images and characters and stories became as familiar as bread. Children learned long chapters by heart and usually knew the geography of Palestine before they knew their own. Lloyd George recalled how in his first meeting with Chaim Weizmann in December 1914, place names kept coming into the conversation that were "more familiar to me than those of the Western front." Lord Balfour's biographer says that his interest in Zionism stemmed from his boyhood training in the Old Testament under the guidance of his mother. Could it have been as rigorous, one wonders, as that of Ruskin, who tells on the first page of his autobiography how at the bidding of his mother he had to read the entire Bible "every syllable through, hard names and all, aloud, from Genesis to Apocalypse, about once a year . . . and began again at Genesis the next day"? Probably he was not aware that he was doing what is done in Jewish synagogues every year (though without the New Testament), but he remembered it as "the most precious and on the whole the one *essential* part of my education."

One cannot fix upon the exact date when England changed, became Anglican, so to speak; when the God of Abraham, Isaac, and Jacob became the English God; when the heroes of the Old Testament replaced the Catholic saints. All Europe was changing in the decades before and after 1500, when the Middle Ages were giving way to the Reformation and the Renaissance or to what men of that time called the New Learning. Some historians date the end of the Middle Ages from the fall of Constantinople to the Turks in 1453, others from the invention of printing by movable type in 1454, or from Columbus' discovery of the New World in 1492, or from the revolt against Rome signaled by Luther's nailing his theses to the church door in 1517. Not any one of these events, but the combination and interaction of all within roughly fifty years, brought about the new era. In England it took the whole of the turbulent sixteenth century to establish the Reformation, with every decade marked by the roll of a severed head upon the scaffold and the flames of a heretic's death at the stake. Among those whose blood was spilled were Tyndale, the Bible's translator, Thomas Cromwell, the King's minister, Sir Thomas More of the old faith, and Archbishop Cranmer of the new. Still the work of translating the Bible went steadily forward, until in the opening years of the new century it reached its highest point in the King James version. It had been achieved at a terrible cost, but, as the Persian poet said, the rose blooms reddest where some buried Caesar bled.

The work that reached fruition in the Bible of 1611 really began with Tyndale in 1525; but his was by no means the first translation into the English vernacular. All the earlier ones, however, had predated the invention of printing and were self-limited by the difficulty of reproducing copies in longhand. Once printing was available, the flood waters were loosed, and the vernacular Bible could no longer be kept from the people, for as fast as the Church authorities could buy them up or burn them more copies could be printed.

The fact that Henry VIII defied the Pope for a divorce and so sanctioned the Protestant revolt was not a cause of the Reformation, but an accident that placed the Crown on the side of the reformers earlier than might otherwise have happened. The Reformation would have taken place if Henry had never lived or never lusted after Anne Boleyn. The spirit of Protestantism was abroad and in England had been strong ever since John Wyclif and his Lollards fought the abuses of the Roman Church in the fourteenth century. Wyclif himself and his disciples had translated the entire Bible from the Vulgate in the 1380's. How immense was their devotion to their cause is plain when one thinks of the work involved. One hundred and seventy manuscript copies of the Wyclif Bible have survived. Many more must once have existed, for many were probably destroyed when the Lollards were being persecuted as heretics and many more lost in later years. Perhaps two, three, or four hundred copies were made, each copied out laboriously by hand (there are approximately 774,000 words in the Bible) and each done in danger of the copyist's life or liberty. Even possession of the vernacular Bible at that time could be used as evidence of the crime of heresy. "Our bishops damn and burn God's law because it is drawn in the mother tongue," accused a Lollard writer of the fifteenth century.

But what concerned the bishops was not so much the reading of the Bible as *who* read it. It was not the translation as such that infuriated the bishops, but the unauthorized translation and the use of it among classes prone to heresy and revolt, who had already shown their temper in the Peasants' Uprising of 1381. The rich and orthodox, whose interest lay in upholding Church authority, were frequently granted special licenses to possess and read the Bible in English. But the upper clerics were concerned to keep it out of the hands of the common man lest he find a direct path to God that by-passed the sacraments of the Church. In 1408 Archbishop Arundel decreed that anyone making or using an unlicensed translation of the Bible was liable to the ultimate penalty of death at the stake; the decree was founded on the notorious *de Heretico Comburendo* passed by the King and Parliament in 1400, the first statute in English law to allow the death penalty for religious beliefs. "Divers false and perverse people of a certain new sect," it said, who "preach and teach these days openly and privily divers new doctrines and wicked heretical and erroneous opinions . . . and hold and exercise schools and make and write books and wickedly do instruct and inform people" shall be handed over to the secular courts and, if they do not abjure, shall be burned "that such punishment may strike in fear to the minds of others." No wonder that Thomas Fuller in his *Church History* says of one of the Wyclifites, John de Trevisa, who made a translation in 1397, that he does not know which to admire the most, "his ability that he could, his courage that he durst or his industry that he did perform so difficult and dangerous a task."

Generally the Wyclif Bibles were of pocket size, intended for the use of the itinerant Lollard priests who went about among the people preaching and reading to them from the Scriptures in the language of daily speech. Records show that the cost of one of the little Wyclif Bibles was about forty shillings, or the equivalent of a hundred and fifty dollars today. The fact that as many as a hundred and seventy were preserved despite the efforts at suppression is further evidence of the value put upon them. Over a century later bits and pieces of the manuscript Bibles were still being used. Foxe in his *Book of Martyrs*, speaking of the year 1520, reports that a load of hay was sometimes paid for a few chapters of the New Testament in English.

Essentially the Lollard movement was an attempt to democratize religion, to bring it to the people direct from Scripture, free of all the tithes, indulgences, pardoners, fat abbots and mitred bishops, and the whole venal empire of the intrenched clerical hierarchy. Wyclif wanted to put the Scriptures into English because he believed that the Bible and not some red-hatted prelate on a Roman throne was the true source of all law, human and divine. Unless it existed in the common tongue it could not serve as a daily guide for all men, as he hoped to make it. But despite the Wyclif translation it would go too far to say that he familiarized England with the Bible, especially with the Old Testament. Copies were too few, their cost too great, and the general level of literacy too low to accomplish any widespread change. Wyclif's great contribution was the *idea* of the Bible as the pre-eminent spiritual authority that every man could consult for himself. His efforts established the deep root growth of English Protestantism that was necessary before the top growth could sprout in the Reformation. But real life for the Bible in English had to wait for the printing press.

In the ages before Wyclif, however, the content of the Bible, especially Genesis, Exodus, and the Psalms from the Old Testament and the Gospels of the New, had been familiar. We have seen how the Celtic Gildas, the earliest British historian, composed every line of his *Epistle* with examples from the Old Testament in mind. Beginning with Bede many translations into Anglo-Saxon of parts of the Old and New Testaments were made in the pre-Conquest period. Bede himself translated the Gospel according to John; King Alfred translated the Psalms and the Ten Commandments as part of his general work of putting Church history and the Fathers into English for the greater education of his people. Various other versions of the psalms and gospels and "Bible stories" were done into Old English; but the motive for these was pious rather than protestant as with the Wyclifites. The education available to the Anglo-Saxon clergy was limited and what Latin they acquired lamentably meager. Preaching in Saxon times was in the vernacular. To aid the semiliterate priests in conducting services and reading sermons, translations of the Scriptures were written in parallel columns beside the Latin or in interlinear glosses. Stories from the Old Testament of Adam and Eve, of the Patriarchs, of Joseph and his brethren, of Moses and the Exodus were also the subject of sermons and homilies and more often of poems sung by the Saxon bards at banquets and of pantomines and miracle plays.

Caedmon, the first English poet, composed many of his sagas on Old Testament themes. In Bede's unforgettable story Caedmon appears as a herdsman called on for a song by a group feasting around the night fire, but he had no skill to entertain them. That night as he slept among the oxen he dreamed that a stranger came and commanded him to sing; and when he protested that he could not, the Lord gave him voice and words, and he arose and took a harp and poured forth a song. Afterwards he remembered the words and repeated them, and they were taken down. "His song," says Bede, "was of the creation of the world, the birth of man, of the history of Genesis. He sang too of the Exodus of Israel from Egypt and their entrance into the Promised Land."

Many of the Caedmonian poems belong to later centuries than the seventh, when Caedmon flourished, but until lately were attributed to him because of the celebrity given to his name by Bede. Written probably by a succession of Saxon bards, these poems take up the incidents of the Old Testament that were the most likely to be appreciated by a Saxon audience: tales of kings and tyrants, hosts and battles and mighty deeds interpreted in terms nearest the experience of the poet and his listeners. During the four centuries before the Norman Conquest the raids of the Norsemen and their local conquests kept some part of England constantly at war. There was hardly a year when a boatload of Danes did not plunge in somewhere along the coast to raid, plunder, kill, and burn; hardly an inhabited spot that at some time had not been left a smoking ruin. That is what the poet has in mind when he tells how Abraham led his "aethelings" and his "fyrd" to battle over the kings in the vale of Siddim. Abraham's victory was a vicarious satisfaction to the too-often-defeated Saxons, and they reveled in the picture the poet drew of "the fowls of prey tearing the flesh of the murderers of freemen" and in Abraham's words to Melchizedek, whose enemies he has slaughtered (as rendered into modern English by Stopford Brooke):

> "For a while thou needest not
> Fear the fighting rush of the foes we loathe—
> Battle of the Northmen!—for the birds of carrion
> Splashed with blood are sitting under shelving mountains
> Glutted to the gullet with the gory death of hosts."

The awful fate of "Pharaoh's fyrd" under the engulfing waves of the Red Sea was another death of tyrants that delighted the Saxon audience. "Famous was that day over the middle earth when the multitude went forth," writes the unknown poet of the Old English *Exodus*. The Israelites tremble as they hear the thunder of the oncoming Egyptian army, but Moses marshals them to the defense, urging them to "don their linked war-coats — dream of noble deeds." Then he parts the waves and the tribes cross over. "Shields these sea-vikings bore over the salt marsh," and behind them the Red Sea closes over the death struggle of the Egyptians — "Highest that of haughty waves! All the host sank deep!"

As the annual terror of the Norsemen lengthened into territorial conquests and the hope of ridding the country of its enemies all but flickered out, last-ditch fighters like King Alfred and religious leaders like the Abbot Aelfric tried to inspire a sense of national resistance among the people. Aelfric, surnamed "Grammaticus" in testimony of his great learning, died in 1020. He has been called "the most distinguished English-writing theologian in his time and for five centuries afterwards." To spread religious education, but also to foster a fighting patriotism among his people, Aelfric turned to the example of the ancient Hebrews. In addition to translating the Pentateuch he epitomized most of the Old Testament in a running narrative and composed homilies based on the books of Judges, Esther, "who delivered her nation," Judith, and Maccabaeus. He explains his choice of the last by "the great valor of that family who prevailed so much in fighting against the heathen forces encroaching upon them and seeking to destroy and root them from the land which God had given them . . . and they got the victory through the true God in whom they trusted according to Moses' law . . . I have turned them also into English so read them you may for your own instruction." Judas Maccabaeus, whose history Aelfric included in his *Lives of the Saints,* was, he says, "as holy in the Old Testament as God's elect ones in the Gospel-preaching because that he ever contended for the will of the Almighty.... He was God's thane that most often fought against their conquerors in defense of their people."

> Judas then girt himself with his shining breast plate
> Even as an immense giant and completely armed himself
> And guarded his host against the foes with his sword.
> He became then like a lion in his strifes and deeds....

Aelfric interpolates in the story explanations to his audience of how these things came to be; and if any should wonder how God's angels could appear to the Jews, they must know that

> The Jews were the dearest to God
> In the old law because they honored
> The Almighty God with worship continually,
> Until Christ, God's son, was himself conceived
> Of human nature, of the Jewish kin,
> Then would not some believe that He was Very God
> But laid snares for His life....
> There were however many good men of that nation
> Both in the old law and eke in the new
> Patriarchs and prophets and holy apostles....

Aelfric may have seen some disturbing signs that the Saxons, through contact with the heathen Danes, were hankering after the pagan gods of their fathers, for he is careful to point out that when Israel of old "forsook the living God they were harried and abased by the heathen nations who dwelt about them," but "when again they called earnestly on God with true repentance then he sent them help through some judge who overcame their enemies and freed them from their misery." He appends a list of English kings, Alfred, Athelstan, and Edgar, as examples of English leaders who, like the judges of Israel, defeated their enemies through God's help.

Likewise the story of Judith, Aelfric explains, "is also arranged in English in our manner as an example to you men that you should defend your land against the hostile host." Aelfric's homily on Judith's heroic tyrannicide was inspired by the most stirring of all the Anglo-Saxon Bible poems, the *Judith*, which is supposed to have been composed in honor of Alfred's stepmother, the young queen Judith whom Alfred's father married in 856. Other scholars have suggested, to the contrary, that the poem postdates Aelfric and was itself inspired by his homily, and that it may have been a eulogy of the queen of Mercia who led her people to battle against the Danes early in the tenth century. In any event the poem, which has been placed with Beowulf in the front rank of old English literature, made Judith a favorite heroine. In the fragment that survives we read how Holofernes, drunk as a typical Saxon thane,

> Laughed and shouted and raged so that all his folk
> Heard far away how the stark-minded stormed and yelled,
> Full of fierce mirth and mad with mead.

Judith enters the tent where the Assyrian king is sleeping off his drunken stupor; down flashes her glittering sword, beheading the tyrant. Triumphantly she holds aloft the black-bearded, blood-dripping head to the people assembled at the city's walls, exhorting them to revolt.

> Proud the Hebrews hew a path with swords
> Through the press thirsting for the onset of the spear.

Victory is won, and the field is left covered with slain Assyrians, meat for the gathering ravens.

Although these Old English versions must have acquainted the people of Saxon England, so far as they could be reached from the pulpit, with the Hebrew origins of Christianity and made a living drama of the history of ancient Palestine, yet the future English Bible owed nothing to these earlier fragments. For one thing, the language in which they were written would have been quite unintelligible in Wyclif's time, not to mention Tyndale's. For another, the Conquest made a break with the past; the culture that preceded the conquerors was ignored and soon largely forgotten. The lack of Latin and the bare literacy that had so distressed King Alfred and Aelfric had been responsible for the early translations, which were simply designed to teach—to acquaint the people with their religious heritage, just as simplified Bible stories are today read to children. But post-Conquest England, with greater Latin and dominated by the dialectics and text-slinging of the Scholastics, was held in strict subservience to the Latin Bible and to the Fathers, at least until the age of Wyclif. Such free paraphasing as Aelfric's *Maccabees* or his epitome of the Old Testament, with all the difficult passages and Levitical laws left out, would have been as good as heresy, even supposing its language could have been understood.

The next attempt, by the Lollards, to make the Bible comprehensible to the people was made, not by the authority of Crown and Church as in Saxon times, but against it, although Wyclif was himself a priest. Fiercely suppressed through the fifteenth century, this attempt at last burst the dykes with the advent of the Reformation, and it changed the history of Europe. Tyndale's proud boast to the "learned man" who upheld papal authority over that of the Bible, "I wyl cause a boye that dryveth ye plough shall know more of scripture than thou doest," contains the essence of the change.

When Tyndale began his work in the 1520's unauthorized translation of the Bible was still a punishable act, for Henry VIII had not yet broken with Rome. It was, then, in exile that the true begetter of the English Bible went to work in a little garret room in Cologne, with Hebrew and Greek grammars open on the candle-lit table. The Wyclifites, working from the Latin Vulgate, had produced a translation of a translation; but Tyndale, who knew Greek and some Hebrew, worked from the original languages. Nor did he have any recourse to the Wyclif Bible: he began afresh. As he explicitly states in his *Epistle to the Reader* prefacing his New Testament, "I had no man to counterfit nether was holpe with Englysshe of any that had interpreted the same or such lyke thynge in the Scripture before tyme." Since Wyclif's time the New Learning had revived the study of Greek and Hebrew, so long ignored in the Latin-dominated Middle Ages. Cardinal Wolsey had just founded a college at Oxford, later to be known as Christ Church, in which Robert Wakefield held the first chair of Hebrew; and at Cambridge Christ's and St. John were also founded to teach in the new trilingual tradition.

At Oxford Hebrew scholarship had flowered briefly during the thirteenth century when the newly founded Franciscan order devoted itself to learning and philosophy under the teaching of the great Bishop Grosseteste. The Jews had had at Oxford one of their largest communities before their expulsion, and both Grosseteste and Roger Bacon, brightest ornaments of the Franciscans, had studied Hebrew with them there. Bacon believed that a knowledge of Hebrew was necessary for true learning, for he said that all knowledge stemmed from the revealed word of God first given to the world in that language. A fragment of a Hebrew grammar believed to have been his work exists. But after the decline of the Franciscans Hebrew learning died out until its revival in the Renaissance.

In the 1480's and '90's new Hebrew Bibles published under the direction of Continental Rabbis were printed. In 1516 Erasmus published a new edition of the original Greek New Testament with his own Latin translation based on it. Luther used the Greek of Erasmus for his German translation of the New Testament, which appeared in 1522. His Old Testament in German (1534) was done from the Hebrew Masoretic text published in 1494.

Tyndale began with the New Testament, and his finished translation was printed in Germany and smuggled into England in 1526. Of some six thousand copies only three have survived into our time, for severe measures were taken to suppress it. In fact, the bishops' anxiety to buy up the copies in order to destroy them provided Tyndale with a steady income while he went to work on the

Old Testament. Hall's *Chronicle* written at the time tells
how Sir Thomas More, then lord chancellor, was examining one George Constantine for suspected heresy and said
to him: "Constantine, I would have thee plain with me in
one thing. . . . There is beyond the sea Tyndale, Joye and a
great many more of you. I know they cannot live without
help. Someone sendeth them money and succoreth them,
and thyself, being one of them, hadst part thereof and
therefore knowst from whence it came. I pray thee who be
they that thus help them?"

" 'My Lord,' quod Constantine, 'will you that I shall tell
you the truth?' 'Yea I pray thee' quod my Lord. 'Marry I
will' quod Constantine. 'Truly' quod he, 'it is the Lord
Bishop of London that hath holpen us; for he hath bestowed among us a great deal of money in New Testaments to burn them and that hath been and yet is our only
succour and comfort.' 'Now by my troth' quod More, 'I
think even the same and I said so much to the Bishop when
he went about to buy them.' "

Apart from this unexpected source of funds Tyndale,
and later Coverdale and their associates, received their
main financial support and encouragement from a group
of well-to-do London merchants, representatives of the rising capitalist class, who were as eager as any to throw off
the taxing grip of the Roman bureaucracy. These men supported Tyndale in exile, paid for the printing of the new
Bibles in Germany, and arranged for them to be smuggled
into and distributed in England. Later when official sanction brought the process into the open the entire cost of
printing the Great Bible, the one that Henry VIII ordered
read in the churches, was borne by a rich textile merchant,
Anthony Marler, who incidentally made a good business
speculation of it. He received the exclusive concession for
its sale, was able to fix its cost, which he put at ten shillings
(overruling Cromwell, who wanted to make it thirteen
shillings, four pence) and received back more than his
original investment.

But that was ten years later; at the time when Tyndale's first New Testaments were being smuggled in, the merchants were risking their necks though not their capital, for the demand exceeded the supply. It continued unabated; four years after the first appearance of Tyndale's translation the Bishop's efforts had so far failed to suppress it that he found it necessary to stage a public burning of the book in St. Paul's churchyard. In that year, 1530, Tyndale finished his translation of the Pentateuch, which was printed at Marburg and sent on its way to eager hands in England by the busy agents across the Channel.

Meanwhile on the political front, under the masterly engineering of Thomas Cromwell, events were gradually being pushed toward the final break with Rome. After Cardinal Wolsey—who would or could not give Henry what he wanted—was executed in 1530 Cromwell's rise began. Within a short time he gave his sovereign a new wife and a new title. The marriage with Anne was performed in 1533, the submission of the clergy to the King followed by act of Parliament in 1534, and in 1535 the Act of Supremacy confirming Henry as "Supreme Head of the Church of England." At once efforts were made to provide an official English Bible. Tyndale's work could not be recognized, because his barbed marginal comments pointing out how original meanings had been twisted in the Vulgate to suit Catholic doctrine had already made it too controversial. The clergy petitioned the King in 1534 for a new translation "to be meted out and delivered to the people for their instruction." This was met by the so-called Matthew Bible, which was really a composite of Tyndale's translation, as far as it had gone, and of Miles Coverdale's work, which took up the Old Testament where Tyndale left off. Brought to England in printed sheets and issued in 1535–36, it was revised and reprinted under the direction of Archbishop Cranmer in 1538–39, the first complete authorized English Bible printed in England. Known as Cranmer's Bible or the Great Bible, this was the book that figured in the King's

proclamation of 1538, and it bore on the title page the culminating line of a hundred and fifty years' struggle: "This
is the Byble apoynted to the use of the Churches." It was
also provided with an elaborate frontispiece designed,
some say, by Holbein, which shows a crowd of little figures
receiving the book with cries of "Vivat Rex!"

While this was happening Tyndale, the gallant, devoted,
stubborn scholar, the "apostle to England" as Foxe called
him, was burned for his share in unchaining the Scriptures. His death was not at the hands of the English, but
ironically enough, it was the result of the English Church's
having now come around to his position. Charles V, Holy
Roman Emperor, in whose dominions the English translators had done their work, sent Tyndale to the stake as a
representative of the now heretical Church of England,
which dared to secede from Rome. For another irony, Tyndale's execution followed by only a few months that of his
great opponent, Sir Thomas More, who laid his head on the
block in England for refusing to acknowledge the King as
Supreme Head of the church. More, trying to hold back the
wave of Protestantism and Tyndale doggedly, passionately
determined to spread it, had clashed in a bitter, brilliant
controversy contained in More's *Dialogue* and Tyndale's
letters in reply. Both accepted death for their faith, but on
opposite banks of the great schism. Despite More's greater
fame Tyndale left the greater mark, for his work was to
echo through the English-speaking world forever after.

"It was wonderful to see," wrote Strype a century later,
speaking of the Great Bible, "with what joy this book of
God was received, not only among the learned sort, but
generally, all England over, among the vulgar and common people and with what greediness God's word was read.
Everybody that could bought the book and busily read it or
got others to read it to them." As the biographer of Archbishop Cranmer Strype was giving a prejudiced view, actually a good half or more of England was still at heart faithfully Catholic and regarded the vernacular Bible with the

same horror it would a snake. An example is the story in Foxe's *Book of Martyrs* of fifteen-year-old William Maldon of Chelmsford, in Essex, whose secret reading of the Bible enraged his father almost to the point of murder. "I and my father's prentys," goes the boy's account, "layed our money together and bought the newe testament in engelyshe and hidde it in our bedstrawe . . . then came my father up into our chamber with a great rodde. . . . Then said my father to me serra who is your scholmaster tell me, forsooth father sayd I, I have no scholmaster but God." The infuriated father failing to extract an admission of sin by beating his son, then cried, "Fette me a haulter, I will surely hang him up . . . and my father cometh up with ye haulter and my mother intretyted him to lette me alone but in no wise he wolde be intretyd but putte the haulter about my neke I lyinge in my bedde and pullyd me with the haulter almost clene out of my bedde then my mother cryed out and pullyed him by the arme and my brother rycherd cryed out and laye on the other syde of me and then my father let go his holde and let me alone and went to bede. I thynke VI dayes after my neke greved me with the pullyng of the haulter."

Closer in sympathy to William's father than to the boy, King Henry and the bishops were soon aghast at the flood of Lutheranism let loose by their authorization of the Great Bible. Henry himself was a Protestant only up to the point of getting rid of the Pope, not in doctrinal matters. He allowed a translation of the Bible only because the English Bible would be a symbol of the displacement of papal authority by his own. He regarded himself more or less as pope in England and was as anxious to subdue doctrinal rebellion as if he had been pope in Rome. In fact, in 1540 he burned three Lutherans for heresy at Smithfield on the same day he executed three papists for treason. Luther commented on this occasion: "What Squire Harry wills must be an article of faith for Englishmen for life or death."

But the dam had been breached, and even Squire Harry could not stem the flood. Despite proclamations warning his subjects to use the book "humbly and reverently," to read it only in a quiet voice and not to go disputing and arguing over its puzzling passages in alehouses, "nor having thereof any open reasoning in your open Tavernes," the people, at last given open access to the Scriptures in their own tongue, were consumed with excitement and interest. They clustered around the huge folio volumes chained to every pulpit and listened avidly to whoever could read them aloud, as men today listen to the World Series results. In St. Paul's, where six Bibles had been fastened to "divers pillars, fixed unto the same with chains for all men to read in them that would," the scenes of enthusiasm appalled the authorities. Foxe says that these Bibles were much resorted to by the people, "especially when they could get any that had an audible voice to read unto them." One John Porter, "a fresh young man of big stature," became very expert in this "godly exercise," and "great multitudes would resort thither to hear this Porter because he could read well and had an audible voice." Such lay preaching was hardly welcome to the clergy. Porter was arrested, charged with making expositions on the text and attracting crowds and causing tumults contrary to the King's proclamation. He was thrown into Newgate prison and "laid in the lower dungeon of all, oppressed with bolts and irons where within six or eight days after, he was found dead."

An act of Parliament followed, expressly forbidding unauthorized persons to read the Bible aloud. It stipulated that noblemen and gentlemen householders might have the Bible read aloud quietly to their own families; that noblewomen, gentlewomen, and merchant householders could read it privately but not aloud to others; but that people of the "lower sort"—women, artificers, prentices, and others under the degree of yeomen—were forbidden to read it privately or openly unless the King, seeing that their lives were amended by the practice, gave them special liberty to do so.

There was about as much chance of enforcing this act as of enforcing Prohibition. Not that the population as a whole became Bible readers over night. But enough convinced Protestants, or Lutherans as they were called then, made free and individual access to the Scriptures a basic article of faith to nullify Henry's attempt at suppression. Especially during the Catholic reaction under Mary, in whose reign the Bible was torn out of the churches and proscribed, it acquired the extra life that always attaches to words that tyrants have endeavored to stifle. As the "good Doctor Taylor" went to the stake he called to the people who had been his parishioners: "Good people! I have taught you nothing but God's holy word and those lessons that I have taken out of God's blessed book, the Holy Bible; and I am come hither this day to seal it with my blood." In that flaming year, 1555, sixty-seven Protestants were publicly burned in Mary's vain attempt to enforce the resubmission to Rome. Some, like Rowland Taylor, died in unswerving loyalty to their principles, some like Cranmer recanting previous recantations, but all through the manner of their death were to live on as heroes and martyrs. Bishop Latimer's last words at the stake signalized Mary's failure: "We shall this day, by God's grace, light in England such a candle as I trust shall never be put out."

Then in the reign of Elizabeth everything was turned upside down again, the reforms were restored, and the Bible put back in the churches. A new version was commanded, but its editors were cautioned to follow the Great Bible and "not to recede from it but where it varyeth manifestly from the Greek or Hebrew original." Thus their version carried forward for another generation the continuity of Tyndale's translation. Known as the Bishop's Bible, this Elizabethan edition held the field until the reign of King James. By that time the rise of the Puritan sects that favored a Calvinist version called the Geneva Bible brought about a situation in which the official Bible read in the churches did not agree with the Bible read privately in many homes. At the Hampton Court Conference in 1604 a new version was petitioned; and so was set in motion the immense task, shared by fifty-four scholars, that was to result in the King James version.

Almost a century had passed since Tyndale began his work, and in that time much new research into ancient texts and many new grammars, dictionaries, and treatises had resulted from the advance in Greek and Hebrew scholarship. Among the revisers were Edward Lively, Regius Professor of Hebrew at Cambridge; Lancelot Andrewes, Dean of Westminster, who knew Hebrew, Chaldee, Syriac, Greek, Latin, and some ten other languages; William Bedwell, fellow of St. John's College, Cambridge, the greatest Arabic scholar of Europe; and at least nine others who were then or afterwards professors of Hebrew or Greek at Oxford or Cambridge. The revisers were grouped in six companies of nine each, two sitting at Oxford, two at Cambridge, and two in London. For their guidance was laid down a set of thirteen rules that shows the workmanlike approach of these seventeenth-century divines and scholars. Each company was given a number of books to work on, and each man was to work by himself on a designated number of chapters. Then all were "to meet together, confer what they have done and agree for their Parts what shall stand." Next the several companies were to exchange their finished books "to be considered seriously and judiciously for His Majesty is very careful on this point." If any point was in disagreement afterwards, then the revisers were to write each other their doubts, "note the Place and withal send the Reasons to which if they consent not, the Difference to be compounded at the General Meeting which is to be of the chief Persons of each Company at the end of the Work." Further elucidation might be asked of any learned person outside the group. Every bishop was instructed to send news of the project to any scholar of ancient tongues that he might know of, encouraging him to send in helpful observations to the "companies."

In their preface to the finished work as it appeared in 1611 the "workmen," as the revisers styled themselves, state simply that they tried "to make a good translation better, or out of many good ones, one principall good one, not justly to be excepted against; that hath bene our indeavor, that our marke." They did not disdain, they said, "to revise that which we had done, or to bring back to the anvill that which we had hammered." Nor did they bind themselves to a rigorous precision in using exactly the same English word every time for the same original word of the text, "for is the kingdom of God become words or syllables?" Their freedom of language preserved the work of their predecessors; in fact, the first of their thirteen rules sealed the style set by Tyndale by explicitly ordering that the Bishops' Bible was "to be followed and as little altered as the truth of the original will permit." How basically honest was the attempt to get as close as possible to the original meaning set down in ages past in Palestine, how astonishingly free of doctrinal partisanship, is evident from the instructions to the revisers. Names of prophets, for example, and all other proper names were "to be retained as nigh as may be, accordingly as they were vulgarly used." Angled interpretations were prohibited by Rule 6: "No marginal notes at all to be affixed, but only for the explanation of the Hebrew and Greek words." Finally in the preface the revisers acknowledged their constant effort to steer clear both of the "scrupulosities of the Puritans" and the "obscurities of the Papists" and firmly stood by their purpose that "the Scripture may speake like it selfe, as in the language of Canaan, that it may be understood of the very vulgar." This they accomplished, and this was their glory, for their Bible became not only understood by every one from the "very vulgar" to the most educated, but known, remembered, and loved.

CHAPTER VI

MERCHANT ADVENTURERS
TO THE LEVANT

In the age of discovery, when Europe was bursting its
boundaries in every direction, the Elizabethan navigators
and merchant adventurers were in the vanguard. These
"stirrers abroad and searchers of the remote parts of the
world," boasts Hakluyt, "have excelled all the nations and
people of the earth."

"For which the kings of this land before her Majesty,"
he continues, "had theyre banners ever seene in the Cas-
pian Sea? Which of them hath ever dealt with the Emperor of Persia as her Majesty hath done, and obtained for
her merchants large and loving privileges? Who ever saw
before this regiment an English Ligier in the stately porch
of the Grand Signor of Constantinople? Who ever found
English consuls and agents at Tripolis in Syria, at Aleppo,
at Babylon, at Balsara. . . ? What English shippes did
heeretofore ever anker in the mighty river of the Plate . . .
land upon the Luzones in despight of the enemy . . . traf-
ficke with the princes of the Moluccas . . . and last of all
return home most richly laden with the commodities of
China as the subjects of this now flourishing monarchy
have done?"

The return home "richly laden" was the chief factor in
Elizabethan expansion. The impetus that drove the explor-
ers was trade; their goal was the merchandise of the East.
Palestine for the time being was forgotten in its character

as Holy Land and became but a trading post, a way station in the commerce opened with the Ottoman Empire. Crusaders fired with zeal to split the heads of Turks gave way to gift-laden ambassadors who sued the Turk for trading privileges with soft words and promises. In the course of the commercial and diplomatic relations established between England and the Sultan's empire at this time the foundations were laid for England's future strategic involvement in the Middle East.

The Crown went into partnership with the merchants and navigators, subsidizing their expeditions and collecting handsome profits on their return. Above all, out of this activity England reaped a navy. As trade expanded, more and more ships were built to carry it and more and more crews trained to sail them.

Meanwhile another instrument of empire, the chartered company, grew up along with the navy. Formed by groups of merchant adventurers, the companies were granted monopoly rights to trading privileges in particular areas in return for an annual tribute to the Crown. The first to be chartered was the Muscovy Company in 1554, and the second was the Levant Company chartered in 1581 to trade in the dominions of the "Grand Senior," the Sultan of Turkey.

Palestine lay within those dominions, but it was a Palestine that had been for a generation neglected, unvisited, and all but forgotten by Englishmen. From Torkyngton, the last of the pilgrims in 1517, to Anthony Jenkinson, the first of the merchant adventurers in 1553, there are no records of English travel in Palestine. That gap of roughly a generation saw the overthrow of the Catholic Church in England and the establishment of Ottoman rule in Jerusalem. These two events were responsible for a new era in England's relations with Palestine. In 1453 the new and more terrible Turks captured Constantinople, which has remained theirs from that day to this. By 1540, at the height of the reign of Suleiman the Magnificent, the Turks ruled in Damascus, Jerusalem, and Cairo, in Budapest and Belgrade, in Rhodes and Algiers. They straddled all roads to Palestine by land or sea. A Christian traveler was regarded by them as legitimate prey, to be captured as a slave or killed as an infidel whose death assured the perpetrator a place in Paradise.

Not only had the risks of the journey to the Holy Land vastly increased, but also the compelling motive had disappeared. Salvation, according to Protestant theory, was to be won by the soul's journey, not by the body's. "The best pilgrimage," wrote Samuel Purchas, "is the peaceable way of a good conscience to that Jerusalem which is above." Wherever the Reformation took hold, pilgrimages ceased, at least for the time being. Along with the sale of indulgences and pardons they were condemned by the Protestants as the most objectionable of the forms and ceremonies of the Catholic Church — forms whose public performance was substituted for private morality. In that day Protestantism still meant protest, reformation still meant reform; and the most urgent reform was replacing the mechanical means through which Rome bestowed grace with the effort toward an inner virtue. To undertake the physical journey to some pilgrim shrine only endangered the soul's journey, as Purchas said, and he added the awful warning that "to ascribe sanctity to a place is Jewish."

Commerce, not salvation, was the new lure of the East. Where once the pilgrims disembarked, bales of English woolens now rolled onto the quays. Spices and silks, wines and oils, carpets and jewels were brought back in exchange. Caravans from Arabia passed through Palestine, were bartered in the market places and transshipped at the ports to the waiting vessels of European merchants. The land of Palestine itself contributed little to the new commerce. Under the Turkish despotism the devastation of the land that had followed the various Arab, Seljuk, Christian, and Tartar invasions and battles went on apace.

Terraced vineyards crumbled away, hillsides eroded, cisterns and aqueducts choked up with silt. The land that had supported the gardens and palaces of Solomon, and all the "crowded, busy world" of Biblical times, was but a backwater of the Ottoman empire. Even its ports, Jaffa and Acre, though still busy, were secondary to Scanderoon, port of Aleppo, on the one hand and to Alexandria and Algiers on the other.

But the future fate of Palestine was involved in the development of the Levant trade as a whole. When England first entered the "Turkie trade" in the reign of Elizabeth the foundations of her future empire in India and the Middle East were being laid, however unwittingly. The merchants of the Levant Company opened the Middle East to England's commerce. Pushing ever eastward, the same group twenty years later founded the East India Company, whose role in the development of the British Empire is well known. In this instance, a reversal of the usual order, the flag followed trade. The road to India, the Suez Canal, the oil fields of Mosul, the whole complex of political and strategic requirements that drew Britain into Palestine in 1918, began with the enterprise of the Elizabethan merchant adventurers. It was they who first put England into official diplomatic relations with the Ottoman Empire. The religious attachment to Palestine that had played so great a role hitherto and would do so again—this was for the moment absent. It is a striking fact that in all the correspondence of the Queen and her ministers with the "Turkie" merchants regarding negotiations with the Sultan, appointment of ambassadors, terms of the company's charter, there is, except for a casual reference in passing, no mention whatever of the land for which so many generations of crusaders had fought and died, the goal of a thousand years of pilgrimages.

Before the reign of Elizabeth the "Turkie trade" was largely monopolized by the Italian city republics, whose practiced fleets knew every wind and tide, every cove and port of the Mediterranean. Although Hakluyt lists several sporadic voyages by "divers tall ships of London to Tripolis and Barutti in Syria" in the early sixteenth century, the English made no concerted effort to break the Italian shipping monopoly until the balance of power in the Mediterranean was changed by the battle of Lepanto in 1571. When the battle was joined the combined forces of the Spanish Hapsburgs, the papal states, and the Italian cities under the command of the dashing Don John of Austria, brother of the Spanish king, numbered 270 galleys and 80,000 men. At the end of that terrible day, wrote Knolles, Elizabethan historian of the Turks, "the sea was stained with blood and covered with Bodies, Weapons and fragments of broken Gallies." The Turks' fleet was destroyed, their sea power in the Mediterranean smashed. They lost 220 ships, 25,000 men killed, 50,000 taken prisoner, and 12,000 Christian galley slaves released by the victors. "Never," claims the historian Lafuente, "had the Mediterranean witnessed on her bosom nor shall the world again see a conflict so obstinate, a butchery so terrible, men so valiant and so enraged." The victory aroused glittering visions of reviving the throne of Constantine and sweeping the Turk clean out of Europe and the Levant, back into the Scythian wilds whence he had come.

Don John saw himself an emperor in Byzantium. But the Turk, despite his defeat, remained a danger to Europe for over a century, until turned back at the doors of Vienna in 1683, and, even after that, a great power for over two centuries more. Still the toppling of the Turkish fleet in the Bay of Lepanto cleared the way through the Mediterranean. When news of the victory reached London, Holinshed reports, "There were bonfires made through the citie with banquetting and great rejoycing as good cause there was for a victory of so great importance to the whole state of the Christian commonwealth."

Naval supremacy did not, however, stay with the victors long. Venice, whose monopoly of the spice trade had been broken by the Portuguese, was already on the descent from the peak of her mercantile and maritime greatness. Within the next decade Spain's haughty Armada was to be scattered and sunk by the English. In that event the hindsight of history recognizes the passing of control of the seas to the Protestant countries, with results that Lecky, in a burst of conscious righteousness, called "an almost unmingled benefit to mankind." Of course the shift in power did not take place overnight. Spain remained a power to be reckoned with for some time; but the loss of the best part of her fleet, following a similar loss to the Turks and coinciding with the decline of Venice, served to open England's sea road to the Middle East.

England's merchants had not waited for Drake's smashing blow at the "Inquisition dogs and the devildoms of Spain." Already the victory at Lepanto had awakened them to opportunities in the Levant. Two rich merchants of London were soon busy assembling men, money, and ships for a collective assault on the "Turkie trade." One was Edward Osborne, a leading member of the Clothworkers' Company, and the other was Richard Staper, whose tombstone describes him as "the greatest merchant in his tyme; the chiefest actor in the discoverie of the trades of Turkey and East India." Behind them was Lord Burghley, Elizabeth's astute treasurer, whose eye was fixed on the gold that would accrue to the Crown when the Mediterranean trade winds should fill English sails. By 1579 Osborne and Staper had organized a group ready to invest in the new venture, and in that year, as their first act, they sent an agent to Constantinople to secure trading privileges from the Sultan.

William Harborne, an M.P. for Great Yarmouth who two years earlier had visited Turkey and returned with a letter from the Sultan inviting the friendship of the Queen of England, was the man selected for the mission. It was an inspired choice. England's whole future in the Middle East, and with it the future of Palestine, was touched by the diplomatic genius, the grit, the superb Elizabethan self-confidence of the first English envoy to the Porte. Off he went to a virtually hostile country and to a court of sinister reputation. Although the Sultan had once been gracious, the moods of Amurath III were notoriously unreliable. Access to him was guarded by jealous viziers and trigger-fingered janissaries. Other European envoys already established at the court were all inimical to Harborne's purpose and certain to intrigue against him. Yet within a year he was home bringing a full treaty of twenty-two articles empowering the English subjects to trade in Turkish dominions. Later he served six years in Constantinople as ambassador. He "firmly laid," says A. C. Wood, historian of the Levant Company, "the foundations of his country's influence in the Near East and never again was it in any real danger of extinction by rival influence."

With Harborne's treaty in their pockets Staper and Osborne petitioned the Crown for incorporation as a chartered company that would give them exclusive trade rights in the Levant. They pointed out the advantages to the state that would result from increased customs and an increased navy. In support of their petition Secretary Walsingham drew up a memorandum entitled "A Consideration of the Trade into Turkey," in which he spelled out for the Queen the reasons why the project should receive official backing. "First," he wrote, "you shall set the great number of your greatest ships in work whereby your navy shall be maintained, one of the principallest strengths and defence of this realm, which otherwise were like to decay." In addition, he continued, an English company would eliminate middlemen from the carrying trade so that "you shall vend your own commodities with most profit which before did fall into strangers' hands." For that very reason moreover it might be worth using the Levant trade to incline the Sultan toward England and away from his uneasy alliance with King Philip of Spain.

Convinced of the political advantages to be secured, and lured by the profits to be expected, Elizabeth on September

1, 1581 duly granted to Staper and Osborne and ten other merchants a charter as "The Company of Merchants of the Levant." According to its terms only members of the company, by virtue of their having "found out and opened a trade in Turkey not known in the memory of any man now living to be frequented by our progenitors," were thereafter permitted to enter the Turkey trade. Osborne was named governor and the membership limited to twenty. The company's ships were to fly the royal ensign and their ordnance and crew to be under supervision of the Admiralty. In return for the monopoly conferred by the charter the company was to pay the Crown a yearly tribute of £500.

More than a year's delay followed while the Queen and the company quarreled over who was to pay the ambassador's expenses. Beside salary and handsome presents for the Sultan he would also have to be provided with what is nowadays inelegantly called a slush fund. It was too much for Elizabeth's unconquerable parsimony, and she flatly refused to accredit an ambassador unless his expenses were paid by the company. Osborne and his fellows refused in their turn to lay out another shilling.

Finally the merchants, with their capital tied up in the waiting ships loaded with good wool cloth, gave in and decided to send Harborne at their own expense. In January 1583 the *Great Susan* set sail for Constantinople with Harborne on board and, as gifts for the Sultan, three mastiffs, three spaniels, two bloodhounds, "two little dogs in coats of silk," two silver popinjays, a jeweled clock valued at £500, and other ornamental objects and rare treasures. Elizabeth stingily contributed a knighthood and letters of credential to the new ambassador.

Once arrived, Harborne again justified the merchants' faith. By his persuasiveness, his presents, and his craft in circumventing the machinations of his rivals he not only regained the Sultan's favor and a restoration of the trade treaty, which had been canceled in his absence, but also secured terms more favorable than those enjoyed by the other Europeans and a reduction in export duties as well. "The mercurial breasted Mr. Harborne," wrote the journalist playwright Tom Nash, "so noised the name of our island among the Turks that not an infant of the cur-tailed, skin-clipping pagans but talk of London as frequently as of their prophet's tomb at Mecca."

Such fame was good for business as well as for diplomatic bargaining. The "Turkie merchants," in their first five years of operation, made twenty-seven voyages to ten Levant ports, realizing on some shipments a 300- or 400-per-cent profit and paying to the Crown a total of £11,359 in customs duties. Osborne, governor of the Company, was knighted and elected Lord Mayor of London. The charter was renewed twice, the second time at a profit to the Crown of 800 per cent. A consulate was opened at Aleppo to handle the commerce of Aleppo, Damascus, Aman, Tripolis, Jerusalem, and "all other parts whatever in the provinces of Syria, Palestine and Jurie [Jewry]." To such estate had the Holy Land fallen—one of half a dozen trading posts lumped together equally under a consul's jurisdiction.

Not every voyage was a triumph. Pirates and "the dreadful touch of merchant-marring rocks" that ruined the Merchant of Venice and put him in bond to Shylock fell upon the English as well. Of three Levant Company ships that set sail in 1591 only one returned. Another under Captain Benjamin Wood, bound for Cathay with a letter from Elizabeth to the emperor of China, never was heard of again. How anxiously must Staper and Osborne have awaited word of the safe arrival of their ships! How often must they have paced the wharves scanning the horizon for the first distant glimmer of incoming sails! But if their ships did escape shipwreck and storm, plunder by Turks and corsairs, ambush by Spaniards or Venetians, and made home port safely, then their return ensured lush profits to the Turkey merchants. One argosy brought a cargo of "Rawe silks, Indico Bleue, all sorts of spices, all sorts of poticary druggs, grograynes, cotton yarns, cotton wooll, some Turkye Carpitts, cotton clothe and Gawles [jewels]," according to the same report made to Cecil. "Her Majestie's custome," the company added, "will amount to, at the least, for soe wee dare adventure to give for the same, the sum of £3,500."

Particularly important to England's future was raw cotton, a strange new plant fiber which the Turkey merchants found for sale at Acre and Sidon. According to a contemporary account, "divers people in this kingdom, but chiefly in the county of Lancaster have found out the trade of making fustians, made of a kind of bombast or down, being a fruit of the earth growing upon little shrubs or bushes brought into the kingdom by the Turkey merchants." Such were the beginnings of Lancashire cotton weaving, which in the day of spinning jenny and power loom was to become England's leading industry.

From Persia by way of the Levant the company brought plants, rare then, a commonplace now in everyone's garden: lilies, irises, crocuses, hyacinths, daffodils, and laurel. One commodity that was to become famous in English life, which the Turkey merchants unaccountably passed up, was coffee. Agents of the company noted it as a popular drink among the Turks. They sit chatting most of the day, wrote the traveler Sandys, sipping it "as hot as they can suffer it; black as soote and tasting not much unlike it." But the English coffeehouse had to wait until the East India Company, a later offshoot of the Levant Company, began importing the coffee bean in quantity.

The East India Company, destined to transform England into an empire with vital effect on the fate of Palestine, was founded by the Levant Company merchants in an effort to break into the Far Eastern trade. The Dutch and Portuguese monopolized this trade. The fabulously profitable spices of the Indies, the silks of China, the muslins and jewels of India were shipped across the Indian Ocean and thence by caravan overland to the Levant cities, where English merchants could pick them up. But not an ounce of pepper or a single emerald could be transshipped by the Levant Company without paying handsome profits into foreign pockets. Already the price of pepper had doubled under the Dutch monopoly. The English determined to break open their own routes to the East. In 1601 the Turkey merchants founded the new company as a separate enterprise to develop the direct sea trade with India and the Indies.

The history of the East India Company so far as it determined England's policy in the Middle East belongs to a later chapter. In the meantime the affairs of the Levant Company brought England into more or less formal diplomatic relations with Turkey. Elizabeth, despite her miserly reluctance to pay an ambassador, made full use of Harborne and his successor, Sir Edward Barton, to try to win over the Grand Senior to England's side against Spain. "The Queen of England is exerting herself," wrote the Venetian ambassador at Constantinople in a dispatch of 1590, "by making large promises to persuade the Sultan to attack the King of Spain. . . ." He goes on to report signs of great preparations, much shipbuilding, and almost daily conferences between the Grand Vizier and the English ambassador. Intrigues were rife among the rival European diplomats, each trying to shift Turkey's weight this way and that in the uneasy balance of Continental alliances. On one occasion the French ambassador was struck accidentally by a snowball thrown in the course of a game among some Greeks. "He fell into a great choler," reports the English ambassador, Barton, and, "supposing it to be done by one of my servants," he went home, armed his retinue, and set them upon the English with daggers, staves, and swords, "manifesting his great fury and malice against our nation."

In spite or perhaps because of incidents like *l'affaire snowball* Barton, who had become ambassador after Harborne's death in 1568, equaled and even improved on his predecessor's success with the mercurial tyrant of the Sublime Porte. Although the Sultan was regularly reminded by the other European ambassadors that their English colleague was a mere "stipendiary of merchants," being still a paid agent of the Levant Company, this status did not prevent his being held in "extraordinary esteme" by the Sultan. He even left his post to accompany Mahomet III, the fratricidal successor of Amurath III, on one of his local wars. In fact, so far did Barton adapt himself to the life of the Sublime Porte that reports reached home complaining that the English embassy had taken on the character of a Turkish harem in which the staff "plied their whores, that at one time was rumoured to be in the house 17; but the ambassador caused all to depart except his owne, with whome and alchemy he waisted his alowance."

The lax-moraled Sir Edward Barton seems to have been the only person who actually enjoyed his stay at "this happy Porte," as he called it. To his countrymen at home the Ottoman Empire was looked upon as the "present terror of the world," in the words of Knolles. The Turks were "a most wicked people," thought the merchant Staper. The general attitude of the English toward the despotism that had succeeded that of the Saracens was one of fascinated horror, a mixture of fear, hate, and awe, in some part a hangover from the Crusades but augmented by reports of cruel and lascivious iniquities unheard of before. The zeal with which Mohamet III, on his accession in 1595, carried out the heir apparent's customary elimination of possible rivals to the throne by murdering all nineteen of his brothers caused thrills of horror in Europe. A flood of eyewitness accounts from ambassadors fresh from scenes of throat-slit bodies tumbled on bloody marble stairs spread through the Western capitals and echoed for years afterward with a steady accretion of gory detail in plays and verse. Spine-chilling villainies were always the role of characters impersonating Souleiman the Magnificent or Bajazet or Selim the Grim or various Janissaries, Mamelukes, and eunuchs who strode across the Elizabethan and Jacobean stages exhibiting every variety of wickedness and lust.

The stereotype of the "terrible Turk" that developed during this period remained fixed in British minds for long after. It is relevant to our story, for the real Turk was the temporal ruler of Palestine for some four hundred years. The sixteenth-century alliance made in the days of Ottoman glory and power when Britain was just beginning her overseas career and challenging the dominance of Spain was not necessarily useful in the nineteenth century, when Turkey and Spain had both sunk into second-rate powers. But through sheer force of habit Britain persisted in it through the long agony of Turkey's decline and decay, committed to the support of a decrepit potentate despite every argument of changed circumstance and historical logic. The policy that made sense in Harborne's and Barton's time made no sense at all when Turkey had become the Sick Man of Europe; but the less workable it became, the more desperately the Foreign Office clung to it, until at last the Turks themselves deserted the alliance in 1914. Then at last Britain found herself, almost against her will, aiding and abetting the demise of the empire that she had so long been propping up, and ultimately replacing Turkish rule by her own in the crucial area from Syria to Suez, which included the long-smothered "vilayet" of Palestine.

Even Sir Francis Bacon, the keenest mind and most learned man of his time, so far shared the general awe of the terrible Turk as to call for a new crusade against the Ottoman despot. This "cruel tyranny" he raged, "bathed in the blood of their emperors upon every succession; a heap of vassals and slaves; no nobles; no gentlemen; no freemen . . . a nation without morality, without letters, arts or sciences; that can scarce measure an acre of land or an hour of the day . . . a very reproach of human society." They have "made the garden of the world a wilderness," he accused, for "where Ottoman's horse sets his feet, people will come up very thin." This diatribe, called *Advertisement Touching an Holy War*, was published in 1623 after

Bacon's fall from power as Lord Chancellor. It is of particular interest as anticipating almost to the very words Gladstone's more famous "bag and baggage" speech denouncing the Turks two hundred and fifty years later.

Yet the inveterate English travelers could not be altogether put off, even by such a dire and awful picture as Bacon's. Some were agents of the Levant Company, like John Sanderson, a merchant adventurer who traveled about the East in the years 1584–1602 and found himself eventually acting as *chargé d'affaires* when Barton was absent on campaign with the Sultan. Some were chaplains of one or another of the English "factories," like William Biddulph, chaplain at Aleppo, whose travel diary appeared in Purchas's collection. Others were simply tourists eager for strange sights and far-off lands. William Lithgow, a Scot, journeyed on foot throughout the Middle East over a period of nineteen years, covering, according to his own calculations, 36,000 miles. Fyne Morison, Sir Henry Blount, George Sandys, and Henry Timberlake were well-to-do gentlemen who, following the routes opened up by the Levant Company, voyaged out of curiosity to the classic lands of Greece and the Aegean, the Biblical lands of Palestine and Egypt, and the fabled wonders of Constantinople, ancient seat of the Eastern Empire.

They toured in a very different spirit from that of the pilgrim forerunners—a spirit derisive of the religious legends attached to the holy places, skeptical of miracles and relics, and almost to a man careful notetakers and diary-keepers. Their journals, published with alacrity on their return home and read avidly by the English public with its eternal curiosity about the East, did much to keep alive acquaintance with the Holy Land during a period of otherwise general neglect. At each night's lodging the traveler sat down to write his notes of the day's sights, to pick apart the superstitions and fables of monkish guides and try to interpret what he had seen in the new light of reason, history, and probability. Lithgow, for example, in his *Delec-*

table and True Discourse of an Admired and Painefull Peregrination, remarks that the fissure in the rock on Mt. Calvary "lookes as if it had been cleft with wedges and beetles" rather than by a miracle. Timberlake, who made the tour in 1603, impressed by the barrenness of the country around Gaza, thought it improbable that the kings of Egypt and Judaea fought many great battles in that area, "there being no forrage for an army there but sand and salt water." Sanderson was disappointed in the cedars of Lebanon, which he found "of indifferent bigness but not very hudge"; but the same trees impressed Lithgow by their grandeur. Their tops, he said, "seem to kiss the clouds." The chaplain Biddulph typified the change from devout pilgrim to critical reporter when he classified the sights and stories of Jerusalem as "Apparent Truths," "Manifest Untruths," and "Things Doubtful." Passages like these exemplify the new inquiring spirit of the Renaissance tourist.

Factual detail was a characteristic of all their accounts. The better to enable his readers to visualize Palestine, Timberlake compares the distances between places of the Bible and familiar distances at home. "The river Jordan (the very nearest part thereof) is from Jerusalem as Epping is from London. . . . The Lake of Sodom and Gomorra is from Jerusalem as Gravesend is from London."

The homebound public could never be satiated. They loved every inch-by-inch detail—possibly the reason why the travelers kept such voluminous journals. It was expected of them. In the *English Traveller*, a play by the prolific Jacobean dramatist Tom Heywood, staged in 1633, the title character entertains his friends with tales

> About Jerusalem and the Holy Land:
> How the new city differs from the old,
> What ruins of the Temple yet remain,
> And whether Sion and those hills about,
> With the adjacent towns and villages,
> Keep that proportioned distance as we read.

The natural features and local customs of the country interested these travelers far more than the religious traditions. Sanderson refused even to enter the Church of the Holy Sepulcher, "by reason I had a great controversie with the Popish friars." Lithgow ridiculed the antics of the Greek and Latin Catholic friars worshiping and kissing the "wooden portrait of a dead corpse representing our Saviour, having the resemblance of five bloody wounds." He called the ceremony a "singular dottage of the Romish folly," noting with approval how the Turks derided the spectacle, "laughing them to scorne in their faces." The adventurous Timberlake even preferred prison to accepting the help of the Greek Patriarch. Becoming entangled in some scrape with the Turks, he was advised to declare himself a Greek in order to acquire the Patriarch's protection, but he refused "because I protested that I would rather be protected by the Turk than by the Pope or himself." A friendly Moor who had traveled on Timberlake's ship eventually interceded and procured his release.

Yet the aura of the Holy Land sometimes overtook even these determined skeptics. Fynes Morison found his mind filled with "holy motives" on first touching Palestine's soil, and his brother Henry, though a thorough Protestant, instinctively fell upon his knees in the traditional pilgrim attitude and kissed the ground, so impetuously in fact that he bumped his head and "voided much blood at the nose."

Few among the travelers of this period showed any curiosity about the original inhabitants of the Holy Land. The position of the Jews was already as bad under Ottoman rule in the Levant as it was under Christian rule in Europe. In any Moslem city, according to Hakluyt, "the surest lodging for a Christian . . . is in a Jew's house, for if he have any hurt, the Jew and his goods shall make it good, so the Jew taketh great care of the Christian for fear of punishment."

John Sanderson, factor of the Levant Company, gives an account of a journey in 1601 in company with seven or eight Jewish merchants from Smyrna, Damascus, and Constantinople. The chief of these was "Rabby" Abraham Coen, "who favored and much regarded me," fortunately for Sanderson, a quarrelsome man who was forever getting into trouble with "Popish friars" and "villainous Moores." On several occasions Rabby Abraham managed to save Sanderson from the consequences of his irritable temper and once even bought his way out of gaol, where Sanderson had been put by "the grisly Turke and his rascally terrible attendants." No doubt some of the 10,000 or 12,000 ducats that "my ritch companion Jews" had sewed into the quilted undergarments of his servants on leaving Damascus, for fear of "theeves who abound in those countryes," were used to effect Sanderson's release.

Sanderson records during the journey many visits to his companions' houses of worship and "coledges or scoles of lerninge" and how his fellow travelers were forever buying "holie books of the declaration of their law," enough to load two or three pack mules. He tells how the Jews endow their "great doctors and scoles" with a yearly stipend, how they try at least once in a lifetime to visit Palestine or send their bones there to be buried, how the "graver and better sort of Jewes" who were his companions never discussed religion for fear of displeasing him, but that from others he learned their opinion of Christians, whose most learned men could not expound the letter A, whereas Jewish scholars could write whole volumes on the first letter only.

It was his companions' custom, he noted, to give alms to needy fellow Jews wherever met; Rabby Abraham at Sefet gave 2,000 dollars (sic) and 1,000 at Jerusalem, and the others according to their ability. Indeed Rabby Abraham "was so respective, kind and courteous that never in any Christian's company of what degree soever, I ever did receive better content." They parted company with moist eyes. "A most devout, zealous, and softhearted man he was. I cannot speake too much good of him in regard to his great humanitie and extraordinarie charitie, his measure being more in those performances than is to be found in many of us Christians."

One final word Sanderson has left us of a people already 1600 years old in exile. "They know, they said, that Jerusalem shall be built againe and their Messias come and make them princes, as they have bine in time past, but then to govern all the wourld."

The year after Sanderson's return home Queen Elizabeth died, forcing upon the Levant Company the necessity of obtaining a new charter from the new sovereign. So the long-drawn-out quarrel over the responsibility for maintaining and paying an ambassador began all over again with James, the first Stuart. If there was one thing in which the Stuarts equaled the Tudors, it was in being tight-fisted. And James, with his limited views, saw no reason for keeping an ambassador to the "heathens" at all. The Turkey Merchants for their part, most of whom now had funds tied up in the new India Company, were unwilling to continue carrying the expense; but as they could get their charter on no other terms they were forced to acquiesce even in the Crown's right to name the ambassador, whom the company paid. Finally in 1605 a charter was granted to "The Governor and Company of Merchants of England Trading into the Levant Seas." Each time it came up for renewal the old dispute was revived, and as shortage of funds was a chronic condition of the Stuarts they could never be got to assume full responsibility for the embassy.

Whether wholehearted support from the Crown would have many any difference in the eventual decline of the Levant trade is questionable. There is no doubt that the aggressive commercial policy pursued by Colbert, first Minister of the French Crown under Louis XIV, succeeded in drawing much of the Turkey trade from England into French hands. Beginning in the seventeenth century France began to assume the role of England's rival that had been filled by Spain in the sixteenth century. When England's new and firmly Protestant king, William of

Orange, brought to an end the Stuart century of popish plots, French mistresses, and royal longings for Catholic connections, he inevitably ushered in the period of wars with France that began in the seventeenth century, lasted throughout the eighteenth, and carried over into the nineteenth century, until the final defeat of Napoleon in 1815. During England's wars with Louis XIV Turkey was won over as an ally by the French, and in the intervals of peace French goods replaced English. Following the disruption of French trade resulting from the French Revolution, England's Levant trade enjoyed a brief revival, but its day was past. By now British energy and money, withdrawn from the West since the loss of the American colonies, was fully diverted to India. The theories of free trade proclaimed by Adam Smith marked a new era in which the protected trade of chartered companies was an anachronism. Mercantilism was dead. The century of imperialism had opened. The Levant Company, after a century of half-life in the shadow of its greater scion, the East India Company, languished to a final demise; and in 1825 its charter was terminated.

CHAPTER VII

ON THE EDGE OF PROPHECY:

Puritan England and the Hope of Israel

IN THE YEAR 1649, the very peak and mid-point of Puritan rule in England, two English Puritans of Amsterdam petitioned the government "That this Nation of England, with the inhabitants of the Netherlands, shall be the first and the readiest to transport Izraell's sons and daughters in their ships to the Land promised to their forefathers, Abraham, Isaac and Jacob for an everlasting Inheritance." The petition further requested that the Jews "may again be received and permitted to trade and dwell amongst you in this Land."

What moved Joanna and Ebenezer Cartwright, authors of the petition, to ask not only that England assist in the restoration of Israel to Palestine but also repeal Edward I's act of banishment, which had been in force for some three hundred and fifty years? To understand their motive one must realize the transformation wrought by the Bible acting through the Puritan movement. It was as if every influence on thought exerted today by press, radio, movies, magazines were equaled by one book speaking with the voice of God, reinforced by the temporal authority of the Supreme Court. Particularly the Old Testament, with its narrative of a people unalterably convinced of having been chosen by the Lord to do His work on earth, governed the Puritan mind. They applied its narrative to themselves. They were the self-chosen inheritors of Abraham's cov-

enant with God, the re-embodied saints of Israel, the "battle-ax of the Lord," in the words of Jeremiah. Their guide
was the prophets, their comfort the Psalms. Their devotion,
their obedience, their inspiration were owed not to the
Heavenly Father of Jesus, but to Jehovah, the Lord God
of Hosts. Scripture, the word of God revealed to His chosen
people, was their command, on the hearth as on the battlefield, in Parliament as in church.

In the period covered by previous chapters, up to 1600
let us say, Palestine had been to the English a land of
purely Christian associations, though lost to the Christian
world through the unfortunate intrusion of Islam. Now it
came to be remembered as the homeland of the Jews, the
land carrying the Scriptural promise of Israel's return.
Interest now centered on fulfilling the Scripture. Starting
with the Puritan ascendency, the movement among the
English for the return of the Jews to Palestine began.

The movement was not for the sake of the Jews, but for
the sake of the promise made to them. According to Scripture the kingdom of Israel for all mankind would come
when the people of Israel were restored to Zion. Only then
would the world see the advent of the Messiah or, in Christian terms, the Second Advent. The return was visioned,
of course, only in terms of a Jewish nation converted to
Christianity, for this was to be the signal for the working
out of the promise. Such was the hope that animated the
Cartwrights, as they plainly stated: "Your Petitioners being conversant in that City [Amsterdam] with and amongst
some of the Izraell race called Jews . . . by discourse with
them and serious perusal of the Prophets, both they and
we find that the time of her call draweth nigh; whereby
they together with us, shall come to know the Emanuell,
the Lord of Life, light and Glory. . . . For the glorious man-
ifestation thereof and pyous meanes thereunto, your Petitioners humbly pray. . ." and so follows the passage already
quoted.

Re-entry of the Jews into England was proposed for two

reasons: First, the Puritans believed that, because their doctrines were closer to Judaism, the Jews, once in contact with Puritanism, would no longer resist conversion. "The English are more gifted to convince them," Henry Jessey, a prominent Puritan divine, wrote in 1656. Secondly, strict bibliolaters insisted that the Jews could not start on their return to Zion until their scattering to every country was complete. Therefore they must be brought to England before they could get to Palestine.

The Cartwright petition, in embodying these ideas, was not a single eccentricity, but a typical and natural product of its time. England, between the sailing of the Mayflower in 1620 and the restoration of the Stuarts in 1666, was in a fanatical mood, perhaps the only fanatical period in her history. It was the England, in Carlyle's phrase, of "awful devout Puritanism," the England of the Great Rebellion, of the regicide that produced such a national sense of guilt as has kept England a monarchy ever since; the England of Oliver Cromwell, "like a servant of the Lord with his Bible and his sword."

With the Puritans came an invasion of Hebraism transmitted through the Old Testament, but distorted by the effort to apply to post-Renaissance England the ethics, laws, and manners native to a Middle Eastern people of more than two thousand years earlier. In their devotion to chapter and verse of the Hebrew testaments the Puritans, undaunted by the mental jump of two millennia, adapted to themselves the thoughts of tribal herdsmen groping their way out of idolatry toward monotheism in the time of Abraham, or of slaves triumphing over Pharoah in the time of the Exodus, or of warriors carving the frontiers of a new state in the time of Saul and David. It did not matter that the narrative of the Hebrews' struggle to achieve a code for communal living according to law, to become a nation, to withstand enemies, to climb like Sisyphus again and again from the slough of sinfulness to the way of the prophets, was a narrative of fierce and far-off times. It did not matter that it covered a period, from Abraham to Maccabaeus, of nearly a millennium and a half; the Puritans swallowed the whole with equal zeal.

It was not a narrative ideally suited for transplanting word for word, as principle and precedent, to seventeenth-century England. But that was what the Puritans attempted. As early as 1573 one of their articles of faith, according to the indictment of Sandys, Bishop of London, was that "the judicial laws of Moses are binding on Christian princes and they ought not in the slightest degree to depart from them." They followed the letter of the Old Testament for the very reason that they saw their own faces reflected in it. They too were a group led by God in the struggle against idolators and tyrants. His word, His guidance, His law to fit every occasion was written in the Old Testament, and the more closely they hewed to it the more steely and impenetrable was their conviction of righteousness. "The Lord himself hath a controversy with your enemies," Cromwell wrote to one of his generals. "In this respect we fight the Lord's battles."

The Puritans' mania for the Old Testament developed directly out of their experience of persecution by the Established Church. The Church hounded and harried them, even to the gibbet, because of their refusal to acknowledge any authority other than the Bible and their own congregation. They hated the episcopacy with the same passion that the first Protestants hated the prelacy of Rome, and for the same reason: that the hierarchy, whether episcopal or papal, were self-anoited intruders between man and his God—intruders whose perquisites and power, all too clearly of human origin, made a mockery of religion. The essence of the Puritan faith was the right of every man to interpret God's law, as embodied in the Bible and only in the Bible, directly to himself and to appeal to that law over any other, whether temporal or ecclesiastic.

Church and state being one, the Crown necessarily joined the Church in attempting to suppress the Independents; that is, those Puritans who, distinct from the Presbyterians, demanded the right to form self-governing congregations. King James in his famous retort, "No bishop, no King," recognized their ultimate danger to monarchy before they did themselves. Inevitably, as hatred of monarchy was added to hatred of episcopacy, they were led to republicanism. Their religious principles were the seed and root of their political principles. As disavowal of the divine right of episcopacy led them to disavow the divine right of kings, so affirmation of the individual's right to liberty of conscience led them to reaffirm man's civil liberties. It was but one step, as Macaulay put it, from the belief that "as power in church affairs is best lodged in a synod, so temporal power is best lodged in a parliament."

Persecution, Macaulay continues, "produced its natural effect upon them. After the fashion of oppressed sects . . . they imagined that in hating their enemies they were hating only the enemies of heaven." In the Old Testament "it was not difficult for fierce and gloomy spirits to find much that might be distorted to suit their wishes." They began to feel for the Old Testament a preference that showed itself in all their sentiments and habits. They paid a respect to the Hebrew language that they refused to the language of their Gospels and of the epistles of Paul. "They baptized their children by the names not of Christian saints but of Hebrew patriarchs and warriors. They turned the weekly festival by which the church had from primitive times commemorated the resurrection of her Lord, into the Jewish Sabbath. They sought for precedents to guide their ordinary conduct in the books of Judges and Kings."

Macaulay waxes more and more indignant as he lays on with his pen against all the unlovable traits of the Puritan: "His gait, his garb, his lank hair, the sour solemnity of his face," his prohibition of all innocent merriment, his nasal twang and peculiar cant in which Hebraisms were "violently introduced into the English language and metaphors borrowed from the boldest lyric poetry of a remote age and country were applied to the common concerns of English life."

Ordinarily too schooled a mind to allow his powerful rhetoric to run away with his prejudices, Macaulay on this occasion does not balance the scales fairly. He tells nothing of the evils of the old system that the Puritans were striving to overcome, or of the ideals that led them on. In this he is unfortunately typical. Because the Puritans were not likable, few have done them justice. As a target for ridicule they are as a barn door to a marksman. Nevertheless they gave permanent underpinning to two principles that are at the basis of democratic society: for one thing, the security of parliamentary government; for another, the right of nonconformity or freedom of worship, as we call it today. The principle of toleration is theirs even if they did not practice it—the principle formulated by Browne and Foxe and Roger Williams that brought the Pilgrim Fathers to America and formed the moral basis of a new society in a new world.

If the Puritans discarded mercy and forgiveness in favor of the more bellicose qualities of the Old Testament, it was because they too were fighting against odds to establish a principle and a way of life. The cry of Joshua's trumpet suited their circumstances better than the plea to turn the other cheek. In the Old Testament they found not only justification for slaying their enemies, but also exhortation to it. Saul "gathered an host and smote the Amalekites and delivered Israel out of the hands of them that spoiled them." But when he spared the life of Agag, King of the Amalekites, did not the prophet Samuel seize upon Agag, saying, "As thy sword hath made women childless so shall thy mother be childless among women"? "And Samuel hewed Agag in pieces before the Lord in Gilgal."

Charles I was Agag, or equally Rehoboam, successor of Solomon, who hearkened not unto the people but answered them roughly, "My father chastised you with whips, but I will chastise you with scorpions," and upon that the Ten

Tribes revolted with the cry, "To thy tents, O Israel!" Charles driving along Whitehall found a paper thrust into his carriage inscribed "To thy tents, O Israel!"

Or Charles and the Royalists might figure as Pharaoh and his host, and the first victories at Marston Moor and Naseby were celebrated in the words of Moses' song of triumph over the Egyptians: ". . . Thy right hand, O Lord, is become glorious in power; thy right hand, O Lord, has dashed in pieces the enemy." Likewise the Royalists were the children of Edom or Moab or Babylon. "Cursed be he that keepeth back his sword from blood," raged Jeremiah against Moab. "Thou shalt be cut down, O madmen; the sword shall pursue thee. . . . For thus saith the Lord, I will send the sword after them till I have consumed them. . . . Behold I will punish the King of Babylon and his land and I will bring Israel again to his habitation . . . and Babylon shall become heaps, a dwelling place for dragons, an astonishment and an hissing, without an inhabitant."

The English have never really liked themselves in moods of enthusiasm, and later ages have been almost ashamed of the Puritans. Cunningham in the classic work on English economic history wrote: "The general tendency of Puritanism was to discard Christian morality and to substitute Jewish habits in its stead." The Puritans, he continued, followed "the letter of an ancient code instead of trusting to the utterances of a divinely instructed Christian consciousness . . . and there was in consequence a retrogression to a lower type of social morality which showed itself at home and abroad." Whether Puritan morality as exemplified by the massacre of the Irish at Drogheda and similar unedifying exploits was any lower than the morality exemplified by Henry VIII's execution of Fisher and More, or by the massacre of the Huguenots on St. Bartholomew's Eve, or by the tortures and burnings of the Inquisition, all done in response to a "divinely instructed Christian consciousness," is a comparison that Cunningham does not venture to make.

Certainly the vengeful qualities of the ancient Hebrews that the Puritans chose to emulate were on a lower ethical plane than the ideals of the Sermon on the Mount, just as they were on a lower plane than the Ten Commandments given to Moses on Mt. Sinai. The Israelites in all their ups and downs were no better able to abide unswervingly by the ideals of Mt. Sinai than the Christian world has been able to conduct itself according to the ideals of Jesus. The only trouble with Christian morality is that Christians on the whole do not practice it. Whereas the Ten Commandments represent a code that men *can* follow if they try, the Sermon on the Mount has been, so far, a code beyond the grasp of society.

Although the Puritans did not by any means reject the New Testament, some of the extremists among them did reject the divinity of Jesus, and some went to the stake firm in that denial. Even the moderate Puritans included as one of their demands in the millenary petition to James I that they be no longer required in church to bow at the name of Jesus. In their effort to "purify" religion of vestments, sacraments, genuflections, and so on, the extremists returned to a belief in a God whose divinity could not be shared, the same belief expressed in the synagogue: "Hear, O Israel, the Lord thy God, the Lord is One." Truth in religion is not a thing to be argued about. The Independents in their preference for an older form have found few champions. Carlyle alone among English historians found them sympathetic. "The last of all our heroisms," he called them, "the last glimpse of the God-like vanishing from this England; conviction and veracity giving place to hollow cant and formulism—antique 'reign of God' which all true men in their several dialects and modes have always striven for, giving place to modern reign of the No-God whom men name the Devil."

But Carlyle was an oddity; like the Puritan, a passionate, not a reasonable man. A truer estimate of the Puritan effect on the English mind was made by the man of sweet reasonableness, Matthew Arnold. Puritanism, he wrote in *Culture and Anarchy,* was a revival of the Hebraic spirit in reaction to the Hellenic spirit that had animated the immediately preceding period of the Renaissance. Arnold's own bent was to Hellenism, which he defined as "to think right," in contrast to Hebraism, which was "to do right within the law." Puritanism, he said, was a reaction to the loss of moral fiber that accompanied the Renaissance. In its yearning for obedience to a law it showed "a signal affinity for the bent which was the master-bent of Hebrew life." It left a lasting imprint on the nation. "Our race," Arnold declared, "has yet (and a great part of its strength lies here) . . . a strong share of the assuredness, the tenacity, the intensity of the Hebrews. This turn manifested itself in Puritanism and has had a great share in shaping our history for the last two hundred years."

A notable turn in the history of the restoration of Israel took place with the settlement of Puritan refugees in Holland, beginning in 1604. For they said, wrote Daniel Neal, their first historian: "It is better to go and dwell in Goshen, find it where we can, than tarry in the midst of such Egyptian bondage as is among us."

To Holland also had come during the preceding century the Jewish refugees turned out of Spain and Portugal by the Inquisition. They had a flourishing community in Amsterdam numbering many prosperous merchants who played an important role in the trade of the Dutch colonies and the general European trade with the Levant. In Holland the Puritan settlers who walked in the footsteps of the ancient Hebrews became acquainted with modern Jews, and the Jews became acquainted with this odd new variety of Christians who advocated religious freedom for all, including Jews. (So long as they were the persecuted ones, the Puritans believed in toleration; after they came to power they began to see its disadvantages.)

Actually, in doctrine alone as distinct from ritual observance, there was little to divide the Independents from

Judaism, a fact recognized by members of both faiths. Sects arose among the extremist Puritans who proclaimed themselves Jews in belief and practice according to Levitical law. Some determined individuals went abroad to study under Continental rabbis and acquaint themselves with Talmudic law and literature. In 1647 the Long Parliament appropriated five hundred pounds to buy books "of a very great value, late brought out of Italy and having been the Library of a learned Rabbi there."

In the course of the approach of Judaism the Puritans came to include the Jews among those who had a right to protection under the banner of toleration. One of the Amsterdam exiles, Leonard Busher, made this point in his tract *Religious Peace or a Plea for Liberty of Conscience,* which appeared in 1614 and is the earliest publication advocating full freedom of worship. Roger Williams in a more famous tract, *The Bloudy Tenent of Persecution for the Cause of Conscience* (1644), said in his opening statement of principles: "It is the will and command of God that since the coming of his Son the Lord Jesus, a permission of the most Paganish, Jewish, Turkish or anti-Christian consciences or worships be granted to all men in all nations and countries. . . . God requireth not a uniformity of religion to be enacted and enforced in any civil state. . . . True civility and Christianity may flourish in a state or kingdom notwithstanding the permission of divers and contrary consciences either Jew or Gentile."

Williams wrote from a brave new world across the Atlantic. In England only the wild, schismatic, fanatic sects, what Bishop Hall earlier called "the cobblers, tailors, feltmakers and such-like trash," really believed that such ideas could be put in practice. A "Council of Mechanics" in 1648, during the heady months following Pride's Purge and the victory of the Independents, voted a resolution in favor of "toleration of all religions whatsoever not excepting Turkes, nor Papists, nor Jewes." But idealism once again bowed to practical politics. The plea for religious liberty was lost in the throes of Cromwell's struggle with the Puritan extremists. For fear of encouraging the lunatic fringe, sects that were demanding his own overthrow to make way for the millennium and the kingdom of the saints, he dared not enact in legislation the brave principles of toleration. "I would rather Mahometanism were permitted amongst us than that one of God's children be persecuted," the Protector once said; but the Levelers and the Fifth Monarchy Men were too much for him.

Meantime certain Puritan theorists evolved the scheme of recalling the Jews to England in order that their conversion under the proper auspices might proceed as soon as possible. What could be more stunning proof to the world at large of the righteousness of the Puritan cause than the accomplishment of this long-delayed event? "Our desires and hopes of the Jews conversion to Christ" would have to be given up, was an argument that Roger Williams used in making his case against an enforced state religion. That the restoration of Israel would follow conversion was part of accepted theology. As early as 1621 there had appeared a treatise called *The World's Great Restauration or Calling of the Jews and with them of all Nations and Kingdoms of the Earth to the Faith of Christ*. Its author was Sir Henry Finch, a sergeant-at-law or legal officer of the king, who predicted the restoration in the near future of temporal dominion to the Jews and the establishment by them of a world-wide empire. It remains the first of all English projects for the restoration of Israel. According to Finch's contemporary, Tom Fuller, the book was interpreted as implying that "all Christian princes should surrender their power as homagers to the temporall supreme Empire of the Jewish nation." In view of James I's sensitivity on the royal prerogative it is no surprise that Finch was promptly arrested, tried for treason, and eventually released only after disavowing any passages that might be considered derogatory to the King's sovereignty.

What influence the book had, if any, cannot be deter-

mined. Its suppression may have prevented any spread of
its ideas; on the other hand, the fact of suppression and
the author's trial may have stimulated interest. In any
event the idea did not die. During the next generation the
Independents—that is, the left wing of Puritanism, which
eventually came to power under Cromwell—were growing
each year more numerous, influential, and infuriated. As
the movement grew the Hebraic invasion spread. The more
surely they felt themselves the reincarnated chosen people
called to do God's work among the Philistines, the more
Hebraic they became in speech and habit. A wave of Old
Testament nomenclature broke over the heads of England's infants. Guy, Miles, Peter, and John gave way to
Enoch, Amos, Obadiah, Job, Seth, and Eli. Mary and Maud
and Margaret and Anne lost out to Sarah, Rebecca, Deb-
orah, and Esther. A Chauncy family of Hertfordshire is
recorded whose six children were named Isaac, Ichabod,
Sarah, Barnabas, Nathaniel, and Israel. The Bible was ran-
sacked from beginning to end; there seems to have been a
particular liking for the more obscure or outlandish examples, like Zerrubabel or Habbakuk and even Shadrach,
Meshach, and Abednego. The playwright Cowley, satiriz-
ing the fashion, has a character named Cutter in one of
his plays who turns Puritan and announces: "I must not
be called Cutter any more . . . my name is now Abednego.
I had a vision which whispered to me through a key-hole,
'Go, call thyself Abednego.'" Especially names of wicked
and suffering characters had a great vogue, presumably as
a form of self-punishment. Children were named for
Tamar, who was raped by her brother, Jael, who drove the
nail through Sisera's head while he slept in her tent, and
Job, the man of affliction.

Old Testament fervor did not stop at the baptismal font.
Biblical scholarship and exegesis became the chief intellectual activity of the age and Hebrew one of the three holy
tongues necessary to the theological study that now choked
the universities. An ordinance of 1644 required candi-

dates for the ministry to be examined in reading the Scriptures in Hebrew and Greek. Hebrew even invaded the grammar schools. A contemporary play satirizes the schoolmistress of the time who "teaches to knit in Chaldee and works Hebrew samplers." Milton began his study of Hebrew as a schoolboy, and in his essay *On Education* recommends its teaching to grammar school pupils, "that the Scripture may be read in the original." That invaluable gossip, John Aubrey, says of Milton that after he became blind he had a man read aloud to him on his first waking up and that "the first thing he read was the Hebrew bible . . . then he contemplated."

The scholar Matthew Poole used to rise at three or four in the morning, eat a raw egg, and study till evening while preparing his *Synopsis Criticorum Bibliorum*. This monolith when finally published filled five folio volumes of over five thousand double-columned pages. Following the lead of the King James translators, the next generation of scholars delved deeper into ancient languages and folklore. Like hounds on a scent they scurried, nose to ground, through fields of Syriac, Chaldee, and Arabic texts. Archbishop Ussher from his study of the ancients worked out a scheme of universal chronology. John Selden tracked down every idol deity mentioned in the Old Testament to produce an exhaustive work on heathen faiths. Edward Leigh in 1646 published the *Critica Sacra*, the most complete Hebrew dictionary that had yet appeared. In the next decade appeared the great Polyglot Bible, a massive multiauthored achievement using altogether nine different ancient tongues including Samaritan, Ethiopic, and Persian.

One of the Polyglot compilers was Edward Pococke, who had been chaplain for the Levant Company at Aleppo in 1630–35. Pococke's profound learning won him appointment to both the professorship of Hebrew and the first chair of Arabic at Oxford. His pioneer history of the Arab world, *Specimen Historiae Arabum,* and his edition of Maimonides' commentary on the Mishna were the first

works printed by the Oxford University Press to use Arabic
and Hebrew type respectively. Like living fragments from
the days of Solomon, a fig tree and cedars that Pococke
planted from cones he brought back from Syria were still
flourishing in Christ Church garden at Oxford three hundred years after his death.

All this vast erudition was not kept the private preserve
of scholars: it was spread among the people through epit-
omes, treatises, concordances, lectures, and such a din of
sermons by clergy, lay preachers, or anyone who felt the
spirit move him as has never been heard before or since.
Adults and children knew long passages of the Bible by
heart and lived their daily lives according to its ordi-
nances. It was open to all, it needed no priestly intervener
to interpret its meaning, it transfigured moral life.

The psalm-singing, Bible-carrying habits of the Round-
head soldiers are well known. Sir Charles Firth in his book
on Cromwell's army quotes a contemporary account of
"good sermons and prayers morning and evening under
the roof of heaven to which the drums did call for bells."
Morning and evening from the tents came "the sound of
some singing psalms, some praying and some reading
scripture." At Marston Moor a company of Royalists flee-
ing in confusion almost flung themselves into the arms of
the Roundheads, but "by their singing of psalms perceiving who they were, they all most fiercely fled back again."
Soldiers and officers alike were so given to preaching each
his own theology that the chaplains constantly complained, especially when officers preached from horseback,
but they were answered: "If they have not leave to preach
they will not fight."

Cromwell and his officers, on drawing up a plan of battle, literally consulted Scripture for guidance and precedent. A council of war included prayers and Bible reading.
The battle cry was "Lord God of Hosts!" and victory was
celebrated on the field by a halt for psalms in praise of
God. Cromwell himself, as we know from his speeches,

was a great quoter of psalms and prophets, and his talk, as Scott wrote, "had a marvelous twang of doctrine about it." Indeed, the Cromwell whom Scott put into his novel *Woodstock* is probably not too exaggerated. He speaks of himself as "a man who is called to work great things in Israel," of the Stuarts as having "troubled Israel for fifty years," of "the whole Sanhedrin of Presbytery," of England as "our British Israel" and "our English Zion." He orders his soldiers to march in silence "as Gideon marched when he went down against the Midianites." He rages against a Cavalier family who hid and protected Charles as having "aided Sisera in his flight when Israel might have been delivered of his trouble forever." He is called "England's son of Jesse" by his soldiers, constantly likened to David in faith and strength and wisdom. Likewise the soldiers call the Royalists "Baalists," rush into battle crying "Perish Babylon!" and refer to extremists on their own side as "dissenting Rabbis."

Scott's vivid picture of the era in *Woodstock* is not contemporary evidence, but it has a wonderfully true ring. This intense familiarity of the Puritans with the names, the lives, and the personal histories of the people of the Old Testament made them acquainted with the history and traditions of the Jews that focused on the perennial hope: "Next year in Jerusalem." Among the Jews themselves at this time there was a prevailing sense that the time was imminent. It was widely believed in England and other Protestant countries that the year 1666 was going to be decisive in the fate of the Jews, either by their conversion or by the restoration of their temporal kingdom, which would be the signal for the downfall of the Pope.

This excitement communicated itself to the Jews, and it accounts for their susceptibility to the false Messiah, Sabbatai Zevi, who in fact chose the year 1666 to lead his benighted brethren on their tragic fools' journey to the East. Previously, in 1650, the Jews of Europe had held a great council in Hungary to discuss the expected coming

of the Messiah. An English observer who was present, one
Samuel Brett, wrote a report of the council on the assumption that it presaged the conversion of the Jews. Even the
Pope, aroused by the ferment, sent six Catholic priests to
"advise" the council in their discussion of whether the
Messiah of prophecy had come or was yet to come. They
were allowed to expound their doctrine, reports Brett, but
the assembly would have none of it. Nor were the Jews
able to reach any conclusion among themselves; they disbanded on the eighth day, agreeing only to meet again
three years later. Mr. Brett's chief point in his report to
the English public is that Rome "is the greatest enemy of
the Jews' conversion," because it is an idolatrous church
with woman gods and graven images, but that Protestantism could yet effect the conversion.

The Cartwrights, in Amsterdam, had already determined on a practical step toward this goal. Their "Petition
of the Jews for Repealing the Act of Parliament for their
Banishment out of England" was presented to Lord Fair-
fax and the Council of War in January 1649. It was lost
sight of in the agony and turmoil over the King's execution, which took place that month. But in the new stage
now reached in England's affairs, new factors began to
operate toward the consummation that the Cartwrights
wished. Now for the first time a Jew entered the picture,
and his efforts, fitting neatly into certain circumstances
of the time, combined to reopen England to Jewish settlers.

Manasseh ben Israel, a learned rabbi of Amsterdam,
touched perhaps by a tinge of the Messiah complex or at
least by the conviction that he was called to hasten the
coming of the Messiah, published in 1650 a remarkable
book entitled *Spes Israeli*—in the English edition *The Hope
of Israel*. What Manasseh had in mind was the extension
of the Jewish diaspora to England in order to complete the
world-wide dispersion that was necessary before the in-
gathering of the exiles could begin. As he explained in a
letter of later date, it had been foretold in Deuteronomy

(28:64) how "the Lord shall scatter thee among all people from one end of the earth even unto the other," and he added: "I conceived that by the 'end of the earth' might be understood this Island," meaning England.

Manasseh's messianic expectations had been aroused by the narrative of a Jewish traveler, Antonio de Montezinos, whom he had met in 1644 and who had told him a tale of Indian tribes in the West Indies who practiced the rituals of Judaism, recited the Shema, and though somewhat "scorched by the sun" were indubitably Hebrews. These Indians, Montezinos persuaded his listener, were none other than the tribe of Reuben, one of the ten lost tribes of Israel. For some time Spanish missionaries in South America had been propounding the theory that the American Indians were indeed the Ten Lost Tribes who had somehow made their way westward across Asia to China and thence to America. (Present-day anthropologists defend the thesis that the American Indians were in fact originally Mongolians who crossed over by the Bering Strait.) Montezinos, no doubt acquainted with such talk, selected himself, like the character in *The Mikado,* to add "corroborative detail and artistic verisimilitude to an otherwise bald and unconvincing narrative." Names, places, dates, and details of local color adorn his story of an Indian guide secretly revealing himself to be a fellow Israelite; of a week's journey across jungle, rivers, and mountains to a meeting with a bearded community of Hebrew-speaking Indians. On the request of the Amsterdam synagogue Montezinos even signed on oath an affidavit as to the truth of his eyewitness report.

This tale, which soon spread among the Amsterdam Puritans, especially excited the members of the Millenarian sect, who were confidently awaiting the Kingdom of the Saints. According to their prevailing interpretation of Biblical prophecy the return out of exile must include the Ten Lost Tribes, who had seceded in the tenth century B.C. Only when they were reunited with the sons of Judah, as they had been under David and Solomon, could the Messiah, the son of David, appear on earth.

Montezinos' marvellous find was seized on by Manasseh as proof that the dispersion had indeed been accomplished "among all peoples" and thus as a signal that the time for the reunion of the Twelve Tribes under the Messiah was approaching. Was it not written in the Book of Daniel, "And when the dispersion of the Holy People shall be completed in all places, then shall all these things be finished"? Such was the thesis of *Spes Israeli* as Manasseh first wrote it in Spanish. But there was still one portion of the earth empty of Jews. The idea of using his thesis to secure the recall of the Jews to England evolved from Manasseh's conversations with his Puritan friends. He rewrote his book in Latin, adding a dedication to "The Parliament, the Supreme Court of England, and to the Right Honourable, the Councell of State." In it he asked for their "favor and good will," so that "all those things which God has pleased to have foretold by the Prophets do and shall obtain their accomplishment . . . so that Israel at last being brought back to his owne place, the Peace which is promised under the Messiah, may be restored to the world."

Encouraged in their hope of the approaching millennium, Manasseh's English disciples had his book translated into English and printed in England, where two editions were rapidly sold out. It came at an opportune time. Cromwell was then engaged in a war with Portugal, the first in a long series of trade wars with Continental powers that the Commonwealth undertook to restore British maritime supremacy and repair broken trade ties with the colonies. During the prolonged struggles of the Civil War England had fallen 'way behind in the powers' competition for foreign trade. The business and commercial class, almost exclusively Puritan, was particularly jealous of the Dutch, who had seized the opportunity to push into first place in the Levant and Far Eastern trades and in the carrying trade with the European colonies in the Americas as well.

Dutch success was aided by the Jewish merchants, ship-owners, and brokers of Amsterdam, who brought in busi-ness through their Hispanic and Levantine connections. Their value was not lost on Cromwell, particularly as there were several Marrano families in England who had al-ready been of use to him.

The Marranos or crypto-Jews were refugees from the Inquisition who had settled in other countries, where they lived publicly as Spanish nationals practicing Catholicism in the embassy chapels while privately practicing Judaism in their homes. Traces of such families in London and Bristol can be found as early as the years immediately fol-lowing the expulsion from Spain in 1492. In Cromwell's time several prosperous Marranos were active in the City, of whom the most prominent were Simon de Caceres and Antonio de Carvajal. The latter was grain contractor for Cromwell during the Civil War and controlled most of the import of gold bullion from Spanish sources. His ships were expressly exempted from seizure during England's war with Portugal and in fact were granted special facili-ties by the Council of State to continue their commerce abroad. Cromwell, plagued by "ship money" as much as Charles I had ever been, needed capital, which he hoped to get from the Jews. Also he believed that they could be useful to him as "intelligencers" whose connections, threading across Europe, would bring him information on trade policies of rival countries and on royalist conspira-cies abroad.

Official contact with Manasseh was opened in 1650, soon after his book appeared. A mission to Holland headed by Oliver St. John, whose purpose was to negotiate an alli-ance with the Dutch, was authorized to treat with Manas-seh on the side. St. John had several conversations with the Rabbi, with the result that Manasseh addressed a for-mal petition to the Council of State for readmission of the Jews to England.

Events were now hurrying to a climax. The proud and

prosperous Dutch rejected the upstart English republic's offer of union. Thereupon the Commonwealth, operating on the principle, if you can't join them, lick them, promptly passed the Navigation Act, which excluded foreign ships from commerce with England and her colonies. This hit the Dutch where they lived, and war with England followed within a year. Anticipating it, Cromwell, on the day after passage of the Act, sent Manasseh ben Israel a passport to come to England to advocate his cause in person. The coincidence in time, as Cecil Roth has pointed out, is worth noting. Cromwell was anxious for the transfer of the Amsterdam Jewish merchants to London as a measure that would benefit England in the trade race with Holland.

Before Manasseh could come over, however, the Dutch war erupted, and while it lasted no further action on his proposal was taken. If it could have been taken up at this time, the results might have been startling, for in the year 1653, with the calling of the Barebone Parliament, the "remarkablest" of the modern world according to Carlyle, the peak of Hebraism was reached. The little band of stern, impassioned men hand-picked by Cromwell convened on July 4, 1653 with the set purpose of so remaking England's constitution as to put into actual practice Mosaic law and the pristine principles of Jesus. On the Exchange, in the courts, in the markets, the Englishman was willy-nilly going to love his neighbor as himself. It was, says Lord Morley in his life of Cromwell, an attempt "to found a civil society on the literal words of Scripture . . . the high-water mark of the biblical politics of the time."

Cromwell himself was inspired by the mood, and in his opening speech to the Little Parliament he seemed almost carried away by a vision of himself bringing, like Elijah, a nation back to God. "Truly you are called by God as Judah was to rule with Him and for Him," he told the members as they sat rapt in a sense of high mission and a historic moment. "You are at the edge of the Promises and Prophecies," he went on, and quoted the Sixty-eighth

Psalm: "There it prophesies that 'He shall bring His people again from the depths of the Sea' as He once led Israel through the Red Sea. And it may be, as some think, God will bring the Jews home to their station, 'from the isles of the sea' and answer their expectations 'as from the depths of the sea.'" And he rose in eloquence, quoting psalms and prophets in every other sentence and assuring his hearers that the triumph promised in the Sixty-eighth Psalm to God's people of old would be realized by the Commonwealth, God's people now on earth.

Had Manasseh ben Israel been in England to present his case to men thus exhorted, what might not have happened? But in the little space of six months they were finished. Their earnest, hopeless effort to put Scripture into practice was denounced as a "judaizing" of English law, and having clashed with property rights it went down to inevitable defeat. Cromwell himself, standing on the spot where he had said they were "on the edge of Prophecy," summarily dismissed them. They have come down in history as an object of ridicule typified by the nickname taken from one of their members, Praisegod Barebone.

Although the peak of Biblical Puritanism was now passed, the issue of the Jews' recall was not dropped. The Dutch war was over, but the Spanish war, another matter of trade rivalry, was in the offing. Cromwell still pressed for a decision on the Jews, whose mercantile connections with Spain and Portugal remained close. In 1654 Manasseh sent his brother-in-law, David Dormido, and his son to present his petition to the Council of State. Because of opposition among his own people, who cleaved to the orthodox Jews' position and sternly disapproved any human efforts to hasten the Messiah's coming, he felt obliged to lie low for a while. But when the Council, despite Cromwell's request for "speedy consideration" and "all due satisfaction," rejected Dormido's petition, Manasseh decided, on Cromwell's urging, to come over himself. Accompanied by three fellow rabbis he arrived with new arguments for his cause, ready written in a *Humble Address to the Lord Protector*. In it he gave the rabbinical weight of his authority to the argument that the Jews were scattered throughout the world "except onely in this considerable and mighty Island" and "that before the Messiah shall come and restore our Nation, that first we must have our seat here likewise."

Next he took up "profit which is a most powerful motive" and pointed out how useful the Jews could be as channels of influence in trade vis-à-vis Holland, Spain, and Portugal. He stated the affection in which the Jews held the Commonwealth because it offered more toleration than monarchies. He answered familiar accusations with the remark that Christians themselves were accused of blood rituals by Roman emperors and pointed out the uncomfortable truth that "Men are very prone to hate and despise him that hath ill fortune." Finally he specifically asked for protection by the government, a "free and publick" synagogue and cemetery, freedom to trade, civil jurisdiction by the Jews over their own community with final appeal to the English courts, and abolition of any existing laws that might disallow any of the foregoing.

Publication of the *Humble Address* provoked a tumult of controversy in which the pros were loudly outpamphleteered by the cons. All the old charges were revived and some new ones, including the charge that Cromwell was a Jew and that the Jews were going to buy St. Paul's and the Bodleian Library. They were an ignoble race whom even God had constantly to chastise for their wickedness; their exile was divine punishment for the killing of Christ (and the Puritans would reap the same punishment for killing King Charles); if recalled to England they would vilify the Christian religion and cause a movement away from Christian principles and customs, falsify coinage, create unemployment, ruin English merchants, and destroy foreign trade. Advocates, on the other hand, maintained that the Jews were "the most honorable Nation of the world, a people chosen by God"; that the high priests only were responsible for the crucifixion, not the Jews as a nation; that their return to England would "bless" the country; that the Civil War had been God's punishment on England for the expulsion of His people and that the recall would appease His wrath and bring peace; and that the Jews as merchants would lower prices and increase trade and prosperity, for it was well known that "those nations who treat the Jews best flourish most and abound in wealth and strength." Chiefly, however, the advocates based their case on its weakest point: the argument that only by bringing the Jews to England could their conversion be accomplished. The opponents, led by the bitter, brilliant William Prynne, whose *Short Demurrer* is an archetype of the rest, ridiculed the idea of the Jews' ever being converted, on which point, of course, they were right. The whole thesis of the Jews' convertibility, which was to reappear so strongly in the nineteenth century, was totally unrealistic. Yet, ironically, it was the strongest of all the motives that conditioned England to promote the restoration of Israel.

Be that as it may, at Whitehall on December 10, 1655 Cromwell convened a special committee of judges, clergy, and merchants to consider Manasseh's petition. In the following fourteen days' debate the delegates, who were about evenly split pro and con, wrangled to a stalemate. But on one point at least a clear conclusion was reached. Cromwell had laid down the agenda: "Whether it be lawful to receive the Jews," and "If it be lawful, then upon what terms is it meet to receive them?" On the first question Justices Glyn and Steel handed down the opinion that there was no legal bar to the readmission—a great point gained. But as to terms under which the Jews could take up residence in England there was, as Cromwell scolded, "a babel of discordances." The clergy, most of whom favored readmission, argued that "The good people of England did generally more believe the promises of the calling of the Jews and more earnestly pray for it than any other nation," and should admit them in order to bring about this "calling" or conversion. Moreover England should atone for its past cruelties to the Jews, who had indeed been invited in by William I, the more so as "We are children of the same Father Abraham, they naturally after the flesh, we believers after the spirit."

The merchants were adamant against it. Rumors of sinister results that would follow readmission had been spread both by Dutch and Spanish agents, who understood its purpose as aiding the Navigation Act, and by Royalist agents, who hoped to thwart it because "the Protector was earnestly set upon it." Influenced by these rumors, the merchants predicted the direst results, insisting that Jewish trade would enrich foreigners and impoverish England. As for conversion, they said, the people were so prone nowadays to run after strange new doctrines that the Jews would probably make more converts to Judaism than the reverse. Finally the only agreement that could be reached was a resolution permitting the re-entry, but under such disabling trade and financial restrictions as would have made it useless to Cromwell.

The door was flung open. In stalked the Protector, disgusted once more with the inability of human weaklings to come to the point, to get action, to see what he wanted and let him have it. Was it not, he berated them, every Christian's duty to receive the Jews into England, the only nation where religion was taught in its full purity, and "not to exclude them from the light and leave them among false teachers, Papists and idolaters"? This argument silenced objectors among the clergy. Then he poured his contempt upon the City men. "Can ye really be afraid that this mean and despised people should be able to prevail in trade over the merchants of England, the noblest and most esteemed merchants of the whole world?" "Thus he went on," says an observer, "till he had silenced them too. . . . I never heard a man speak so well in his life."

But Oliver had had enough, and he dismissed the shamefaced committee as he had dismissed the Long Parliament and the Little Parliament when they could not serve his purpose. Actually he had secured part of what he wanted in the judges' decision, and he was probably not anxious to push the matter farther for fear of stirring up more agitation. Students of the episode agree that Oliver had probably made up his mind to accomplish his purpose more or less unofficially and to allow the re-entry, as a contemporary said, "by way of connivancy." In fact, this was the impression at the time. "Now were the Jews admitted," wrote the diarist John Evelyn on December 14, 1655, apparently in reference to the judges' admission of no legal barrier.

Everyone was glad to be allowed to drop a prickly subject without a clear-cut decision—with one lone exception. To Manasseh ben Israel, who had put all his passion, his learning, his persuasiveness into the plan, all the ancient longing of his people plus a new urgency because of recent persecutions in Poland—to him a compromise was worthless. He went back to Holland, aged, penniless, defeated; and in little over a year, at the age of fifty-three, he was dead, perhaps of that elusive complaint, a broken heart.

The immediate consequences of Cromwell's "connivancy" are no part of this story. Because of the indecisiveness of the result no large-scale immigration took place at the time; but in 1656, when England went to war with Spain, the Marranos were enabled to throw off their Spanish disguise and, despite renewed agitation, to win official permission for an open synagogue and limited rights as English residents. Manasseh's nephew was admitted as a broker on the Royal Exchange in the same year in which his uncle died of despair. In fact, Cromwell's compromise, a typical English solution, illogical but workable, was fortunate for the Jews when Commonwealth gave way to Restoration. There being no statute on the books for Charles II to cancel, he reasonably allowed things to go as they were, ignored petitions for re-expulsion of the Jews, and, since many Jewish families of monarchist sympathies had helped the Stuarts in exile, refused to consider any restrictions, and in short connived, like Cromwell, at a condition that was useful to him.

Gradually, over two centuries, the Sephardic community increased; and bit by bit, though always against new Prynnes and *Demurrers,* civil emancipation was won piecemeal.

These first stirrings in Puritan England of interest in the restoration of Israel were unquestionably religious in origin, born out of the Old Testament reign over the mind and faith of the party in power during the middle years of the seventeenth century. But religion was not enough. No practical results would have come out of the Puritans' sense of ghostly brotherhood with the children of Israel or out of their ideals of toleration or out of their mystical hopes of hastening the millennium, had not political and economic expediency intervened. Cromwell's interest in Manasseh's proposal was dictated by the same factor that dictated Lloyd George's interest in Chaim Weizmann's proposal ten generations later: namely, the aid that each believed the Jews could render in a wartime situation. And from Cromwell's time on, every future episode of British concern with Palestine depended on the twin presence of the profit motive, whether commercial, military, or imperial, and the religious motive inherited from the Bible. In the absence of either, as during the eighteenth century when the religious climate was distinctly cool, nothing happened.

CHAPTER VIII

ECLIPSE OF THE BIBLE:

The Reign of Mr. Worldly Wiseman

When the power of the Puritans was broken their earnestness and deadly seriousness went out of fashion, though not out of England. The dominant tone of Restoration and eighteenth century was set by the curled black wig, the cool intelligence, the casual shrug of Charles II. After nearly fifty years of being intense, England with a sigh of relief determined to be gay, to be good-humored — to be anything but serious.

But Puritanism, like a subterranean river, carried on among the Dissenters. Ejected from the re-Established Church, excluded from office, from the universities, from society, deprived even of civil rights until 1689, they still preserved a living tradition that was to emerge again in the nineteenth century. In the intervening period loosely called the eighteenth century Dissent lived in the shadows; aristocracy held the place in the sun. It was the age, says Trevelyan, of "aristocracy and liberty; the rule of law and absence of reform"; a "classic" age, orderly, mannerly, rational, and as un-Hebraic as possible.

The eighteenth century, if it is to have a coherent character, must be allowed to divest itself of strict chronological limits and wriggle itself into the period from 1660 to somewhere in the 1780's; that is, from the Restoration to the decade when the American Revolution triumphed, the

French Revolution began, and the Industrial Revolution got under way with Cartwright's power loom and Watt's steam engine. It was the age of reason and free thought. Science with its discovery of natural laws began to challenge the Bible. Not God but gravity, Isaac Newton discovered, brought the apple down on his head. The awful logic of John Locke opened new realms of uncertainty. Under the impact of these new thought processes the supreme authority of Scripture melted away like butter in the sun. Security of faith gave way to the insecurity of knowledge. Deism tried to supply a substitute for the Bible as Revelation. With youthful faith in the power of human reason to overcome religious controversy, the Deists offered a God whom all men of reason could believe in—a God whose existence was proved by all the wonders of the natural world and who needed no miracles, prophecies, or other supernatural revelations to show himself to mankind.

In reaction to "awful devout Puritanism" the Hellenic mood had returned. It left men clear-headed but uncomfortable with the craving for some omnipotent Authority unsatisfied. And the "moral depravity" that Arnold noted in the Renaissance returned too. While the tarnished silver of Restoration comedy held the stage, the government of England was left in the hands of the lordly and unprincipled Cabal. The Bloodless Revolution that unseated the Stuarts for good and brought in the Bill of Rights was an opposite tendency, but it slowly slid down to a nadir of political morality under the German Georges. Their time is memorable for its South Sea Bubbles and rotten boroughs, its fortunes in slave trade and its ministers so busy jockeying for power under a half-crazy king as hardly to notice that they were losing an empire in America. Though called the Augustan Age by literary critics, it was also the gin-soaked age of Hogarth's rakes and trollops. In a world of Yahoos, said Swift, the only angry voice of the time, "decency and comeliness are but conventions."

In its official religion the age was High Church, polite, and satisfied to serve no other purpose than to offer its preferments as a refuge to the nobility's younger sons and deserving relations. Gone was Independency. The order and legality of a state Church, however empty of fervor, was preferred to the anarchy of a dozen self-governing congregations, however sincere and devout. What chance had the Bible in a Church personified by Jane Austen's immortal curate, Mr. Collins? The people of the Bible, New Testament as well as Old, were, like the Puritans, extremists. There is not a comfortable or complacent person among them. In eighteenth-century England the divine rage of the prophets could not penetrate what Gibbon called "the fat slumbers of the church."

Yet a strong current of enthusiasm, of yearning for moral rectitude, ran underneath the urbane surface of the eighteenth century. The Wesley brothers' Methodism and hymn singing were as much a product of the time, though of a different class, as Pope's *Rape of the Lock* or Lord Chesterfield's *Letters to His Son*. And how can one generalize about a period that included at its beginning Bunyan's *Pilgrim's Progress* and at its end Gibbon's *Decline and Fall*, two of the most remarkable books of any era? Gibbon represents the skeptic, the scientist, and the anti-Christian, Bunyan the believer, the enthusiast, the apostle of virtue. One is knowledge, the other faith, or, as Arnold would say, one is Hellenic, the other Hebraic. *Pilgrim's Progress* is probably the most widely read book ever written in English after the Bible. Indeed, it was like a second Bible, in the cottage if not in the manor house. The educated class ignored it, but in the end it proved to be, in Macaulay's words, "the only book about which the educated minority has come over to the opinion of the common people." It is somewhat startling to find that this epitome of piety appeared in the same decade as Wycherley's *Country Wife* and *Plain Dealer*, the epitome of profligacy. Although Bunyan belonged to the older Puritan genera-

tion, his book belongs to later generations who loved it
and lived with it. He was both the heir of the Puritans and
the predecessor of the Methodists—the bridge that carried
Puritanism over to the Evangelical Revival of the nineteenth century.

But while the common people read eagerly of Christian's progress to the Heavenly Gate, it was Mr. Worldly
Wiseman who presided over the country and the time. He
was unconcerned about the Messiah whose promised advent so exercised the Puritans. Not unnaturally, he was
equally unconcerned about the restoration of Israel and
the Jews. In fact, the only evidence of interest in the Jews
during the eighteenth century was the antagonism aroused
by the Naturalization Act of 1753. The Jew Bill, as it was
called, proposed to "enable all Jews to prefer bills of naturalization in Parliament without receiving the sacra-
ment." One opponent warned that allowing Jews to become landowners would give the lie to New Testament
prophecy, which, according to Christian interpretation,
implied that the Jews must remain wanderers until they
acknowledged Christ as the Messiah. Another speaker
added: "If the Jews should come to be possessed of a great
share of the land of the kingdom how are we sure that
Christianity will continue to be the fashionable religion?"
Yet the bill was passed by the Commons and, with the
bishops' approval, by the Lords. Such a storm of protest
from pamphleteers and howling mobs met the Act that it
was repealed the following year and not finally re-enacted
until the Emancipation Act of 1858, over one hundred
years later.

Initial passage of the Act, regardless of its repeal, re-
flects the latitudinarian spirit of the eighteenth-century
enlightenment, the spirit of live and let live. At the same
time eighteenth-century rationalism was working against
the fulfillment-of-prophecy argument that had favored the
restoration of Israel. Rationalism found the whole argument from prophecy untenable. Rationalist writers on the-

ology, Hobbes, Hume, and others, discovered as they examined one by one the bases of Christian dogma that the allegorical interpretations that made Jesus the fulfillment of the Hebrew Messianic prophecies were "irrational"; that the elaborate scheme of reading into every line of the Old Testament an allegory of some yet-to-come event in Christian church history must fall apart under the light of reason. Anthony Collins in a *Discourse on Freethinking* (1713) dared to announce that the Book of Daniel was not autobiographical, but was authored in Maccabaean times—an interpretation that sheds a very different light on its prophecies. Other dangerous thinkers began to suspect that Moses did not personally indite the whole Pentateuch; and the farther they delved and studied, the more they were forced to the conclusion that Christianity's hope of the Second Advent, so far as it was based on Hebrew prophecy, was a hope in vain.

While the rationalists held the field little interest could be aroused in restoring the Jews to Zion. Nevertheless through the rationalists' study of the historic foundations of the Bible new interest in Palestine as a country was created. Its archaeological remains were now studied, not as relics, but as mirrors of the life of the past. One of the earliest of the investigators' works on the Bible lands was the worthy Dr. Fuller's *A Pisgah-sight of Palestine*. Although published in 1650, it has nothing in common with Puritanism, and in fact Fuller, by temperament and interest, leaned toward the Royalists. No Puritan could have written of the Bible's homeland with his detachment. The marvellous good humor and wit that break through the lines of even his weightiest works and the urge to be fair (which in life enabled him to keep out of trouble with both sides, even in the hottest days of the Civil War) separate Fuller from his time. His motive, he says, in writing a descriptive work on Palestine is to contribute to the true understanding of the Bible, even though, he asserts, "these corporall (not to say carnall) studies of this terestriall

Canaan begin to grow out of fashion with the more knowing sort of Christians." He carefully describes the animal
and vegetable life, the mineral resources and geographical
formation of the terrain, correcting common misappre-
hensions as he goes along. In fact, the country is no desert,
he points out, despite the frequent use of the word in Scripture. "Indeed the word Desert sounds hideously to English
eares: it frights our fancies with apparitions of a place
full of dismall shades, savage beasts and dolefull desolation, whereas in Hebrew it imports no more than a woody
retiredness from publick habitation; most of them in extent not exceeding our greater Parks in England, and more
alluring with the pleasure of privacy, than affrighting
with the sadness of solitariness."

He tries to clarify "cubit" and other terms of Hebrew
measurement; he discusses the ancient laws and customs,
household habits, farming methods, food, and clothing.
There are many maps dotted over with tents, temples, battle sites, and turreted cities; plans of buildings, such as
Solomon's Temple shown with all its furniture, utensils,
and treasures; plates of dress and ornaments purporting
to show the exact design worn by each class of person—
maid, wife, widow, and harlot, for example. Fuller's book
was at least scientific in purpose if not in results. He concludes with a chapter disputing the Jews' hope of Restoration, maintaining that the return out of the Babylonian
exile fulfilled all prophecies and that if any further promise remains it must take the form of the Jews' conversion
to Christianity without, however, the "temporall regaining" of their old country. This, he maintains, must remain
a dream. As to conversion, he is not sure whether God
really intends it or not, but since there is nothing revealed
to the contrary it is best to suppose that He does, and in
that event Fuller is sure that, all obstacles notwithstanding, as soon as God wishes it, "in the twinckling of an eye,
their eies shall be opened." But with that burst of the fair-
ness that he can never repress, he admits that conversion

is unlikely as long as Christians exclude Jews from the community: "There must be first conversing with them before there can be converting them."

Another popular book was *Two Journeys to Jerusalem,* published in 1704 by Nathaniel Crouch, editor of a series of penny histories that Dr. Johnson called "very proper to allure backward readers." The book contained, in addition to the travel diaries, some "Memorable remarks upon the Ancient and Modern state of the Jewish Nation," Samuel Brett's account of the Jews' Council in Hungary, an account of the "Wonderful Delusion" of the Jews by Sabbatai Zevi, and a report of the Council's debate on Manasseh ben Israel's proposal in 1655. One of the two journeys was the "strange and true" adventures of Henry Timberlake already mentioned (Chapter VI); the other was a reprint of the travels of fourteen Englishmen in 1669, which had first appeared in 1683. The whole collection seems to have had a steady audience, for it kept on being reissued, once even in a Welsh translation, at various times over the next hundred years, with a final edition in 1796.

Crouch, who himself wrote the "Memorable Remarks" under the name Robert Burton, plunges into the problem that puzzled generations of writers on Palestine: how so barren a country could ever have supported the busy, prosperous population of Biblical, Roman, and Byzantine times. In our own day, when the White Paper cut Jewish immigration on the pretense that the land could not support any more people, the same problem under the awesome name of "economic absorptive capacity" produced endless debates in Parliament. But Burton (or Crouch), writing two hundred years before it was necessary to worry about appeasing the Arabs or about a "political upper limit," approached the question in the realistic spirit of his time. Assuming a revival of the careful cultivation practiced by the "ancients," he calculated that an acre of good ground will easily feed four men for a year, allowing each two pounds, six ounces of bread a day, "but since our

Israelites were great eaters let us allow them double the nourishment, that is to say four pounds, twelve ounces a day," or two men to an acre. The area of the ancient kingdom of Judea he estimates at 3,365,000 acres, and, deducting half of this as noncultivable, he concludes that it could still support the equivalent of one man to an acre for the whole. Curiously enough, this figure of three and a half million is not far from that which the present government of Israel is aiming at, though ridiculed as fantastic and impossible by all the White Paper experts.

The general impression of Palestine as barren, Burton went on, was due to the fact that travelers usually saw only the country between Jaffa and Jerusalem, which was never famous for fertility; and "for want of culture and tillage among the barbarous Infidels . . . who by their continuous wars and ravages have made it almost desolate and like a desert" it has become "like a place forsaken by God." Yet in Bible times it flowed with milk and honey, thanks to the husbandry of the Israelites, who terraced and fertilized it and wasted none of it in "parks for hunting, nor Avenues, nor Bowling greens, nor grass-plats."

The general decay under Islam was noticed, too, by the group of fourteen Englishmen, members of the Levant Company's factory at Aleppo, whose tour is reported in the book. Passing through Caesarea and the country north of Jaffa, they found it "now ruinate and inhabited by a company of savage Arabs." Jaffa, for which Richard fought so valiantly, where Venetian galleys once massed in the bay to disembark their pilgrim crowds, was, these merchants thought, a poor second-class harbor. Its chief trade was in potash for soap and in cotton and cotton yarn. Far from falling on their knees or thinking solemn thoughts, these travelers of three hundred years ago behaved exactly like the guided bus tourists of today. At Jerusalem they crowded around the visitors' book to look for familiar names and counted a hundred and fifty-eight English visitors since the year 1601. At the site of the Garden of Eden "we spent some time in cutting sticks and setting our names on the great trees." On the Bethlehem road they fell in with some local Christians "whose art is to make the figure of our Saviour's sepulchre or what Holy story you please upon your Arm; they make it of a blew color and it is done by the continual pricking of your Arm with two needles." Everyone in the group selected a pattern from prints shown and was accordingly tattooed.

In 1776, over a hundred years later, another party from the Aleppo factory came through, and their account, by one Richard Tyron, is still as matter-of-fact in tone as if they had been visiting London from the provinces. They are not bothered by questions of ancient prophecy or future fulfillment. Tyron, remarking on the general rack and ruin, notes briefly that the land "is now under a curse" and leaves it to that. Between these two visits a century apart few Englishmen were coming out to Palestine; the fashionable tour was rather to Greece and Rome, the lands of classical antiquity. Only factors or chaplains of the Levant Company already resident in the East occasionally wandered through Palestine, looking less for religious experience than for knowledge and information about the country.

Thomas Shaw, for example, a chaplain from Algiers, who published his tour of the Holy Land in 1738, was chiefly concerned in sketching botanical species, which adorned his book in splendid copperplate illustrations. Likewise Henry Maundrell, chaplain at Aleppo, indulges in no religious raptures, but is more interested in copying ancient inscriptions, examining ruins, and uncovering traces of old cisterns and aqueducts. His *Journey from Aleppo to Jerusalem*, first published in 1697, went into three editions and was reprinted in many travel collections during the next century. Although Palestine is now, he reports, "a most miserable, dry, barren place," yet it is "obvious for anyone to observe that these rocks and hills must have been anciently covered with earth and cultivated." He gives an admirable little lecture on soil erosion, showing how the ancients, "for the husbandry of these mountains," built walls to form "many beds of excellent soil rising gradually one above another from the bottom to the top of the mountains." At the Dead Sea Maundrell confutes old legends by making his own observations. Birds fly over the sea and do *not* fall dead into its waters, he reports, and he finds oyster shells and other signs of marine life on its shores. He takes practical note, too, of the Turks' method of governing subject peoples by sowing division among them (a method not unfamiliar in the later British Empire), "by which art they create contrary interests and parties amongst the inhabitants, preventing them from ever uniting under one prince, which, if they should have the sense to do (being so numerous and almost the sole inhabitants thereabouts) they might shake off the Turkish yoke and make themselves supreme lords of the country."

By far the most learned work of the eighteenth century dealing with Palestine was written by Richard Pococke, son of the great Hebrew and Arabic scholar. His *Description of the East* appeared in 1743–45 in three magnificent folio volumes, of which the second dealt with Syria and Palestine.

Nothing could be more typical of the eighteenth-century attitude toward Palestine than that Pococke, who was to become a bishop, chose to dedicate his volume on the Holy Land to that prototype of the material virtues, the Earl of Chesterfield. The Holy Land is, after all, he says by way of preface, "a very interesting subject," with many places "of which we hear mention every day and generally take pleasure in acquiring the least knowledge in relation to them." In this spirit he sets out from Egypt to cross the wilderness in the footsteps of the Exodus, determined to give an accurate eyewitness picture of that famous route. He notices every landmark, describes the vegetation in detail, and sketches innumerable plans and maps from every elevation, showing every tree and rock. He copies rock inscriptions and tries to identify each stopping place and the site of each incident of Moses' forty-year march. Avoiding the Bedouins as "a very bad people," he finds hospitality with a tribe of "Seleminites" who seem to adhere to the Jewish religion and who, he surmises, might be descended from Jethro, Moses' father-in-law.

Once arrived in Jerusalem, he examines each local tradition to see if it conforms with known facts, history, and probability, accepting nothing on faith. His masterly attack on the supposed pillar of Absalom, a popular tourist attraction, is like Sherlock Holmes's elucidation of a muddy footprint; "Josephus calls it a marble pillar; but as he says it was two furlongs from Jerusalem, though this vale, in which Kedron runs, might be the King's dale; yet as the distance does not agree, it may be doubted whether this was really the monument; and it seems more probable that it was farther to the south-west, beyond the vale of Gehinnon. But if this was the King's dale in which Melchisedeck, King of Salem, came to meet Abraham, it would be a circumstance to prove that Jerusalem was the ancient Salem." And in conclusion he notes that the pillar's Ionic style indicates an origin considerably later than the time of Absalom.

Pococke traversed the whole country from the Dead Sea to Galilee, missing nothing, studying everything for what it could reveal of the famous past. Cisterns, pools, and wells that he found in the Plain of Esdraelon showed him how the land was once irrigated. Struck by the beauty of a field of tulips in bloom near Ramleh, he was led to surmise that these must have been the "lilies of the field" that outshone Solomon in all his glory. This was breathing life into the pages of the Bible. More than all his elaborate engravings of mosques and sepulchers (which later archaeologists have proved largely incorrect) Pococke's tulips began the process of unwrapping Palestine from the cerements of the past.

CHAPTER IX

THE EASTERN QUESTION:

Clash of Empires in Syria

In the closing year of the eighteenth century Englishmen were once again fighting on the beach before Acre, five hundred years to the decade since the Crusaders had lost Acre for the last time. The famous fortress dominating the seaward approach to Palestine and the military highway along the coast had been a prize of arms uncounted times during its embattled career of some thirty centuries. In 1291, the last Europeans were expelled by the Turks, and the key to Palestine, and with it all the Holy Land, were finally enveloped in the Turkish empire.

Now, suddenly, after five centuries of Islamic sleep, British gunboats boomed in the harbor and fierce Mamelukes desperately defended the walls while a European army laid siege by land. This time, oddly enough, the British were defending the fort, not attacking it. They were fighting on the side of the Turks against a European foe, and their guns were aimed not at the walls of Acre, but at the army of Napoleon beneath them.

Palestine's geography had returned to plague it. It lay across the road to India, where Napoleon was determined to plant his foot, cut off his arch-enemy, Britain, from the wealth and commerce of the East, and rule unchallenged over a second Alexandrian empire. Egypt and Syria were essential to his plan, and to the same degree it was essential to Britain to keep them out of his clutches. The very army Napoleon took on his expedition to Egypt was the army that he had assembled for the invasion of England. At the last minute that fatal hesitancy to dare the Channel dash that overcame Hitler, too, at the water's edge in 1940, turned Napoleon eastward in the hope of stabbing Britain from behind, exactly as Hitler was to turn to North Africa in pursuance of the same vain strategy.

In fact, the parallels fall so thick and fast between the Napoleonic and the Hitlerian campaigns that one is often under the impression of seeing double. In both epochs the strategy that swirled around Palestine was the same—and still is. Reduced to the simplest terms, it amounts to this: Whatever swelling despot—non-British, of course—threatens to gain the mastery of Europe must be kept at all costs from likewise controlling the Middle East. This was as true in Napoleon's time as in the Kaiser's, as in Hitler's, and as today in Russia's. The area from Cairo to Constantinople, inclusive, must be kept out of the hands of any would-be world ruler who could convert the Mediterranean into a private lake and close the approaches to the Far East. From the strategic point of view little Palestine must fit into the larger pattern for the Middle East, regardless of who holds the country. Once it was the Turks, then the British, now Israel. It does not matter which—as far as power politics are concerned—so long as it is not the power dominating Europe.

Oversimplified perhaps, this in essence is the problem known to nineteenth-century diplomacy as the Eastern Question. The name has an old-fashioned flavor; it almost seems to wear Victorian sideburns. One thinks of Castlereaghs and Cannings, Talleyrands and Metternichs, of "incidents" and secret treaties, of czars, pashas, and beys, of the Crimea, of Disraeli and the Suez Canal. Sometime during World War I the name fell into disuse along with all the rest of the star-and-garter glitter of nineteenth-century diplomacy. Today there are new actors on the stage—oil and Arabs, Israel and the United States—but the plot is basically still the same as when England, toward the end of the eighteenth century, first planted her "Keep Out!" signs along the frontiers of the Middle East. In those days and for more than a century thereafter the policy took the form of keeping the already ailing Turkish empire intact against all comers. After the final collapse of the empire in 1918 England simply determined to substitute herself for the Turk and hold the area either directly or through Arab puppets, a method that worked well enough until World War II, after which nothing worked in the old way any more. We are now too close to events to see clearly who or what is the coming power in the Middle East; it may be Arab nationalism, or Russia, or, if you are an Arab, the lurking figure of "World Zionism." The proper business of the historian, however, is the past, not the future.

The first antagonist to force England to take a position on the Middle East was not Napoleon, but Russia. In fact, if one is looking for parallels, one can turn the pages of history at any point since about 1780 and never fail to find Russia inching down toward an egress on the Bosporus. Not that Russia had any pretensions to Palestine as such, but Palestine's fate was bound up with that of the Turkish empire, of which it was a part. Whenever the lengthening shadow of the Kremlin edged over Turkish frontiers, at once a furious activity would ensue in the chanceries of Europe, as if they had suddenly sensed a chill and a darkness away in the East. Attachés scurried between embassies, dispatches crisscrossed between capitals like files of ants. A count of all the incidents, ultimatums, wars, congresses, treaties, and settlements concerned with one or another aspect of the Powers' relations with the Turkish Empire during the nineteenth century would show that the Eastern Question absorbed more diplomatic maneuvering, intrigue, and energy than any other single issue of foreign policy. (The term "nineteenth century" is another verbal convenience of some elasticity. If you want it to mean a century, you use it to cover the period 1815–1914. The quarter-century from Bastille to Waterloo, 1789–1815, is then fitted in as a sort of entr'acte between eighteenth and the nineteenth, featuring a special performance by the French Revolution and Napoleon.)

The future of Palestine, which was to see the restoration of Israel, was being played out during the long period of the Powers' strategic involvement in Turkey's affairs. They hovered at the frontiers like jealous heirs waiting for a rich uncle to breathe his last. "Wheresoever the carcase is there will the eagles be gathered together." But the Turkish carcass obstinately continued to breathe, without, however, altogether deterring the hungry eagles from nibbling at its extremities.

When England first realized the strategic necessity of being top eagle in the Middle East she was reacting to the ambitions of Russia under Catherine the Great. Catherine, having given Turkey a beating in one of those confused sets of wars that the wilful monarchs of the eighteenth century were constantly engaging in, was determined to possess herself of a piece of Turkish territory known to diplomatic historians as the "Oczakoff district," thus totally obscuring its sense to modern readers until, with the aid of an atlas, they discover that Oczakoff was Odessa and that what Catherine was driving at was a warm-water port on the Black Sea. Pitt, who may or may not have been England's greatest statesman, but whose career was a single-minded devotion to steering England clear of Continental wars, and who felt the same regard for Catherine that Western statesmen feel today for her successor in the Kremlin, was passionately determined that she should not get it. He risked war and his personal career on an ultimatum demanding that Catherine disgorge the Black Sea port. He failed because popular opinion was not with him, and though he twisted a vote of confidence out of Parliament it was clear that they did not want to go to war for "a far away place about which we know nothing," as

Neville Chamberlain once said about Czechoslovakia. Pitt was forced to back down and allow Catherine to keep Odessa, but the rule he formulated at this time of resisting at any cost any encroachment on the territories under Turkish rule became the fixed focus of British policy on the Eastern Question thereafter.

Most Englishmen did not like it, because of their distaste for what Burke called "this wasteful and disgusting empire." But it was a choice between supporting Turkish misrule and allowing rivals to close in on Britain's road to India. Pitt called the choice, although until that time the English had preferred almost anybody to the Turk. In an earlier Russo-Turkish war in 1770 Pitt's father, the Earl of Chatham, had written to a colleague: "Your lordship well knows I am quite a Russ. I trust the Ottoman will pull down the House of Bourbon in its fall." But in the next decade, with the loss of the American colonies, the whole direction of British imperialism was changed, turned eastward to concentrate on India and the lands along the road thereto. From then on Britain committed herself to keeping her way clear through the Middle East by supporting Ottoman "integrity" against whatever Czars or Napoleons might try to break in. In 1799, when France invaded the East, Pitt promptly concluded a secret treaty with the Porte guaranteeing the integrity of Turkish dominions for eight years. And that explains how British soldiers came to be fighting at Acre on the coast of Palestine in the year 1799.

It also brings us back to "the hope of Israel," for who, of all people, should suddenly declare himself the sponsor of a restored temporal kingdom of the Jews but General Bonaparte! Among all the other records set by this astonishing man is the little-known fact that he was the first head of state* to propose the restoration of a Jewish state in Palestine. Of course, it was a self-serving gesture only, and totally empty of religious significance. Bonaparte

*Soon to be. In 1799 Bonaparte was still a general of the Directory.

cared nothing for the Bible or prophecy, for Judaism or Christianity. As a nonbeliever, he found all religions alike, and he would as soon have declared himself a Mohammedan—and in fact did when he landed in Egypt—if it served his purpose. His proclamation to the Jews, whom he addressed as "the rightful heirs of Palestine," was, to begin with, simply a military stratagem like his previous call to the Arabs to rise against their Turkish overlords. But in all his proclamations Bonaparte could never resist the overtones of glory, and he expanded his call to the Jews into a promise to restore the ancient kingdom of Jerusalem. This was pure play-acting. "Israelites, arise!" he proclaimed. "Ye exiled, arise! Hasten! Now is the moment, which may not return for thousands of years, to claim the restoration of civic rights among the population of the universe which have shamefully been withheld from you for thousands of years, to claim your political existence as a nation among nations, and the unlimited natural right to worship Jehovah in accordance with your faith, publicly and most probably forever." He called on them to flock to his colors and offered them the "warranty and support" of the French nation to regain their patrimony and "to remain master of it and maintain it against all comers.*

Given the circumstances of Bonaparte's impossible venture in Syria, the proclamation was a meaningless gesture, as artificial as any heroic strutting on the stage. Yet it set a pattern that was to unroll to a no less heroic but quite real climax in our time when Israel finally did become again "a nation among nations." For after Napoleon it became axiomatic that whenever the powers fell to fighting

*The original of this Proclamation has never been found. Its wording remained unknown until a manuscript copy in German translation came to light in 1940 in the archives of a Viennese family with rabbinical connections tracing back to Napoleon's entourage in the East. Until then only the fact of the Proclamation was known through two dispatches concerning it that appeared in May of 1799 in *Le Moniteur*, the official organ of the French Directory.

in the Middle East someone would propose the restoration of Israel, and equally axiomatic that the someone would be indulging himself in a happy dream not only of acquiring thereby a sphere of influence over a vital strategic area, but also of drawing to his own side all the supposed wealth and influence of world Jewry. Political effort on behalf of the Jews was never exerted except as a by-product of other nations' quarrels, as when the British assumed the Palestine Mandate in the twentieth century. But one cannot deny Napoleon credit for the idea.

He came to it from an old French dream of acquiring dominion over the Levant. As long ago as 1671 Louis XIV had been seriously interested in the advice of Leibnitz, who, hoping to divert him from aggression against Germany, told him to reconstruct the ancient canal connecting the Mediterranean with the Red Sea across the isthmus of Suez. "It is in Egypt that the real blow is to be struck," wrote Leibnitz. "There you will find the true commercial route to India . . . there you will secure the eternal dominion of France in the Levant." In trade the French did in fact become paramount in the Levant, while the British neglected it to concentrate rather on trade with India by the Cape route. But in the next century the French too had acquired dominions and ambitions in India, which came to a head-on collision and finally defeat in the Seven Years' War (1756–63) with England. In that struggle Choiseul planned for France to gain control of Egypt and Arabia, to cut through a canal to the Red Sea, to win "spheres of influence" over Syria, Mesopotamia, and Persia, and thus to wipe out the British in India. And so a generation later it was Bonaparte's turn.

But he dreamed with a difference—a flamboyant dream of himself as a second Alexander re-creating Alexander's empire from Egypt to the Indus or perhaps even to the Ganges. He saw Egypt as the vantage point from which England could be destroyed, *et que Dieu en soit benit.* He would cut through a new Suez Canal that would transform the Mediterranean into a French lake and channel all the commerce of the Indies and the Levant into French hands. Europe was too narrow; only in the East with its vastness, its riches, its teeming populations was real empire to be won. The East was ever the field of glory where the epic, the imperishable reputations had been made. It was not commerce or riches or even power that Napoleon craved: it was immortality, the immortality of Alexander and Caesar. "Everything here passes away; my glory is already declining," he said to his faithful reporter, Bourienne. He was not quite thirty at the time. "This little corner of Europe is too small to supply it. We must go to the East. All the great men of the world have there acquired their celebrity."

And so at thirty, the same age as Alexander's, he set out for Egypt, conquered Cairo, and, even as his fleet was destroyed by Nelson in the Battle of the Nile, turned his back on that verdict and pushed on in the massive pretense that he could still conquer Syria, then Turkey, Persia, and India, and at last return to Europe with a new empire at his back to become master of the world. In February 1799 he took El Arish in the Sinai peninsula between Egypt and Palestine, invaded Palestine a few days later, captured Jaffa on March 7, and reached the walls of Acre on March 18. "The fate of the East is in the fort of Acre," he said. Once Acre was in his hands he would march on to Damascus, Aleppo, and Constantinople. "Then I will overthrow the Turkish empire and found a great new empire in the East which will preserve my place in posterity." He never got over that vision. Twenty years later as he sat amid the rocks of St. Helena dictating his memoirs he repeated: "Acre once taken . . . I would have reached Constantinople and the Indies. I would have changed the face of the world."

It was with these grandiose prospects crowding his mind that Bonaparte, encamped at Ramleh, 25 miles from Jerusalem, issued his proclamation to the Jews. What more fitting than that the man of destiny should re-establish the throne of David by a stroke of his pen, or rather a wave of his sword? The appeal of the time, the place, and the circumstances was irresistible. And the circumstances were such that Bonaparte may really have believed that he was about to enter Jerusalem.

His siege of Acre had bogged down against the fierce defense of the Mamelukes, supported by a British naval squadron under the command of Sir Sidney Smith. But on April 16 Bonaparte had won a great victory at Mount Tabor, utterly routing a Turkish army that had come down from Damascus to the relief of Acre. At once he saw Acre surrendering, all of Palestine falling into his hands, and a triumphal entrance into Jerusalem. So confident was he that he allowed an official dispatch to be sent to Paris dated April 17, the day after Mount Tabor (it was to appear in *Le Moniteur* of May 22), stating: *"Bonaparte a fait publier une proclamation dans laquelle il invite tous les Juifs de l'Asie et de l'Afrique à venir se ranger sous ses drapeaux pour l'etablir l'ancienne Jerusalem."* Moreover the actual Proclamation, dated April 19, was issued as if from "Headquarters in Jerusalem," where he must have expected to be by that day. But Bonaparte was never to set foot in Jerusalem, or even in Acre. For, with his eyes fixed ahead on glory and immortality, he tripped up on what was right under his feet—the British guns of Sir Sidney Smith. "That man made me miss my destiny," he said in curt and bitter summary when it was all over. For Acre refused to fall, and at the end of another month of siege Smith, mustering every available sailor from the gunboats, stormed ashore, pike in hand as Richard had stormed ashore at Jaffa six hundred years before. The French army, decimated by disease, starvation, and all the ills that had plagued their predecessors under Philip IV, was routed, and on May 20 Bonaparte acknowledged defeat and turned back with the pitiable, straggling remnant of his army the way he had come. The dream was over, the empire unattained. It was Napoleon's first and bitterest defeat, and even at the height of later triumphs he could not forget it. *"J'ai manqué à ma fortune à St. Jean d'Acre,"* his brother Lucien heard the Emperor murmur in regret in the moment of victory at Austerlitz.

Perhaps in the bitterness of retreat he tore up the original document of his grandiloquent promise to the Jews, and no doubt subsequent measures taken to cover up the episode were due to reluctance to be reminded of the whole humiliating adventure. But the Eastern expedition was to have important results. It aroused widespread interest in the East, productive of some valuable feats of exploration as well as of much romantic poetizing. The Rosetta stone, key to translation of Egyptian hieroglyphics, was found by one of the corps of scientists, engineers, and scholars that Napoleon had brought along to make the blueprints of empire in the wake of his armies. In 1803 Ulrich Seetzen went to Syria to spend two years learning the speech and manners of the Arabs so that he could travel as a native for four years more throughout Palestine and Sinai, down to Cairo, and even across the Red Sea to Mecca disguised as a pilgrim. Seetzen's remarkable researches exist only in scattered letters in German periodicals or in unpublished manuscripts moldering in German museums, save for excerpts in English translation published as *A Brief Account of the Countries Adjoining Lake Tiberias, the Jordan and the Dead Sea* in London in 1813. But Chateaubriand, dashing through in 1806, produced a best seller in his *Itinéraire de Paris à Jérusalem*, which also was translated and widely read in English.

In 1810 Lady Hester Stanhope, niece and long-time secretary of William Pitt, in grief at her uncle's death, left England forever to take up her fabled residence in the mountains of Lebanon. "I cannot tell why it should be," wrote one who knew her, "but there is a longing for the East very commonly felt by proud-hearted people when goaded by sorrow." This remark of Kinglake's distills the romantic notoriety Lady Hester shed upon the East in that romantic era. Like a prophetess she lived in the mystic seclusion of a private kingdom, which dwindled from palaces and gardens guarded by a thousand slaves to the impoverished solitude in which she died, after thirty years of waiting with her sacred white mule to accompany the Messiah through the gates of Jerusalem. Every visitor to the East of sufficient prominence to gain an introduction would as soon have missed calling on Lady Hester as seeing the pyramids.

The Palestine Association had already been founded in London in 1804 with the purpose of promoting exploration and researches in the Holy Land, but because of the hazardousness of travel in the country at the time little was accomplished. The Association petered out in a merger with the Royal Geographic Society in 1834 but, as will appear, it was to re-emerge with aplomb in the Palestine Exploration Fund of later years. The Palestine Association did, however, have to its credit the publication of Seetzen's letters, which in turn inspired the journey of the most remarkable of the early nineteenth-century explorers, John Lewis Burckhardt. Like Seetzen he spent years in the East equipping himself to pass as a native, his ultimate purpose being to pass himself off as a Bedouin in order to explore central Africa on behalf of the African Society. He died before he could do this, but in the course of his preparations he spent six years wandering through Syria and Arabia and even succeeded in entering Mecca, so successful was his disguise and so minute his knowledge of the Koran and of native manners. His daily jottings and diary were posthumously published in 1822 as *Travels in Syria and the Holy Land* and *Travels in Arabia*. Here in the notes of this solitary, indefatigable figure, walking along the dusty roads, sleeping in Arab villages, following a goatherd to find the stones of some ruined temple, is the material of the true field archaeologist. His book has no consecutive plan; facts on Arab customs and character, on current crops and ancient artifacts, tracings of rock inscriptions, architectural plans plotted from ruins, geographical and geologic findings are all jumbled together. But one constant theme—the relevance of each day's journey, each fallen pillar and abandoned well, to some incident of the Bible—holds the whole together.

No more absolute contrast to Burckhardt could be imagined than Byron, who in the same years came romping through the Levant with Hobhouse and went home to make himself famous—and the East fashionable—with *Childe Harold's Pilgrimage* in 1812 and *The Giaour* in 1813. A chance by-product of Byron's trip was the reopening of Petra, ancient capital of Biblical Edom, to modern archaeology. Once a flourishing city, the crossroads of all the caravan commerce from the Persian Gulf to the Levant, Petra had been abandoned for hundreds of years. William Bankes, a Trinity College friend of Byron's, probably inspired by his friend's adventures, started off for the East in 1812 with letters of introduction from Byron. Perhaps the tales of a lost city, perhaps some rumors of Burckhardt's entrance into Petra, not as yet known in England, determined him to find Petra for himself. On a second voyage in 1816 he brought with him two English naval officers, Captains Irby and Mangles, and despite the most determined non-co-operation of Turkish officials, from the sultan, the pasha of Damascus, and the governor of Jerusalem, who refused to give safe-conducts, down to the lowliest guide and camel driver, who warned of savage Bedouins eager for the blood of Franks to use as medicine for their women, the English party set out on their own, "resolved to trust to their numbers and force." Through a narrow canyon, overgrown with thickets of tamarisk and wild fig, they pushed and hacked a path to one of the great capitals of the ancient world, now empty in vine-covered marble solitude. Temples, tombs, and palaces echoed only to the eagles' scream, saw only the sudden silent flight of owls; but thereafter Arabia Petraea yielded up its treasures.

These were the pioneers. The full tide of Holy Land ex-

ploration, of field geographers and historians "proving" the
Bible, of earnest tourists intent on following "in the footsteps of the Lord," did not break over Palestine until after
1840. In the meantime Napoleon's expedition had had
other results. The return of Europeans to a battleground
in the Middle East caused an eruption in the affairs of that
region that has not yet subsided. Brewing ever since Napoleon's departure, it exploded in 1830 in a fullfledged
European crisis over the Eastern Question that kept the
powers in turmoil for ten years, brought England and
France to the very hair's breadth edge of war, and restored
the East to life in the popular imagination as it had not
been since the Crusades.

Central figure of the crisis was Mehemet Ali, the first
memorable Moslem since Saladin, the extraordinary Al-
banian freebooter who made himself ruler of Egypt and
pretender to the Caliphate, and single-handed almost broke
up the Turkish Empire a hundred years before its time.
His career engages us less because it shook up the capitals
of Europe than because it pulled Britain permanently into
the Middle East and provided the opportunity for the first
English effort—artificial though it was—to replant the Jewish nation in Palestine. Lord Shaftesbury's experiment in
premature Zionism belongs to the next chapter, but it can
only be presented against the background of the political
and strategic circumstances of the Mehemet Ali episode.

Essentially the issue was who would be the "occupier of
the road to India," as Lord Palmerston put it. Mehemet,
having risen from nowhere to become a vassal more powerful than his sovereign, was ready to throw off the Sultan's
suzerainty and declare himself independent ruler of a new
Moslem state covering Egypt, Syria, and Arabia. Ever-
hungry Russia was aching for the opportunity to support
Turkey against this presumptuous challenge, in the course
of which she could conveniently establish a protectorate
over the Porte and enclose the Dardanelles in her own
embrace. Ambitious France, still yearning after Napoleon's

dream of Eastern dominion, was equally eager to establish
a protectorate over Mehemet by supporting this Eastern
Napoleon who was about to make good the conquest their
own vanished hero had missed. Britain, who wanted
neither Russia nor France, still less Mehemet, to gain influence in or control of this vital region, was bent on stopping all three. A weak and aging and therefore malleable
Ottoman was still a better occupier of the road to India
than an independent French-oriented "active Arabian sovereign," again to use Palmerston's words.

Curiously enough, had it not been for the British, Mehemet's career might have been cut short almost before
it had begun. In 1798, as a regimental commander of
bashi-bazouks fighting against Napoleon in Egypt, he was
driven into the sea in the Battle of the Nile and only rescued from drowning by a dory put out from the ship of
Sir Sidney Smith, the future victor of Acre. Forty years
later Mehemet's own dream of empire was smashed under
the guns of another British admiral at Acre. But, to go
back for a moment to his early career, we find Mehemet
emerging as Egypt's strong man out of the chaos left by
Napoleon's retreat. By 1805 he had become pasha of Egypt,
and he went on to extend his personal rule over the Sudan
and Arabia, including the holy cities of Mecca and Medina.
By 1830 he was ready, with an army and a fleet trained by
French officers, to challenge his overlord the Sultan. In his
path the blood-sated soil of Palestine once more became a
battlefield.

On November 1, 1831 the Egyptian army crossed the
frontiers of Syria, met the Egyptian fleet under the command of Mehemet's son Ibrahim at Jaffa, and at once advanced to lay siege to the inevitable Acre. This time Acre
fell. Ibrahim, having taken Gaza and Jerusalem as well,
swept forward to take Damascus, Homs, Hama, and
Aleppo. By the summer of 1833 he was master of all Syria
and pressing against the gateway to Constantinople. In a
panic the Sultan turned to Britain for help, offering an

offensive and defensive alliance, but Palmerston, who at this stage contemplated the possibility of Mehemet's becoming a British protégé, held back. In his last agony the Sultan, as a drowning man might clutch at a boa constrictor, accepted the help of his long-loathed enemy the Czar. Russian troops, poised for this moment, were on tiptoe at the Turkish border, and in no time a Russian army was blocking Ibrahim's path to Constantinople, Russian advisers appeared at court, Russian officers strutted in the streets, Russian engineers manned the fortifications along the Straits. "It is manifest," wrote home Lord Ponsonby, the British ambassador in Constantinople, "that the Porte stands in the relation of vassal to the Russian government." Worse than that, what deal had the Turks made about the Straits? Lord Ponsonby and the French ambassador, it is told, each went to his window on arising, "the one at six in the morning, the other at six in the afternoon," prepared to see without surprise that long-dreaded sight of the Russian fleet anchored under their eyes in the Bosporus. And the dread was not an empty one, for Russia, as the price of her help, had extracted from Turkey the famous Treaty of Unkiar Skelessi, which provided in a secret clause that, on demand by Russia, Turkey would close the Dardanelles to all other warships.

Palmerston's chagrin was immense, and he now agreed with Ponsonby that it was "wholly erroneous" to think that "Russia could act with moderation in these matters or cease for one moment to aim at the subjugation of Turkey." To stem the Russian advance became the overriding concern—the same problem that was to bring on the Crimean War twenty years later and still today brings nightmares to diplomatic pillows in the Middle East. Britain now bent every nerve to replace Russian intervention with a united front of the Powers that would settle the Turco-Egyptian crisis by joint action and at all costs prevent further opportunities for private raids. Mehemet was temporarily halted, but in 1838 he started in again; a Turkish army that came against him in Syria was wiped out, the Turkish fleet surrendered to him at Alexandria, and the old sultan promptly died of shame in Constantinople. France resounded with the glories of the pasha, and it looked indeed as if he would soon be master of an empire equal to Saladin's, with the tricolor flying in his van. Fortunately the Czar, who despised above all men that bourgeois gentilhomme, Louis Philippe, with his dangerous democratic ideas, was willing to go to any lengths to frustrate him, especially to any that would widen the breach between England and France. Therefore he fell in with Palmerston's plan for joint action, along with Prussia and Austria, even if it meant giving up his private privileges in the Straits. And so in London, while the French King and Thiers were noisily championing Mehemet's demands on the new boy sultan, the four powers quietly signed an agreement to unite in support of Turkey and compel Mehemet to content himself with Egypt and the administration of southern Syria for his lifetime. On the announcement of these terms France, bursting with outraged honor, was on the point of declaring war when Syria rose in revolt against the tyrannical Ibrahim. In support of the revolt a British fleet materialized out of the fog, bombarded and took Beirut, sent ashore a storming party commanded by Sir Charles Napier to capture ancient Sidon, and then sailed southward to turn its guns on that most calamitous fortress in history, St. Jean d'Acre. Ibrahim was defeated without a siege; whereupon his father's almost consummated empire collapsed like a house of cards. "Napier forever!" crowed Palmerston, and a colleague found him "very merry" with sundry jokes about Beyrouth and Acre and confident that the French King and Thiers "are beat and there is an end of the matter."

So it proved. Despite all Thiers' raging Louis Philippe, as Palmerston had gambled, was not prepared to go to war for an Eastern goal that kept eluding France like a mirage. He acquiesced in restoring Syria and Arabia to the Porte and in confining the aged Mehemet, who was soon to lapse into insanity and death, to the hereditary pashalik of Egypt under Turkish sovereignty. On these terms the whole crisis was resolved in a new five-power treaty, to which France was now a party, signed at London in July 1841. For the time being the Turkish Empire was preserved, tattered but intact, from the claws of the gathering eagles. It was triumph unalloyed for Palmerston, and for Britain the opening of a road that was to lead to Suez and, eventually, Jerusalem.

C H A P T E R   X

LORD SHAFTESBURY'S VISION:

An Anglican Israel

Lord Palmerston, in the midst of his manipulations to prevent a sudden coming apart of the Ottoman Empire, wrote a letter to his ambassador at Constantinople about the Jews. "There exists at the present time among the Jews dispersed over Europe, a strong notion that the time is approaching when their nation is to return to Palestine. . . . It would be of manifest importance to the Sultan to encourage the Jews to return and to settle in Palestine because the wealth which they would bring with them would increase the resources of the Sultan's dominions; and the Jewish people, if returning under the sanction and protection and at the invitation of the Sultan, would be a check upon any future evil designs of Mehemet Ali or his successor. . . . I have to instruct Your Excellency strongly to recommend [the Turkish government] to hold out every just encouragement to the Jews of Europe to return to Palestine."

As the Foreign Secretary saw it the Jews, given a landed interest in their ancient homeland, would act as a prop at the center of the sprawling, collapsing structure that was the Turkish Empire and would, for their own sakes, lend all their considerable effort to keep the structure standing; and this, as we have seen, was the object of British policy.

Palmerston's letter was dated August 11, 1840. On August 17 the *Times* published a leader on a plan "to plant the Jewish people in the land of their fathers," which, it said, was now under "serious political consideration." It commended the efforts of Lord Ashley (later Lord Shaftesbury), author of the plan, as "practical and statesmanlike" and quoted a canvass he was making of Jewish opinion designed to find out how they felt about a return to the Holy Land, how soon they would be ready to go back, and whether Jews "of station and property" would join in the return and invest their capital in the land if the Porte could be induced to assure them law and justice and safety to person and estate and if their rights and privileges were "secured to them under the protection of a European power."

There was no doubt as to the identity of the European power the *Times* had in mind. The article created a sensation. "The newspapers teem with documents about the Jews," recorded Lord Ashley in his diary twelve days later, "What a chaos of schemes and disputes is on the horizon. . . . What violence, what hatred, what combination, what discussion. What a stir of every passion and every feeling in men's hearts!"

Obviously neither Palmerston nor the *Times* had come up with the same idea within a week of each other by pure chance. Each had been led to it, pushed, persuaded, wheedled, and argued into it, by Anthony Ashley Cooper, seventh Earl of Shaftesbury, the most influential nonpolitical figure, excepting Darwin, of the Victorian age. His motives were religious, the Foreign Secretary's imperial. Shaftesbury represented the Bible, Palmerston, so to speak, the sword. The time was 1840; Syria, at once Holy Land and geographical crux of rival pathways of empire, was the place. Here Shaftesbury envisaged an Anglican Israel restored by Protestant England, at one stroke confounding popery, fulfilling prophecy, redeeming mankind. Palmerston would have been content to confound the French and redeem the Turk.

It was said of Lord Shaftesbury that he had "the purest, palest, stateliest exterior of any man in Westminster." His cold and classic face always called forth comparison to a marble bust. Every separate dark lock of hair, said one acquaintance, seemed to curl from a sense of duty. Yet this impeccable peer was in reality a compassionate, deeply religious man who based his life on literal acceptance of the Bible. The Bible, he said, "is 'God's word written' from the very first syllable down to the very last and from the last back to the first. . . . Nothing but Scripture can interpret Scripture. I should reject it if announced to me by man. I accept it, believe it, bless it, as announced in Holy Writ . . . and like the Israelites, I bow the head and worship."

This was what made him a philanthropist: the Bible enjoined him to be exactly that—to love his fellow man. Born into the ruling aristocracy, related by marriage to the two great Whig prime ministers of his time, sought after by both parties for cabinet office, which he consistently refused in order to remain above party for the sake of his welfare work, Lord Shaftesbury was the personification of *noblesse oblige*. He really believed he *was* his brother's keeper—especially the wretchedest brother's. He really believed that his endowments of rank, ability, and influence obligated him to help the underprivileged. He really believed that the charity and love preached by the gospels was the sum total of all man needed to know or practice, and he practiced them. To say that he was a friend and benefactor of the poor is to use one of those overfamiliar phrases that will pass under a reader's eyes unnoticed. Yet Lord Shaftesbury was literally and exactly what the phrase says: a doer-of-good to the poor, to thieves, to lunatics, to cripples; to children, chained at five years old to coal carts underground, to wizened "climbing boys" squeezed into soot-filled chimneys, to all humans who existed in the half-starved, ragged, sick, shivering sixteen-hour-a-day squalor that was the life of the laboring class in those happily unregulated days. It was Lord Shaftesbury who forced through Parliament the Ten Hours Bill (the Factory Act), credited with staving off revolution in the industrial counties, as well as the Mines Act, the Lunacy Act, and the Lodging House Act, which Dickens called the finest piece of legislation ever enacted in England up to that time.

What has all this to do with Palestine? it will be asked. The point is that Lord Shaftesbury's zeal for "God's ancient people," as he always styled the Jews, was the outcome of this same entire acceptance of the Bible that had made him a philanthropist. He worked just as hard to restore the Jews to Palestine as he did to pass the Ten Hours Bill, though not one in ten who ever heard of Lord Shaftesbury is aware of it, famous men being generally remembered for their successes rather than their failures. But, despite all his zeal on the Jews' behalf, it is doubtful if Lord Shaftesbury ever thought of them as a people with their own language and traditions, their own Torah and law and spiritual guides honored through a hundred generations. To him, as to all the Israel-for-prophecy's-sake school, the Jews were simply the instrument through which Biblical prophecy could be fulfilled. They were not a people, but a mass Error that must be brought to a belief in Christ in order that the whole chain reaction leading to the Second Coming and the redemption of mankind might be set in motion.

Belief in the Second Advent, Lord Shaftesbury told his chosen biographer, Edwin Hodder, "has always been a moving principle in my life, for I see everything going on in the world subordinate to this great event." And privately he wrote: "Why do we not pray for it every time we hear a clock strike?" Since, according to prophetic Scripture, the return of the Jews was indispensable to this great event, Lord Shaftesbury, says Hodder, "never had a shadow of a doubt that the Jews *were* to return to their own land. . . . It was his daily prayer, his daily hope. 'Oh, pray for the peace of Jerusalem!' were the words engraven on the ring he always wore on his right hand."

Like all men in the grip of an intense belief, Lord Shaftesbury felt the touch of the Almighty on his shoulder, a commandment to work personally for the "great event." In company with other great Victorians he never doubted that human instrumentality could bring about Divine purposes. This was a principle as yet unacceptable to the Jews. Not until they came to perceive, beginning in the 1860's, that they would have to act as their own Messiah did the return to Israel actually become realizable and ultimately realized. Previously the Christians had been in more of a hurry to hasten the coming of their Messiah, either because they felt more in need of salvation or because the fatalism born of an old exile had not laid its deadening hand on them.

The urgency was felt again in England at the time of the Evangelical Revival. For now the pendulum had swung back again, after the Hellenic interlude of the eighteenth century, to the moral earnestness of another Hebraic period. Eighteenth-century skepticism had given way to Victorian piety; eighteenth-century rationalism was again surrendering to Revelation. And as the inevitable accompaniment of the return to Hebraism we find Lord Shaftesbury espousing the restoration of Israel in almost the same terms as the Cartwrights and the Puritan extremists. This was not because Hebraism in Matthew Arnold's sense had anything to do with modern Jews, but because it was an ethos inherited from the Old Testament. And whenever Christians returned to the authority of the Old Testament they found it prophesying the return of its people to Jerusalem and felt themselves duty-bound to assist the prophecy.

The England of Lord Shaftesbury's generation was almost as Bible-conscious as the England of Cromwell. The religious climate had warmed up considerably since the casual days when Pitt held cabinet meetings on Sunday. (A Shaftesbury would as soon have failed to keep the Sabbath as would an orthodox Rabbi.) During the eighteenth century the old religious fervor of the Puritans flickered only among the Nonconformists. After the shock of the "atheistic" French Revolution it came back to the Established Church, warming its cold hearths, infusing a new piety into its fox-hunting, place-hunting complacency. This was the Evangelical Revival that now began to take hold on the propertied class, who, frightened by what was happening in France, were anxiously mending their fences, spiritual as well as political. To escape rationalism's horrid daughter, revolution, they were only too willing to be enfolded in the anti-intellectual embrace of Evangelicalism, even if it demanded faith and good works and a willing suspension of disbelief. Churchgoing, preaching, absolute belief in the Bible became fashionable again. Trevelyan quotes a passage from the *Annual Register* of 1798: "It was a wonder to the lower orders throughout all parts of England, to see the avenues to the churches filled with carriages. This novel appearance prompted the simple country people to enquire what was the matter."

The matter was neo-Puritanism, and once again England was to choke on an overdose of holiness. The Evangelicals, like the Puritans, have inspired ridicule by their fervor, their sense of mission, their preaching, Sabbath-worship, and bibliolatry. A wit has said of the Puritans' struggle with the Crown that one side was wrong but romantic, the other right but repulsive, and we tend to think of the Evangelicals in the same light. A lot of ridicule has stuck to the reputation of Lord Shaftesbury, the archetype as well as the acknowledged lay leader of the Evangelical party. It hurts the economic historians, the Marxians and Fabians, to admit that the Ten Hours Bill, the basic piece of nineteenth-century labor legislation, came down from the top, out of a private nobleman's private feelings about the Gospel, or that abolition of the slave trade was achieved, not through the operation of some "law" of profit and loss, but purely as the result of the new humanitarianism of the Evangelicals. But take a historian who is not riding the economic hobbyhorse and you will find him concluding, like Halévy, that it is impossible to overestimate the influence of the Evangelicals on their time. Granted that they were not thinkers, not reasonable or graceful or elegant; granted that, including Lord Shaftesbury, they were in some ways rather silly. Yet they were the mainspring of early Victorian England, and their effect remained long after their heyday was over. Even the opponents of religion in the nineteenth century were religious. Throughout the prolonged battle between faith and science, between the defenders of the Bible as Revelation and the discoverers of the Bible as history, which convulsed the Victorian age, splitting families and friends as sharply as any physical civil war, both sides shared equally the seriousness and high moral purpose inherited from the Puritans. There was nothing lax or latitudinarian about either.

In our day it has become almost impossible to appreciate justly the role of religion in past political, social, and economic history. We cannot do it because we have not got it. Religion is not part of our lives; not, that is, comparably to its part in pretwentieth-century lives. But the twentieth century is the child of the nineteenth, and if England in the twentieth century undertook the restoration of Israel to Palestine, it was because the nineteenth was by and large religiously motivated. Trevelyan chose as the four popular heroes of the age Shaftesbury himself, Gladstone, General Gordon, and Dr. Livingstone, because all of them regarded life as a religious exercise. Strachey, whether he admits it or not, chose his four Eminent Victorians, Cardinal Manning, Florence Nightingale, Dr. Arnold, and General Gordon, for the same reason. Both Gladstone and Manning had Evangelical beginnings, and though one ended High Church and the other Roman Church, both acknowledged Shaftesbury's inspiration. Manning, in fact, named him *the* representative figure of the age.

"I am an Evangelical of the Evangelicals," proclaimed Lord Shaftesbury, and, as the name implies, his was a missionary movement. It was bound and determined to bring everyone else to acceptance of the same faith, to a share in the same salvation—especially the Jews.

For the Jews were the hinge. Without them there could be no Second Advent. They were the middle member of the Evangelical's unbreakable syllogism. Biblical prophecy = Israel converted and restored = Second Advent. Of course, if rationalism, which cuts the prophetical connection between New Testament and Old, leaving only a historical connection, is allowed to crack the syllogism, the whole thing falls apart. Therefore rationalism must be held at bay. This Lord Shaftesbury understood well enough. "God give me and mine grace," he prayed, to stem "the awful advance of saucy rationalism." Thirty-odd years later he still had no use for the new "science" that men were trying to put on a par with God. Especially he disliked apologists for the Bible who attempted to reconcile it with science. A diary entry of 1871 says: "Revelation is addressed to the heart and not to the intellect. God cares little comparatively for man's intellect; He cares greatly for man's heart. Two mites of faith and love are of infinitely higher value to Him than a whole treasury of thought and knowledge. Satan reigns in the intellect; God in the heart of man."

This remarkable passage expresses the core of the dominant religious philosophy in the first half of the Victorian epoch. It explains how it was possible for the Evangelicals to waste so much energy and good will on the delusion of converting the Jews. More intellect and less soul would have shown the project to be of doubtful success; but, as Shaftesbury would have said, to admit doubt was to admit Satan's foot inside the door. And so they did not doubt. On the contrary, Charles Simeon, clerical leader of the Evangelical party, regarded conversion of the Jews, according to his biographer, "as perhaps the warmest interest of his life."

Of all the gospel societies spawned around the turn of the century, the London Society for Promoting Christianity among the Jews was for many years the most popular. Its list of noble patrons glittered like a court circular (including one Sir Oswald Mosley, vice-president of the Society in 1850). Its cornerstone for chapel and school buildings was laid in 1813 by the Duke of Kent, brother of the King and the father of Queen Victoria. It was considered by Basil Woodd, the great Evangelical educator, as his "favorite institution" among the swarm of groups that claimed his membership. Its prestige threatened to overshadow even that of the Church Missionary Society, whose preachers were compelled to take as their text, "Is He the God of the Jews Only?"

The Jews' Society, as it was familiarly called, was to become the chief rostrum from which Lord Shaftesbury and his fellow enthusiasts pursued their darling object; establishment of an Anglican Bishopric in Jerusalem and restoration of an Anglican Israel on the soil of Palestine. Founded in 1808 in an upsurge of evangelical enthusiasm that produced the British and Foreign Bible Society, the Religious Tract Society, the Church Missionary Society, and many others, the Jews' Society set about its avowed purpose with a series of "demonstration sermons" every Wednesday and Sunday evening, designed to prove Jesus as the Jews' Messiah. A church was leased from the French Protestants and renamed the Jews' Chapel. A free school was established in the hope that Jewish families might be sufficiently attracted by the offer of free education to send their children. Within three years the school could boast nearly four hundred pupils, of whom, however, only the most uncharitably inquisitive would pause to note that fewer than a fifth were Jews.

After five years of existence the Society had a list of some two thousand contributors, whose names fill fifty pages of small type and whose donations ranged from a few shillings to one hundred pounds. It had acquired its own real estate, a square renamed "Palestine Place," in which the Chapel, schools, and Hebrew College for Missionaries were erected. It published its own monthly periodical, *Jewish Intelligence.* By 1822 its reputation was such that the annual meeting was held at Mansion House with the Lord Mayor officiating. By 1841 the Archbishops of Canterbury and York and twenty-three bishops, or "nearly all the Episcopal bench," were added to the list of patrons, as well as one duke and assorted marquises, earls, viscounts, reverends, and right honorables. By 1850 the Society had seventy-eight missionaries employed in thirty-two branch offices from London to Jerusalem and an expenditure of twenty-six thousand pounds.

In the Society's annual reports, from which these proud and happy facts are taken, the only modest claim is the number of converts; sometimes this is shyly omitted altogether. In 1839, after thirty years of operation, the Society had collected a total of two hundred and seven adult converts in London, or an average of six or seven a year. For its foreign missions it could report, for example, from Bagdad: Jewish population, 10,000, three missionaries, two converts. Or from Smyrna, Jewish population 1,500, no converts, mission closed. The Society was a success, of course, but not at the receiving end. However, that did not matter. Its beneficent sponsors continued to propagate Christianity among the Jews, intent on St. Paul's dictum that the Church would be forever incomplete without them and unaware that this was a prospect of very little concern to the Jews.

Indeed, it is quite striking how optimistic the Society's workers were in a task in which the greatest of all missionaries had conspicuously failed. They constantly quote Paul's Epistle to the Hebrews in justification of their work, but they never seem to have questioned why his own people denied him the success he later had among the Gentiles, or to ask themselves why the Jews, after 1800 years of none too happy association with Christianity, should find the Society's arguments any more convincing than they had Paul's. Yet their sincerity and serious purpose were unmistakable. The Reverend Alexander MacCaul, executive head of the Society's missionary work and professor of Hebrew at King's College, London, was not only the greatest Hebrew scholar of his day in England, but also a man who had lived and worked among the Jews of Russia and Poland and knew Judaism at first hand, a rare distinction. Lewis Way, a wealthy barrister who devoted his fortune to the Jews' Society and is credited with "the first great impulse given in the Jewish cause," burned with an equal conviction of the benefit to the whole world that would be conferred by the ultimate success of his work.

Way came to the Jews' Society in a manner typical of the exalted antirational spirit of the Evangelicals. According to the legend retold at every annual meeting (though later disputed) he had admired a magnificent stand of oaks during a day's ride from Exmouth to Exeter, and was told by a companion that a former owner of the property, one Jane Parminter, had given orders in her will that it was never to be cut down till the Jews should be restored to Palestine. Struck by this quaint notion, Mr. Way went home to reread his Bible and came so under the thrall of prophecy that he gave up the law, studied divinity, took orders, donated thirteen thousand pounds to bring the Jews' Society out of debt, and thereafter remained for twenty years its principal financial backer. He financed publication of the Bible in Yiddish and of the Church of England Liturgy in Hebrew and visited both the Russian Czar and the King of Prussia to obtain their official influence in behalf of the Society's work.

It was while Way was collecting a library of Hebrew literature that he became acquainted with MacCaul, then a student of Hebrew at Trinity College, Dublin, and persuaded him that conversion of the Jews represented "the highest good of the Jewish people and through them of the whole world." To the disgust of the Dublin dons, who had high hopes of this brilliant young scholar, MacCaul deserted the University to go to Warsaw as a missionary to the Jews. On the voyage out, his daughter tells in her memoirs, he read Paul's Epistle to the Hebrews thirteen times, and such was his determination to become proficient in Hebrew script that in the accumulated spare hours of his lifetime he wrote out the whole of the Pentateuch eight times in longhand. It is hardly to be wondered at that his daughter, who was born in Warsaw, learned Hebrew at three, at four could read the Bible and speak German and Yiddish, and at twelve taught Hebrew in the Mission school at "Palestine Place."

Back in London in 1831, MacCaul was appointed president of the Society's College of Missionaries and took an active part in making the condition of the Jewish people known to the English, who, says his daughter, "knew very little about it and cared less." Still straining to convince the reluctant beneficiaries of his mission, MacCaul published a weekly tract, called *The Old Paths,* expounding the thesis that Christianity remained the logical outcome of the faith of Moses, whereas medieval rabbinical writings had departed from the true Mosaic law. Mrs. Finn, his daughter, recalls the excited conferences in her father's study on Saturday afternoons, when Jewish gentlemen came to discuss religious matters while she, aged eight, and her younger brother listened at a crack in the door. This young lady, who later made her home in Jerusalem for eighteen years as wife of the British consul there and worked with her husband to reopen the Holy Land to "its lawful owners, the Hebrew nation," was to be a living link between Shaftesbury and Balfour. At fifteen she had copied out Shaftesbury's historic letter to Palmerston proposing England as sponsor of the Jews' return, on "cream laid foolscap with gilt edges," as a gift for her father. She died in 1921 at the age of ninety-six, having lived to see Britain assume the Palestine Mandate.

It is impossible not to admire the learning, devotion,

and good will of men such as MacCaul and Shaftesbury.
The latter, after he became president of the Jews' Society
in 1848, attended every annual meeting for thirty-seven
years until his death and even took lessons in Hebrew from
his friend "Rabbi MacCaul." Yet one is left with an impression of the immense disproportion of earnest endeavor to
minuscule results. The impressive edifice was built on
sand and, so far as "promoting Christianity among the
Jews" was concerned, was dedicated to a goal no more
substantial than a drifting mirage in the desert.

There were critics of the Society who voiced their doubts
from the beginning. In its annual report for 1810 the Society admits to having been ridiculed for "foolish and Uto-
pian expectations" and to being open to the charge of "enthusiasm." In fact, on one occasion membership in the
Society was offered as evidence of insanity in a case
brought before the Lunacy Commission in 1863. "Are you
aware, My Lord, that she subscribes to the Society for Conversion of the Jews?" "Indeed," replied the Chairman,
none other than Lord Shaftesbury, "are you aware that I
am president of that Society?"

Such critics held that, if the Jews were to be converted,
it could only be by a miracle, some stroke of divine intervention such as delivered them from Pharaoh, and that
human efforts to anticipate this were presumptuous (incidentally the same objection as that urged by orthodox
Jews). So much time and money, growled the critics, were
better spent in the service of the Christian Church than in
hankering after the Jews. Angriest of all was a Reverend
Henry Handley Norris, who in 1825 published an entire
book reviling the Society and all its works through six hundred and ninety pages of furious invective. This gentle-
man, known as the "Bishop-maker," happened also to be
chaplain to Shaftesbury's estranged father, the sixth Earl,
a harsh old autocrat—a fact that may possibly have initiated the son's warm adoption of the opposite point of view.

In answering these attacks the Society's defenders repeatedly urged the duty of making good the long wrong done to "God's ancient people." They had convinced themselves that converting Jews to Christianity somehow represented an act of retribution for Christianity's persecution of them. An unacknowledged sense of guilt for ill requiting the gift of the Gospel was certainly a factor. The Society's centennial historian, Reverend W. T. Gidney, for example, discusses all the historical references to Joseph of Arimathea or to one or more of the apostles' having preached the gospel in Britain, and insists that, since the original message of salvation came from a "Hebrew Christian," Britain out of gratitude if nothing else should return the gift of Christianity to the Hebrews of today.

The Society had, in fact, a double task. It had to convince Jews of "the errors and absurdities of their present mistaken opinions," and it had to convince suspicious Christians that the Jews, though admittedly a stiff-necked, dark-hearted people, sunk in moral degradation, obduracy, and ignorance of Gospel, were not only worthy of salvation but also vital to Christianity's hope of salvation. This they accomplished by a kind of inversion that enables the missionary mind to transcend logic. Paul had said: "As concerning the Gospel they are enemies for your sakes; but as touching the election, they are beloved for the father's sakes." The old forgotten fact that Jesus' message was addressed to his "kinsmen according to the flesh" became the basic text of the Evangelical preachers. Charles Simeon, in a sermon in 1818, startled his hearers with the reminder that "it is a Jew who is at this moment interceding for us at the right hand of God." For His sake they should regard the Jews as "the most interesting of all people and, under God, the greatest benefactors of the human race." Similarly at the Society's jubilee celebration in 1858 Canon Edward Hoare congratulated the members as being "those who love the Jewish nation, and, above all, Christians who love the Jewish King."

Actually it was not love for the Jewish nation, but concern for the Christian soul, that moved all these good and earnest people. They were interested only in giving to the Jews the gift of Christianity, which the Jews did not want; civil emancipation, which the Jews did want, they consistently opposed. During the first half of the nineteenth century the Emancipation Bill, permitting Jews to enter Parliament without taking the usual oath "on the true faith of a Christian," was debated many times before its final enactment in 1858, and each time found Lord Shaftesbury speaking against it on the ground that waiver of the oath was a violation of religious principles. It was not the Evangelicals with their love for "God's ancient people" who favored admitting the Jews to full citizenship on equal terms, but the less pious Liberals. It was Lord Macaulay arguing from history, not Lord Shaftesbury arguing from prophecy, who made that eloquent speech for Emancipation which recalled that when Britain was "as savage as New Guinea . . . the Jews had their fenced cities and cedar palaces, their splendid Temple, their schools of learning"; and if they are now reduced to low circumstances, "shall we not rather consider it as a matter of shame and remorse to ourselves?" (Parenthetically it should be added that Shaftesbury accepted Emancipation gracefully when it was ultimately voted by both Houses and promptly proposed Sir Moses Montefiore for a peerage. "It would be a glorious day for the House of Lords," he wrote to Gladstone, "when that grand old Hebrew were enrolled on the lists of the hereditary legislators of England," a view in which the Lords did not concur. Shaftesbury was unconventional as always.)

If the Jews' Society had concerned itself only with conversion we could ignore it. It was that vital linked factor, the restoration of Israel, that gives the Society's work historical importance. The year after Victoria came to the throne, 1838, was that in which things began to move; the year, as we recall, when Syria (including Palestine) was caught in the turmoil of Mehemet Ali's defiance of the

Sultan and the resulting European intervention. In that
year Britain became the first European power to appoint a
consul to Jerusalem. The appointee was only a vice-consul,
but it was a beginning. It happened that in March 1838
the simmering Turco-Egyptian feud began to boil toward
another crisis when a local Arab revolt against Mehemet's
viceroy and son, Ibrahim Pasha, encouraged the Sultan to
arm for a last attempt to crush his upstart vassal. Palmerston, to aid the Sultan, concluded a commercial treaty
with the Porte and, with Lord Ashley (as Shaftesbury then
was) jogging his elbow, included provision for a British
consulate in Jerusalem. One can be sure that anything to
do with Jerusalem originated with Ashley, and he, in fact,
had conceived the idea as a first step toward his great goal
of Israel restored. It was Palmerston's pen that instructed
the consul "that it will be part of your duty as British vice-
consul at Jerusalem to afford protection to the Jews generally and you will take an early opportunity of reporting
. . . upon the present state of the Jewish population in
Palestine"; but it was not Palmerston's idea. The Foreign
Secretary, as Ashley privately regretted, "did not know
Moses from Sir Sydney Smith," but he could be appealed
to in terms of practical British self-interest. In this case
Ashley emphasized the usefulness of having a British
agent on the spot at such a crucial time and put into
Palmerston's head the idea of using the Jews as a British
wedge within the Ottoman Empire. He kept his own more
sublime motive to himself, recording privately in his diary
that "God put it into my heart to conceive the plan for His
honour and gave me influence to prevail with Palmerston."

Ashley's influence was, curiously, always greater with
Palmerston, who was of the opposite party, than with the
Conservative ministers of his own party, and not so much
because he was Palmerston's stepson-in-law as because
the two oddly contrasting men, one with his eyes fixed on
this world, the other on the next, were genuinely fond of
each other. Palmerston valued the younger man's advice

on religious issues and as prime minister, it is said, never appointed a bishop except on Ashley's recommendation. Ashley, for his part, knew that his dashing, exuberant chief could be counted on for the bold or original gesture, the plan of scope and daring, which cold Peel or cautious Aberdeen would only view with alarm.

His own exuberance at the consul's appointment is recorded complete with Victorian italics and exclamation points. "Took leave this morning of Young, who has just been appointed her Majesty's Vice-Consul at *Jerusalem!* What a wonderful event it is! The ancient city of the people of God is about to resume a place among the nations, and England is the first of Gentile kingdoms that ceases 'to tread her down.'"

It may seem a large message to have read into the appointment of a vice-consul, but Ashley saw him not as a mere functionary of the Foreign Office, but haloed with the rays of prophecy, "accredited, as it were, to the former kingdom of David and the Twelve Tribes." He had in fact arranged it so that the consul's jurisdiction should cover the whole country within the ancient limits of the Holy Land and that the chosen consul should be a person sympathetic to the cause. Young entered on his duties with enthusiasm and soon reported back a census of 9,690 Jews all of whom, he said, were sufficiently poor and oppressed and stateless to be eligible for British protection. In fact, he followed his instructions with such zeal that his superior, the consul-general at Alexandria, complained to the Foreign Office that Mr. Young was "granting British protection in an indiscriminate manner to all Jews." The Foreign Office upheld Young with a promise of "all proper support."

Meanwhile Ashley had been reading Lord Lindsay's just-published *Letters from Egypt, Edom and the Holy Land,* the first in that flood of Holy Land travel books that over the next forty years was to saturate the British public with an average of some forty books a year. He took the opportunity of reviewing the book to present publicly his vision of restoration of the "Jewish nation" under the aegis of the Anglican Church. The political regeneration of Palestine as a British sphere of influence had hardly yet taken shape in his mind, but the first green shoots of the idea that was to become the British Mandate appeared in the article on Lindsay's book that he wrote for the *Quarterly Review* of December 1838.

Using as evidence a letter written to him by a convert recently arrived from Warsaw, he spoke about the resurgence of the feeling among the Jews of Russia and Poland that the time "for the turning of their captivity was nigh at hand," about the upsurge of Christian interest in the Holy Land, about what he insisted was "a new and tender interest in the Hebrew people" among Christians and what he insisted was an approximation toward Christianity among Jews. He told of the Society's plan to build an Anglican church in Jerusalem, "if possible on Mt. Zion itself," for which funds were now being collected. Already the Society's missionaries were on the spot conducting services in Hebrew where no Protestant services had ever been held before, and a "small but faithful congregation of proselytes hear daily the Evangelical verities of our Church on the Mount of the Holy City itself in the language of the prophets and in the spirit of the Apostles." Surely, Ashley glowed, this event is "one of the most striking that have occurred in modern days, perhaps in any days since the corruptions began in the Church of Christ." As heralding the conversion of the Jews under Protestant auspices it would establish forever "the pure doctrines of the Reformation as embodied and professed in the Church of England."

Leaving the religious question, he then calls attention to the significance of the recent consular appointment and suggests that "the soil and climate of Palestine are singularly adapted to the growth of produce required for the exigences of Great Britain" — cotton, silk, madder, and olive-oil. "Capital and skill are alone required," and these he sees as forthcoming from Britain now that Palestine enjoys "the presence of a British officer and the increased security of property which his presence will confer." Why, then, shall the world not see at last the return of the Jews, "who will betake themselves to agriculture in no other land, and having found in the English Consul, a mediator between their people and the pasha, will . . . become once more the husbandmen of Judea and Galilee"?

We may smile at Ashley's faith in the ability of a lone vice-consul to move empires by his mere presence, but the Victorian self-confidence, like the Elizabethan, built the British Empire. The consul represented Britain. What more was necessary?

For one thing, the Jews themselves, the essential ingredient, were necessary but still missing, for as yet there was no mass movement for the return. Not until a generation later, when political anti-Semitism as a state policy was resorted to by the czars as a vent for popular discontent, was enough pressure built up to push the Jews into active Zionism. But the battles, intrigues, and clashing ambitions now reverberating around Palestine determined one Jew to investigate for himself the possibility of reopening the land to his people. This was Ashley's fellow philanthropist Sir Moses Montefiore, who out of religious feelings as deep and fervent as Ashley's, if less mystical, believed also in the literal restoration of the Jewish state, though (it seems hardly necessary to point out) for different reasons. Montefiore was a believing Jew of the most orthodox description who daily attended synagogue at seven A.M., dated his letters by the Jewish calendar, and refused to attend his own inauguration as sheriff because it fell during Rosh Hashana. But, having made his way in the business world, he was accustomed to work for what he wanted, not wait for it. "Palestine must belong to the Jews and Jerusalem is destined to be the seat of the Jewish Empire," he is quoted as saying by his biographer Lucien

Wolf. But, being a practical man, he also said: "Begin in the first instance with the building of houses in Jerusalem; begin at once."

Conversion, Ashley's motivating idea, he would probably have regarded, like the learned counsel, as lunatic. Yet otherwise they were not far apart. The "Jerusalem" engraved on Ashley's ring appeared on Montefiore's carriage crest in Hebrew letters of gold. Both believed that the Jews, once they felt the soil of Palestine beneath their feet, would again become agriculturists, restore the vine and the fig tree, and reclaim their homeland from decay. Both were, in a sense, Zionist-before-the-fact; and to be a Zionist in the 1830's was something like being an antifascist in the 1930's—"premature." Ashley was right for the wrong reason; Montefiore was right, but too soon.

In November 1838 he set out for Palestine, where, thanks to his prestige and wealth and the memory of his munificence on a previous visit, his passage through the country was like a royal progress. Its climax was entry into Jerusalem on a prancing Arab steed provided by the Turkish governor, which bore him down the Mount of Olives through two lines of mounted Turkish soldiers in ceremonial uniform. Between parades and oriental courtesies Montefiore, always businesslike, surveyed housing, sanitation, and possibilities for work and land reclamation available to the wretched Chalukah community, who so far had lived on prayers, wailing, and reciting the Talmud and on pennies from "Jerusalem boxes" abroad.

Proceeding to an audience in Egypt with Mehemet Ali, who had once asked Montefiore to be his business agent, he laid before the Pasha a plan for land purchase described in detail in his diary on May 24, 1839:

"I shall apply to Mohammed [Mehemet] Ali for a grant of land for fifty years; some 100 or 200 villages; giving him an increased rent of from 10 to 20 per cent, and paying the whole in money annually in Alexandria, but the land and villages to be free, during the whole term, from every tax or rate either of Pasha or Governor of the several districts. The grant obtained, I shall, please heaven, on my return to England form a company for the cultivation of the land and the encouragement of our brethren in Europe to return to Palestine. . . . By degrees I hope to induce the return of thousands of our brethren to the land of Israel. I am sure they would be happy in the enjoyment of the observance of our religion in a manner which is impossible in Europe."

Mehemet, smoking his diamond-studded pipe, promised him "any portion of land open for sale in Syria" and agreed to "do everything that lies in my power" to support his project. But within little more than a year Mehemet's power too was broken; Syria reverted to the sultans, and not until their miserable dynasty was at last extinguished was the opportunity to come again.

Meanwhile the Damascus Incident had erupted, growing out of a charge of ritual murder against the Jews in the death of a Capuchin friar. All the ferocious hallmarks of the pogrom followed—riots, sacking, imprisonment, and torture to extract confessions, instigated and kept going by French agents and the local Catholic orders. It was part of the boiling over of the Eastern Question, which now, in the years 1839–40, reached its crisis, with France set against the other powers. Though the Damascus Incident was historically important in the development of nineteenth-century Jewish nationalism, arousing Jews the world over to the need of united action, it is relevant here only so far as it provided opportunity and motive for British intervention on behalf of the Jews in the Turkish Empire and awakened public opinion to their situation.

A memorial addressed to the Protestant Monarchs of Europe appealing for the restoration of the Jews was published in full in the *Times* of March 9, 1840. It drew attention to the Eastern crisis and "other striking signs of the times" as providing an opportune moment for "what may be the probable line of duty" of Protestant Christianity to the Jewish people. Shortly afterwards the General Assembly of the Church of Scotland published a report by two of its missionaries on the condition of the Jews of Palestine that attracted much attention and followed it with a memorial addressed to Palmerston, also carried by the *Times* (December 3, 1840). It commended him for appointing a consul to Jerusalem and extending British protection to the Jews and expressed the hope that the current crisis in Syria "will result in the more firm and more extensive establishment of British influence in that interesting land."

Meanwhile Montefiore, hardly back in England, hurriedly set out again for the East, resolved to obtain release of the Jewish prisoners in Damascus dungeons, not with a pardon, which he scorned, but with acquittal on the blood accusation as well as reparation and a general order from the Sultan protecting Jewish life and property. Montefiore was not a man to be stopped, whether by French intrigue, Mohammedan red tape, or war. To the astonishment of the world he obtained not only full acquittal, but also a firman, granted grudgingly by the Sultan, assuring to the Jews equality of treatment with all Turkish subjects. "The Magna Charta for the Jews in Turkish dominions," Montefiore proudly, if too hopefully, acclaimed it, and he took particular pleasure in stopping off at Paris on the way home for the purpose of personally presenting to Louis Philippe a copy of the firman obtained at the cost of that discomfited monarch's ambitions in the East. The moment must have given him even more satisfaction than the "supporters" to his coat of arms granted by Queen Victoria on his return, in specific recognition of his "unceasing exertions in behalf of his injured and persecuted brethren in the East and of the Jewish nation at large."

The Queen's interest may have been personal,* but Pal-

* While Victoria was still princess she and her mother had dined at Montefiore's country home in Kent, where he was a neighbor. In the year of her accession she had consciously broken precedent to knight him, the first professing Jew to receive a title. Before his departure for Damascus the Queen received him in private audience to encourage his mission.

merston's instructions about the Jews were not. While Montefiore was in the East Palmerston was sending to Ponsonby and other envoys at Turkish posts the series of dispatches that mark the beginning of official British intervention on behalf of the "Jewish nation" and of its resettlement in Palestine. Already in July he had concluded the Treaty of London, pledging the Four Powers' help to the Sultan against Mehemet, which had so infuriated France and had precipitated the final phase of the Eastern crisis.

While Palmerston was chortling at his bold stroke and Montefiore was charging forth like a medieval knight to save his fallen brethren, Ashley, still wrapped in prophetic visions, was using the occasion too.

"Anxious about the hopes and prospects of the Jewish people," he wrote in his diary on July 24. "Everything seems ripe for their return to Palestine. Could the Five Powers of the West be induced to guarantee the security of life and possessions to the Hebrew race, they would flow back in rapidly augmenting numbers. Then, by the blessing of God, I will prepare a document, fortify it by all the evidence I can accumulate and, confiding to the wisdom and mercy of the Almighty, lay it before the Secretary of State for Foreign Affairs."

On August 1 he dined with Palmerston and "propounded my scheme, which seemed to strike his fancy; he asked some questions and readily promised to consider it." Ashley confesses that he used political, financial, and commercial arguments, for these are the considerations that strike home to the Foreign Secretary, who "weeps not like his Master over Jerusalem" and is unaware that he has been "chosen by God to be an instrument of good to His ancient people and to recognize their rights without believing their destiny."

Palmerston comes through handsomely. On August 11 he writes to Ponsonby, ambassador at the Porte, the dispatch, quoted earlier in this chapter, urging the advantages to the Sultan and to Britain of resettling the Jews in Palestine. On the same day the British fleet arrived off the coast of Syria. On the 17th appeared Ashley's article in the *Times*, followed by the flood of replies that it provoked. One anonymous correspondent suggested that Britain should buy Palestine for the Jews. Another urged their restoration as a matter of practical politics on the optimistic theory that if the Jews repossessed Syria it would be removed as a bone of contention among the powers and thus contribute to the general peace.

On September 25 Ashley formally presented to Palmerston his document for "recall of the Jews to their ancient land." Its tone is uninspired, for Ashley, in trying to make out a case for official policy, carefully restrained his pen from raptures about "God's ancient people" and "Christ's coming Kingdom." Nor, being an anti-imperialist at heart, could he force himself to any enthusiasm about advancing the British flag. He simply proposes the plan as a means of "adjusting the Syrian question" and promoting the fertility of "all the countries between the Euphrates and the Mediterranean Sea." He affirms that the Hebrew race believes the time is near for their restoration to the soil of Palestine, and that only fear for their persons and estates holds them back. He proposes that the "Governing Power of the Syrian provinces" (who this would be was still uncertain at the time he wrote) should enter into a "solemn engagement to establish the principles and practises of European civilization"; that this power should be induced to enact "equal laws and equal protection to Jew and Gentile"; that the Four Powers should guarantee performance and that an article ratifying their guarantee should be included in the final treaty in settlement of the Eastern Question. Such a guarantee would call forth the "hidden wealth and industry of the Jewish people." Lands now worthless as a source of revenue would be settled and developed. More effort could be expected from the Jews than from others, because of their "ancient reminiscences and deep affection for their land." Their industry and persever-

ance are prodigious, they can subsist on the smallest pit-
tance, they are accustomed to suffering and trained in
"implicit obedience" to arbitrary rule. "They will submit to
the existing form of government."

Ashley, like the framers of the Balfour Declaration,
makes no mention of the possibility of a developing Jewish
state. In the Balfour Declaration the omission was deliberate, and, as it proved, it was the fatal error that was to
cause all the trouble. But it is doubtful if Ashley ever imagined a self-governing state. On the contrary, he assures
Palmerston that the Jews will acknowledge present ownership of the land by its "actual possessors," being content
to obtain interest on it by rent or purchase. He adds: "They
will return at their own expense with no hazard but to
themselves," that it will be "the cheapest and safest mode"
of colonizing Syria, that no "pecuniary outlay" will be demanded of the guarantors, and that the "benefits to be
derived from it would belong to the whole civilized world."

This is not Ashley at his best. In trying to be worldly he
only succeeds in sounding mercenary. His estimate of the
Jews is ludicrous; at least we know it to be so in the light
of their subsequent history. But it must be remembered
that Ashley was writing at a time when the Jews themselves had not yet conceived the idea of a state. It was
another fifty-five years before Herzl's *Judenstaat* burst
upon his own people, and they gasped with the shock of
it. Ashley was writing twenty years before Herzl was even
born and forty years before the first Jewish organization
for sending colonizers to Palestine was formed. Moreover
his peculiar ideas of Jewish submissiveness were not only
the product of his time, but also the product of his own
thinking, which regarded the Jews as somehow passive
agents of the Christian millennium. If Ashley had been
more politically minded he might have remembered the
Maccabees and how Abbot Aelfric had long ago used their
example to inspire the struggle for English nationhood.

Meanwhile events were hurrying to a climax in Syria.

On October 3 Beirut, bombarded by Napier's squadron, surrendered, and a month later Acre fell and inspired Ashley to see God manifest in the British sailor as he had previously seen Him guiding the hand of the Foreign Secretary: "It is really heart-stirring to read of our successes in Syria, the forward valour, the iron-steadfastness, of our countrymen! One midshipman does more than a hundred Turks. . . . What materials for greatness! What instruments, should it so please God, for the alliance and protection of His ancient people and for His final purposes on earth!" In his diary Ashley runs true to form.

In the following months, during which Napier chased Mehemet's army back to Egypt and forced his return of the Turkish fleet to the Sultan, British influence at the Porte was naturally at its peak. Palmerston was now pursuing Ashley's plan under his own steam. In November he reminded Ponsonby of Britain's role as protector of the Jews under Turkish rule. In February 1841 he authorized the ambassador to allow Jews "to transmit to the Porte, through British authorities, any complaints which they might have to prefer against the Turkish authorities."

In the same dispatch he again urged Ashley's project almost in Ashley's words: "It would be highly advantageous to the Sultan," wrote the Foreign Secretary, "that the Jews who are scattered through other countries in Europe and Africa, should be induced to go and settle in Palestine, because the wealth and habits of order and industry which they would bring with them would tend greatly to increase the resources of the Turkish Empire and to promote the progress of civilization therein." The Sultan must be pressed into giving some "real and tangible security," and as a starter Palmerston suggested that the protégé relationship with British officials be offered for a specific period of twenty years. In April he followed this up with a circular letter to all British consuls stationed in the Turkish Empire, informing them that the Porte had guaranteed equality of treatment to Jewish subjects and had agreed to "attend to" any instance of maltreatment brought to its notice by British officials. He instructed all envoys to make "diligent enquiry" into any such case brought to their attention, to "report fully" on it to the ambassador at Constantinople, and to make it clear to the local Turkish authorities that "the British Government feels an interest in the welfare of the Jews in general."

What had sprung from Ashley's cloud-touched "Evangelical verities" had now hardened into official policy. But Ashley had rubbed his lamp too soon for history; his short-lived dream had but a moment to walk the earth before it was stuffed back into the bottle. The guarantee that he had hoped for was not included in the final five power treaty. Because of the immense difficulty of hammering out an agreement among the five powers with five different axes to grind, the treaty, to be known as the Straits Convention, was confined solely to the question of control of the Bosporus and the Dardenelles. Encouragement of the Jews' recall to Palestine got no farther than Palmerston's last dispatch on the subject in February. Ponsonby, cold to the idea, made no effort to pursue it, the Sultan was equally antipathetic, and the ultimate blow came when the jaunty Palmerston, having withstood the roaring of French war threats and accomplished his five power treaty in July, was carried out of office with the defeat of the Whig government on a domestic issue in August. His "intrepidity in jumping into hot water on all occasions," which won him *Punch's* Prize for the Session and delighted the British public (though it sadly vexed the Queen), was replaced at the Foreign Office by the "antiquated imbecility" (Palmerston's phrase) of Lord Aberdeen.

Aberdeen regarded his predecessor's interest in the Jews with frigid distaste, much as Asquith seventy-five years later was to shudder at the "fantastic" scheme for Palestine presented to the Cabinet by Lloyd George. He instructed Young, the consul at Jerusalem, henceforth to limit consular protection to "British subjects, or agents, alone."

Palmerston had of course outreached conventional practice when he authorized protection of Jews who were not
British subjects, but he did it deliberately. By encouraging
the virtually stateless Jews in the Turkish Empire, ignored
by the Turkish authorities and rejected as nationals by the
other European consuls, to look to Britain for protection
that they could get nowhere else, he was laying the ground
for Britain to move in as protector of a future Jewish resettlement of Palestine.

Aberdeen, however, did not regard it as the proper function of the Foreign Office to have ideas, especially new
ideas, and he saw no reason to go beyond the letter of the
law. In practice his timidity had little effect on the men
on the spot. Both Young and his successor at the Jerusalem
consulate, James Finn, the son-in-law of "Rabbi" MacCaul
and enthusiastic disciple of Ashley, continued to intervene
on behalf of God's ancient people, whether British subjects
or not, whenever occasion arose.

Indeed, the prospect for Israel's restoration, from Ashley's point of view, now looked brighter than ever, despite
the change in government. For he had at last succeeded in
his dearest wish: the creation by the Church of England
of an Anglican bishopric in Jerusalem, with a converted
Jew consecrated as its first bishop. This was to be the
crowning achievement of the Jews' Society, the signal for
the restoration of the ancient kingdom of Israel as a diocese of the Church of England. It was the receptacle of all
Ashley's hopes, "an accomplishment," he ardently believed,
"of the prophecy of Isaiah."

The bishopric had the eager sponsorship of the Protestant king Frederick William of Prussia and of his envoy,
Chevalier Bunsen, appointed to England for the special
purpose of aiding Ashley in the project. Their utmost joint
efforts were required to overcome opposition arising from
doctrinal issues, now long since dead, that kept the Victorian atmosphere steaming. The whole Anglo-Catholic
party of Tractarians and Puseyites attached to the Oxford

Movement, which was trying to reconcile the Church of England to Rome, bitterly resented the bishopric as a step for the advancement of "Low Church" Protestantism. Gladstone, then a powerful young voice of the High Church party, was "beset with scruples," which he communicates in a twenty-four page letter to Bunsen. It asserts that "the novelty and (as yet) the dimness of the scheme has made it act powerfully on the nerves of my countrymen."

Bunsen hurries around to call and tries to exorcise the scruples in a two-hour conversation. He is not above using as an argument the political advantages to be gained in Syria. "Would you do nothing," he asks Gladstone, "to avail yourselves of political conjunctures which it is not presumptuous to term providential in their coincidence with these symptoms of Zion's revival?" Concealed in the Germanic turgidity of this remarkable sentence is a glimmer of realism.

Next Ashley arranges a meeting between Bunsen and Peel, who will be the new prime minister, anxiously confiding to his diary the hope that Peel will have a heart, "like Solomon's, large as the sands of the sea," for here is matter enough to fill it—the opportunity "to plant under the banner of the Cross, God's people on the mountains of Jerusalem."

Peel makes no objections, and a week later (July 19) it is Bunsen's turn to record, after an interview with Palmerston, who is still in office: "This is a great day . . . the principle is admitted. So the beginning is made, please God, for the restoration of Israel."

Now comes Ashley's greatest moment as bishop-maker, for Palmerston will accept whomever he designates. MacCaul had been suggested by the King of Prussia but had declined on the ground that the position should go to one of the Hebrew race. Ashley is of the same opinion, and his choice falls upon the Reverend Doctor Alexander, "an Israelite belonging to Church of England" and professor of Hebrew and Arabic at King's College.

The choice is accepted and then is followed by a setback when Ponsonby writes from Constantinople that the sultan is sure to refuse permission to build a church in Jerusalem. But Palmerston insists. "I wrote to Lord Ponsonby," he tells Ashley, "and desired him to put not one shoulder but both shoulders to the wheel"—an injunction that had the desired effect on both the Ambassador and the Sultan.

On September 23 the Bill creating the Bishopric of Jerusalem is passed by Parliament. Ashley receives a letter telling him of "the prodigious sensation the Jewish Question is creating in Liverpool. Twenty-four sermons on *one* Sunday in our behalf!" Reclaiming the Jews had indeed become a favorite project of "the mass of English society." But the zeal was not universal. While the Puseyites opposed it on doctrinal grounds, there were still a few figures who retained an eighteenth-century scorn of all religious fervor and regarded the whole affair as misplaced enthusiasm. "All the young people are growing mad about religion," grumbled Lord Melbourne, the outgoing Whig prime minister.

But the new Conservative ministry headed by Peel was swept along in the tide of enthusiasm if not practically blackmailed into acquiescence by Ashley. He told Peel that opposition now from a Conservative government would form "a most pernicious contrast" to the warm support given to the cause by Palmerston, and he warned Aberdeen of the "strong feeling of the country and the consequences of obstruction." He himself believed that the "love for God's people" incarnated in the bishopric "is the truest Conservative principle and will save the country." This seems to have been his recipe for the current crisis brought on by the wheat famine that was then gripping the country.

At any rate his efforts, for the moment at least, were successful. Peel assured him that he would offer no obstacles, and "even Aberdeen relaxed." Bunsen confesses being "moved to tears" by the spectacle of his dear friend Ashley, "a future Peer of this realm," accomplishing so much good. (There is a kind of German sentimental snobbery that becomes transfixed before the image of an English nobleman, of which Bunsen seems to have been the original example.)

Everything is now ready for the consecration. Letters gush between the King of Prussia, Ashley, and Bunsen. "Never since David has a King uttered such words," exclaims Ashley on receiving an encouraging message from Frederick William. Even many of the High Church party have come around, including the future Cardinal Manning and, at last, Gladstone. According to Ashley he "stripped himself of a part of his Puseyite garments, spoke like a pious man," and proposed a toast to the new Bishop. According to Bunsen he made an exquisite speech that flowed like "a gentle and translucent stream," a most improbable description of Gladstone's oratory.

The Archbishop of Canterbury, who is to perform the ceremony, sits together with Ashley "in the library for two hours talking of the Jews. The dear old man is full of Zeal and piety for the cause" and affirms that "the question is deeply rooted in the heart of England." On November 12 the solemn service takes place. Everyone is overcome with emotion. To Ashley it is the climax of all his labors. He finds it "nearly overwhelming to see a native Hebrew appointed by the Church of England to carry back to the Holy City the truths and blessings which Gentiles had received from it." Puseyites may ill conceal the fact that "they cannot stomach the notion of a *Jew* elevated to the Episcopate. . . . Be it so. I can rejoice in Zion for a capital, in Jerusalem for a church and in a Hebrew for a King."

On November 18 Bishop Alexander preaches the first sermon of the "Jewish Church" as Ashley calls it, and on the 29th he starts for Jerusalem. At the last minute a hitch developed when Peel refused a Government steamboat to carry the Bishop to Syria, which Ashley thought the dignity of his position demanded. Peel "talked of provoking the Ottoman Porte—he talked of doing things quietly.

" 'I don't see,' said he pettishly, 'why we should be called upon to give a steam boat.'

" 'I will tell you why,' I replied. 'A foreign potentate [the King of Prussia] has contributed half the endowment of an English bishopric, the British public has contributed the other half; there prevails the deepest, most intense interest I ever knew in the country and *all* we ask of our *own* government is the loan of a steam boat to carry out the Bishop.'

"Peel said he would speak to Aberdeen. Thus ended a short interview equally unpleasant and odious, I should think to both parties." But to his surprise Ashley had prevailed, for three days later Peel issues the necessary orders to the Admiralty enabling the Bishop to embark under government steam.

Then came news that the Porte had canceled its permission to build a church. But Ponsonby "for once" proved vigorous and sent a "bold and threatening" message to the Sultan, and "even Aberdeen" resented the insult. Later, however, he reverted to his accustomed timidity and ordered Young in Jerusalem to "carefully abstain" from identifying himself, as a servant of the Crown, in any way with the Bishop's mission or from assisting in any scheme of "interference" with the Jewish subjects of the Porte in which Bishop Alexander might possibly engage.

But no one paid much attention to Aberdeen, and as far as Ashley was concerned the great object had been attained, "for the consolidation of Protestant truth, the welfare of Israel and the extension of the Kingdom of our Blessed Lord."

And what then? What of the great hopes to be realized, the great truths to be propagated, the great light that was to beam upon the world from the Anglican See in the Holy City beckoning home God's ancient people? The painful fact is that nobody saw it. Popery did not wither away, Protestantism was not visibly advanced, Judaism remained untouched. This extraordinary and now forgotten episode that added so many degrees of heat to Victorian religious controversy found its ultimate epitaph in a report by an English traveler, E. Warburton, author of *The Crescent and the Cross*. In 1844 he visited Bishop Alexander's church in Jerusalem and found a total congregation of eight converted Jews and one or two tourists. "The Hill of Zion is not a likely place for a Jew to forsake the faith of his fathers," a Hebrew told Warburton. No one in England seems to have thought of that.

Only Ashley, mourning the untimely death of Bishop Alexander in 1845, allowed a sliver of doubt to penetrate his mind. "Have we," he wondered, "conceived a merely human project and then imagined it to be a decree of the Almighty?"

CHAPTER XI

PALESTINE IN THE PATH OF EMPIRE

Yet Ashley had not labored in vain. There was a valid political idea at the core of his scheme, even if there was little sense to the form that he hoped it would take. Through the agitation that his proposals had aroused the British public was gradually made aware of the strategic advantages to be gained from a sphere of influence in the Middle East. Napoleon's expedition, Nelson's victory at the Nile, the romantic history of Mehemet Ali's rise and fall punctuated by the echo of British naval guns, Palmerston's neat triumph in the Syrian crisis, the visionary prospects aroused by the Evangelical craze for conversion of the Jews and the Jerusalem bishopric, all these events centering in the Holy Land combined to create almost a proprietary feeling about Palestine. The idea of a British annex there through the medium of a British-sponsored restoration of Israel began to appeal to other minds than Ashley's. His followers, however, invariably stressed the strategic arguments that he had added only half-heartedly to the old religious objectives.

The most far-sighted and sensible of Ashley's successors was Colonel Charles Henry Churchill, a grandson of the Duke of Marlborough (and thus an antecedent of Winston Churchill) and an officer in the army that overthrew Mehemet. Churchill was captured by his idea when he was stationed in Damascus at the time of the furor over the ritual murder trial and Montefiore's visit. It was Churchill to whom Montefiore sent the Sultan's firman of 1840 for presentation to the Jewish community of Damascus. In recognition of Churchill's help in their cause during the year of terror the Damascus Jews gave a banquet honoring him, together with the fourteen victims of the blood accusation just released from prison. His speech on this occasion and, more particularly, a letter to Montefiore that he wrote shortly afterwards, already mark a change from the Evangelicals' visionary nonsense to a more realistic point of view. He seems to have been concerned with restoring the Jews for their own sake rather than as agents of prophecy, and he nowhere mentions their conversion as a precondition or corollary of the return to Zion. He hoped, he told the Damascus group, that the hour of the liberation of Israel was approaching, when the Jewish nation would once again take its place among the powers of the world. England, he added, was the only country friendly to Israel's hopes.

Then, in a letter to Montefiore dated June 14, 1841, he makes the point that had escaped everyone so far: namely, that "It is for the Jews to make a commencement."

"I cannot conceal from you," he wrote, "my most anxious desire to see your countrymen endeavor once more to resume their existence as a people. I consider the object to be perfectly obtainable. But two things are indispensably necessary: Firstly that the Jews themselves will take up the matter, universally and unanimously. Secondly that the European powers will aid them in their views."

Next he hit on a second truth: the essential fallacy of Britain's policy of propping up the Turkish Empire—a fallacy that was to plague her diplomacy throughout the nineteenth century. The effort is doomed to "miserable failure," Churchill predicts. Syria and Palestine must be rescued from the "blundering and decrepit despotism" of the Turks and Egyptians and taken under European protection. When that day came the Jews should be ready and able to say: "Already we feel ourselves a people." He "strenuously urged" Montefiore as president of the Jewish Board of Deputies, the governors of London's Sephardic community, to start the wheels turning in this "glorious struggle for national existence" and to stir up the deputies to meet, petition, and agitate.

In a second letter a year later he took up Ashley's idea of a guarantee and suggested that the Jews of England and the Continent should petition the British government to appoint a resident commissioner for Syria to watch over the interests of Jews residing there and protect the security of their property, and thus to encourage colonization "under the auspices and sanction of Great Britain."

Such a step was too much for the courage of the deputies. They could be aroused to action in behalf of distressed or persecuted Jews in cases like the Damascus affair, but they were too concerned in the struggle for civil emancipation at home to look any farther ahead toward Jewish nationhood. In later years, of course, the more emancipated they became the less (with certain notable exceptions) they liked the idea of nationhood in any form. But that is another story. In 1842 even Montefiore could not move them, and they adopted a resolution regretting that the Board was "precluded from originating any measures for carrying out the benevolent views of Col. Churchill." They added that the Jews of Eastern Europe and the Near East would have to make their views known before the British Jews could venture any step in support. Churchill replied that they might "endeavor to ascertain the feelings and wishes of the Jews in the rest of Europe on a question so interesting and important" as the "prospective regeneration" of their country, but there is no evidence that the suggestion recommended itself to the Board. The rest, as far as the records show, is silence.

The Jews of the West would not listen; the Jews of the East behind their ghetto walls could not hear; nor did Churchill have the ear of the Foreign Secretary or the opportunity to influence state policy over the dinner table as Ashley had done. In fact, during the half-century or so after the Ashley-Palmerston opening move in 1840 there were no advocates of restoration eminent in high councils apart from Ashley himself. As Lord Shaftesbury he continued to bestride the Victorian heights for nearly another fifty years. He never abandoned the cause and indeed made the finest expression of it near the end of his life.* His association with Palmerston, who was soon back in the Foreign Office and went on to a ten-year reign as prime minister, remained as close as ever, but both were absorbed in those years by larger matters. In any case the heyday of Evangelical enthusiasm for converting the Jews was over, and with its passing Shaftesbury's own particular motive had become out of date.

Later advocates of Israel's restoration were more concerned with its relation to Britain's imperial progress eastward than to her spiritual progress upward. "It must be clear to every English mind," wrote Colonel Churchill in his book *Mount Lebanon,* "that if England's oriental supremacy is to be upheld, Syria and Egypt must be made to fall more or less under her sway of influence." The book, which was the product of his fifteen years of residence in the Middle East, was published in 1853, the year before the Crimean War, when rumblings from the East were, as usual, interpreted as the death rattle of the Turkish Empire. When Palestine ceases to be Turkish, predicted Churchill (correctly if prematurely), it must become either English or an independent state, and the prospect stirs him to a burst of Ashleyan eloquence: "The land of Jacob's might and Ishmael's wandering power, of David's lyre and Isaiah's strain, of Abraham's faith and Immanuel's love—where God's mysterious ways with man began and where in the fullness of time they are to be accomplished—it also has claims on England's watchful vigilance and sympathising care and already invokes her guardian Aegis."

His was not the only voice trying to summon that Aegis

* See below, page 250.

to a destiny in Palestine. Hardly a returned traveler from
the Grand Tour of the East failed to make the point. In
1844 everyone was reading Warburton's *Crescent and the
Cross,* a book that was to go into seventeen editions over
the next forty-odd years. It epitomized the experience of
generations of pilgrims to the Holy Land when the author
spoke of "a sort of patriotism for Palestine." The emotions
aroused by place names familiar from early childhood and
the thrill of being received "by Sheiks of Abraham's fashion
who feast him on the fare that was set before the Angels"
do not obscure from this observant traveler the fact that
Abraham's footsteps mark what is now the shortest route
to India. Where the Crusades failed to establish a foothold,
he remarks, "The interests of India may obtain what the
Sepulchre of Christ has been denied." Admitting that "this
is perhaps a delicate subject," he hurriedly passes on to
other matters, only to come back to it again. Everywhere
in his travels, he reports, he has met the expectation that
England is coming to the East. When the mad old Pasha
Mehemet Ali dies, England should not allow Egypt to be
restored to the "imbecile tyranny of the Porte," but "boldly
assert" her right of way through Egypt to India, bringing
in her wake prosperity to the country and freedom to the
people—a relative phrase when used by an English author,
meaning freedom from the Turks.

Warburton does not notice in the Jews a possible *avant-
garde* of England's imperialism. His predecessor by a few
years, Lord Lindsay, whose book inspired Ashley's ground-
breaking article in the *Quarterly Review,* came closer to it.
As he follows "in the steps of the Israelites to the Promised
Land," as he experiences the "strange and thrilling pleasure" of rereading the passage of the Red Sea "with the
sight before my eyes," as he camps at night in the desert
and never drives a tent pin "without thinking of Jael and
Sisera," the future of the chosen people begins to occupy
his mind. He is convinced that the barrenness and decay
everywhere around are due, not to a curse on the land, but

simply to "the removal of the ancient inhabitants." He believes that it is the will of the Almighty that the "modern occupants should never be so numerous" as to prevent the return of the "rightful heirs" and that the once fertile land "only waits the return of her banished children and the application of industry commensurate with her agricultural capabilities to burst once more into universal luxuriance and be all she ever was in the days of Solomon."

Another enterprising traveler, Lady Francis Egerton, finds herself pricked into curiosity about the condition of God's ancient people as she wanders through the country seeing on every hand living images of Moses and Elijah. In Jerusalem she pokes into Jewish homes and synagogues, asks questions of the London missionaries, discusses the Damascus persecutions and theories of the restoration. Repeatedly she notices the feeling, recorded in so many travel books of the period, that these were "fateful" times, that something extraordinary was about to happen, vaguely connected in some way with the fulfillment of prophecy and the return to Zion. Lady Francis puts it down to the common expectation of the downfall of the Ottoman Empire and the belief that the ensuing vacuum in Palestine would be filled by the return of the Jews to temporal power. She finds, however, that the impression prevailing in England of Jews "flocking" to the country is imaginary and concludes that in her opinion the Jews will never be restored until they are converted. Her book, intended, she says, only as a private diary, was published in 1841 at the earnest solicitation of friends for the benefit of the Ladies Hibernian Female School Society and found its way to the bed table of the unctuous Baron Bunsen when he visited the queen dowager, showing, he said, "the exquisite hospitality of a Queen surrounded by English noblemen of the right sort."

The report of the Turk's death, which seemed so imminent in the 1840's, proved to be greatly exaggerated; his coma continued chronic for some seventy years more. But it was believed at the time that the Holy Land would soon be available for new ownership. What more convenient and natural than the return of the old tenant with a new landlord? The idea appealed to a variety of English minds. "Were the Ottoman power to be displaced the old commercial route would reopen," wrote Dr. Thomas Clarke in a treatise called *India & Palestine: Or the Restoration of the Jews Viewed in Relation to the Nearest Route to India.*

"Jews," he continued, "are essentially a trading people. What so natural than that they should be planted along that great highway of ancient traffic . . . and in what more skillful hands could exchanges betwixt the East and the West be placed? . . . Syria would be safe only in the hands of a brave, independent and spiritual people, deeply imbued with the sentiment of nationality. . . . Such a people we have in the Jews. . . . Restore them their nationality and their country once more and there is no power on earth that could ever take it from them."

A similar pamphlet entitled *A Tract for the Times, being a Plea for the Jews* was published in 1844 by the Reverend Samuel A. Bradshaw, proposing that Parliament should grant four million pounds, provided the churches should collect another million, for the restoration of Israel. In the same year a committee was convened in London for the purpose of forming a "British and Foreign Society for Promoting the Restoration of the Jewish Nation to Palestine." Although it was apparently stillborn, it is interesting to note that the opening address by the chairman, a reverend with the delightful name of T. Tully Crybbace, urged that England secure from Turkey the surrender of the whole of Palestine "from the Euphrates to the Nile, and from the Mediterranean to the Desert." What generous ideas Englishmen had in those days, when Palestine belonged to someone else, of the area that should be returned to its ancient proprietors!

When the Reverend Mr. Crybbace spoke of the area from the Nile to the Euphrates what he had in mind, of course, was the original conception of the Promised Land as staked out in that day when "the Lord made a covenant with Abram, saying, Unto thy seed have I given this land, from the river of Egypt unto the great river, the river Euphrates" (Genesis 15:18). This was the old Canaan, the land promised anew to Moses and again to Joshua. The Lord was very explicit. The Twelve Tribes were to push out the Canaanites and the Hittites, the Amorites and the Jebusites, and "every place that the sole of your foot shall tread upon, that have I given unto you"—from the wilderness (that is, the Sinai peninsula) to Lebanon, from the western sea to the Euphrates (Joshua 1:3).

Actually the kingdoms of Judah and Israel, once established, never occupied anything like this area. They extended from Dan to Beersheba and from the Mediterranean to Gilead and Moab east of the Jordan. This was the area considered as Palestine, and it remained the common conception of Palestine until White Papers and Commissions of Inquiry took to chopping it up. To our simple ancestors Palestine was simply the land covenanted to Israel; they gave no thought — happy men — to Abraham's other son, Ishmael. What Victorian thunders would have rolled had the Reverend Mr. Crybbace or Lord Shaftesbury or Colonel Churchill been alive in 1922 to see all of Palestine east of the Jordan lopped off for the benefit of the Arab sons of Ishmael! What explosions of eloquence would have followed upon the partition plan that left Israel without Hebron where the Patriarchs are buried, without Shiloh where the Ark of the Covenant was housed, without Dothan where Joseph was sold, without Bethel where Jacob dreamed, without Jericho where Joshua triumphed, and without Bethlehem. What final awful silence would have met that remarkable Jewish state proposed by the best minds of the United Nations—a Jewish state without Jerusalem!

Of course our ancestors lived in happy ignorance of a wealth beneath the desert floor, a richer liquid than the water that gushed forth in the wilderness to save Hagar and her dying son Ishmael. Perhaps that legendary gush of water was meant as an omen. At any rate, Hagar's son, in the person of the Arab League states, holds today an area outside of Palestine ninety times the size of Israel's inheritance and a sizable chunk of Palestine as well.

However, to get back to the 1840's, there was another event of the time, besides the expected collapse of the Porte, that made the Middle East crucial for control of the road to India. This was the advent of steam navigation. Steamships depended on frequent ports of call for recoaling and therefore used the Mediterranean-Red Sea route with transshipment at Suez (the Canal being not yet cut) rather than the Cape route around Africa. In 1840 the P. & O. opened regular steamship runs from England to India by way of the Red Sea. This too was used as an argument by advocates of the restoration. In 1845 E. L. Mitford of the Ceylon Civil Service proposed the "re-establishment of the Jewish nation in Palestine as a protected state under the guardianship of Great Britain." Among the "incalculable" advantages that he foresaw for Britain was that such a state would "place the management of our steam communication entirely in our hands." It would moreover, he believed, "place us in a commanding position (in the Levant) from whence to check the process of encroachment, to overawe open enemies and, if necessary, to repel their advance."

Another official from another corner of the empire, Colonel George Gawler, a former governor of South Australia, put forward a detailed scheme for the accomplishment of the same purpose. He also urged Jewish settlement in Syria in order to prevent intrusion by a foreign power. England "urgently needs," he said, "the shortest and safest lines of communication. . . . Egypt and Syria stand in intimate connection. A foreign hostile power mighty in either would soon endanger British trade . . . and it is now for England to set her hand to the renovation of Syria, through the only people whose energies will be extensively and permanently in the work—the real children of the soil, the sons of Israel." Gawler, like Colonel Churchill, returned time and again to his thesis, urging it on all sides. He became acquainted with Montefiore and accompanied him on a survey of Palestine in 1849. He went farther than Shaftesbury, who saw no "pecuniary outlay" by the guarantor-state and proposed that the powers should undertake financial support of the scheme in expiation for their treatment of the Jews. He urged the Jews to come forward in the event of the collapse of Turkey and "boldly enforce" their claim to Palestine, serving notice that "This portion belongs to the God of Israel and to his national people" and eventually "to hold their own upon the mountains of Israel against all aggressors."

It is a notable fact that clergymen and military men—men of the Bible and men of the sword—dominate these discussions of Israel's return to Palestine. An odd little echo of the military's interest occurs in Mrs. Finn's memoirs of the British consulate in Jerusalem. In 1858 a distinguished party came up from the British frigate *Euryalus*, anchored at Jaffa. The fourteen-year-old Prince Alfred, a younger son of the Queen, was on board as a cadet and was escorted, with his tutor Major Cowell and the ship's commander, Captain Tarleton, on a tour by the Finns. "All the way to Bethlehem," Mrs. Finn recalls, "there was chat with Major Cowell and the Captain (both of whom knew their Bible very well) on the prospects of this land and of the Jews."

The Major and the Captain are heard of no more. Meanwhile Consul and Mrs. Finn, still carrying on the Shaftesbury tradition in the field, were pursuing their local effort to enable the Jews to take root in their own land. The Finns, like Montefiore, tried to begin with the material at hand, the old Jewish community of Jerusalem. It consisted of some four thousand Sephardim, descendants of the Spanish Jews expelled in 1492 who had been allowed to settle in Jerusalem by Suleiman the Great, and of some three thousand Ashkenazim, poor stragglers from central Europe who came to lay their bones in Zion. Largely they were sunk in "hopeless pauperism," partly due to the local inhabitants' refusal to give them work and partly to a rabbinical dictatorship that chained them to the condition of a medieval ghetto. Against this obstacle the Finns, still dedicated to conversion, could make little headway. They were tactful. Mrs. Finn says she was careful to keep the Cross out of sight of the Jewish wet nurse whom she had for the children, for she "quite understood the feelings of our Jewish friends on the subject." How at the same time she could "fully believe and expect that some day Israel would fulfill the Divine conditions" is a paradox that I will not attempt to explain. Whatever the reasoning, it held them to the conviction, to use Mrs. Finn's words, "that this work will progress and that the Holy Land will again be peopled by its lawful owners, the Hebrew nation, and will again 'blossom as the rose.'"

And so they went ahead. They organized work projects, not only to give unemployed Jews paid labor, but also to make headway toward land reclamation. Land was rented for an irrigation project, though with pitiful results, for most of the beneficiaries were too weak to walk the mile to the field. An English surgeon, Mr. Sandford, one of the Finns' little band of helpers, made the discovery that the high mortality rate among the Jews was "chiefly due to want of food." And if they accepted work from the gentiles, they were disowned by the rabbis. Still the Finns persisted, and Mrs. Finn wrote constant letters home trying to enlist financial support from England. It was discouraging to find that few people at home could be convinced that "the Jews would work or that the Holy Land was worth cultivating."

Enough were found, however, to finance purchase of a tract of land, which they named Abraham's Vineyard; but not much was accomplished beyond temporary relief of the most destitute. Yet for years they persisted, and the Society for the Promotion of Jewish Agricultural Labor in the Holy Land, which they formed at this time, continued in existence under various names right up to the Mandate.

Consul Finn, as long as he was in Jerusalem, also kept up political activity on behalf of the Jews. In 1849 he induced the Foreign Office to grant him powers to take over protection of all Russian Jews in Palestine when the Russian government discarded them. He was always ready to make the Pasha enforce Jewish rights or to take up any case of persecution. Once he succeeded in getting a Turkish soldier publicly reprimanded and punished before the whole garrison for an offense committed against a poor Jew fourteen months before, which "greatly astonished the population." In 1857 he tried again to revive Shaftesbury's old plan and forwarded to the then foreign secretary, the Earl of Clarendon, a detailed scheme "to persuade Jews in a large body to settle here as agriculturists on the soil . . . in partnership with the Arab peasantry." As the word "persuade" indicates, the time was still not ripe, the necessary volition being not yet present among the Jews of Europe.

While it was in the making, one figure in England was also preparing for a role that was to bring the British Empire to the frontiers of Palestine. It has been said that there was no one apart from Lord Shaftesbury in a position to influence policy among the nineteenth-century advocates of Anglo-Israel dominion in Palestine. But there is one glittering exception. One of the most provocative figures in English history, the personage in question is of course Disraeli. Though he was unconnected with the restoration of Israel, it would be as absurd to leave him out of the story as to leave the ghost out of Hamlet. But in relation to it, as in his relation to his time and his country, he almost defies classification. Alone among eminent Victorians he was not primarily a religious man. Judaism he abandoned; Christianity, adopted for expediency, hardly touched him;

prophecy was nothing to him. Yet he felt the age-old pull of Palestine in his bones. He wrote passionately in *Alroy* of a revived kingdom of Israel; yet he never took a political step toward its modern achievement. He took no notice of the proposals of the Shaftesbury-Churchill school. He took no share in Montefiore's enterprises. He does not belong with the Jewish nationalists, because his nationalism was individual and unique. He was the trumpet of Israel's heritage, not of her destiny. He was concerned with the world's debt to the Jews, not with the Jews' future in the world.

"Where is your Christianity if you do not believe in their Judaism?" he asked the House in the debate on Jewish Emancipation. "On every altar . . . we find the table of Jewish law. . . . All the early Christians were Jews . . . every man in the early ages of the Church by whose power or zeal or genius the Christian faith was propagated, was a Jew. . . . If you had not forgotten what you owe to this people . . . you as Christians would be only too ready to seize the first opportunity of meeting the claims of those who profess this religion." He jeopardized his political career to make the speech. As a private member, dependent for advancement on the higher-ups in his party, he nevertheless, alone among the Tories, spoke for the Bill and each year when it came before the House crossed the floor to vote for it with the Liberals, against his own party.

Pride in his race and its heritage appears repeatedly in his novels, in prefaces to the later editions, in the famous chapter on the Jews that suddenly erupts in the midst of his political biography of Lord George Bentinck. "The world has by this time discovered that it is impossible to destroy the Jews . . . that it is in vain to attempt to baffle the inexorable laws of nature which have decreed that a superior race shall never be destroyed or absorbed by an inferior." Like Matthew Arnold, he believed that England's strength and purpose derived from the moral laws of the Hebrews transmitted through the Bible. England, he said, "despite her deficient and meagre theology has always re-membered Sion."

Ultimately it was not as a Jew at all, but as an empire builder, that he contributed to British progress toward Palestine. Even above the lure of Palestine he felt the lure of empire. Britain's eastward expansion in the latter nineteenth century was under his guidance, largely his doing. Long ago Richard the Lion-Heart had stopped off to take Cyprus on the way to the Holy Land. When Disraeli re-acquired it for Britain in 1878 he knew that the logistics of empire would bring the next advance to Palestine. His purchase of the Suez made that advance inevitable.

But in the 1840's all this was still a generation ahead and Disraeli still a junior M.P. known for his ornamental novels and for a certain uncomfortable power that left the House uneasily aware that the odd duckling in their midst would one day turn out to be an eagle. In 1831 he had been on a Byronic Eastern tour from Greece to Egypt, where every stopping place was a hall of ancient fame, every day's journey along an imperial pathway of the past. The Acropolis, the Pyramids, the roadsteads of Alexander and Caesar and Mahomet, the graves of the Crusaders, above all the tombs and ruined Temple of his race glowed like crown jewels in his mind. In Constantinople he had an audience with the Sultan, in Alexandria one with the Pasha, Mehemet Ali. From Cyprus he had sailed down the coast of Syria, past Beirut, Tyre, and Acre to Jaffa, and finally, "well mounted and well armed," he had ridden up through the desolate hills until "the city on which I gazed was JERUSALEM!"

The next days were among the most enraptured of his life. All the accumulated glories of the past, all the nostalgia of exiled centuries poured over him. He stayed only a week, but before he departed he had already begun to write a novel on "a gorgeous incident in the annals of that sacred and romantic people from whom I derive by blood and name"—that is, the Jewish rebellion led by the pseudo-

Messiah, David Alroy, "Prince of the Captivity," against
the Caliphate of Baghdad in the twelfth century. Disraeli's
heroes are often autobiographical in spots, and it is difficult not to see in *Alroy* an autobiographical reflection of
an inner dream.

"You ask me what I wish," says the Jewish sage, Alroy's
eminence grise: "My answer is, a national existence, which
we have not. You ask me what I wish: my answer is, the
Land of Promise. You ask me what I wish: my answer is
Jerusalem. You ask me what I wish: my answer is, the
Temple, all we have forfeited, all we have yearned after,
all we have fought for, our beauteous country, our holy
creed, our simple manners, and our ancient customs."

Disraeli wrote that speech with real feeling. In contrast
with the rest of *Alroy's* purple prose, decorated with silks
and scimitars, Afrites and Cabalists, fountains of quick-
silver and voluptuous princesses, it stands out starkly.
Alroy, its author once said cryptically, represented his
"ideal ambition." Indeed, it would be strange if the young
Disraeli, with his pride of race, his burning ambition,
standing amid the exalted surroundings where his ancestors had ruled, had *not* dreamed that he himself might be
destined to win back nationhood for his people.

If he did, the realities of English politics soon super-
vened. Four years later he entered Parliament determined
to be prime minister, nothing less. ("By God," said Lord
Melbourne, "the fellow will make it yet.") When next he
published an eastern novel, *Tancred*, it shows him on the
way to his goal, concerned no longer with a kingdom of
Israel, but with an empire for England. He had intended
Tancred as a novel of "Young England's" search for spiritual rebirth. The hero, a world-weary duke's son, has
shaken the dust of England from his boots and come to
Jerusalem to penetrate the "Asian mystery." But hero and
author soon forget all about that and become immersed in
the swirling politics of the Middle East and in the over-all
question of how England shall control the road to India.

The Syrian crisis was still fresh; the surging currents stirred up by Mehemet Ali's bid for a sovereign Arabian state had not been quieted by his defeat. Curiously enough, Disraeli sees England's opportunity in Arab rather than in Jewish nationalism. Half sardonically but with a foresight that is almost uncanny he pictures the possibilities.

Speaking through the mouth of Fakredeen, the emir of Lebanon, a wily, ambitious Syrian whose only religion is one "which gives me a sceptre," he says: "Let the Queen of the English collect a fleet . . . transfer the seat of her empire from London to Delhi. . . . In the meantime I will arrange with Mehemet Ali. He shall have Bagdad and Mesopotamia. . . . I will take care of Syria and Asia Minor. . . . We will acknowledge the Empress of India as our Sovereign and secure for her the Levantine coast. If she like she shall have Alexandria as she now has Malta; it could be arranged. Your Queen is young: she has *avenir*. . . ." Indeed she did. Thirty years later the author of *Tancred* officially added the title "Empress of India" to the Queen's other titles.

Tancred includes other startling glimpses into the future. Two comic characters are discussing world politics:

" 'Palmerston will never rest till he gets Jerusalem,' said Barizy of the Tower.

" 'The English must have markets,' said the Consul Pasqualigo.

" 'Very just,' said Barizy of the Tower, 'I think of doing a little myself in cottons.' " Disraeli was joking, of course— or was he? Farther on a Jew of Jerusalem tells Tancred: "The English will not do the business of the Turk again for nothing. They will take this city; they will keep it." The English public of 1847 may not have taken *Tancred* seriously, but history did.

CHAPTER XII

ENTER THE JEWS:

"If I am not for myself, who will be for me?"

So far the people of Israel had taken no active part in the gradual reopening of the path to Palestine. On the occasion of the first return from exile, when Persia was the intermediary power, they were ready as soon as King Cyrus gave the word, and they went back from Babylon forty thousand strong with their basins of gold, their vessels of silver, their servants and horses and camels and asses. But then they were near at hand, and the separation from Zion had lasted only fifty years. The second exile had lasted 1800 years, and its people were scattered over every latitude of the globe, dulled by the desperate effort simply to stay alive, *not* to be absorbed, not to lose their identity. They succeeded—the only people on earth ever to retain national identity without a national territory—but at grim cost. Survival was won only by turning inward, encasing themselves within a hard shell of orthodoxy, concentrating every thought on the only thing they could bring out of their country: its heritage and its code, the Torah and the Talmud, the Law. Other men could plow or build or fight. Without land, such occupations were closed to the Jews. What land could they seed and reap, or build on or fight for? When the Temple was pulled down, according to an old rabbinical legend, a splinter from its stones entered the heart of every Jew. That stone in their hearts was their only country.

But with changing times it was not to be enough. "Without a country," said Mazzini, the prophet of nineteenth-century nationalism, "you have neither name, voice nor rights nor admission as brothers into the fellowship of peoples. You are the bastards of humanity—Ishmaelites among the nations." He was addressing the Italians, not the Jews, but his cry was the spirit of the age, and the Jews began to hear it too.

Until 1800 the centuries had gone by in passive waiting for supernatural intervention. The prayer "Next year in Jerusalem" had marked the passing of each year since 70 A.D. like the dripping of water on a stone. But now it began to dawn on first one and then another that only their own hands on their own bootstraps would pull Israel out of exile. "The Jewish people must be their own Messiah," wrote the historian Heinrich Graetz in 1864. Many forces were at work in the nineteenth century to produce this revolutionary idea.

It is almost impossible to attempt even the briefest survey of the modern resurrection of the Jewish people without getting hopelessly mired in internal Jewish controversies and external European politics. Europe in the wake of the French Revolution brought the Jews into the period of the "Enlightenment" and emancipation, but also into a period of religious and social conflict that tore apart the unity of Judaism, so fiercely hugged over the centuries of imprisonment, only to be lost forever in the emerging struggle for freedom, citizenship, and finally statehood. The background is the history of Europe under Napoleon, then the reaction to the disappearance of Napoleon, the futile attempt by the Holy Alliance to clamp down autocracy, the revolutions of 1830 and '48, the rise of Nationalism, Liberalism, Socialism, the Commune in France, Bismarck and Pan-Germanism, the convulsions of Russia in the last stages of Czarist senility. All these forces acted upon the Jews as the spasms and contractions of labor pains, driving them into the painful process of rebirth as a nation.

The process begins with the "Enlightenment" initiated by Moses Mendelssohn in eighteenth-century Germany, which shattered the protective shell of orthodoxy and opened the way to acquaintance with Western culture and participation in Western affairs. The reign of the Talmud and the rabbis was broken. All over Europe the shuttered windows were flying open. Jews read Voltaire and Rousseau, Goethe and Kant. The Reform movement followed, shedding the old rituals, trying to adjust Judaism to the modern world. Civil Emancipation became the goal. In 1791 the French Constituent Assembly had decreed citizenship for the Jews; Napoleon confirmed it wherever he had dominions. Reaction rescinded it, and thereafter it had to be fought for separately in each country. Civil Emancipation was won around the middle of the nineteenth century, and if it had been a success, Judaism would have ended there. But it was not; and in the process of discovering why not, the Jews discovered nationalism. They became aware that Judaism was dying; on the one hand petrifying into a dry husk of rabbinical mumbo jumbo, and on the other dissolving in the open air of Western "enlightenment." If it were to be kept alive, it was in urgent need of a new soul. Nationalism provided it. From then on the movement toward Palestine slowly, hesitatingly, unhappily got under way, not out of enthusiasm but out of necessity. It was never a single movement along a straight line: it was an infinite splintering off of contradictory tendencies and groups: Reform against orthodoxy, nationalists against assimilationists, both against anti-Zionists, and, on the heels of all, the baying of the hound of anti-Semitism.

Political anti-Semitism was a creature of the nineteenth century. It rose like a black phoenix from the ashes of the

Napoleonic conquest, with Germany, it is no surpise to learn, as the scene. The "Hep! Hep!" that resounded through the streets of Heidelberg and Frankfort in 1819 to the accompaniment of riots and pillaging of Jewish homes went on down the century through the Damascus affair, through the May laws, the Pale and the pogroms of Russia, through the Dreyfus case to the ultimate holocaust of Hitler. Always it was pushing, pushing the Jews, some toward nationalism and Palestine, others toward escapism and assimilation.

This pressure was what proved enlightenment and emancipation illusory. Despite the nineteenth century's fervent and touching belief in Progress, anti-Semitism did not disappear. The orthodox had once believed that they had only to wait long enough and the Messiah would appear and miraculously restore them to Zion. The assimilationists now believed that they had only to wait long enough and that if they were quiet, well-mannered, and cultivated, if they bothered no one, anti-Semitism would inevitably disappear in a haze of Progress and the brotherhood of man. But somehow it didn't. Neither did it vanish before the magic wand of Marxism and the Socialist International. The Jews twisted and turned, seeking a solution in a dozen different directions, striving to be ordinary citizens of whatever country they lived in, yet still to be Jews; to find an escape for their persecuted brothers in the East, yet to keep their own hold on the measure of freedom and of the good life that they had found in the West. These pulls and tugs produced a tragic factionalism in Jewry unknown since the last days of the Temple, when Pharisees, Sadducees, and Zealots fought one another while the city fell about their ears. Divisions deepened, splinters multiplied, internal antipathies increased, hampering the effort toward nationhood as they hamper the nation today. But the baying of the hound kept the movement going. Herzl hearing it in enlightened France went home in agony of mind to write the *Judenstaat* and to call the Zionist Congress that was to launch "the vessel of the Jewish state upon its way." But fifty years earlier Moses Hess had heard it at Damascus.

Hess, like Herzl after him, was an "emancipated" Jew— one of the early German socialist leaders who thought of themselves as socialists first, Germans secondly, and Jews last if at all. Suddenly the Damascus affair hit him like an unexpected blow from behind. It showed that Jews could still be imprisoned and tortured and a whole community despoiled over a pretense dug up from medieval superstition. It spread a black shadow over every Jewish community from New York to Odessa. "Then it dawned upon me for the first time in the midst of my socialist activities," Hess wrote later, "that I belong to my unfortunate, slandered, despised and dispersed people . . . and I wanted to express my Jewish patriotic sentiment in a cry of anguish." But he was not content with anguish. He wanted a solution. There was only one. "Without a country . . . you are bastards of humanity"—Mazzini's yet unwritten dictum was already inescapable. Emancipation was emptiness. No matter how bitter the truth, it had to be spoken. In 1862 Hess published *Rome and Jerusalem,* subtitled *The Latest National Question.* "The hour has struck," he wrote, "for resettlement on the banks of the Jordan." Country was a necessity. "With the Jews, more than with other nations, which, though oppressed, yet live on their own soil, all political and social progress must necessarily be preceded by national independence. A common native soil is a primary condition. . . ."

But he knew what the Shaftesbury enthusiasts never asked: that his people were far from ready. The Jewish masses were still locked behind rabbinical shutters that must be broken open from within; the "progressive" Jews were hiding behind vain hopes that would only be shattered "by a blow from without, one which world events are already preparing." It was clear that "the main problem of the Jewish national movement is . . . how to awaken the

patriotic sentiment in the hearts of our progressive Jews
and how to liberate the Jewish masses by means of this
patriotism from a spirit-deadening formalism." Only when
this is achieved will "the restoration of the Jewish state
find us ready for it."

Hess went on from there to outline plans for colonizing
Palestine. He hoped for the support of the powers in pur-
chasing the Holy Land from the bankrupt Porte; but it
was France in particular, where he was then living and
where Louis Napoleon was already hungering after dominion in Syria, that he thought of as the intermediary
power. With French support he foresaw colonies "extending from Egypt to Jerusalem and from the Jordan to the
Mediterranean."

While Hess was working out his solution a very different type of Jew was coming to the same point independently. Rabbi Hirsch Kalischer of Thorn in Prussia, an admired scholar of the old school, suddenly announced from
the pinnacle of his Talmudic authority the doctrine of self-
help. "Let no one imagine," he wrote in 1860, "that the
Redemption of Israel and the Messiah will suddenly appear from heaven and that amid miracles and wonders he
will gather the Israelites of the Diaspora to their ancient
inheritance. The beginning of the Redemption will take
place in a natural way by the desire of the Jews to settle in
Palestine and the willingness of the nations to help them
in their work."

In the same year he assembled a conference of rabbis
and community leaders at Thorn to promote revival work
in Palestine. Although little physical progress was made,
Kalischer's *Quest of Zion*, like yeast in a lump of dough,
began to take effect. Other orthodox rabbis joined in the
new attitude toward the Return, and through his disciples
and associates Kalischer's ideas began to penetrate the
shadowy life inside the Pale. Only the Jews' own efforts on
the desiccated soil of Palestine, he taught, would make
possible the final Redemption. He wanted Jewish soldiers

to guard Jewish settlers. He had no great belief in the benevolence of the Western powers. He preferred help from his own kind. He wrote letters to Montefiore and the Rothschilds urging them to finance colonization societies, to buy land, transport immigrants, settle those who knew farming on free tracts of land, employ teachers to train the others, make loans until the settlements became self-supporting, establish a police system, a military guard, an agricultural training institute.

A beginning on this pattern was made by the *Alliance Universelle Israelite,* founded that same year, 1860, in Paris. It was the first of the welfare and protective societies subsequently formed in the other Western capitals. Their philosophy was paternalistic, not patriotic in the sense that Hess and later Herzl demanded. Patriotism was a new idea—or at least one so long dead that it was hard to revive —and it took a long time to catch hold; but philanthropy or, more exactly, community responsibility for the needy had been a continuing tradition of Israel as old as the tribe. It now began to work in the direction of Palestine. Montefiore, working alone, had already made three trips there before the days of railroad and steamship and was to make seven altogether before he died, the last at the age of ninety. Whenever and wherever misfortune or persecution fell upon a Jewish community the old "Prince of Israel" would set off, to Constantinople at the age of seventy-nine, to Morocco and Spain at eighty, to Rumania at eighty-three, to Moscow at eighty-eight. Neither distance nor plague nor rioting mobs dismayed him, neither snows nor desert. But no matter how grand the gesture or how revered the person, by himself he could accomplish little of lasting effect. Damascus, however, and similar instances repeated elsewhere, had by now awakened the collective conscience of the emancipated Jews of the West. As far as Palestine was concerned their object was as limited as possible: to provide a refuge for the persecuted Jews, not for themselves.

The *Alliance* established an agricultural training school near Jaffa in 1870. And meanwhile a trickle of colonists was beginning to come out from Russia, where colonization societies were springing up under the influence of writers inspired by the ideas of Hess and Kalischer. In Vienna a periodical, *Ha Shahar* (The Dawn), was the organ of these new voices. Its editor, Perez Smolenskin, published a book in 1873, *The Eternal People,* that had great effect among the Eastern Jews. It ridiculed the pet theory of the assimilationists that Israel survived only as a religion and insisted that the Jews were a living people. Its text, taken from *Ecclesiastes,* "A living dog is better than a dead lion," has since been used over and over to express the cleavage between nationalists and assimilationists. In the same year Moses Lilienblum, another contributor to *Ha Shahar,* wrote his *Rebirth of the Jewish People in the Land of its Ancestors;* and other voices in Russia, Poland, Germany, Austria, France, and Italy picked up the theme. Books, articles, and periodicals in Hebrew sprouted in Eastern Europe in the seventies. They indulged the Jewish passion for controversy, but they were dedicated in the main to the colonization of Palestine as a basis for the regeneration of Judaism.

They set people to thinking, but not yet to moving. The baying of the hound did that. Now it burst into the shrill chorus of yelps that precedes the kill. In Germany in the late seventies polemical anti-Semitism had been raging in party politics and the press, indulging the pseudoscientific theories in which the German mentality delights to wallow. Bismarck showed how it could be used to political advantage. In Easter week of 1881 in Russia the lesson was put into practice, and there began the modern era of political anti-Semitism in the form of conscious national policy instigated and fostered by the state. Within three days all of Western Russia from the Black Sea to the Baltic was smoking with the ruins of Jewish homes (to use the graphic words of Lucien Wolf). From Warsaw to Kiev to Odessa, through one hundred and sixty small villages, a mass savagery on a scale and to a degree of brutality unknown since the Middle Ages exploded upon the Jews and echoed around the world through the horrified reports of foreign envoys and journalists. Hitler added the concentration camp and the gas chamber, but otherwise he invented nothing. It had all been done before in Czarist Russia. Even the Nürnberg Laws had their prototype in the May Laws of 1882, which deliberately intended to make the Jews' lives untenable, snatched homes and livelihood away, set whole villages to wandering, destroyed their already precarious economy, and constituted under the name of "Temporary Orders" a permanent pogrom.

The reasoning behind the outbreaks was the same as the Nazis': to use the Jews in the classic role of scapegoat, to create a diversion from oncoming disaster, to draw off mass discontent from the governing class.

In the course of two years, 1881–82, the great majority of Jews in Russia learned what it took the Jews of Western Europe nearly a hundred years to learn: that emancipation would be illusory as long as it did not have the dignity of statehood to back it up. They came more quickly to nationalism because, not having won emancipation or committed themselves to assimilation, they had no cherished illusion that they could not bear to give up. They were not haunted by the specter of "double loyalty": after the massacres and edicts and the mobs, what loyalty to Russia was left?

As Damascus called forth Hess, the 1881 pogroms called forth the famous pamphlet *Auto-Emancipation* by the Odessa physician Doctor Leo Pinsker. He sounded his call in the words of Rabbi Hillel, Judaism's last great teacher before the fall of the Temple: "If I am not for myself who will be for me?" The Jews must emancipate themselves, Pinsker proclaimed. "We must re-establish ourselves as a living nation." For long the Jews have lacked the desire to become a nation as a sick man lacks appetite, but the desire must be created. Without it they will remain a ghost people, ghosts of a dead nation walking alive among the living. The Jew is the eternal foreigner. Other foreigners always have a country somewhere that claims their patriotism. Only the Jews have not, and without it they remain aliens everywhere. "What a contemptible role for a people that once had its Maccabees!" There is no use complaining of anti-Semitism; it will go on as long as the Jew remains a ghost and an alien. "There is something unnatural about a people without a territory just as there is about a man without a shadow."

Pinsker urged that the existing Jewish societies call a national congress that should form a stock company to purchase land and organize the emigration and resettlement. He believed that the leaders of the movement must come from among the Western Jews who had the power, the money, the knowledge of affairs, although he did not expect them to join in the emigration. They were comfortable where they were and would stay there. Mass support would come from Russia and Poland, but no leaders: the environment could not produce them.

The leaders Pinsker hoped for were not yet ready, but the rank and file were stirring, and among them his efforts took effect. He called a conference at Kattowitz, near Cracow in Poland, and it convened on Montefiore's hundredth birthday in 1884. It failed to produce a national congress, but something less was formed, an association for colonization in Palestine, of which Pinsker was named president. Later known from its headquarters as the Odessa Committee, it began the real work of gathering recruits for the Return. The workers called themselves Chovevé Zion (Lovers of Zion). Their meetings, proscribed by the police, were held by candlelight in little villages throughout the Pale. Students tramped the muddy roads distributing leaflets. At last the uprooting and the trek began. Little groups of settlers who had never cleared a field or ploughed a furrow were given the terrible labor of beginning the revival of a long-dead nation on the half-dead soil of Palestine.

As yet it was not a national movement. Herzl was still in his twenties, a dandy of the Viennese salons, writing graceful *feuilletons* and toying with the theater. He never read Pinsker. Others among the emancipated Jews who did read him resented and resisted the idea of a nation and a country. "It is a joke . . . you are feverish, you need a medicine," said Dr. Adolf Jellinek, a famous Jewish scholar of Vienna when Pinsker went to see him. Jellinek recorded the conversation:

"I don't see any other solution," said Pinsker.

"But progress, civilization! Russia cannot forever remain as reactionary as it is!" Jellinek pleaded.

That was what they wanted to believe: that anti-Semitism was a phase. Progress would banish it in the end. Take care of its victims in the meanwhile. No radical solution was necessary.

Help from the West came, but no leadership. The grand dukes of Jewry would finance anything except political action. Baron de Hirsch tried to direct a mass emigration to the Argentine. Baron Edmond de Rothschild, almost alone among the Westerners, helped the infant settlements in Palestine. That they were able to gain a toehold at all and hold on to it was due to his support. He was regarded, for his pains, as an eccentric if not worse. The revival of Palestine at that time aroused no enthusiasm in the emancipated community. "With one alone it was a passion," President Weizmann wrote later in his autobiography, "and that was Baron Edmond of Paris. A dozen men of his stamp and his capacity to help would have changed the history of Palestine and would have overcome completely the handicap of the anti-Zionist Jews and the hesitancies and oppositions in the non-Jewish world. We did not get them."

For the moment we must stop in the eighties, for the real launching of the Zionist movement belongs to another

era, and meanwhile England was slowly developing toward
the future role of intermediary power. Emancipation had
been a reciprocal process, acquainting the Jews with the
culture of the West and beginning to make the West acquainted with the modern representatives of "God's ancient
people." Lessing's *Nathan der Weise* was modeled on his
friend Mendelssohn. Byron's *Hebrew Melodies* fix on the
fatal lack of country half a century before Hess:

> The wild dove hath her nest, the fox his cave,
> Mankind their country – Israel but the grave!

Byron, who died in the fight for Greek independence, was
the champion of the generation that rebelled against tyranny of the Holy Alliance. He plucked the spirit of nationalism from the air and put it into verse. Mazzini in jail
had three books with him, Tacitus, the Bible, and Byron.
Nowhere else does the bell of liberty, the knell of the tyrant
ring so loud and clear as in "The Destruction of Sennache-
rib," best-known of the *Hebrew Melodies*. Nor was it merely
a poetic rendering of heroic moments from the Old Testament. Byron seems somehow to have caught the still living
spirit of Judaism, the pride that Disraeli was to express,
the scorn of the gentile: "Live on in thy faith, but in mine
I will die."

There is the same spirit in Tom Moore's lines:

> Sound the loud timbrel o'er Egypt's dark sea!
> Jehovah hath triumphed! His people are free!

And Scott put it into Rebecca, who runs away with *Ivanhoe*
though Rowena gets the man.* How Rebecca thrilled the
avid public of the Waverley novels when she jumped to
the parapet and defied the villainous Bois-Guilbert to take
another step! And when she laments her people's submission to their fate and regrets that "the sound of the trumpet
wakes Judah no longer" she is expressing the nationalism

*Scott felt obliged to explain in later editions that he was forced
to let Ivanhoe marry Rowena rather than Rebecca for the sake of
historic verisimilitude.

of Scott's and Byron's generation, which was to reach the modern Jews several decades later.

When it did reach them it found an echo again in Victorian England as on the Continent. In France Dumas fils, the most popular playwright of his time, turned from love and consumption among the demimonde in *La Dame aux camélias* to, of all things, Jewish nationalism in *La Femme du Claude*. "The fixed territorial fatherland is again necessary to us," announces the hero of this play written in 1873. In England a year later George Eliot turned to the "latest national question," as Hess had called it, for the theme of one half of her peculiarly schizoid novel *Daniel Deronda* (1876). Its hero has hardly discovered his Jewish ancestry before he becomes overnight an ardent advocate of nationhood. "The idea that I am possessed with," he says, "is that of restoring a political existence to my people, making them a nation again, giving them a national centre." Like all the productions of non-Jewish enthusiasts for the Return, Daniel never hesitates a moment over the problems that so harassed actual Jews—assimilation, anti-Semitism, Judaism as religion or as nationality, living dog or dead lion. The problem of reviving the desire for nationality never occurs to them, any more than the economics of the business—the actual physical process of getting to Palestine, of acquiring land, of making a living. They skip over all that to plunge at one stride into Palestine, where a revived Israel will emerge full grown like Athena. "Revive the organic centre," exhorts Mordecai, Daniel's inspirer, "look toward a land and a policy . . . a national life which has a voice among the peoples. . . . Redeem the soil, set up a standard . . . the world will gain as Israel gains . . . a new Judea poised between East and West, a covenant of reconciliation."

George Eliot, like Shaftesbury and his followers, was taken with the idea, which seems so ironic today, that the new state would be a pacifying factor in the Middle East; as Mordecai says in the novel, "a neutral ground for the enmities of the East as Belgium is for the West." In fact, her debt to Shaftesbury, though unacknowledged, must be considered. Her early years were hotly evangelical, and the favorite cause of the evangelical leaders can hardly have escaped her notice. Direct inspiration of the novel, however, came from her husband, George Lewes, who during a residence in Paris had been an intimate friend of Moses Hess.

Daniel Deronda, unlike Rebecca, conspicuously fails to run away with the novel. He is a wooden creature, far too noble and good for human nature's daily food. George Eliot's readers were much more interested in the marital adventures of the gorgeous Gwendolyn, whom Daniel ultimately rejects in favor of the Holy Land. On the whole the book did not impress the critics. Sir Leslie Stephen for one considered Daniel's goal of restoring nationality to his people as "chimerical," and the author's choice of theme struck him as "showing a defective sense of humor." If the book fails to come off by literary standards, it nevertheless had immense effect on the Jewish national movement. Lucien Wolf probably overrates its effect when he says that the book gave the movement "the strongest stimulus it had experienced since the appearance of Sabbatai Zevi." Yet the American poet Emma Lazarus, when she adopted the cause of Jewish nationalism in 1883, referred to it as "the idea formulated by George Eliot," as if it had originated with her.

Though Daniel and the consumptive Mordecai remain mock figures, George Eliot was in earnest. She developed the idea that was to play a role in Balfour's thinking,* of the necessity of requiting a moral debt owed to the Jews. She was disgusted, she wrote to Harriet Beecher Stowe, to find educated people who "hardly know that Christ was a Jew" or who suppose that he spoke Greek. "A whole Chris-

*Balfour incidentally was among the undergraduates at Trinity College who met George Eliot on her visit to Cambridge in search of material for her studies of Deronda and his friends.

238 / BIBLE AND SWORD

tian is three-quarters a Jew," she says in the novel. But she
finds little recognition of the debt among average Englishmen, who regard Judaism as "a sort of eccentric fossilized
form . . . something (no matter exactly what) that ought
to have been entirely otherwise." She deliberately chose
the theme of *Daniel Deronda* in a conscientious effort to
improve the status of Jews vis-à-vis the English; and in a
later article, "The Modern Hep Hep," she hits upon the
essential fact that only nationhood will solve the problem
of the dispersion. The world needs "Some new Ezras, some
modern Maccabees, who will know how to use all favoring
outward conditions, how to triumph over the indifference
of their fellows and the scorn of their foes and will stead-
fastly set their faces toward making their people once more
one among nations."

CHAPTER XIII

THE RUSH FOR THE HOLY LAND

In 1862 the Prince of Wales, the future Edward VII, made a tour of the Holy Land, the first heir to the British throne to set foot in Palestine since the crusade of Edward I in 1270. He came in the same year that Moses Hess proclaimed that "the hour had struck" for the revival of the Jewish nation. The two events were of course totally unconnected, but they are evidence that history was propelling the convergence of the Exiles and the Intermediary Power. Edward's tour, which included a visit to the Mosque at Hebron, where the Patriarchs' tombs had been taken over as a Moslem holy place, broke the barrier against Christians' entering the sanctuaries and "may be said to have opened the whole of Syria to Christian research." These are the words of the prospectus issued by the Palestine Exploration Fund, which, founded three years after the Prince's tour, opened the Holy Land both to modern archaeology and to modern mapping and surveying.

Nothing could be more typically English than the dualism of the work of the Palestine Exploration Fund—undertaken for the sake of Biblical research, it was carried out by army officers designated by the War Office. Colonel Conder, the most notable of the field workers, was said to have contributed more to knowledge of the Bible than anyone since Tyndale translated it; his maps meanwhile were published by Army Ordnance — maps used by General Allenby, the victor of Jerusalem in 1918. Here are Bible and Sword working together unmistakably. In fact, Colonel

Conder is a sort of epitome of British experience in Palestine, always a double thing composed of Biblical nostalgia and imperial thrust. It was like a print of a twice-exposed negative — two pictures discernible but impossible to separate.

Inevitably the Palestine Exploration Fund field workers, as over years of search and excavation they gradually uncovered the true shape of Palestine's highly civilized past, became themselves caught up in the prospects for the country's future. Conder concluded rightly that little effort toward the revival of Palestine could be expected from the local Jews, who were "still bound by the iron chain of Talmudic law, a people . . . whose veneration for the past appears to preclude the possibility of progress or improvement in the present." The urge and the man power would come from the Jews of Eastern Europe; if they could survive under the czars, he said, they could survive and prosper under the Sultan. His companion officer, Sir Charles Warren, veteran of many Exploration Fund expeditions, went further and proposed that Palestine be developed by the East India Company with "the avowed intention of gradually introducing the Jews pure and simple who would eventually occupy and govern the country." He called his book *The Land of Promise* and maintained that with good government and increased commerce the population could increase tenfold, and "yet there is room." Productiveness of the land, he predicted, "will increase in proportion to the labor bestowed upon the soil, until a population of fifteen million may be accommodated there." Warren's book appeared in 1875, while George Eliot was writing *Daniel Deronda* and in Vienna the *Ha-Shahar* group were calling for the rebirth of their nation.

But the mainspring of England's interest was still Biblical, though in a very different form from Shaftesbury's; indeed, in direct opposition to it. "Saucy rationalism" had by now triumphed over Evangelicalism, but to the accompaniment of such furious controversy as made the Bible a

fighting document and the Holy Land an arena as embattled as the Roman forum. The champions of rationalism, determined to prove the Bible as history, went charging out to the Holy Land both literally and figuratively, to
uncover the necessary evidence. Since they rejected the
Bible as revelation and therefore as infallible, they rejected prophecy, too; but the basis for the restoration of
Israel was not carried away by this new wave, for in the
course of their investigations into the past they rediscovered the Jews as a people and as a nation. An early herald
of the Higher Criticism was the Reverend Henry Hart Milman's *History of the Jews* (not, be it noted, history of the
Hebrews or Israelites or "God's ancient people"), and the
howl that arose when he was found to have called Abraham a sheik was stupendous. Milman died as Dean of St.
Paul's, famous and respected, but when his book first appeared in 1829 it was regarded almost as a national insult.

The recovered factual history of the Jews, Milman held,
was not sacred ground, exempt from scientific treatment
because of its connection with divine revelation: on the
contrary, it was "part of the world's history." The functions
that the Jews have performed, he said, in the progress of
human development and civilization "are so important, so
enduring" that it becomes the duty of the Christian historian to investigate their history as the only safe way to
attain the highest religious truth. The ancient Hebrews
were human beings, spoke with human voices, heard with
human ears, and in short (to lead the reader at full tilt
into the famous sentence) "Abraham, excepting in his
worship and intercourse with the one true God, was a
nomad sheik." And hard upon that, another blow: the part-
ing of the waters of the Red Sea was no more a miracle
than the storm that came up in the Channel to destroy the
Spanish Armada at precisely the right moment.

Coleridge, in the same vein, had discovered Jesus to be
a "platonic philosopher." Fresh from his studies in Göttin-
gen, where historical criticism of the Bible was marching

sternly on with the heavy tread of German scholarship, he pronounced worship of Biblical infallibility to be "if possible still more extravagant than that of papal infallibility." Through his essays and table talk he immensely stimulated the new spirit of investigation. Churchmen began to worry, and when in 1832 the First Reform Bill marked the triumph of Liberalism they became thoroughly frightened. A Liberal climate was not considered healthy for ecclesiastical authority. In response, the Oxford movement was launched in 1833 in a desperate effort to strengthen, by a renewed emphasis on faith, the defenses of revealed religion against the onrushing forces of rationalism. Keble preached his famous Assize sermon, and in the same year he and Newman and Pusey issued the first of the *Tracts for the Times*. What passion and erudition were poured out over such vexed questions as the authorship of the Pentateuch, the validity of the Book of Daniel, the moral attitude to be adopted toward the all too human behavior of David at his worst or Jacob at his most conniving! Newman regarded anyone who raised such questions as a heretic; Keble decided that only very wicked persons could engage in inquiries that undermined the divinity of Scripture; Pusey even went to Germany to study the historical method, the better to combat it, and on being appointed Regius Professor of Hebrew at Oxford gave nine lectures a week to teach divinity students a full idiomatic knowledge of the language of the Old Testament for the better understanding of God's word.

But in the long run it was all of no use. The Tractarians were essentially reactionary, *against* rather than for the times, and the times prevailed over the Tracts. Newman's surrender to Catholicism in 1845 (followed by Manning's) was the logical outcome. Infallible authority was to him necessary for faith, and when the Bible no longer possessed it Rome became the only refuge. Keble and Pusey struggled on, striving to keep adherents of the Oxford movement from following Newman over the edge. Even as late as 1860 two of the seven authors of *Essays and Reviews*, the famous counterblast of the rationalists, were actually tried for heresy. Their acquittal by the Privy Council in 1864, after years of fuming and fulminating on all sides, marked the doom of the old order—of the authority that had reigned with the Puritans, was revived by the Evangelicals, and uttered its swan song in the Oxford movement.

Now the rationalists galloped with the bit in their teeth, and their road led to Palestine and to a new understanding of Judaism as the human source of Christianity. Dean Stanley, the leading liberal theologian of his age, began his course in Church history at Oxford with "the call of Abraham." Inevitably he sought out the spot itself, and after a two-year tour of the Holy Land he published his *Sinai and Palestine* (1857). Palestine, he wrote, was the "scene of the most important events in the history of mankind." Here the word of God came directly to the Jewish people, and here alone could be studied the surroundings that formed the character "of the most remarkable nation which has appeared on earth." Here where the traveler recognizes the wild broom of the desert as the shrub under which Elijah slept, where he stands on Pisgah and sees the view that Moses saw, where at every hand he finds the local features that "have become the household imagery of Christendom," here indeed are to be found the evidences that prove the flesh-and-blood reality of the Bible.

Dean Stanley returned to Palestine as chaplain and guide to Prince Edward during the royal tour in 1862. His passion for historic origins was rewarded when permission was at last arranged for the party to visit the Tomb of the Patriarchs at Hebron, which no European had entered since 1187. "There was a deep groan from the attendants when the shrine of Abraham was opened, redoubled at the shrine of Jacob and Joseph.* You may imagine my feelings

* Presumably Dean Stanley meant Isaac and Jacob; Joseph's tomb is not at Hebron.

when I thrust my arm down as far as I could reach into the rocky vault, and when I knelt down to ascertain how far the tomb of Abraham was part of the native mountain." The Prince, on being thanked by Stanley for making the visit possible, replied: "Well, high station, you see, has, after all, some merits."

Three years later Stanley's *History of the Jewish Church* explored and further uncovered the Jewish roots of Christianity; and the subject was pursued by W. R. Smith, who wrote the article on the Bible for the famous ninth edition of the Encyclopaedia Britannica, of which he was the editor. He expanded the historical method in his books *The Old Testament in the Jewish Church* and *The Prophets of Israel*. Meantime Dean Stanley's friend and Oxford colleague, the great Jowett, one of the contributors to *Essays and Reviews*, was also presenting the Jewish prophets as our civilization's "schoolmasters." "They taught men the true nature of God, that he was a God of love as well as of justice, the Father as well as the judge of mankind." We owe our intellectual framework to the Greek philosophers, said Jowett, and our moral feelings to the Jewish prophets.

If this sounds like Matthew Arnold, the likeness is not accidental. He too was a professor (of poetry) at Oxford in the exciting sixties; and here, with Jowett, Regius Professor of Greek, on his left and Pusey, Regius Professor of Hebrew, on his right and the air crackling with the feud between the two champions, it is no wonder that Arnold developed his thesis stated in "Hebraism and Hellenism," the "two points between which our world turns." He brought to the surface a conscious recognition of the Hebraic content in English culture and followed Milman and Stanley in treating Christianity as "modified Hebraism." All of Victorian England's religious obsession and the intellectual battle that it provoked are contained in Arnold's books that followed one another rapidly in the next five years: *St. Paul and Protestantism, Literature and Dogma* (which he subtitled *An Essay towards a Better*

Apprehension of the Bible); and lastly *God and the Bible,* in rebuttal to critics of the previous book.

There was heard, too, the loud voice of that passionate apostle of rationalism, Lecky, whose hatred of dogmatic theology led him to admire all its victims, especially the Jews. Writing of the Inquisition, he says: "Certainly the heroism of every other creed fades into insignificance before this martyr people, who for thirteen centuries confronted all the evils that the fiercest fanaticism could devise, enduring the infliction of the most hideous sufferings rather than abandon their faith. . . . Persecution came to the Jewish nation in its most horrible forms . . . but above all this the genius of that wonderful people rose supreme." Lecky's prose rises to heights of enthusiasm as he portrays the Jews pursuing the path of knowledge, keeping alive the torch of Greek Learning through the Arabic conquest till it could be relit in Europe, while the intellect of Christendom was "grovelling in the darkness of besotted ignorance" and occupied with "juggling miracles and lying relics." There was nothing palely "objective" about the great nineteenth-century historians; when they espoused a point of view they pulled no punches.

Lecky's *History of Rationalism* appeared in 1865, the same year as Stanley's *Jewish Church,* and in that same year the Palestine Exploration Fund was founded, the direct outcome of the new flesh-and-blood approach to the Holy Land. Remember that, only the year before, the judges had decided in the heresy case that it was not penal under the law for a clergyman to affirm that authorship of the books of the Bible was human, not divine. The dikes were down. To recover the real past and the real people of the Book was the task the P.E.F. set itself. Not only Palestine's archaeology, but also its topography, meteorology, botany, zoology, and every other -ology was to be, said the P.E.F.'s prospectus, within its scope. It sternly announced, in asking for funds, that it would be bound by three guiding principles: field work was to be carried out on scien-

tific principles, the Fund was to abstain from religious controversy, and it was not to be conducted as a religious society. Oxford University, naturally, led the list of donors
with £500, Cambridge £250, the Syria Improvement Committee £250, the Queen £150, and the Grand Lodge of
Freemasons £105.

Curiously enough, although the P.E.F. was founded in
the spirit of rationalist investigation, its original impulse
came from the evangelical Finns and their friends in Jerusalem. They had founded a Jerusalem Literary Society for
the study of local "antiquities," and it had rapidly become
the center for all the Biblical historiographers who came
in those years, like a pack of excited bird dogs, to flush the
relics of the far-off time when "the documents of our faith
were written." Local members of the Society went on exca-
vating trips and dug up enough artifacts to start a little
museum. A library of a thousand volumes was collected.
The Archbishop of Canterbury became a patron. The
Prince Consort sent £25. Learned foreigners and distinguished archaeologists become corresponding members.
Prominent visitors — Ernest Renan, Holman Hunt, Dean
Stanley, de Lesseps, Layard the discoverer of Nineveh—
came to its meetings.

As a result of all this bustling and digging the true im-
mensity of Palestine's past and the size of the task necessary to uncover it began to be understood. Concerted and
professional effort must replace the enthusiastic amateur.

In 1864 the War Office was persuaded to appoint an
officer of engineers (without however, paying his expenses) to begin a survey of Jerusalem and its vicinity.
Sir Charles Wilson volunteered, and the results of his work
(which included a plotting of the difference in levels between the Mediterranean and the Dead Sea) constituted
the first publication of the P.E.F., organized in the following year. Wilson went again to survey the Beirut and
Hebron area, and many years later, after a military career
that included command of the expedition that failed to

rescue General Gordon in the Sudan, he returned to Palestine in 1899 and 1903 to locate the controversial sites of Golgotha and the Holy Sepulcher.

After Wilson the P.E.F. sent out Sir Charles Warren, whose researches led him to the conclusion, already quoted from his *Land of Promise,* that Palestine could again be the productive land it had been of old. In 1872 the basic and most extensive work of surveying was begun by two officers of the Royal Engineers in their twenties, Lieutenant Claude Conder and one destined to greater world fame in another sphere, Lieutenant Kitchener. Kitchener surveyed Eastern Palestine; Conder took the territory west of the Jordan and in three years mapped an area of 4,700 square miles. He located the previously unknown sites of a hundred and fifty Biblical place names, plotted the boundaries of the Twelve Tribes, traced the routes of armies and migrations, and deciphered ancient inscriptions. For two years more, back in England, he and Kitchener worked together preparing their material for publication. The historical findings were issued in seven volumes of *Memoirs* by the P.E.F., beginning in 1880; the maps were printed by the Ordnance Survey Office. Conder published his own account, *Tent Work in Palestine,* illustrated with his own drawings, and went back again and again to the Holy Land. The rest of his life, between tours of military duty in Egypt and South Africa, he devoted to bringing into the light the lost history of the land and its people. In 1882 he was chosen to guide Prince George, later George V, on a Holy Land tour, as Dean Stanley had guided Edward twenty years earlier.

His erudition was enormous, his mind searching and original, his interests limitless, his prose lively. He could speak and write Hebrew and Arabic and was expert in ancient cuneiform. He translated the Tel-Amarna tablets, the primary source material for pre-Hebraic Palestine. He could trace the history of every place he visited from the Crusades back through to the Bible, peeling off Moslem,

Byzantine, Roman, and Assyrian layers one by one. He could write with authority on geology, archaeology, philology, medicine, agriculture, art, architecture, literature, and theology. Unconcerned with proving or disproving doctrinal dogmas, he loved to dig down to the history beneath the religious façade. Instead of bowing before the Church of the Holy Sepulcher he called it that "grim and wicked old building," cause of more human misery and spilling of blood than any other edifice in the world. Short of a whole chapter on Conder, the best résumé of his work can be gained just from listing the titles of some of his works: *Judas Maccabaeus and the Jewish War of Independence* (1879), *Primer of Bible Geography* (1883), *Syrian Stone Lore* (1886), *The Canaanites* (1887), *Palestine* (1891), *The Bible in the East* (1896), *The Latin Kingdom of Jerusalem* (1897), *The Hittites and their Language* (1898), *The Hebrew Tragedy* (1900), and *The City of Jerusalem* (1909) the year before he died.

Besides all this he helped Sir Charles Wilson gather and edit material for the Palestine Pilgrims Text Society, an offshoot of the P.E.F. Early accounts of Palestine by pilgrims from all lands from the fourth century to the fifteenth were translated and, after eleven years' work, eventually published in a twelve-volume series.

Conder, when he wrote on the prospects for the regeneration of Palestine through Jewish colonization, brought to the subject the practical common sense of a man who knew the ground. His flat statement that "there is not a mile of made road in the land from Dan to Beersheba" is enough in itself to reveal the awful extent of the task that would be required to make Palestine livable again. Roads, said Conder, to allow transport by wheeled vehicles were the first necessity. Irrigation and swamp drainage, restoration of aqueducts and cisterns, sanitation, seeding of grass and reforestation to check soil erosion were all, he pointed out, essential to a colonization program.

Until the work of the Palestine Exploration Fund began

to be published there were few practical people who
thought the land could be revived at all. It was the great
contribution of the P.E.F. (apart from its historical findings) to show that Palestine had once been habitable by
a much larger population and a more advanced civilization than was commonly supposed and therefore could be
again. When the work started the common picture of Palestine was of a deserted tract left to the desolation predicted by Isaiah, "an habitation of dragons and a court for
owls." The infertile ground left the impression that even
in Biblical times the land had been an obscure, unproduc-
tive country inhabited by simple people of simple pursuits.
But gradually the true grandeur of the past hidden beneath
the surface was scraped out. Outlines of old cities, of temples and vineyards, kingdoms and thoroughfares, markets
and bazaars emerged, and a civilization, "with its settled
institutions, priests, kings, magistrates, schools, literature
and poets," was revealed. Fields of grain had once covered
the plains, and even the Negeb had supported, in Byzantine times, six towns of from 5,000 to 10,000 population,
with many smaller settlements in between. The country
was not under a curse, the archaeologists found. It had
reverted to the nomad and gone to decay for a simpler
reason: lack of cultivation. The Arab conquest had swept
out the last of Byzantine civilization "as a locust swarm
devastates a corn-field," leaving the land to Bedouins and
goats.

The implications of the P.E.F.'s work could not escape
Palestine's venerable champion, and the P.E.F. itself did
not long escape Lord Shaftesbury. Ten years after its
founding he became, inevitably, its president. And here in
the closing years of his life he could still expound more
eloquently than anyone else the hope of Israel. "Let us not
delay," he told the Fund in his opening address, "to send
out the best agents . . . to search the length and breadth of
Palestine, to survey the land, and if possible to go over
every corner of it, drain it, measure it, and, if you will,

prepare it for the return of its ancient possessors, for I must believe that the time cannot be far off before that great event will come to pass. . . .

"I recollect speaking to Lord Aberdeen when he was prime minister, on the subject of the Holy Land; and he said to me, 'If the Holy Land should pass out of the hands of the Turks, into whose hands should it fall?' 'Why,' my reply was ready, 'Not into the hands of other powers, but let it return into the hands of the Israelites.' "

Lord Shaftesbury was perfectly aware that he did not have the full sympathy of his audience, many of whom were interested more in Israel's past than in its future. (One in the audience was the famous and erratic Captain Burton, Arabian explorer and translator of the *Arabian Nights*, whose views on the Jews were distinctly unfriendly. Speaking after Lord Shaftesbury, he made the point, fairly taken, unfortunately, that the "Israelites of Europe" were not going to prove too ready "to unloose their purse strings for the benefit of Judea.") But Shaftesbury, evangelical to the last, refused to be intimidated by scientists and archaeologists. All over England, he told them, were people like himself, animated by "a burning affection for that land" [Palestine]; its revival should be a goal equal in importance to the recovery of its past; and on this question he concluded: "My old age is not much tamer than my early life."

Tamer he certainly was not. In 1876, nearly forty years after his first article on the subject in the *Quarterly Review*, he wrote another that reveals how much, for all his still fervent Evangelicalism, he had learned from the rise of Jewish nationalism in the intervening years. It is perhaps the classic expression of England's role in the revival of Palestine:

"Syria and Palestine will ere long become most important. The old time will come back . . . the country wants capital and population. The Jew can give it both. And has not England a special interest in promoting such a restora-

tion? . . . She must preserve Syria to herself. Does not policy then—if that were all—exhort England to foster the
nationality of the Jews and aid them, as opportunity may
offer, to return as a leavening power to their old country?
England is the great trading and maritime power of the
world. To England, then, naturally belongs the role of
favouring the settlement of the Jews in Palestine. . . . The
nationality of the Jews exists; the spirit is there and has
been for three thousand years but the external form, the
crowning bond of union, is still wanting. A nation must
have a country. The old land, the old people. This is not
an artificial experiment; it is nature, it is history."

CHAPTER XIV

CLOSING IN:

Disraeli, Suez, and Cyprus

England's purchase of the Suez Canal in 1876 as the opening gun of Disraeli's premiership ushered in a quarter-century of imperial expansion unequaled since the conquests of Alexander the Great. Following logically after Suez came the Cyprus Convention in 1878. By this treaty Britain committed herself to a military guarantee of Turkish possessions in Asia. Thus the historic area from the Nile to the Euphrates, staked out by the Lord for Abraham, was embraced as a British sphere of influence. Palestine was to remain under Turkish rule for another forty years, but after Suez and Cyprus its ultimate physical possession by Britain was a foregone conclusion.

England had become officially an empire after the Indian Mutiny of 1858; from India and around India and along the paths to India, all the rest followed. Under the "imperious and irresistible necessity of acquiring defensible frontiers—in the words of Lord Cromer, a senior partner in empire-building—Britain acquired a million and a quarter square miles in the ten years 1879–89. Afghanistan to block Russia off from India on the north, Burma on India's eastern frontier, Egypt to protect the Suez Canal, were brought in during these years. Next came Africa, from the Transvaal at the bottom to Egypt at the top, with enough in between to complete a road of British red the length of the Dark Continent from the Cape to Cairo. The vast horizon of empire was pushed outward not only for the sake of defensible frontiers, but also under the equally imperious necessity of acquiring markets for Manchester cotton goods. What made the combination irresistible was the imperious, and often genuine, belief that Britain was fulfilling her manifest destiny to extend the civilizing benefits of rule by the British race. It is, said Joseph Chamberlain unhesitatingly, "the greatest of governing races the world has ever seen."

"God's Englishman" was the phrase made famous by Lord Milner, the spokesman of empire. Lord Rosebery saw in imperial expansion "the finger of the Divine." Doctor Livingstone opened up central Africa as a missionary. General Gordon went to his death in the Sudan with the Bible in his pocket and read it as often as did Oliver Cromwell. W. T. Stead in his opening manifesto for the *Review of Reviews* proclaimed the imperialist's creed that "the English-speaking race is one of God's chief chosen instruments for executing coming improvements in the lot of mankind." On the other hand the "Little Englanders" of the Gladstone wing saw nothing but a "mania for grabbing" and "a fatal lust for empire."

But the trend was against them, and the Suez Canal was its initial impulse. By giving Britain command of the Red Sea route to India and the Far East it made the southeast corner of the Mediteranean the most vital strategic spot in the Empire. Henceforth the Holy Land became its military left flank, even as Egypt and the Sudan became its right flank and were accordingly occupied in the eighties. It becomes understandable why the War Office was ready to send Royal Engineers to map Palestine in the interests of Biblical research.

The second step, the guarantee of Turkey-in-Asia under the Cyprus Convention, is less well known but of equal importance. It meant that Britain now recognized as paramount her interests in the Palestine area; and it led eventually to her occupation of it, under a variety of mandates, after World War I. Guarantees mean a willingness to fight; in fact, they generally imply an assumption that a fight is looming. Witness Britain's guarantee of Poland in 1939. Thus the Cyprus Convention marks the point at which Britain decided that the region including Palestine was worth a war if it should come to that. Actually the Cyprus Convention did not work out that way. Russia, the aggressor against whom it was aimed, was on the down grade and by the end of the nineteenth century had been superseded by Germany as Britain's chief imperial rival. When it did come, the war whose outcome was to make Britain the inheritor of Turkey-in-Asia and the occupier of Palestine was fought, not against Russia in support of Turkey, but against Germany and Turkey itself.

But through the middle of the nineteenth century, between Napoleon at its beginning and the Kaiser at its end, Russia was the chief opponent, not so much of the British Isles as of the British Empire. It was Russia's old restless hunger for the south that brought her into collision with Britain's path of empire. It had gnawed at every Russian ruler since Catherine the Great. Pitt had risked war to keep Catherine from Odessa; Palmerston defeated Nicholas I's grab at the Black Sea in the 1830's. The Crimean War was fought over the same issue in the 1850's, and Disraeli came to the very brink of war for the same cause in the 1870's. The Russians never gave up. When Nicholas I visited England in 1844 he proposed to the foreign secretary, Lord Aberdeen, a joint partitioning of the Turkish Empire, Russia to become protector of Turkey's European possessions in the Balkans, England to have Egypt and Crete, and Constantinople to become a free city "temporarily occupied" by Russia. Nicholas, a simple autocrat, saw no harm in giving history a push, since everyone was momentarily expecting the breakup of the Turkish Empire anyway. But his delightful plan, appealing as it might be, was not possible to England under parliamentary government. Despite a reputation for deep-laid scheming, England has always been under the necessity of composing a policy to fit events rather than vice versa, and she managed to conquer half the world in a series of haphazard fits and starts, if not altogether in that "fit of absence of mind" of Seeley's ingenuous explanation.

Jerusalem itself provided the excuse for Russia's next attempt to break into the Ottoman house. The quarrel over the Holy Places that brought on the Crimean War was one of the most ridiculous causes of a major war in all history. "Tout pour un few Grik priests," shrugged Princess Lieven. Trivial as it was, it could never have burst into such a flame had not Nicholas I and Napoleon III both been breathing hard upon the coals. Russia had traditionally been protector of Greek Orthodox institutions in the Holy Land, France of the Latin or Roman Catholic. The various monastic orders, priests, and pilgrims of both rites were forever clashing over access to the Holy Places and shrines. France had secured dominant rights for the Latin clergy under capitulations originally granted to Francis I in 1535 by Suleiman, but had suffered them to decline during the anti-Christian policy of the French Revolution and Napoleon I. The Orthodox, purposefully supported by the Czar, had encroached more and more, and now Nicholas, using them as a wedge to penetrate the Ottoman empire, demanded that the Sultan confirm him as protector of the Holy Places and of all Orthodox Christians in Ottoman dominions.

But Europe's newest imperial pretender, Napoleon III, wearing uneasily the crown that he had just taken out of storage to place on his own head, had Eastern longings no less than his uncle. He, too, was insecure, on his throne, in his person, and in the awful shadow of his namesake. He needed glory. A war, a victory, a gift to France of territory in the East, would settle him in the saddle and establish the Napoleonic dynasty at last. He pressed for the Latin rights to the Holy Places. The poor Sultan, caught between the two emperors, offered a compromise solution that was satisfactory to neither. The Czar wanted a war with Turkey so that he could extract the Balkan provinces as the price of victory and stand at last on the mouth of the Danube. He issued an ultimatum. The Sultan turned to Britain for help. Britain, determined as ever to keep Russia from access to the Mediterranean and unwilling to let France win or lose alone, dispatched her fleet to the Dardanelles. The Czar, wrongly supposing that British public opinion would never support a war, moved his fleet from Sebastopol and slaughtered a Turkish squadron at Sinope, on the Asiatic shore of the Black Sea. The British public got wildly excited. Britain rang with Russophobia. Palmerston, chafing in the Home Office, to which he had been relegated by party politics, was asked by the Queen if he had any news of the strikes in the north of England. "No, Madam," he replied in anguish, "but it seems certain the Turks have crossed the Danube." The Crimean War, with Britain and France allied in support of Turkey against Russia, was soon in full swing.

It ended in a defeat of Russia's aims, ratified by the Treaty of Paris in 1856, which bound all signatories to respect the independence and territorial integrity of Turkey and admitted Turkey to the concert of European powers in return for equal rights for Christian subjects of the Porte and the usual solemn promises of reform. The treaty was supposed to usher in a rejuvenation of Turkey, but the "Sick Man" continued to deserve the contemptuous phrase that Czar Nicholas had coined for him. The government of the Porte remained as despotic, as corrupt, as unreformed as ever. And the eagles continued to hover in hopes of a corpse. In fact, the Treaty of Paris not only changed nothing, but also provided a spark for the next crisis.

Moslem indignation at the granting of equal rights to Christians reached a pitch among the bellicose Druses of Lebanon and exploded in 1860 in a three-day massacre of the Maronites, a Christian sect that had been under the special protection of France since the crusade of St. Louis. Here was another opportunity for Napoleon III, who immediately offered to send troops to restore order, as the Turks showed no interest in doing. Palmerston and Russell, deeply suspicious of Napoleon's eagerness to protect the Maronites, yet unable to say No when Christians were being massacred, reluctantly agreed to an international convention authorizing French troops to occupy Lebanon for six months for pacification purposes. Mutual mistrust breathed in every line of the protocol in which the powers proclaimed their "perfect disinterestedness" and declared that they did "not intend to seek for and will not seek for any territorial advantages, any exclusive influence or any concession with regard to the commerce of their subjects. . . ." Napoleon secured an extension of another four months, which only deepened English suspicions. "We do not want to create a new Papal state in the East and to give France a new pretext for indefinite occupation," wrote the foreign secretary, Lord John Russell. He could not rest till he got the French out of Syria, and for putting British interests above the safety of Christian lives he has earned a posthumous scolding from the *Cambridge History of British Foreign Policy*. But he had his way. By forcing the Porte to grant semiautonomy to Lebanon under a Turkish Christian governor nominated by the Powers, he removed the basis for the French occupation.

Napoleon withdrew his troops in 1861, but the prestige that France had gained by coming to the rescue of the Christian community gave the French a foothold in Syria that lasted down to the French mandates of our own time. Meantime Napoleon had not given up his dream. He commissioned Gifford Palgrave, the English Jesuit missionary and explorer, who had settled in Syria and brought out firsthand reports of the Damascus massacres, to travel through Arabia in 1862–63 to report on the Arabs' attitude toward France. Nothing came of this. But meanwhile he pursued another and older dream of his predecessors. In

1866 he secured the Sultan's consent to cut a canal connecting the Mediterranean with the Red Sea. By 1869 de Lesseps had triumphed. The Suez Canal was a reality. On November 17, 1869 the Imperial yacht, with the Empress Eugénie on board, led the opening procession through the locks. It was the Second Empire's last hour of glory. Within eight months came the Franco-Prussian War; Napoleon was broken by Bismarck, a new conqueror emerged on the Continent, a new era of German expansion had begun.

Meanwhile the Canal was an accomplished fact. Britain had long dreaded it and long opposed it. It had always been the symbol of France's Eastern ambitions from Louis XIV to Napoleon, and again when France tried to realize them through Mehemet Ali as her protégé. The Pasha had hoped to build up a Suez route to the Red Sea by connecting railway and canal lines. Viewing this project as a blind for the occupation of Egypt by France, Britain had attempted to build up an alternative route to the Red Sea by the Euphrates and connecting railways. Despite repeated experiments, this never proved practical. But anything rather than the Canal was Palmerston's settled conviction; he feared that the Canal would create a new source of rivalry in the Middle East and make the Eastern Question more insoluble than ever. "I must tell you frankly," he said to de Lesseps, "that what we are afraid of losing is our commercial and maritime pre-eminence, for this Canal will put other nations on an equal footing with us."

It almost seemed as if the old man would be prime minister forever, but at last in 1865 he died. Room for many new ideas and new men was made. Some ten years later the author of *Tancred* succeeded to the premiership. "Mr. Disraeli," the Queen discovered with pleasure, "has *very large ideas* and *very lofty views* of the position this country should hold." Mr. Disraeli saw the Canal as an imperial pathway to the East, and he resolved that it should be controlled by Britain. In a stroke so bold, so individual that one can conceive of no other statesman of the time who could have done it, he bought the Canal for Britain on barely a few days' notice.

"Zeal for the greatness of England," said Lord Salisbury on Disraeli's death, "was the passion of his life." As *Alroy* had been his ideal ambition, England was his ideal Israel. Odd that, by acquiring the Suez Canal for England, he should have started the Intermediary Power on the path that was to reopen Palestine to the real Israel.

The circumstances were sudden. The Khedive Ismail, Mehemet's grandson, was bankrupt. Agents rumored that his shares in the Canal might be offered for sale and that the French were negotiating. A telegram to the Foreign Office confirmed that the Khedive would sell; the price was £4,000,000. Disraeli dined with Rothschild. Then he called the Cabinet. His private secretary, Montagu Corry, was waiting outside the room for a prearranged signal. When Disraeli put his head outside the door and said "Yes" Corry went off to New Court to tell Rothschild that the Prime Minister wanted £4,000,000 "tomorrow."

Rothschild paused, so runs Corry's account, ate a grape, and asked: "What is your security?"

"The British Government."

"You shall have it."

Next day Disraeli had a letter confirming the loan, £1,000,000 down on December 1, less than a week off, and the remainder during December and January, the banker to receive 2½ per cent commission and 5 per cent interest until the advance was repaid. The Queen was in "ecstasies," the *Times* was "staggered," the country on the whole, except for Mr. Gladstone, enthusiastic. The Queen's "Uncle Leopold," king of the Belgians, felicitated Victoria on "the greatest event of modern politics," and her daughter, the Crown Princess of Germany, wrote enclosing a letter from the future Kaiser Wilhelm II, then sixteen:

"Dear Mama: I must write you a line because I know you will be so delighted that England has bought the Suez Canal. How jolly! Willy."

Parliament met and, after hearing Disraeli defend his purchase of the Canal as a vital link in the chain of fortresses along the road to India, voted the £4,000,000 without a division. Thereafter the hinterland of the Canal, "from the Nile to the Euphrates," was to be an area of acute sensitivity to Britain. To hold the Ottoman gates against any rival intruders was now more than ever essential, unless Britain were prepared to take over the Nile-to-the-Euphrates region herself. For fear of offending France, in view of French interests in Syria and Egypt, and in view of the anti-imperialism of the Liberals at home, this was not yet feasible. The only possibility was to keep the Sick Man on his feet and sufficiently upright to keep Russia off his back.

But already there were rumbles from the North. A Bulgarian revolt in 1875 against the Turkish despotism acted on Russia like that ringing of the bell that makes the dog's mouth salivate. It has set "everything again in flame," wrote Disraeli, "and I really believe the Eastern Question that has haunted Europe for a century . . . will fall to my lot to encounter—dare I say to settle?" The "peace with honour" that he brought back with such renown from the Congress of Berlin was the result of this encounter. But to "settle" the Eastern Question was beyond even Disraeli's power—beyond, it seems, any human power, for it still haunts the world today. However, one result of Disraeli's efforts was the acquisition of Cyprus, 150 miles off the coast of Palestine, as *quid pro quo* for the British guarantee of Turkey's dominions in Asia. The Russo-Turkish War of 1877 provided the opportunity, but, on the useful principle of sidestepping all Balkan wars whenever possible, let us hasten to its conclusion. Turkey was beaten, Russia occupied her European provinces, and the powers called a Congress to limit Russia's gains.

Why did not Britain fight in support of Turkey, this time as before? For one thing, she nearly did. Russophobia reached the wildest extremes. The Queen, at the prospect of Russian entry into Constantinople, described herself as "feeling quite ill with anxiety" and expressed her *great astonishment* and her extreme *vexation and alarm* at this, and must solemnly repeat, that if we allow *this, England would no longer exist as a great power!!*"

The music halls resounded with the chorus:

> We don't want to fight but by Jingo if we do—
> We've got the ships, we've got the guns,
>   we've got the money too—
> Russia shall not have Con-stan-ti-nople!

The "Jingoists" were all for war. But the Cabinet was split, and so was the country, for by this time Turkophobia was raging too. Turkish atrocities in Bulgaria had so inflamed public opinion, at least that part of it represented by the Liberals, that to make a public ally of Turkey was impossible. Who could withstand the crashing chords of Mr. Gladstone in that most intoxicated of all his perorations, the pamphlet on the *Bulgarian Horrors*? The Turk, he roared, was "the one great anti-human specimen of humanity," who had blackened Europe with his "fell Satanic orgies, his ferocious passions, his daily gross and incurable misgovernment." The government's policy of preserving Turkish rule simply meant "immunity for her unbounded savagery, her unbridled and bestial lust," a continuation of "fiendish misuse" of power, of "loathsome tyranny" of men "incorrigible in sin." Let it be over. Let them clear out of Europe with "their Bimbashis and their Yuzbashis, their Kaimakanis and their pashas, one and all, bag and baggage, from the province they have desolated and profaned." There was not a criminal in a European gaol, not a cannibal in the South Sea islands, whose indignation would not rise at a recital of Turkish crimes. The Turks must be driven from the soil they have left "soaked and reeking with blood," for nothing less can bring relief "to the overcharged emotion of a shuddering world."

Obviously this specter at whom cannibals shuddered

was far from a suitable ally; nevertheless when the Russian fleet approached Constantinople Disraeli managed to overcome Cabinet opposition sufficiently to send the British fleet into the Bosporus, bring up Indian reinforcements as far as Malta, and call out the reserves. *Punch* portrayed him standing with Britannia at the edge of a precipice labeled "War" and asking her to move "just a leetle nearer." Lord Derby agreed with *Punch* and resigned, allowing Disraeli, at last, to appoint a foreign secretary in his own image: his future successor as prime minister, Lord Salisbury.

Lord Salisbury was the architect of the secret treaty by which Cyprus was acquired and Turkey's dominions in Asia guaranteed. Even before he assumed office Disraeli and Layard, the Mesopotamian archaeologist, now ambassador to Constantinople, had been privately searching for "some territorial station conducive to British interests" which the Sultan in his extremity could be induced to assign to England. Many years before, during the Eastern crisis of 1840, the *Times* had carried public correspondence on the suggestion that Britain should annex Cyprus and Acre in compensation for the aid then rendered the Sultan in recovering Syria from Mehemet Ali. History was now offering a second chance under very similar circumstances, and Disraeli was not the man to hesitate. "These are times for action," he says in a private letter. "We must control and even create events."

Cyprus was a small place, and it was never developed into a military base as Disraeli and Salisbury had intended. Its importance is rather in having carried Britain a long step forward toward Palestine. A distinguished diplomatic historian* believes it to be a "reasonable assumption that in securing Cyprus for Britain, Disraeli felt that sooner or later the step would bring Palestine and Syria within the orbit of British control."

---

*Sir James Headlam-Morley, C.B.E., Historical Adviser to the Foreign Office, in his *Studies in Diplomatic History*.

The reasoning behind the step is stated with stern precision by Salisbury.

In a letter to Layard he warned that Turkey ruled over places vital to British security, including the neighborhood of the Suez Canal; that the Turkish government was now almost entirely subject to Russia; that the Sultan's only chance to maintain himself in Asia was to secure the alliance of England; and that if England hoped to keep Russia off the road to India she must make such an alliance with Turkey.

"We shall have to choose between allowing Russia to dominate over Syria and Mesopotamia *or taking the country for ourselves,* and either alternative is formidable."

I have inserted the italics to mark a moment in history when a decision was being made, a return to the goal from which Richard I, hiding his eyes from Jerusalem, had turned back. Alone at his Foreign Office desk, the black-bearded, frock-coated Salisbury writes it down, his pen scratching in the silence of the room. This alternative, though not then acted on, became inevitable from then on.

For the moment Salisbury proposed, instead of either alternative, a defensive alliance with Turkey, "but for that purpose it is absolutely and indispensably necessary that she [England] should be nearer at hand than Malta." Four days' sail from Malta to the Syrian coast makes "utterly impossible efficient and prompt military action." The Turks must cede Cyprus as the price of an alliance. However unpalatable, an alliance is necessary, for any lesser promise that would not bind the Liberals would allow the Middle East to slip away. An alliance "will pledge the national honour of England" so that "when the moment of decision comes" no peace-at-any-price party can urge the government of the day not to act; a "direct national promise" will have to be honored.

On June 4, 1878 the Cyprus Convention was signed, pledging Britain to defend "by force of arms" any attempt by Russia "at any future time to take possession of any further territories of H.I.M. the Sultan in Asia"—and engaging the Sultan to cede Cyprus "to be occupied and administered by England."

With this document safely in their pockets Disraeli and Salisbury went off to Berlin to join the other European powers in tightening an international noose that forced Russia to disgorge the gains ill gotten from defeated Turkey. *"Der alte Jude, das ist der Mann,"* said Bismarck in reluctant admiration. Disraeli, for his part, found the German Chancellor with "one hand full of cherries and the other full of shrimps, eaten alternatively, complaining he cannot sleep and must go to Kissingen." When all delicate issues of the Congress were finally wrapped up in treaties, Disraeli revealed to a stunned but generally appreciative Europe the existence of the Cyprus Convention.* It was hard not to applaud this one more daring stroke of the old master that so largely restored British prestige in the East. It "made a great impression on the world and greatly rejoiced the friends of England," wrote the invaluable King Leopold to Victoria. The Queen was so delighted that she offered Disraeli a dukedom.

There were exceptions. Prince Gortchakoff of Russia went away "deeply disappointed and dejected." At home, a friend reported to Disraeli, the Liberals "have been raving about the awful crime you have committed," calling it unconstitutional and threatening a dissolution. Gladstone fumed, protesting that no despot would have dared do what

---

*Evidence that Disraeli intended to bring the question of Palestine, together with a plan for restoring the Jews, before the Congress has recently been brought forward. Its authenticity is dubious. On the basis of newly found memoirs of the period a claim is made that Disraeli was the author of an anonymous German pamphlet published in Vienna in 1877 under the title *Die jüdische Frage in der orientalischen Frage* (The Jewish Question within the Eastern Question) which proposed that in any reapportionment of the Turkish territories following a collapse of the Ottoman Empire Palestine should be given to the Jews, and further that Disraeli proposed to put such a plan on the Agenda of the Congress but was dissuaded by Bismarck. The evidence has been published by Dr. N. W. Gelber

Disraeli had done, that he had overstepped the ministerial prerogative, that the secret negotiations were "an act of duplicity," and that by so far extending Britain's responsibilities he had committed her to an "insane covenant."

Disraeli was stung to the memorable retort that if it were a question of insanity, the more likely candidate was a "sophisticated rhetorician, inebriated with the exuberance of his own verbosity." As to the wisdom of the guarantee of Turkey-in-Asia, he replied that it was better to warn aggressors in advance at what line Britain would stand firm and say "Thus far and no farther." That was what the Cyprus Convention had done; it was well done, and he would stand by it. He was upheld by Parliament, which, despite a further heavy dose of Gladstonian oratory, endorsed the treaty. And it had the desired effect. Russia was stopped from attempting any further advances through European Turkey toward the Mediterranean or through Asia Minor toward Syria, Mesopotamia, and the Persian Gulf. It would be pleasant to be able to say with Mr. Buckle, Disraeli's biographer, writing in 1920, that these movements were "definitely stopped and have never been renewed by arms," but, as of 1955, one wonders.

As far as the nineteenth century was concerned, Russia was soon to be finished as a serious threat to the British Empire. Gladstone himself opened the way for Germany to take its place. His horror of imperial commitments led him to try vainly to abrogate the Cyprus Convention as

---

in a Hebrew brochure, subsequently translated by T. H. Gaster as *Lord Beaconsfield's Plan for a Jewish State,* New York, 1947. But Mr. Cecil Roth, a leading English authority on Jewish history, in his life of Disraeli (1951) pokes several large holes in its credibility. He finds the anonymity, the appearance in German, the withdrawal at Bismarck's request, all unlikely and the lack of any mention in the Beaconsfield papers or the papers relating to the Congress inexplicable if the authorship were in reality Disraeli's. Certainly if Disraeli had elected at the height of his power to put the theme of *Alroy* into practical politics he would not have gone about it anonymously, secretly, and in a foreign language.

soon as he came to office in 1880. Frustrated in this by Parliament, he could at least, in his detestation of everything Turkish, sever all British contact with the horrid Turk. He recalled Layard from Constantinople, allowed British influence at the Porte to lapse altogether, and alienated Turkey into the waiting arms of the Kaiser, whose glittering gaze was already fixed on a Berlin-to-Bagdad path of empire of his own.

Disraeli was dead by this time. But Palestine was within the British orbit.

CHAPTER XV

THE EAGLES GATHER:

The Sultan's Dilemma

The intrusion of Germany among the contenders for the Turkish inheritance, the growth of England as a power in the Moslem world, and the first appearance of Jewish colonizers infiltrating Palestine, all combined to exacerbate the Sultan's nerves. His problem was to hold on to his slipping dominions. He needed support. But whom could he invite in who would not settle down as a permanent resident and take over the house? He was frightened of England, he considered the Jews; in the end he plumped for Germany.

"Wheresoever the carcase is, there will the eagles be gathered together." When Crown Prince Frederick of Prussia, the future emperor of Germany, turned up in Jerusalem it was a feather in the wind that promised the arrival of a new eagle to join the group hovering over the Turkish body. *Unser Fritz* visited Jerusalem in 1869, shortly after the visit of his brother-in-law the Prince of Wales. Some thirty years later his son, Kaiser Wilhelm II, came on a much more imposing visit, a royal progress through Palestine culminating in the Sultan's gift to him of lands at Jerusalem. The gift was symbolic. By this time the Kaiser was the new kingpin on the Continent. The Sultan had made his choice and doomed his empire.

Imperial Turkey went down with Imperial Germany in the defeat of 1918. Sultan Abdul Hamid's shift away from Britain in favor of what seemed a more promising protector in Germany at last accomplished the crash that Europe had been awaiting for a hundred years. The crash freed Palestine from centuries of Moslem neglect and opened a new era in its history. Britain, as the conqueror on the spot, became, at least temporarily, the inheritor of Turkey-in-Asia. But if the Turks had not gone in on the wrong side, this might never have happened. And logically, if England's consistent policy from Pitt down to the eve of 1914 had any logic, Turkey should have been allied with England on the winning side. If she had been, what, one wonders, would have been the modern fate of Palestine?

Fortunately British diplomacy failed; Turkey chose the loser; and at last the Ottoman Empire, which for nearly five hundred years had, first in strength and then in senility, harassed the West, was destroyed. The result was of lasting benefit to everyone concerned, not the least to the Turkish people themselves. Once rid of a corrupt autocracy, they were able to prove themselves in the remarkable rejuvenation of their country, the most virile and capable nation of the Middle East.

The roots of Imperial Turkey's wrong choice, which was so vitally to affect the fate of Palestine, go back to the Congress of Berlin. Abdul Hamid was hardly happy in having to accept British protection under the conditions of the Cyprus Convention. He began to feel that he could improve upon the Porte's traditional policy of accepting a British embrace in order to avoid a Russian rape. He was impressed by the choice of Berlin as the seat of the Congress and by the prestige that accrued to Prince Bismarck as its presiding officer. Here was a new rising power on the Continent and one that had so far no history of Eastern ambitions. The fact that Germany up to 1880 had shown no Eastern longings should not have deceived the Sultan as to the future. As soon as Prussia reached the position of

a great power at the head of a federated Germany she became afflicted with the Eastern disease as chronically as
Russia, France, or England. In 1888 Willy, who had
thought it so "jolly" that England had bought the Suez
Canal, came to the throne as the Emperor Wilhelm II. He
soon had a no less jolly Eastern dream of his own: the
Berlin-to-Bagdad railway. Though coming late on the scene
of imperial expansion eastward, he made up for it in push-
fulness.

Railway concessions became the favored method of penetration. Abdul Hamid, soon after the Congress of Berlin,
had determined to solidify his Asiatic dominions, of which
he considered Syria the key, by a planned program of mod-
ernization. He began to increase garrisons and multiply
guards, to build roads and railways for military transport,
linking Syria to Constantinople, Mesopotamia, and Arabia.
He improved Syrian port facilities, paved streets, built
modern buildings, added tramways. All this opened a grab
bag to European concessionaires and carpetbaggers, chiefly
German. The newly established Deutsche Palästina Bank
became headquarters for an army of German commercial
travelers, commission agents, exporters and importers,
and a superabundance of consular officials. The French
predominated in building the major railways of Syria, but
Berlin won the concession for the Bagdad railway, being
favored over Britain, which had previously held options
for rail development of the Euphrates valley. Berlin-to-
Bagdad has a romantic oriental sound that brings to mind
cloak-and-dagger adventures on the Orient Express; but its
significance to Britain was sinister enough in fact. Its proposed route would put a rival European power in control
of communications leading to the head of the Persian Gulf,
which opens upon the Indian Ocean. It was a direct threat
to the road to India.

Britain's strategic effort in the Middle East during this
period focused on Egypt. Her approach to Palestine had
stopped, for the time being, at Cyprus. Palestine was in

any event not a conscious goal of imperial policy. Along
the Nile Lord Cromer, the great modern proconsul, was
busy sinking the eagle's claws into a more easily detachable
part of Turkey's non-European empire. He guided the in-
tricate business of extending the foothold gained at the
Suez Canal to a position as virtual ruler of Egypt while
still maintaining the khedive on his throne and the legal
fiction of Turkish over-all sovereignty. It had to be deli-
cately done in order to keep the jealousy of the other European powers below the boiling point. By the time European
rivalries finally boiled over in 1914, Britain from her base
in Egypt commanded the classic approach to Palestine,
the route that Moses took to possession of the Promised
Land.

England had become suspect in the Sultan's eyes after
the Cyprus Convention. In casting about for a new prop
Abdul Hamid, listening to the persuasive arguments of an
unofficial Englishman, Mr. Laurence Oliphant, considered
for a while the possibility of using the Jews. Oliphant was
a former foreign service officer, a journalist, and a religious eccentric. (It is a curious fact that so many notable
English eccentrics have been drawn irresistibly to the East.
Perhaps it was because most of them, like T. E. Lawrence,
the archetype, were voyaging on some private religious or
metaphysical quest of their own and, like Disraeli's *Tancred,* sought spiritual rebirth in the place where three great
religions were conceived.)

Oliphant's religious aberrations verged on the ridiculous,
but he was at the same time an experienced and brilliant
young man of affairs. He seemed to young Henry Adams,
who met him at a house party, "exceptionally sane, and
peculiarly suited to country houses where every man would
enjoy his company and every woman adore him." This
worldly creature threw himself into the promotion of Israel's restoration from the same religious motives as Lord
Shaftesbury's, though like Shaftesbury he tried to conceal
them behind arguments based on strategy and politics.

Born of fervent evangelical parents, he entered the diplomatic service, served in posts ranging from Canada to Japan, traveled through India, the Turkish Empire, Europe, and the United States, covered the Crimean War as correspondent of the *Times*, aided Garibaldi and Cavour in Italy, and became an M.P. in 1865. Suddenly he resigned his seat in Parliament and disappeared. The shock rocked London when it became known that this ornament of society, famous for his charm, his flirtations, his far-flung adventures, had gone off to dig ditches in a religious community in New England.

Actually Oliphant had embarked on a recurring endeavor of the disillusioned: the attempt to forsake the world and live the humble life of the first Christians. It did not suit him, and he was allowed to return to the world as a proselyte. Although his association with the shady prophet of the Brocton colony was a prolonged mortification involving his mother, two wives, and several lawsuits, he remained to the end of his life dedicated to the "regeneration of humanity." He denied that his advocacy of the Jews' return to Palestine had anything to do with this or even that it was based on Scriptural grounds. But the second Mrs. Oliphant, who was subject to visions and voices, was less reticent. She described a vision of a Jew on a White Horse; the horse, she explained, symbolized power, the color white stood for righteous power. This she took to mean that Israel, "redeemed" by Christ, would be restored to power in Palestine and, thus "illumined," would become a "splendid Jewish-Christian race wielding religious power, for none but true Christians may fittingly govern the Holy Land."

Oliphant himself stated the case on more earthly terms. The fact that it coincided with "a favorite religious theory," he said, "does not necessarily impair its political value." In 1879, the year after the Congress of Berlin, he was in Rumania during a series of anti-Semitic outbreaks. He saw the gathering of refugees at Brody and Lemberg and, caught up in their tragedy, he went to a Chovevé Zion conference at Jassy. Enthralled at the glimpse of Biblical prophecy coming true, he immediately set off for Constantinople to persuade the Sultan to grant lands to the Jews under a charter for colonization. Next he went to Palestine to survey the land and in 1880 published his book, *The Land of Gilead*, proposing Jewish resettlement, under Turkish sovereignty and British protection, of Palestine east of the Jordan.

Oliphant believed that England, acting through the Jews could—indeed, must—revitalize Turkey-in-Asia if it were to be held against the advance of a rival imperial power. He had in mind Russia, in that day still the leading menace, but his predictions hold good equally for the rival that he did not foresee. "The day is probably not far distant," he warned, "when it may be found that the most important interests of the British Empire may be imperilled by the neglect to provide in time for contingencies which are now looming in the immediate future."

It was unfortunate, he admitted, that English efforts to bolster Turkey-in-Asia—Disraeli's policy—"should be misconstrued at Constantinople into a desire to obtain possession of Asia Minor." But that risk must be taken. Palestine's strategic and prestige value leap to the eye. It is the logical place to begin, and the Jews are the logical colonists. "It remains for England to decide whether she will undertake the task of exploring its ruined cities, of developing its vast agricultural resources, by means of the repatriation of that race which first entered into its possession 3,000 years ago and of securing the great political advantages which must accrue from such a policy."

Describing the existing condition of the country, as he saw it in 1880, he proposes a million-and-a-half-acre colony east of the Jordan, connected by rail to a port at Haifa and eventually, through future railways, to Akaba on the Red Sea and to the Suez Canal. East of Jordan the land is more fertile than on the near side, less settled, and therefore easier to acquire. The problem of the existing Arab population he disposes of easily. The war-like Bedouins can be driven out, the peasant Arabs conciliated and placed on "reserves" like the Indians in Canada. Elsewhere the fellahin can be used, as Colonel Conder suggested, as a source of labor, under Jewish direction. In any event the Arabs "have very little claim to our sympathy [having] laid waste to the country, ruined its villages and plundered its inhabitants until it has been reduced to its present condition."

The incoming Jews would become Turkish subjects and Syria eventually a semi-independent province. Opened to colonization by an enterprising, energetic people of known "business intelligence, industry and wealth," it would become a source of strength to Turkey.

Contrasted with the painful realities of the first Jewish colonies, in which at that moment the half-starved settlers stared helplessly at their crops withering in the sun, Oliphant's prognosis was perhaps optimistic. He was a victim of the same misconception shared by all non-Jews, that the Jews would be united in the desire to go to Palestine and that Jewish wealth would finance the return. He argued that it would be advantageous to any power likely to become involved in the "impending complications" in the Middle East to secure as an ally this "wealthy, powerful and cosmopolitan race." He forgot, as Shaftesbury and other predecessors had forgotten, that nine tenths of the Jews were not Montefiores and Rothschilds, but submerged minorities living on the edge of subsistence. These enthusiasts failed to realize that the Jews who wanted to go to Palestine had neither money nor influence (indeed, the fact that they had nothing to lose was the reason they wanted to go) and that the Jews who *had* money and influence did not want to go to Palestine.

But Oliphant's talk, during several visits to Constantinople, of Jewish industry, business acumen, and gold pouring like a river of nourishment upon Palestine tempted the Sultan and found favor with the progressive party in Turkey. He won a valuable ally in the English financier, Victor Cazalet, who had interests in the Euphrates Valley railway development. The two men presented to the Sultan a plan to give the Jews a strip two miles wide on either side of the proposed railway. It did not materialize, and in the end, when the baksheesh clique turned out the reform party, all Oliphant's efforts were defeated. His failure lay in the times. In England, where the anti-imperialist Liberals had replaced Disraeli, no one was interested. In Turkey Abdul Hamid, one of the most erratic sovereigns in history, now became frightened at the thought of admitting a new and questionable element into Syria. Was another non-Moslem minority with support from outside to root itself in his dominions? Would it not provide, like the Christians of Lebanon, a perennial cause of Western protests, not to mention an avenue of Western penetration? Lebanon was already gone, detached from his sovereignty in all but name, having been a French sphere of influence ever since the intervention of 1860. The Sultan had no wish to see Palestine become another Lebanon.

Now the diplomatic atmosphere began to warm perceptibly around the representatives of Berlin. England, then enjoying the government of Mr. Gladstone, did nothing to counteract this tendency. Mr. Gladstone was disgusted with the Turks, hated the whole business of imperialism, and appeared to believe that, by ignoring the responsibilities that Britain had acquired for herself through imperial expansion, he could make them vanish. Ireland and Home Rule loomed larger in his eyes than Europe, Asia, Africa, and America put together. Unfortunately the world beyond the English Channel, though Mr. Gladstone turned his back on it, refused to vanish. The death in the Sudan of General Gordon, left to his fate through the tragic ineptitude of the Liberal government, proved that Britain's imperial undertakings could not be ignored out of existence. In a wave of indignation over the Gordon tragedy Mr.

Gladstone and the Liberals were voted out; Lord Salisbury and the Conservatives came back.

This was in 1885. Lord Salisbury took the Foreign Office for himself, and one of his first acts was to call for the file on Turkey to learn what had become of England's position at Constantinople under the previous government. He read it through in silence and laid it down in despair. "They have just thrown it away into the sea," he said, "without getting anything whatever in exchange."

Lord Salisbury did not think restoration of Britain's former influence at the Porte likely or even worth while. He had no faith in the possibilities of Turkish reform and did not believe the empire could hang together much longer. Long ago in his famous afterthought on the Crimean War he had said: "We put our money on the wrong horse." He believed that it would have been better all around had England accepted Czar Nicholas' suggestion to partition the Ottoman Empire in 1840. Why then, did he author England's guarantee of Turkey-in-Asia under the Cyprus Convention in 1878? Lord Salisbury was once called by a perceptive observer the Hamlet of English politics. He suffered from that fatal affliction of being able to see both sides of a question and of being consequently unable to elect wholeheartedly for either. He had no love for Turkey, but he was obliged to contain Russia, which was then pressing down upon her. The Cyprus Convention was not an expression of confidence in Turkey, but a warning to Russia as well as a precaution that would permit England to move in if and when the Turkish collapse came.

Now back in office and (with Disraeli gone) in full command, he determined to waste no more effort on wooing the Sultan. Egypt was the thing. It would be a "terrible blow," he acknowledged to his ambassador at Constantinople, to lose the leading influence at the Porte, but, he asked, "have we not lost it already?" And, "with this sickly, sensual, terrified, fickle Sultan on the throne," it was impossible in any event to maintain a steady policy for two days together. Rather go ahead in Egypt on a step-by-step basis without trying to extract signed agreements from the Sultan, which were worthless anyway and would only provoke opposition from the other powers.

Salisbury sensed that the Sultan's alienation from England was permanent. "He hates us," he wrote again in 1891 to the ambassador, who had complained that never had his influence at the palace been so low or the Sultan's aversion to him so evident. "Egypt and Cyprus would be sufficient to account for this feeling," he goes on, but worse than that, the English have shown that they can govern Moslems better than he. "In Arabia people have begun to talk and move, and to ask themselves whether eternal misgovernment by the Turks is their irrevocable doom. And Arabia is the terror of the Sultan's dreams—the joint in his armour: because it is in Arabia that some day an opposition Commander of the Faithful will be manufactured." He concludes that the Sultan, "to whom his position as the first Moslem of the world is everything," cannot forgive England's intrusion into the Moslem world.

Lord Salisbury's somber eyes saw the truth. The unhappy Sultan saw his empire eroding at both ends: while Egypt was being swallowed by England, the Balkans were slipping away in the north. Consequently he was determined to hold like grim death onto Syria, including Palestine and especially Jerusalem. The Holy City, because of its prestige value, was absolutely vital, for already, as Lord Salisbury had seen, the Sultan's Moslem sovereignty was beginning to fray at the edges and his position as caliph to come into question. Foreign influence had penetrated Syria too far already. More and more "visitors" were flooding the Holy Land. There was a curious accretion of Russian pilgrims; formerly numbered annually in the hundreds, they now began to appear in thousands and to acquire land in Jerusalem on the basis of the old claim as Orthodox protectors of the Holy Places. French Jesuits, English Protestants, American missionaries spreading dangerous liberal ideas through their schools, were increasing in numbers every year. Jewish colonists were buying land. And turning up everywhere with their surveyors' rods and tripods were little bands of British army engineers plotting the lay of the land.

Abdul Hamid tried to stem the tide. In 1887 he detached the *sanjak* of Jerusalem from the provincial governorship of Syria and made it directly dependent on the Palace. In 1885 the Porte announced that it would not permit formation of another Jewish colony and would enforce the edict against aliens' holding or acquiring real estate. But the Sultan was by now a prisoner of the system of government-by-bribe that had corrupted his empire. His edicts stood little chance of enforcement by the venal corps of viziers and governors supposed to administer them and were, in fact, easily circumvented.

The early Jewish colonies founded by the Chovevé Zion societies, small, scattered, and feeble though they were, had gained a toehold in the Jaffa area. In spite of the Sultan's edict they had acquired by 1889 a total of 76,000 acres scattered over twenty-two separate settlements with a population of about 5,000. The figures on paper appear more imposing than the true facts. Actually these Zionists beginnings were precarious and primitive in the extreme. Twenty families in 1882 established Rishon-le-Zion ("First in Zion") on the sand dunes south of Jaffa to begin reclamation of the ancient homeland. Another colony was settled some sixty miles up the coast and a third, Rosh Pinah, far to the north in the mountains above Galilee. Within a year they were floundering close to ruin. The little vanguard from the Russian Pale, fired by an ideal and a hope two thousand years old, had gone out with hardly a thought for the local conditions that they would meet and with little more than their railroad tickets provided. There was hardly a dirt farmer among them. They scratched into the wasted soil of Palestine the same corn and wheat crops that they had seen growing in the rich black earth of the

Ukraine. The crops withered. Malaria forced the abandonment of a colony started by Jerusalem Jews at Petah Tik-
vah. The other colonies were on the verge of abandonment;
some of the settlers had returned, the rest were starving.

A finger of rescue reached out in the form of a gift of
30,000 francs to Rishon-le-Zion from Baron Edmond de
Rothschild of Paris. The finger grew to a hand. He sent
further funds to the other colonies and helped to establish
newcomers on lands that he acquired. So began the effort
that was to keep going the little outposts of Jewish resettlement until, at the close of the century, the Zionist movement was mobilized.

But the difficulties that beset the attempt to revive a
half-dead nation on the soil of a half-dead country were
enormous and all but overwhelming. Quite apart from the
external problems of climate and soil, the colonists' own
inexperience and above all the internal dissension that has
been the curse of Jewish movements nearly ended Palestine's resettlement then and there. While they were starving they were arguing whether they should keep the commandment of a Sabbatical year during which no work on
the fields or among the livestock could be done. If this
seems incredible, it is none the less literally true. The controversy reached furious proportions and consumed oceans
of ink in every Jewish journal throughout Europe. It was
actually provoked and encouraged by the rabbinical clique
of Jerusalem, who were unalterably opposed to the whole
restoration ideal of the Chovevé Zion and hoped to see the
colonization scheme fail. Those of the colonists who resented dependence on Rothschild's bounty (though they
would unquestionably have starved to death without it)
took up the Sabbatical issue as a flag of rebellion against
Rothschild's administrators. Constant quarrels only slightly
less fantastic embittered the early years.

The Odessa Committee, headquarters of the Chovevé
Zion, whose zeal far outran its funds, was amazed at the
sums required merely to keep the first pioneers alive. Des-

perate delegates pleading in the capitals of Europe could collect no more than a few francs. Could Palestine ever be restored to fertility? Comfortably placed Jews, though they did not lack the desire to help their brethren caught under the hammer of the Russian pogroms, declined to put their money on so risky a proposition. Basically they were afraid of Palestine and of the prospects that it stirred up of a restored Jewish nationhood which would endanger the dream of assimilation into Western societies. They preferred Baron de Hirsch's scheme of resettlement in Argentina to Baron Edmond's passion for Palestine.

Among the grand dukes only Rothschild (after the death of Montefiore) had faith in Palestine. "The only salvation of the Jewish people is in bringing them back to the Holy Land," he said. The family scoffed. They called his Palestine colonies *la fantaisie du Baron.*" They wished that he would stick to his art collection, the only other passionate interest of his life, since he refused to concern himself with business affairs in the bank on the Rue Laffitte. Instead Baron Edmond listened to the thinkers and workers of the rising Jewish nationalism—to Pinsker, the author of *Auto-Emancipation*, to Netter of the *Alliance*, to Rabbi Mohilever, hard-working delegate of the Chovevé Zion, to Ahad-ha-Am, Socrates of the movement and the most influential voice speaking for the revival of Judaism as a living culture and a living religion.

So, in the '80's, the return to Palestine began hesitantly, minutely, and without benefit of intermediary power. The movement was self-started by Jews, pushed at last to the realization that they must give up waiting for a miracle and take their fate into their own hands or perish. The pioneers acted on their own. There was as yet no second Cyrus to open the way, to say "Go back, resume your homeland." The Sultan, it is true, had considered Cyrus' role on the mistaken theory that Jewish wealth might be used to rescue his empire from its recurring fits of bankruptcy. Even the Kaiser, in a brief visionary moment when he granted an audience to Herzl in Palestine, toyed with the idea; but he quickly let it drop. English attention was absorbed elsewhere.

The Jews were stirring — talking, writing, persuading themselves. But so far the power, influence, and money required to build homes in Palestine was not behind them. A single Rothschild does not make a summer. It was easier for the average family seeking escape from the Pale to head for city life in New York or London. To stake a family's future on belief in the future of Palestine and the future of the Jews as a nation required a heroic effort that few were prepared to make. Conditions were ready for an Exodus, but the Exodus was not ready for Palestine. Mobilization of a mass movement toward the old land had to wait for pressure in Europe to grow worse and for the emergence of a leader.

It did not have to wait long.

CHAPTER XVI

HERZL AND CHAMBERLAIN:

The First Territorial Offer

Suddenly, explosively, in the year 1896, a voice cracked out like a pistol shot: "I shall now put the question in the briefest possible form: Are we to 'get out' and where to?

"Or may we yet remain? And how long?"

Theodore Herzl, a Viennese journalist, quickly supplied the answer to his own rhetorical question. He stated that the Jews were a nation, must organize and behave as a nation, and must acquire the physical attributes of a nation: land and sovereignty. He cut through fifty years of verbiage in one word: statehood. His pamphlet was entitled *Der Judenstaat* (The Jewish State). A vast hedge of polemics known as the Jewish Question had in the preceding decades risen around the actual sufferers from anti-Semitism in Eastern Europe. Herzl crashed through the hedge on his opening page: "Everything depends on our propelling force. And what is that force? The misery of the Jews." And he announced the remedy: "The Jewish state is essential to the world. It will therefore be created. . . . Let sovereignty be granted to us over a portion of the globe large enough to satisfy the rightful requirements of a nation; the rest we shall manage for ourselves."

Within eighteen months of the publication of *Der Judenstaat* Herzl, unknown till then in the Jewish world, had organized and convened the first Zionist Congress. Meet-

281

ing biennially thereafter, it was to act as the organ of the state until statehood was accomplished fifty years later. With Herzl as president the first Congress of two hundred delegates from fifteen countries met at Basle in 1897 and launched, as was said, "the vessel of the Jewish state upon its way."

Herzl was thirty-six when he wrote the *Judenstaat*. In eight years he was dead, burned out by the superhuman effort to wrest his people out of subjection into freedom. Though warned of a weak heart, he could not rest. The baying hound was running down its victims. A terrible sense of urgency raged in him against the frustrations, the obstructionism, the endless passion for controversy that he met inside Jewry and the delays, disappointments, and defeats that he met from the outside world. Moses survived the same difficulties over forty years and at last brought his nation to the frontier of the Promised Land, but Moses had the pillar of smoke by day and the pillar of fire by night. When his enemies were upon him the Lord opened the Red Sea; when his people muttered and rebelled the Lord thundered and scolded; when they starved He sent down manna in the wilderness. But there was no extra-human assistance available when the Jews set out to recover the Promised Land at the end of the nineteenth century. Herzl emerged as a leader without benefit of burning bush. There were more profound thinkers than he in the movement, wiser men and steadier men and many, before and after him, equally devoted to the goal. But Herzl had that extra endowment that makes a leader, the sense of personal mission and destiny. Napoleon was born with it; Herzl acquired it when he discovered his goal. Moses, slow, reluctant, self-deprecating, lacked it until the Lord appeared to him, talked to him, propelled him. Herzl was no Moses in the sense of being a formative influence on mankind. He was, so to speak, half a Moses—the Exodus half, not the Ten Commandments half.

Neither he nor Moses came from the ranks of the sufferers to lead them out of bondage. Moses was brought up at the court of Pharaoh, Herzl in the comparatively comfortable circle of the emancipated and enlightened Jews of Vienna. Perhaps that was why they were able to lead. It was often said of Herzl that if he had known the Jews better he would never have had the courage for the task he set himself. Ussishkin, an opponent, once said that Herzl was fitted to lead Zionism because he knew neither the Jews, Palestine, nor Turkey, and added: "His eyes must not be opened; then his faith will be great." Herzl's eyes did open; his faith did lessen, but not his determination. No obstacle could daunt him. He never slackened, never stopped until his life stopped. His name and personality so dominate the scene that it is difficult to realize that he was active in the movement less than nine years, whereas Weizmann, for one, the future president of Israel, was active for sixty.

Herzl saw only the beginning. Moses had been shaken into action by the sight of an Egyptian beating an Israelite. For Herzl the blow of the Egyptian was Dühring's brutal book summoning Western Europe to cancel the Jews' civil rights and turn them back into the ghettos. He read it when he was twenty-two, and for twelve years thereafter he struggled with the "Jewish question" in his mind. It haunted his thoughts, intruded itself into the themes of projected novels and plays, pricked the joy of his success as the most admired writer on the staff of the most admired paper in Central Europe, the *Neue Freie Presse*. He had believed in the credo of nineteenth-century optimism, that progress would dispel prejudice, that gradually people would become too civilized to be anti-Semitic. But he read Gobineau, he read Dumont's *La France Juive*. He experienced the anti-Semitic agitation in Austria and Germany. Progress was unaccountably going backward. Slowly the hope shriveled, revealed itself as an empty illusion. In 1890 a Russian edict enforcing the May laws prohibited Jews from residing in rural districts, owning or farming land, entering the universities, practicing the professions, or holding government jobs. But it was not the slow choking of the ghetto Jews that affected Herzl so much as the attacks on the position of the emancipated Jew in Austria-Hungary, in Germany, and even, bitterest disillusion of all, in France, the capital of reason.

Herzl was Paris correspondent for his paper when the Chamber rocked with the violence of the debates on the Panama scandal, in which Jewish figures were involved. Then came the Dreyfus Affair. It grew and grew like a Sahara sandstorm till all France was twisted by its violence. "*A mort! A mort les Juifs!*" howled the mob as Captain Dreyfus was led to trial in December 1894. Herzl, who was covering the trial, heard it then and for the rest of his life. "Where?" he wrote later in retrospect. "In France. In republican, modern, civilized France, a hundred years after the Declaration of the Rights of Man. . . . Until that time most of us believed that the solution of the Jewish question was to be patiently waited for as part of the general development of mankind. But when a people, which in every other respect is so progressive and so highly civilized, can take such a turn, what are we to expect from other peoples, which have not even attained the level France attained a hundred years ago?"

A "curious excitement" began to seize him; a sense of things coming clear, of being on the edge of revelation, of the answer being within his grasp. He felt himself destined to be the instrument. For the next two years he grappled with it, he poured out schemes in his diaries, buttonholed friends and Jewish leaders, argued passionately, wrote letters to the Rothschilds, to Bismarck, to his editor, confronted Baron de Hirsch with a plan for a "Jewish national loan" to finance a mass emigration. But it must be emigration to a land under Jewish sovereignty: otherwise, he foresaw, the immigration could be stopped at any time—as was proved by the future experience under the British Mandate. Ideas raced through his mind, tumbled out upon scraps of paper wherever he was, "walking, standing, lying down, in the street, at table, in the night . . . more than once I was afraid I was going out of my mind."

In five days he wrote a sixty-five-page pamphlet originally called *Address to the Rothschilds*, outlining a state complete from political independence to territorial integrity, with flags, parliament, army, laws, courts, "where we can live at least as free men on our own soil." A friend, finding him sleepless and disheveled, was forced to listen while Herzl read the *Address* from beginning to end. The friend decided that it was the product of an overstrained mind and advised Herzl to rest and see a doctor. Herzl shook him off and went to work on a memorandum to be transmitted through a diplomatic acquaintance to the Kaiser. He entered into negotiations with the new Austrian prime minister, Count Badeni. He read the pamphlet to another friend, Güdemann, the chief Reform rabbi of Vienna, sitting on the edge of a hotel bed in Munich. Dazed, the Rabbi wondered if perhaps he had seen Moses reborn. He offered timid encouragement. Others told Herzl that he was mad or "impractical." The Rothschilds were silent, de Hirsch disapproving. His own editor refused to print a word on the subject. A visit to London brought encouragement. He was invited to address the Maccabaean Society, won adherents, and was asked to contribute an article to the *Jewish Chronicle*. In England this paper became, prophetically enough, the first to publish, in condensed form, the material later to appear as the *Judenstaat*. A month afterwards, under that title, a revised version of the pamphlet was published in Vienna.

This remarkable document and its extraordinary author, between them, accomplished what no one had been able to do so far: the political organization of a body of Jews for the purpose of regulating their own fate under their own authority. The banner was unfurled in the opening sentence: "The idea which I have developed in this pamphlet is a very old one: it is a restoration of the Jewish

State." There follows a discussion of anti-Semitism as the "propelling force." The rest is a blueprint for building the state down to the last specification: creation of a governing society (the future Congress), financing, political planning, acquisition of land and a charter, gathering of emigrants, reception and organization "over there."

Herzl hardly envisaged any difficulty in acquiring title to Palestine from the Ottoman Empire. He airily assumed that the Sultan would be open to a deal under which the Jews would "undertake to regulate the whole finances of Turkey." Then, once the funding corporation was established, all plans "systematically settled beforehand," provinces delimited, town sites chosen, streets laid out, the mass migration could begin. The first settlers, disposed and directed by the governing agency like a body of troops, would build roads, till the land, irrigate, build homes; gradually more would come, industries would be established, trade attracted, and through trade more settlers, and so on and on and up and up until there would arise "a State founded in a manner as yet unknown to history and with possibilities of success such as never occurred before."

Der Judenstaat is full of flights of grandeur on wings of wishful thinking. Herzl was spectacularly wrong about the society, or future Congress, when he pictured it as a homogeneous body composed entirely of people in agreement with each other, with "no voting necessary." He was even more mistaken in his analysis of anti-Semitism, which he naively believed would assist the emigration. "The governments of all countries scourged by anti-semitism will be keenly interested in assisting us to obtain the sovereignty we want," he wrote. Perhaps it is unfair to subject Herzl's first thoughts to the unkind glare of hindsight. It is clearer now that no anti-Semitic government in any country has ever helped its scapegoats to leave by any other door than death.

But Herzl made the one great necessary contribution:

the intransigent insistence on land, sovereignty, and state-hood. He insisted that the Jews come out in the open as a nation, that they act as a nation to obtain for themselves the legal rights that go with nationhood. Hitherto they had attempted to make gains by infiltration, by not arousing opposition, by being rewarded for good behavior. Emancipation was essentially a handout and as such, as Herzl realized, revocable. He activated the movement toward autonomy, compelled the Jews to abandon dependence on philanthropy and to organize according to modern recognized political rules for the management of their own destiny. "The basis," he told the first Congress, "can only be that of recognized right and not of sufferance. We have had our fill of toleration. Our movement . . . aims at a publicly recognized, legal guarantee."

Herzl expected antagonism and debate, but hardly the fury that the *Judenstaat* aroused. Generally speaking, the emancipated Jews felt themselves threatened by this wild man who would dispel the illusion of ultimate assimilation. They raged and stormed, called Herzl a madman, his state a chimera, his proposals, in the words of Rabbi Isaac M. Wise, founder of Reform Judaism in the United States, "the momentary inebriation of morbid minds." At one moment Rabbi Güdemann, who could never resist Herzl's spell, almost seemed won over.

"You have me completely on your side," he said, as recorded in Herzl's diary.

"'Good,' I said, 'then speak in your Temple about it.'

"'Excuse me!' he cried out, terrified. 'That won't do. The people just don't want to hear about it.'"

Even the Chovevé Zion, wedded to modest piecemeal colonization, were surly and critical. They were the pioneers; who was this elegant frock-coated Dr. Herzl of Vienna, who knew nothing of Palestine and did not even write in Hebrew, to come along and tell them how to do it better? He had never even read Hess or Pinsker. (Astonishingly, this was true: Herzl confessed later that if he had

4

88 / BIBLE AND SWORD

read the *Auto-Emancipation* first, he would never have
written the *Judenstaat*.) The disciples of Ahad-ha-Am's
"cultural Zionism," who believed that the soul of Judaism
had to be revived before the body and that the Jews must
learn to feel themselves a nation before they could act as
one, were aghast at Herzl's plunging program. It went too
fast, it skipped the soul, it would not work.

Yet the more the debate raged the more widely known
the tract became. Inevitably its basic appeal—the appeal to
dignity, to self-help, to stand up like a man—took hold.
This was the quality in Herzl's own personality that impressed itself the most on others and reached out to something basic in Jewry, the conviction of superiority; the
factor that, though hidden beneath centuries of humiliation, accounts for the unique phenomenon of their survival. In Herzl it was not hidden at all. Rather he insisted
on it, as when, during an interview at the Vatican, he refused to kiss the Pope's hand, or when he ruled that delegates to the first Zionist Congress must appear in frock
coats and white ties. This gesture, although it irritated
many, was deliberately planned to impress on the delegates themselves the dignity of their role as founders of a
nation.

In Herzl himself the quality was hard to resist. It pushed
him into leadership of the movement, brought him lieu-
tenants, rallied followers to his banner. On his way to and
from Constantinople, to which he went in the summer of
1896 to open negotiations with the Sultan, masses crowded
the railroad platforms to see him, hailed him as Messiah
and King, shouted the age-old cry "Next year in Jerusalem!" Already the rays of legend began to gather around
him. By the time the Congress met at Basle enthusiasm,
tension, and expectation, mounting over the last months,
focused on him alone. "Everyone sat breathless as if in
the presence of a miracle," wrote an observer. When the
magnificent figure, black-bearded like an Assyrian king,
walked to the dais for the opening address, there was a

burst of wild applause. His dark splendor, his spell-binding
eyes were well known; but at that moment there was something more—an aura of royalty, as if the long-awaited scion
of King David had appeared.

Here it is not necessary to go into the internal history
of Zionism. Its goal was stated by the first Congress under
a four-point declaration of principles known thereafter as
the Basle Program. "The aim of Zionism," it proclaimed,
"is to create for the Jewish people a home in Palestine
secured by public law."

Meanwhile it became evident from Herzl's experience at
Constantinople that the Sultan was hardly prepared simply
to hand over the sovereignty of Palestine to an emissary
who, for all his dignity and aplomb, had not two farthings
of grand dukes' gold to jingle in Turkish ears. It was obviously necessary to gird every effort for another attempt
to bring in the rich and influential Jews. Until the shares
of the proposed Bank or Colonial Trust were subscribed
there would clearly be no co-operation from the Sultan.
Herzl would have "sold his soul to the devil" for success in
floating the loan, he privately recorded. In London, where
he believed the financial key was to be found, leaders of
the Jewish community, who had begun to have an uneasy
feeling that Herzl might possibly be on the right track,
were earnest with advice but timid with funds. They would
go no farther than an offer to come in if he could first get
Baron de Rothschild on the governing board and a check
for ten million pounds from the I.C.A. The Baron, whom
Herzl tried to persuade to take over active leadership of
the movement on condition that he give up piecemeal
colonization in favor of the principle of a national state
into which Jews could immigrate by right, backed away.
"He was a nationalist with a distrust of the nationalist
movement and of the people," Weizmann once said of the
Baron. "He wanted everything to be done quietly."

The hesitancy of the great only served to convince Herzl
that his earlier sense of destiny was correct and that he

himself was the inevitable leader. "I always feel posterity glancing over my shoulder," he noted in his diary. And he was learning fast. He began to realize that Zionism had to become "a movement of the poor" and find its support in the unemancipated Eastern Jews who "were not tortured by the idea of assimilation." He neither knew nor understood them, but he recognized that if he were to lead it would have to be at the head of an army of "beggars and cranks."

Yet he could not get over his fondness for the "portals of royalty" or the belief that he could somehow bring down the state as a gift from above through frock-coated interviews with diplomats, bankers, and prime ministers. A fictional portrait that almost seems to have anticipated Herzl is the exuberant Pinchas in Zangwill's *Children of the Ghetto*.

"We shall no longer be dumb—we shall roar like the lions of Lebanon. I shall be the trumpet to call the dispersed together from the four corners of the earth—yea, I shall be the Messiah himself," said Pinchas, rising on the wings of his own eloquence, and forgetting to puff at his cigar. . . .

"Hush, hush!" said Guedalyah, the greengrocer. "Let us be practical. We are not yet ready for the Marseillaises or Messiahs. The first step is to get funds enough to send one family to Palestine."

"Yes, yes," said Pinchas, drawing vigorously at his cigar to rekindle it. "But we must look ahead. Already I see it all. Palestine in the hands of the Jews—the Holy Temple rebuilt, a Jewish State, a President who is equally accomplished with the sword and pen,—the whole campaign stretches before me. I see things like Napoleon, general and dictator alike."

"Truly we wish that," said the greengrocer cautiously. "But tonight it is only a question of a dozen men founding a collecting society."

Herzl did sometimes tend to "see things like Napoleon." He was concentrating now on the Kaiser, whose forthcoming visit to the Holy Land was the talk of the hour. Could the Kaiser be brought to use his influence with the Sultan, title to Palestine, or at least a charter for colonization, could be won at a stroke. Herzl, whose mind leapt to short cuts, was convinced that he could carry it off. Through the Grand Duke of Baden, uncle of the Kaiser and a fervent, prophecy-minded advocate of the cause, he was lifted to feverish hopes by the report that the Kaiser was favorably inclined to become protector of a Jewish emigration to Palestine and had consented to receive Herzl at the head of a Zionist delegation in Jerusalem. "The Kaiser has informed himself thoroughly on the matter and is full of enthusiasm. . . . He believes the Sultan will accept his advice," the Grand Duke told Herzl. An hour's interview with the Kaiser himself at Constantinople confirmed the Imperial interest, despite the frowns of von Bülow, the foreign minister. Next, in Palestine at a prearranged meeting outside the Mikveh Israel colony, the Kaiser rode up, guarded by Turkish outriders, reined in his horse, shook hands with Herzl to the awe of the crowd, remarked on the heat, pronounced Palestine a land with a future, "but it needs water, plenty of water," shook hands again, and rode off. Finally came the culminating moment of the formal meeting at Jerusalem (where a special entrance had been broken through the Jaffa gate so that the Kaiser could enter the Holy City without dismounting). The interview took place, but the Kaiser was vague, offhand. Herzl's written address had been blue-penciled in advance and all mention of the charter deleted.

Herzl had pinned all his hopes upon the Imperial communiqué, which he had envisaged as a public espousal of his cause by the most powerful man in Europe. Instead it omitted any mention of Zionism, merely referred lightly to a "Jewish deputation" and expressed nothing more than His Majesty's "benevolent interest" in general agricultural improvements in Palestine "as long as these were conducted in complete respect for the sovereignty of the Sultan." For Herzl it meant a total fiasco. But with that gift for seeing double that kept him going after each defeat, he wrote in the midst of his black despair that the Jewish people in the long run would have had to pay "the most usurious interest" for a German protectorate.

The shattering effect of his failure turned Herzl, not all at once, but slowly, toward England. In the interval there were four more years of unremitting efforts—of more congresses, petitions, diplomatic negotiations, speeches, mass meetings; and there were three more trips to Constantinople at the behest of money-hungry Turkish ministers. In a personal interview with Abdul Hamid in 1901 the Sultan agreed, if the Jews would take over the funding of the Turkish debt, to permit them to colonize—but in scattered settlements only, as Turkish subjects without a charter, and in Mesopotamia, not Palestine. "Small, shabby, with a badly dyed beard, long yellow teeth, ill-fitting colored shirt-cuffs, bleating voice, diffidence in every word, timidity in every glance—and that man rules!" Herzl wrote of the Sultan in disgust. He went home, forced at last to admit to himself that nothing useful could be got from the Turk at this time.

But in 1900 the Fourth Congress had been held in London and the Jewish National Fund at last established, though short of the capital of two million pounds that Herzl had thought essential. Speaking in one of those flashes of prophecy that seemed to visit him as if from some outside source, he foretold that "From this place the Zionist movement will take a higher and higher flight. . . . England the great, England the free, England with her eyes fixed on the seven seas, will understand us."

The possibility that a way station to Palestine might have to be sought, while waiting for the further indigence or final collapse of the Turkish Empire, now absorbed his attention. An old idea recurred, centering on Cyprus, from which he had once, in a flight of fancy, dreamed of the Jews' taking back Palestine by force. El Arish or elsewhere in the Sinai Peninsula, known then as Egyptian Palestine and in the Bible as the "Brook of Egypt," were other possi-

bilities. Both were occupied by England. Meanwhile pogroms in Rumania, sending a bloody trail of refugees
across Europe, added to the urgency. A homeland must be
found. For all the Kaiser's melodramatic ambitions, it was
England after all that actually stood on the frontiers of
Palestine. England was, Herzl had once written in one perfect, phophetic sentence, "the Archimedean point where
the lever can be applied."

At that moment England was undergoing pressure to
restrict Jewish immigration out of fear of cheap labor competition. A royal commission had been appointed to investigate and recommend a policy. Lord Rothschild, whose
seat in the House of Lords marked the final victory of
emancipation in England, who was a director of the Bank
of England and the leader of English Jewry, was a member of the commission. Long antagonistic to Herzl, whom
he repeatedly refused to meet, he now saw a use for him.
If the colonization project could be got going, it would
absorb the refugees from Eastern Europe, deflecting even
that small number that headed for London, and would
prevent the royal commission from recommending restric-
tive legislation. Herzl was summoned to the presence. If
invited to testify before the commission, what would he
tell them? Rothschild demanded.

"I want to ask the British government for a colonization
charter," Herzl shouted to his hard-of-hearing host.

"Don't say Charter. The word has a bad sound."

"Call it what you like. I want to found a Jewish colony
in British territory."

"Take Uganda."

"No, I can only use this—" And because there were others
present he wrote on a scrap of paper: "Sinai Peninsula,
Egyptian Palestine, Cyprus." "Are you in favor?"

Lord Rothschild considered. Then, with a pleased smile,
he replied: "Very much." He asked for a written prospectus
to submit to the colonial minister, Joseph Chamberlain,
with whom he promised to discuss the matter.

At that moment "Pushful Joe," the screw manufacturer from Birmingham, dubbed by the public the "Minister for Empire," was the most powerful man in England. The fox-like face, the monocle, the orchid in the buttonhole dominated Westminster, captured the populace, symbolized the peak of imperial self-satisfaction as the nineteenth century turned over into the twentieth. Queen Victoria's sixtieth jubilee in 1897, marked by the loyal presence of colonial and dominion delegates from all over the globe, thrilled Britons with family pride. The Boer War, despite the bitterness of the "Little Englanders" or "pro-Boers" as Chamberlain labeled the opposition, and though hardly a victory to be proud of, carried the triumphal march forward. Chamberlain, the inventor of business imperialism, had opened a vision of the Empire as a vast undeveloped market that if properly exploited (hence his crusade for Tariff Reform), would raise wages and profits for everybody. "Your hope of continuous employment depends upon our foreign commerce," he would say, adding that the future of the country depended not only on maintaining the Empire but "in taking every wise and legitimate opportunity of extending it."

The credo of the time was a happy conviction of England's God-chosen destiny to rule what Kipling called the "lesser breeds without the law." "Take up the White Man's Burden," Kipling proclaimed, while the official laureate, Alfred Austin, celebrated England's noble task "to harvest Empire, wiser than was Greece, wider than Rome!" No less fervent than the poets, Chamberlain, the man of affairs, agreed that England's "national mission" was to become "the predominant force of world history and universal civilization." It was England's obvious duty to extend her rule as wide and as fast as possible for the mutual benefit of conquerors and conquered. The natives, in the course of receiving the benefits of Christianity and civilization would buy Manchester cotton goods, Sheffield and Birmingham export articles in large quantities. This was the lesson that "Birmingham Joe" taught and that English manufacturers, merchants, and workers delighted to learn. In the warm summer rays of the Imperial sun they experienced the delightful sensation of doing the "right thing" and finding that it paid.

With Chamberlain as its prophet, Lord Cromer in Egypt, Lord Milner in Africa as its instruments, Lord Roberts and Lord Kitchener leading the Army as its heroes, and the unfortunate Liberals its unregarded Cassandras, expansion held the day.

The center of this swirl of power was not 10 Downing Street, but the Colonial Office, where Chamberlain, who had risen to fame at the Board of Trade, now chose to reign. Old Lord Salisbury had retired from the premiership in 1902 after successful conclusion of the Boer or "Joe's War," as the Prime Minister privately styled it. He had been succeeded by his nephew, Arthur Balfour, a scion of the Cecil family, which had waited four hundred and fifty years since the two Cecils, father and son, ruled England under Elizabeth, to produce again two successive prime ministers. Mr. Balfour, tall and willowy in his tennis flannels, was the very antithesis of Mr. Chamberlain. He was an aristocratic high-brow, a profound skeptic, and a philosopher who inherited not only his uncle's leadership of the Conservatives but also the qualities for which Lord Salisbury had been called "the most intelligent Englishman of the nineteenth century." There were many who thought that Mr. Chamberlain deserved the premiership rather than the younger Balfour—including, one suspects, Chamberlain himself. He maintained the contrary, insisting that he wanted only to continue at the Colonial Office.

How did it happen that this man should take an interest, casual though it was, in finding a homeland for the Jews? Biblical prophecy was of no concern to Birmingham Joe. Nor was he moved by humanitarian considerations or a sense of moral debt to God's ancient people. If anything, judging by a painful indiscretion reported by the *Times* correspondent, Wickham Steed, he was, to put it politely, unsympathetic. Steed, on one occasion in Rome, arranged a luncheon to bring Chamberlain together with Baron Sonnino, the Italian finance minister, by birth a Jew. Suddenly, over a gap in the general conversation, he heard the clear voice of Mr. Chamberlain, whose favorite subject was the special endowments of the Anglo-Saxon race, saying to Sonnino: "Yes sir, I have been called the apostle of the Anglo-Saxon race, and I am proud of the title. I think the Anglo-Saxon race is as fine as any on earth. . . . There is in fact only one race that I despise—the Jews, sir. They are physical cowards." While Steed kicked the Colonial Secretary under the table, Sonnino had taken up the challenge and was defending the Jews hotly. Later, after the company had disbanded, Chamberlain said to Steed: "Thank you for the friendly kick. It hurt, but I twigged, and now we have had it out."

Two years after this incident Chamberlain, following three meetings with Herzl, agreed to the proposition of Jewish colonization in Sinai if the Zionists could obtain the permission of the authorities in Egypt and, when this failed, himself proposed an offer of territory, with internal autonomy, in East Africa. England thus became the first country to negotiate officially with the Jews as a political entity and the first to make them an offer of territory. Granted that the land was not particularly suitable nor the offer a very generous one. It aroused passionate rejection from a large section of Zionists, was resented by English colonists in Africa, and, really favored by no one, was eventually allowed to lapse and die unmourned. But it was made at a time, following the Kishinev massacre in Russia, of desperate need. And in recognizing the Jews as a people it marked the first step in their relations with the outside world, toward regaining the nationhood lost nearly two thousand years before.

Chamberlain knew nothing of that and cared nothing. But as he listened to Herzl's always sweeping prognostica-

tions he quickly saw in them one of those "legitimate opportunities" for extending the British Empire. He saw in
the Jews a ready-made group of European colonizers available to settle, develop, and hold all but empty land under
the British aegis. From the private papers accessible to his
official biographer Chamberlain's thinking on this issue
has been described not only as an interest in acquiring
colonizers "for the development of what was virtually British territory," but also colonizers who, from a base in
Sinai, "might prove a useful instrument for extending
British influence into Palestine proper, when the time
came for the inevitable dismemberment of the Ottoman
Empire." When the project was switched to East Africa
Chamberlain's interest remained basically that of filling
conquered territory with useful settlers beholden to Britain.

To pretend, as does Mr. Julian Amery, author of the concluding volume of Chamberlain's official biography, that
Chamberlain was both "prophet and pioneer" in his brief
brush with Zionism or that he was the "first among British
statesmen" to see in Zionism both an end to the ancient
Jewish problem and a means for advancing British interests, or that he was the originator of an idea that Balfour
later took over, is absurd. A host of pioneers from Cromwell's day through Shaftesbury's preceded Chamberlain,
even if he (and his biographer), as seems quite likely,
were unaware of them. Balfour's interest stemmed from
his earlier tradition, not from Chamberlain. Balfour was,
of course, prime minister at the time of the Colonial Secretary's offer to Herzl. "I did my best to support it," he
later recalled. But though it was well-intentioned, though
it had many merits, it "had one serious defect. It was not
Zionism."

Herzl found this out for himself. A few months before
his death he wrote in his diary an account of an audience
with King Victor Emmanuel of Italy, during which he reminded the King that Napoleon had wanted to resettle the
Jews in Palestine. "No," said the King, "he only wanted to

turn the scattered people of the world into his agents."

"That," replied Herzl, "is an idea which I also found in Chamberlain."

But two years earlier, after the failure of all his efforts at Constantinople, what a sudden surge of hope had returned when he was informed that an interview with England's Colonial Secretary had been arranged! Before his departure for Constantinople in July 1902, summoned there by the Sultan for more fruitless haggling, he had left with Lord Rothschild an outline of the El Arish and Sinai projects, with a separate letter in which he said: "To avoid all misunderstanding now and for the future, I wish to make it clear that I have submitted this plan only because you are against Palestine. . . . But . . . a great Jewish settlement in the Eastern Mediterranean strengthens our position in regard to Palestine."

On his return to London in October he learned of the interview, arranged for him by Leopold Greenberg, editor of the *Jewish Chronicle,* who was Herzl's most valuable ally, agent, and counselor throughout the English negotiations. At his first conference with the "famous master of England" on October 23, 1902, his voice was inclined to tremble, but gradually it steadied, and "in my shaky English . . . I expounded to the immovable mask of Joe Chamberlain the entire Jewish Question." He next described the protracted dealings with the Sultan. "But you know how it is with Turkish negotiations. If you want to buy a carpet you must drink half a dozen cups of coffee and smoke a hundred cigarettes; then you throw in a few words about the carpet. Now I may have time to negotiate, but my people have not. They are starving in the Pale. I must bring them immediate succour. . . . I then came to the territory which I wanted to get from England: Cyprus, El Arish and the Sinai Peninsula."

Chamberlain replied that Cyprus was impossible; the Greek and Moslem inhabitants would object, and England would be duty bound to take their side. But if Herzl "could show him a spot in the British dominions where there was no white population yet, then we could talk!" As to El Arish and Sinai, Lord Cromer would have to be consulted. What a pity he had already gone back to Egypt.

Herzl's diary record continues: "I drew El Arish for him on a bit of paper that lay on his desk and also my Haifa-hinterland idea. I said that I hoped to induce the Turks to come more speedily to terms with me, if I also turned up by the 'Brook of Egypt' [Sinai]. I might then be able to get the Haifa district cheaper.

"At this the Mask laughed and dropped his monocle. But he had no idea where El Arish was." It amused Herzl to find that the Colonial Secretary "did not completely know his way around the British possessions of which he is at present the undisputed master. It was as though the manager of a big drygoods store was not quite sure whether some slightly uncommon article happened to be in stock." Together they consulted an atlas, and on finding El Arish in Egyptian territory Chamberlain said that there would be the same trouble with the natives as in Cyprus. "No," Herzl told him, "we are not heading for Egypt. We have been there before." At this the Mask laughed again. "It was only now that he understood fully my wish to have a place of assembly for the Jewish people in the neighborhood of Palestine."

With Chamberlain, as with Rothschild, Herzl made no attempt to conceal his concept of Sinai as a jumping-off base for the old homeland. He argued that Arish and Sinai were untenanted; that England could give the area to the Jews and gain an increase in power thereby. This seemed to impress Chamberlain, and on being asked point-blank, "Would you agree to our founding a Jewish colony on the Sinai Peninsula?" he replied: "Yes, if Lord Cromer is in favour. . . ." He asked Herzl to come to see him again the following day.

Herzl left with the impression of a practical, energetic man, not brilliant, not imaginative, but essentially a business man determined to increase his business. Chamberlain, in fact, hardly pausing to consider a problem that had baffled the world for two thousand years, went ahead with the speed of a business tycoon who has been offered a favorable deal. When Herzl arrived at the Colonial Office next morning Chamberlain told him he had arranged a meeting with the foreign secretary, Lord Lansdowne, for that afternoon. "I have prepared the way for you. You will lay the whole matter before him. Be careful to reassure Lord Lansdowne that you are not contemplating a Jameson Raid from El Arish upon Palestine."*

"He positively beamed as he said that. . . . I said, 'Of course there can be no question of that, as I want to go to Palestine only with the Sultan's consent.' He looked at me with amusement, as if to say, 'the deuce you do!' "

Herzl hurried on to his conference with Lord Lansdowne, whose secretary told him that Chamberlain had been most pressing in arranging the meeting. The Foreign Secretary listened affably, repeated everything depended on Lord Cromer, and agreed to arrange for Leopold Greenberg to proceed to Egypt, where negotiations could be carried further on the spot.

In November Greenberg returned and reported that Lord Cromer had not said No but had raised one objection in the fact that the Sinai Peninsula was already the subject of frontier disputes between Turkey and Egypt. Nevertheless Herzl, encouraged by Cromer's having taken the colonization project seriously, drew up the formal declaration of the Zionist program and the El Arish project that he had promised to submit to Lansdowne. The first step should be British consent for a Zionist commission to investigate the locale, the next a land concession from the Egyptian government. Ultimately the terrible problem of

---

*Dr. Jameson's raid on the Transvaal in 1895, planned with the knowledge of Cecil Rhodes, prime minister of the Cape Colony, precipitated the Boer War and was widely believed to have had the secret blessing of the Colonial Secretary.

the Pale would be solved, and England would "benefit materially," but above all the Jews would gain a guarantee of "colonial rights," which would mean more than anything else.

Here Herzl was hinting at statehood, though he was apparently not ready to say so openly to the British government. Lord Cromer, to whom the memorandum was forwarded by the Foreign Office, immediately pounced on this point. "In your letter you remark that you 'will become great and promising by the granting of this right of colonization.' Your letter does not make clear what is to be understood by these words and what kind of rights the colonists will expect." This failure to make statehood an explicit aim was repeated by the Zionist leaders at the Paris Peace Conference in 1918, and it led to endless trouble and bitter recriminations under the Mandate. It is quite possible, however, that an explicit statement would have led to equal if not more trouble, especially from the assimilationist Jews, whom it would have infuriated. This Herzl could not afford to do, since he was still hoping to obtain from them the money for capitalization of the Colonial Trust. Whichever way he turned this problem always baffled his efforts. He could not get the land unless he could show that he had the money, and he could not get the money unless he could show that he had the land.

In any event Lord Cromer had warned that the Egyptian attitude indicated that "no sanguine hopes of success ought to be entertained." And Lord Lansdowne, in his covering letter, pointed out that the colonists would have to accept Turkish citizenship under Egyptian law. Herzl, however, refused to be discouraged. Already he suspected that the Sinai project would not come off, and though he obtained the consent of his Zionist colleagues for the investigating commission, in reply to Lansdowne he began to prepare the ground for some alternative territory. This time he was more, if not wholly, explicit. The land itself mattered less, he said, than the creation of an atmosphere so Jewish in character "that it could guarantee them, as Jews, freedom, justice and security. Your Lordship will, I know, appreciate the immeasurable worth of the national consciousness which in defiance of everyone has rescued our people from the lowest forms of degradation in the past and will lift us out of the unhappy condition in which we find ourselves today."

At a subsequent interview at the Foreign Office early in 1903 he found no ready acceptance of this point of view. He was received by the permanent undersecretary, Sir Thomas Sanderson, "a lean, angular, clever, suspicious old man" who was scared off by the talk of colonial "rights." He tersely remarked that there could be no question of an international guarantee; that the most to be hoped for was a charter from the Egyptian government, of which details would have to be settled by Lord Cromer. "The English government will go as far as Cromer, no farther."

At this time Chamberlain, the chiefly interested party on the English side, was not in London, having left it in November 1902 on a tour of Africa to bind up the wounds of the Boer War. On his travels through Uganda and the Kenya highlands in East Africa he heard from the English colonists of their need for more settlers to strengthen their fingernail hold on the country. Again Chamberlain's quick mind seized on the opportunity. "If Dr. Herzl," he wrote in his diary on December 21, "were at all inclined to transfer his efforts to East Africa, there would be no difficulty in finding suitable land for Jewish settlers. But I assume that this country is too far removed from Palestine to have any attractions for him. . . ." But he mentally filed the thought for future reference.

Meanwhile at Cairo things were going badly for the El Arish project. The crucial question of just how far Lord Cromer was prepared to go was being plainly answered: not very far. The Zionist commission of experts had reported the land quite unsuitable without massive irrigation. The Egyptian government was obstinately against permitting any diversion of the waters of the Nile. Turkish wires at Cairo were being pulled against a charter. Herzl, with his obsessive sense of time running out, himself went to Cairo to see Lord Cromer in March 1903. He knew well enough that pressure from the Proconsul could dispose of all the objections, but Lord Cromer was cool and would go no farther than to say that he would have the irrigation expert of the Anglo-Egyptian administration, Sir William Garstyne, examine the needs further.

Back in London in April Herzl went to see Chamberlain, who had himself just returned from Africa. It was at this meeting that the Colonial Secretary first broached the historic offer. Hearing from Herzl that the Sinai prospects looked gray indeed, he said that in East Africa "I saw the very country for you. The coast region is hot, but the farther you get into the interior the more excellent the climate becomes, for Europeans too. . . . So I thought to myself: that would be just the country for Dr. Herzl."

Exactly what or where was the country Chamberlain had in mind has never been made perfectly clear. It is usually carelessly referred to as "Uganda," but when the Zionists went out to investigate and found that country unsuitable for Europeans much criticism resulted. Herzl's notes on the conversation specifically quote Chamberlain as naming Uganda. Chamberlain's biographer, on the other hand, maintains that he had in mind the Kenya highlands, bordering on Uganda, which were eminently suitable for white settlement, and that in describing it to Herzl he may have mentioned seeing the country from the Uganda railway, or something of the kind, which led to Herzl's misunderstanding. Whatever the truth of the matter, Herzl at that time tried rather to explain to Chamberlain the importance of the Holy Land as the focus of the Zionist movement. Sinai was only a step away, and he urged Chamberlain to swing Lord Cromer toward a favorable decision. Chamberlain promised to try.

This was on April 24, 1903. In the next days the first

reports of the Easter Week pogroms at Kishinev appeared in the newspapers of Europe and America. The shrieks and murders, the stoning of helpless people in flight; women attacked, babies flung on the cobblestones, homes plundered and burned, synagogues defiled; an old rabbi stabbed as, backed against the altar with arms flung out, he attempted to protect the Torah with his body; the sacred scroll torn from him and trampled in filth—these were the reports carried in the press and in the shocked dispatches of diplomats.

On top of this, early in May, Herzl began receiving cables from Greenberg and Colonel Goldsmith, whom he had left in charge of the negotiations in Cairo, presaging their defeat. Garstyne's report had come through, stating that five times as much water was needed for irrigation as originally estimated. Lord Cromer considered the whole project too chancy to make it worth while bringing the heavy pressure necessary to overcome Egyptian objections. Finally, on May 11, came the official rejection.

For Herzl it was a worse defeat than the Kaiser, the Sultan, and all the others. Following upon Kishinev, it was like the implacable doom mounting in a Greek tragedy. In no other circumstances would he probably have considered the East African offer, knowing as he did that the land and the soul of Judaism were, in the end, inseparable. On May 20 Chamberlain repeated the offer on more definite terms in an interview with Greenberg. Herzl authorized him to negotiate further on the basis of a "publicly recognized, legally secured plan of settlement." This would be his answer to Kishinev—"We must play the politics of the hour." Privately he hoped that a show of serious interest in East Africa indicating that the Jews were prepared to go elsewhere might induce the wavering Sultan to reconsider offering them better terms. He began again to work for a Turkish charter, perhaps in Mesopotamia, anywhere within view of Palestine. In the hope of bringing added influence to bear upon the Porte, he even went to Russia to see the man behind the pogroms, the abhorred Von Plehve, minister of the interior, who, he thought, would not be averse to aiding the exit of the Jews from Russia. Herzl would have gone to see the devil himself had he thought he might prove useful.

While he was gone Greenberg carried on the East Africa negotiations. He had few illusions about the place as a geographical solution but he believed that if the offer were made officially it would, as he wrote to Herzl, involve Britain in the first political recognition by a modern state "of our people as a Nation." Even if the Zionist Congress should refuse the offer it would not matter, he continued, because "we shall have obtained from Britain a recognition that it cannot ever go back on," and he added, with a quite remarkable prescience, "they will have to make a further suggestion and this, it is possible, will gradually and surely lead us to Palestine."

Greenberg, thinking along these lines, envisaged the offer being made in the form of an agreement between the British government and the Jewish Colonial Trust, but the Foreign Office, to which Chamberlain had turned over the negotiations, was too wary for him. On the margin of Greenberg's draft agreement, now in the Foreign Office archives, can be read the careful comments of C. J. B. Hurst, legal officer of the Foreign Office, neatly picking out each piece of autonomy asked for. Underneath, Lord Lansdowne, the foreign secretary, has pencilled, "I fear it is throughout an *imperium in imperio*."

After a further interview with Greenberg, Hurst summarized the Foreign Office position in a memorandum of July 23 stating that there would be no objection to a Jewish colony subject to the ordinary laws of a protectorate, "but if the promoters are looking for more than this and want a petty state of their own, I fear there would be great objection." Here is the crux of the trouble that was to reappear in the Mandate.

But Pushful Joe, in a hurry to settle a useful and energetic people in the outposts of Africa, was not the man to worry about implications. He spurred the reluctant Foreign Office, which in August finally confirmed the offer though not in terms of Greenberg's draft agreement. Instead, a letter of August 14, 1903, from Sir Clement Hill, superintendent of African Protectorates for the Foreign Office, was addressed to Greenberg that promised "to entertain favorably proposals for the establishment of a Jewish colony or settlement on conditions which will enable the members to observe their National customs" and, if a suitable site were to be found in East Africa, to make "the grant of a considerable area of land" and appoint "a Jewish official as chief of the local administration . . . such local autonomy being conditional upon the right of H.M. Government to exercise general control."

In the impreciseness of the wording the fatal flaw that was to mar the Balfour Declaration is here already apparent. It was no doubt deliberate. Neither the Jews nor the British government ever wanted to come to grips with the problem in the back of everybody's mind—ultimate statehood. The Zionists, or most of them, were looking ahead to statehood but avoided saying so for fear of endangering whatever negotiations were in progress. The British government, equally, knew statehood to be the goal, in 1903 as Hurst's memorandum indicates, as well as in 1917,* but being traditionally averse to precise definitions, on the theory that the less exactness the more room for maneuver, preferred to leave as much unsaid as possible.

Herzl was notified of the offer on his return from Russia. The Sixth Zionist Congress was to meet at Basle at the end of the month. In a painful moral struggle Herzl tried to convince himself and his colleagues on the Actions Committee (the governing body of the Congress) that they were justified in proposing an offer that was not Zionism, that could not be reconciled with the original Basle Pro-

*See below, pages 346–347 for Balfour's and Lloyd George's explanation of what they meant by the phrase "National Home."

gram. But it was a place to go—a *Nachtasyl*, in the words of Max Nordau, a temporary asylum, a shelter for the night; and would they be justified if they did *not* present the first offer of land ever made to the Jews since the loss of their homeland? No official vote of the Committee in this agonizing situation seems to have been reached, but when the Congress met, the East African offer of the British government was announced by Herzl.

Stunned silence, amazement, followed by a storm of applause, was the first reaction. But as soon as the delegates began to emerge from the shock of actually receiving, as a people, an offer of something from a Great Power, they became disquieted. As the various national delegations met separately to debate the issue, opposition grew, especially in the delegation from Russia, the most devotedly Zionist, the most passionately argumentative of them all. Even the delegate from Kishinev, who had previously told Herzl that, to get out of Russia, the Russian Jews would even go to hell, now rejected East Africa. When the vote was finally taken, not on whether to accept the offer, but whether to authorize the sending of an investigating committee to East Africa, it was carried in the affirmative, 295 to 178. But in a body the negatives rose and left the hall. At a meeting called among themselves there was anger, with cries of "Traitor!" at Herzl's name; but there were also weeping and rending of clothes in the traditional rites of mourning.

The depth of feeling, the principles at stake, cannot be fully understood without a realization of the passionate attachment to Palestine. Palestine was, as Ahad-ha-Am continually preached, not only the land, but also the source —and the only possible source—of the spiritual strength that would re-create a sense of nationhood in the Jews. Back in the days of the first Congress, as a self-proclaimed "mourner at the wedding," he had refused to be swept away by Herzl's political visions and had always maintained that "a cultural center" in Palestine must come first. His influence, particularly on the Eastern Jews, had been profound and was expressed now in their sense of betrayal of the cause. One of them, shouting "Death to the East African!" attempted to assassinate Max Nordau.

A backlog of simmering discontent with Herzl's autocratic leadership, an old antagonism among the Russians for the too worldly, too Western figure who had become their leader, also played a part. They considered his reliance on high-level deals naive. But Herzl was not so much naive as he was in a hurry. His sense of urgency was greater than the Russians' if less realistic. To them persecution was an old story; to Herzl, in whom normal experience was speeded up like a film run too fast, it seemed to require an immediate solution for which he felt personally responsible. Warned by frequent spells of heart trouble, he could hear death hovering at his back. This identification of the movement with himself was his greatest weakness; he was never quite sure that it would go on without him. "Don't do anything foolish when I am dead," he wrote suddenly in the midst of a long letter of instructions to a colleague. Two months later, in July 1904, he died at the age of forty-four.

Actual progress to the Promised Land was to prove slower and more painful than he ever dreamed. Perhaps it was as well that leadership passed to the more patient, more practical, more level-headed Weizmann. Herzl's restless spirit could never have supported another forty years of wandering in the wilderness. It has always seemed startling that the earlier Israelites took so long on a journey that need have been only a straight three hundred miles. When Joseph's brethren came down to Egypt for grain they covered the same distance in a matter of months—and went back and forth several times. The Scriptural if not the historical explanation has been that the Exodus generation, unfit for the Promised Land, was forced to wander round about until a new generation grew up, ready to enter in. The old experience was to be repeated by the modern exiles.

But Palestine was still the only Zion. The East African proposal split the Zionist movement into fractions, although, of course, the lines of division already existed. Under the blow the fractions simply came apart. The negatives, calling themselves "Zion-Zionists," convened a secessionist conference at Kharkov. Subsequently Herzl, whose heart was in Palestine and who, in his last year, was trying again for the Turkish charter, effected a reconciliation with the negatives. As a result another faction, favoring East Africa, split off under the leadership of Israel Zangwill to form a group called the Territorialists.

Meantime a survey of the land in East Africa disclosed many obstacles. In the area originally proposed large tracts were already under option. Protests from English colonists in Kenya began appearing in the *Times*. Empty land offered instead by the colonial administration of East Africa proved to be unsuited to Europeans. There were hints that the British government was none too anxious to follow through on the issue; and Herzl and the majority of the Zionist leaders were glad enough to be disembarrassed of it. For a while haphazard negotiations continued, and the offer, though never officially dropped, was allowed quietly to fade away.

After Herzl's death the Territorialists continued to press for it; but by that time Chamberlain, its progenitor on the English side, whose interest had been only a passing one, had left the government. He resigned at the end of 1903, the better to carry his protective tariff to the public without wrecking the party. Never deeply concerned anyway, he did not make much difference to the fate of the East African scheme by his departure. In not being Palestine it had been born with a congenital deformity, and of this it died.

CHAPTER XVII

CULMINATION:

The Balfour Declaration and the Palestine Mandate

1. Mr. Balfour and Doctor Weizmann

Palestine's fatal geography made it inevitable that Britain would take it over when the Turkish Empire should break up. The unrolling of history from the time when British gunboats shelled Napoleon out of Syria to the time when Lord Salisbury posed the alternative of "taking the country for ourselves" was leading, as we have seen, directly to this conclusion. But that Britain should at the same time reopen the old land to settlement by its ancient proprietors added a new twist to the usual method of annexation.

The ground had been laid in Balfour's mind a decade before the Declaration when, as prime minister, his curiosity was piqued by the Zionists' rejection of Chamberlain's offer of East Africa. His curiosity led him to a fateful meeting with Weizmann and to an understanding of Palestine irredentism. In the intervening years before the war there was stirring and developing in his mind a desire to see England "do something" about the Jews.

Cynical is a word used of Mr. Balfour by people who knew him almost as often as they try to describe his charm, which left everyone feeling happy who talked with him. He had a profound and philosophic mind, he was lazy, imperturbable in any fracas, shunned detail, left facts to subordinates, played tennis whenever possible, but pursued his principles of statecraft with every art of politics under the command of a superb intelligence. As one who belonged among the rulers by birth, owned an independent income and remained a bachelor, he was detached from the scramble of ordinary life. The aloofness together with the impression of his physical height made him seem a lofty being. "He was quite fearless," says Churchill. "When they took him to the Front to see the war he admired the bursting shells blandly through his pince-nez." He adds, "There was, in fact, no way of getting at him."

But the problem of the Jews did in fact get at him.

In Balfour the motive was Biblical rather than imperial. If the Biblical culture of England can be said to have any meaning in England's redemption of Palestine from the rule of Islam, it may be epitomized in Balfour. Though he was the reverse of Shaftesbury, not ardent but a skeptic, not a religious enthusiast but a philosophical pessimist, he was nevertheless strongly infused, like the Evangelicals and the Puritans, with the Hebraism of the Bible. Long before he ever heard of Zionism Balfour, steeped in the Bible from childhood, had felt a particular interest in the "people of the Book." According to his niece, companion, and biographer, Mrs. Dugdale, it was a "life long" interest that "originated in the Old Testament training of his mother and in his Scottish upbringing. As he grew up his intellectual admiration and sympathy for certain aspects of Jewish philosophy and culture grew also and the problem of the Jew in the modern world seemed to him of immense importance. He always talked eagerly on this and I remember in childhood imbibing from him the idea that Christian religion and civilization owes to Judaism an immeasurable debt, shamefully ill repaid."

In 1895 a visitor to the Balfour home at Whittingame, Lady Constance Battersea, a Rothschild by birth, records that after dinner they "talked a great deal about the Jews, alien immigration, synagogues, chorus, churches." Echoing the usual paeans of Balfour's lady admirers, she confides her zest at being under the same roof with "the most delightful of men . . . lovable, distinguished, broad, refined —oh dear, what a gulf between him and most men," and adds that he read a chapter from Isaiah "beautifully and reverently."

The mention of Isaiah is interesting. Nowhere else does the eternal longing for Palestine ring with such sound of bronze as in Isaiah. The cool, aloof Balfour was anything but an Old Testament character himself. But of all the Englishmen who at one time or another helped along the Return he was possibly the only one interested in it from the point of view of the Jews. To him they were neither tools of the Christian millennium nor agents of a business imperialism, but simply exiles who should be given back, in payment of Christianity's "immeasurable debt," their homeland. Not just any land, but the old land. Why Palestine? "The answer is," he wrote, "that the position of the Jews is unique. For them race, religion and country are inter-related as they are inter-related in the case of no other religion and no other country on earth."

Mr. Balfour was not, of course, the only begetter of the Declaration which, as foreign secretary, he was to sign. Indeed, according to whose memoirs one reads, one can come away with the impression that Lloyd George was finally responsible; or, no, that Sir Herbert Samuel really persuaded the Cabinet; or, wait a moment, that of course Dr. Weizmann pulled all the wires behind the scenes. Mr. Balfour left no memoirs and made no claims, but it was not an accident of office that the Declaration bears his name.

It began in 1906 when the Conservative government of which Balfour was prime minister was defeated in Parliament and called a general election. In the course of contesting his seat at Manchester Balfour was brought together by his political agent, a Mr. Dreyfus, with a young scientist and ardent Zionist who was one day to be the first president of Israel. Chaim Weizmann, then an instructor in chemistry at Victoria University in Manchester, was in those days emerging as Herzl's successor in the leadership of the Zionist movement. He was thirty-two and had been less than two years in England, but he had been a worker in the Zionist cause since boyhood days in the Russian Pale, when he distributed leaflets and collected kopecks for the Chovevé Zion societies. Collection time came traditionally at the Feast of Purim in March, when the thaws filled the streets of Pinsk with mud and slush, and the boy in a brother's handed-down overcoat, tramping from door to door, found these earliest steps toward Palestine cold and uncomfortable. Later, as a delegate to the Zionist Congress, when the Uganda issue came up he stood firm for Palestine first, last, and always. To an Englishman many years later he posed the question, apropos of the rejection of Uganda: Would the English, if exiled for centuries, accept as a substitute permission to return to Calais? He could be, acknowledged this man (Sir Ronald Storrs, the governor of Jerusalem), "almost frighteningly convincing."

Weizmann's was the voice of Eastern Jewry, not the cultivated, cosmopolitan voice of Herzl or of the moneyed and influential Western Jew who had hitherto conducted the contacts with Western statesmen. Curiously, it was Balfour who sought the interview, out of an intellectual curiosity to understand what had motivated the rejection of the East African offer. Beneath more pressing issues the question had remained gnawingly unanswered in the back of his mind. Such Jews as he knew personally, of the assimilated Reform group, who shied violently at the very mention of Palestine, would not, if they could, explain the passion and the agony of spirit stirred up by the Uganda affair. Dreyfus, whom he questioned about it, offered to bring along his young friend from the University as a specimen of the "other Jew" and a possible source of enlighten-

ment. It was characteristic of Balfour, as well as illustra-
tive of his unique relation to the Palestine problem, that
he alone came to it, not with ulterior designs to promote,
but rather in the spirit of inquiry. One can hardly imagine
any other figure who, as a freshly deposed prime minister
in the midst of a slam-bang political campaign, would concern himself with a matter irrelevant to votes or to immediate political issues.

Yet, as these things sometimes happen, the meeting
proved historic. In it the Exile and the Intermediary Power
met and briefly joined in a sort of chemical reaction.
Neither expected much of the interview. Balfour, at his
election headquarters in a Manchester hotel, had set aside
fifteen minutes for his visitor. He stayed to listen for over
an hour. Weizmann, for his part understandably nervous
at the prospect of explaining to the renowned statesman
in his shaky English all the history and hopes, the divisions
and cross-currents of his people in fifteen minutes, hardly
hoped to accomplish anything. Balfour, long legs stretched
out in the languid Treasury Bench pose that the cartoons
had made famous, asked why the Zionists were so bitterly
opposed to the Uganda offer. The British government, he
said, was really anxious to do something to relieve the
misery of the Jews; and the problem was a practical one,
calling for a practical approach.

In reply, Weizmann recalls, "I plunged into a long ha-
rangue on the meaning of the Zionist movement . . . that
nothing but a deep religious conviction expressed in modern political terms could keep the movement alive and that
this conviction had to be based on Palestine and Palestine
alone. Any deflection from Palestine was—well, a form of
idolatry. I added that if Moses had come into the 6th
Zionist Congress when it was adopting the resolution in
favor of the Commission for Uganda, he would surely have
broken the tablets once again. . . .

"I was sweating blood and trying to find some less pon-
derous way of expressing myself. . . . Suddenly I said: 'Mr.

Balfour, supposing I were to offer you Paris instead of London, would you take it?'

"He sat up, looked at me and answered: 'But, Dr. Weizmann, we have London.'

"'That is true,' I said. 'But we had Jerusalem when London was a marsh.'

"He leaned back and continued to stare at me. . . . I did not see him again till 1914."

Weizmann's emphasis on Palestine as the center of a faith, his curiously just phrase that a swerving away from it was a form of idolatry, would have bored or bewildered Joe Chamberlain, but it was exactly right for Balfour. "Balfour told me often," writes Mrs. Dugdale, "about the impression the conversation made on him" and how from that time he understood that the Jewish form of patriotism would never be satisfied with anything less than Palestine.

Balfour understood Weizmann. Later, during the war years, the acquaintance was renewed and became intimate. "A statesman with his heart in science," said Storrs, "would take refuge from party routine with a scientist whose soul was in politics and the first seeds of sympathy were sown." At the end when Balfour lay dying, Weizmann was the only friend outside his family circle admitted to see him. "No words passed between them for Balfour was very weak and Dr. Weizmann much overcome." Balfour moved his hand and touched the bowed head of his visitor. In the silence of the room the bond between them could be felt.

Because Weizmann represented the unassimilated Jews who accounted for the bulk of the Zionists, he personified their cause in Balfour's eyes. Never excitable, never extravagant like Herzl, Weizmann was suave, immensely intelligent, and a shrewd negotiator, a "minimalist" who scaled his demands to what was practically obtainable. He was the possessor, too, of a charm as magnetic as Balfour's own. His personality, one suspects, caused Balfour rather to romanticize the movement. "As guardians of a continuity of religious and racial tradition" the Zionists were, Balfour decided, "a great conservative force in world politics."

Immediately following the fateful meeting of the two personalities at Manchester in 1906 Balfour's party lost the general election, and Balfour was freed from the duties of public office. He turned "with the ardor he reserved for his speculative moments" (to quote Mrs. Dugdale) to the new subject that had caught his interest.

Here, he saw, was an opportunity not only of bringing the Holy Land back to life out of the desolation of Moslem rule, but also of "doing something material to wash out an ancient stain upon our own civilization." The phrase is his own, from a critical speech in the House of Lords in 1922, when a well-supported motion to reject the Mandate was under debate. Rising to oppose the motion, Balfour on that occasion produced the one serious defense that he ever attempted of the policy in Palestine that bore his name. He would be unfair to himself, he said at the end, if he sat down "without insisting to the utmost of my ability" that there was a great ideal involved in Britain's sponsorship of the Jews' return to their homeland. "This is the ideal which chiefly moves me . . . that Christendom is not oblivious to their faith, is not unmindful of the service they have rendered to the great religions of the world, and that we desire to the best of our ability to give them the opportunity of developing in peace and quietness under British rule, those great gifts which hitherto they have been compelled to bring to fruition in countries which know not their language and belong not to their race."

Back in the early days of his study of Zionism Balfour was faced with the antipathy of the Jews of his own acquaintance, who were, almost to a man, frigidly anti-Zionist. Never himself having felt insecure, never having known any challenge or possibility of challenge to his own social position, Balfour was unable to understand what upset them so. He questioned Lady Constance, who was visiting Whittingame again in 1911. "A. J. B. is hugely interested in all Jewish questions," she wrote to her sister. "He asked a great deal about Claude [Montefiore; the intellectual leader of the assimilationist group in London]—his books, his attitude, his influence. He wanted me to tell him how C. stood with the Community and how his writings affected the Jewish question." Regrettably, Lady Constance adds, A. J. B. "gets a good deal of information from Natty, naturally very one-sided." The reference is to her cousin Nathaniel, first Lord Rothschild, who, since his contact with Herzl, had become too favorable to the cause, at least in the opinion of the lesser, or intermarrying, Rothschilds. Natty's son was later to be the recipient of the Balfour Declaration, which was issued in the form of a "letter to Lord Rothschild." But most of the English Jews shared the attitude implicit in Lady Constance's *Reminiscences* as well as in another book of memoirs about her family, both published after the event, which, despite their frequent mention of Balfour himself, pass over the Balfour Declaration in tight-lipped silence.

This attitude was to leave its mark on history when its bitter-end spokesman, Mr. Edwin Montagu, was able, from his post in the War Cabinet, not to stop the Declaration altogether, but at least so to blur its wording as to leave unclear and forever controversial exactly what its drafters had in mind. The fatal results of this evasion will appear later. The rationale of the anti-Zionists' position is not our subject, and any attempt to elucidate it stirs such vast muddy waters as to make the attempt unwise, short of a volume. If mistaken, it was at least understandable, though it puzzled Balfour. He felt that the assimilationists' fears that a return to Palestine would "adversely affect their position in the country of their adoption" were groundless. On the contrary, he said, "ancient antipathies" would be lessened only by giving the Jews "that which all other nations possess: a local habitation and a national home."

That much Balfour accomplished, and he rated it above

all else in the fifty-year career that had taken him to the pinnacle of government. "Near the end of his days," reports Mrs. Dugdale, "he said to me that on the whole he felt that what he had been able to do for the Jews had been the thing he looked back upon as the most worth his doing." The burden of the past must have weighed heavily in Balfour's estimate. There was more to it than the satisfaction of righting an old wrong. He felt (one can only suppose) that a special dignity attached to this one act out of all his life's work, when for a moment he had walked in the footsteps of the ancestral heroes of the Old Testament.

2. *The Balfour Declaration: acetone or conscience?*

The popular legend that England's promise of a "National Home" for the Jews in Palestine, as incorporated in the Balfour Declaration, was a reward to Dr. Weizmann for his solution of the acetone shortage is attractively simple but totally inadequate. Responsibility for it rests with Lloyd George, whose *War Memoirs* record how he proposed to recommend Dr. Weizmann for some honor, how Weizmann demurred, how Lloyd George asked: "Is there nothing we can do as recognition of your valuable assistance to the country?" and how Weizmann answered: "Yes, I would like you to do something for my people." This, remarks Lloyd George with a flourish, was the "fount and origin" of the Balfour Declaration.

No doubt the conversation took place, but the "fount and origin" was not in this chivalric episode, but in the hard facts of the war in the Middle East.

The world had gone to war in August 1914. Last-ditch English diplomacy tried hard to secure Turkish neutrality, but the Turks openly joined the Central Powers late in October, having in fact been in secret alliance with Germany for some months. The break was finally made; Lord

Salisbury's harsh judgment of long ago—"we put our money on the wrong horse"—was proved only too true; the wrong horse was now racing in German silks. The Allies, England, France, and Russia declared war on Turkey, November 2–5, England incidentally allowing herself the small comfort of annexing Cyprus. Two weeks later English forces from India took Basra on the Persian Gulf and began the advance toward Bagdad in a general movement to close in on the Turks from the East.

The crucial point, however, was of course the Suez Canal, the hinge on which hung the British Empire. Reinforcements were hurriedly sent out just in time to meet the Turkish troops who had crossed the Sinai Peninsula and launched their attack on the Canal in February 1915. Though thrown back, they remained a threat that was to make the Middle East a major theater of war from then on. The strategy enthusiastically urged by Winston Churchill, seconded by Kitchener and Lloyd George, focused on the Middle East as *the* major theater of English effort, especially in view of the deadlock on the Western front. The Dardanelles campaign was a famous failure. It did not succeed in taking Constantinople or bringing assistance to Russia by the back door. But the land campaigns in Mesopotamia and later in Palestine eventually, after four years of sieges, attacks, and stalled operations, rolled the Turks back, out of Syria, Mesopotamia, and Arabia, back into Turkey proper. On the Mesopotamian front the British succeeded in taking Bagdad in March 1917, but their advance up the Tigris and Euphrates was halted when their Russian allies, supposed to be flanking the Turks from the north, melted away after the Revolution. Meanwhile the other movement, based on Egypt, began the advance into Syria in December 1916. The British after laying a railroad and a pipeline across the Sinai desert, took El Arish and crossed into Palestine. At Gaza on the border, where the Turks had been reinforced by German troops, the British twice met defeat, but at last, after a six months stalemate and a regrouping under a new commander, General Allenby, they took the town of Samson's tragic triumph. Jaffa, where Richard forced the beachhead long ago, was taken next, then Jerusalem in December 1917, and ultimately Damascus, Homs, and Aleppo, until all of Syria was in Allied hands.

Behind and between these military campaigns were carried on some of the war's most complicated, entangled, and mutually conflicting diplomatic maneuvers, of the kind that so disgusted President Wilson with secret covenants secretly arrived at.

This was the moment for which the eagles had gathered. The Turkish carcass was about to be distributed. Russia, France, and England each had claims; and meanwhile two new parties had entered the picture: the Jews and the Arabs, with ambitions of their own that were being simultaneously encouraged by Britain for various strategic reasons. Everybody was negotiating with somebody, and nobody held all the strings in any one hand at any one time. The Foreign Office was negotiating with France and Russia. The War Office was negotiating with the Arabs, sometimes with one set, sometimes with another, sometimes through the Arab Bureau at Cairo, sometimes through Colonel Lawrence in the field. The Zionists were negotiating with various Cabinet members in London. A crisscross of secret treaties, pledges, promises, and "understandings" were made which have never since been satisfactorily untangled. It would be foolish as well as futile to attempt to extract a basic British policy out of this mess. There was no single clear policy except to win the war and to emerge from it as firmly intrenched in the Middle East as possible. This was the goal that the British were pursuing by whatever pragmatic means seemed necessary at the moment or seemed advisable to a particular negotiator in his particular task.

One of the wordiest quarrels of our time—and one of the saddest—has been the result. Endless disputation by op-

posing groups among the British, by Arabs and Zionists
and anti-Zionists, by White Papers, by the Permanent
Mandates Commission, by some seventeen Commissions
of Inquiry; hours, even weeks, of Parliamentary debate,
countless books, columns in the press, reports, mass meetings, legal briefs, have all quite failed to pin down for history exactly what the British intended the future fate of
Palestine to be. The fact is they hardly knew themselves.
They certainly intended that Palestine should come under
British control and that France should be kept out. But as
to what form that control should take they were never too
specific. They rather hoped that time would work it out.
Meanwhile the various negotiators each followed his own
bent. What Colonel Lawrence intended was rather more
sweeping than what his chief at the Arab Bureau, Sir
Henry MacMahon, intended; what Sir Mark Sykes intended was never entirely clear to anybody for long and
tended to veer according to whether he was dealing with
the French, the Arabs, or the Zionists; nor are we quite
sure that what the Foreign Secretary intended was what
the Prime Minister intended. Indeed, we can be sure that
it was not. Balfour's eye was on the revival of Israel, Lloyd
George's on containing the French.

All that we can tell is what happened. At the outbreak
of war Sir Herbert Samuel, the future first high commissioner for Palestine, was a member of Asquith's government. According to his account he felt it incumbent on
himself, as the first Jewish Cabinet minister, to learn
about the Zionist movement, and after some study he
emerged favorably disposed. In November 1914, after the
Turks' entrance into the war, he talked over the possibilities with Sir Edward Grey, then foreign secretary, and
Lloyd George, then at the Exchequer. He argued that England should take the lead in supporting the project because
the geographical situation of Palestine made it important
to the British Empire to have friendly inhabitants there.
Grey showed "a strongly sentimental attraction" for the

plan and Lloyd George was "very keen" on it. The advisability of securing Russia's support in an attempt to regain for the hard-pressed Czar the loyalty of the Russian Jews was discussed, likewise the probable attitude of France. Grey warned that when France came to put forward her claims in Syria, Britain should be careful not to acquiesce in any that might be "inconsistent with the creation of a Jewish state in Palestine." The wording shows that these earliest talks were in terms of a "state," not a "home."

On the strength of this conversation Grey, through his ambassador in Petrograd, asked for the support of the Russian government, but received no encouragement. Meanwhile there entered into the act one who was to play a galvanizing yet a background role: C. P. Scott, the respected editor of the *Manchester Guardian*. He had met Weizmann shortly after the outbreak of war, had acquainted himself thoroughly with the Zionist aims, and quietly but persistently thereafter saw to it that Weizmann and his colleagues met the key people in Whitehall; and his paper kept the problem in the public mind. In December Scott brought Weizmann to London to meet Lloyd George and Samuel.

"Lloyd George began to fire questions at me," runs Weizmann's account, "about Palestine, about our colonies there, about the number of Jews in the country and the number who could go there. Then I had the surprise of my life when Herbert Samuel interposed some helpful remarks. . . . Lloyd George pointed out that I ought to talk with Balfour and the Prime Minister, Asquith. At this point Herbert Samuel said—I could hardly believe my ears —that he was preparing a memorandum on the subject of a Jewish state in Palestine to present to the P.M."

Weizmann had supposed Samuel to be an anti-Zionist; but, though he found him instead an advocate, he seems never to have worked closely with him. The next move, however, was Samuel's. In January 1915 he presented his Memorandum on "The Future of Palestine" to the Prime

Minister. Asquith found it distasteful. Samuel, he noted, proposed "the British annexation of Palestine, a country the size of Wales, much of it barren mountain and part of it waterless. He thinks he might plant in this not very promising territory about three or four million European Jews and that this would have a good effect upon those who are left behind. It reads almost like a new edition of *Tancred* brought up to date. I confess I am not attracted by this proposed addition to our responsibilities, but it is a curious illustration of Dizzy's favorite maxim that 'race is everything' to find this almost lyrical outburst proceeding from the well-ordered and methodical brain of H. S."

More cold water was poured by the British ambassador in Paris, Lord Bertie, whom Weizmann sounded out. Lord Bertie, who was a Catholic, considered the whole thing "an absurd scheme" and trembled as to "what the Pope would say."

Meanwhile Samuel, having revised his Memorandum—though without toning it down, for it still spoke of "an autonomous Jewish State"—sent it back to the Prime Minister, with little effect except to elicit the petulant remark that this "dithyrambic" proposal found its only other partisan in Lloyd George, "who I need not say does not care a damn for the Jews or their past or their future but thinks it will be an outrage to let the Holy Places pass under the protectorate of 'agnostic, atheistic France.'"

Here Asquith was quite wrong, but he was temperamentally incapable of fathoming Lloyd George. In Balfour's opinion Lloyd George's interest was initially caught by the reappearance of the Old Testament in modern politics, and Lloyd George himself confessed that "when Dr. Weizmann was talking of Palestine he kept bringing up place names which were more familiar to me than those of the Western front." Indeed, there was hardly an Englishman to whom Dan and Beersheba did not mean more than Ypres or Passchendaele. In any event Asquith's disapproval did not matter in the long run. Under the stress of the war and divided councils he melted away before the more vigorous Lloyd George and finally disappeared from the scene altogether. For the time being, in a preliminary shake-up, Lloyd George moved nearer to direct control as minister of munitions, and at the same time Balfour entered what was now a coalition government as First Lord of the Admiralty. A year and a half were to pass before the line-up changed again, and it was not until Lloyd George became prime minister and Balfour foreign secretary, in December 1916, that the government began seriously to consider a public statement of policy on Palestine and opened official talks with the Zionists on the question.

But before that happened policy began to take shape in the field. We are still in the spring of 1915. The scene shifts to the Ottoman front. Two figures appear somewhere between Cairo and Damascus—"private eyes," one might call them today, for the War Office. In command at the War Office was a great and imaginative soldier, the onetime surveyor of the Holy Land, the savior of Khartoum, now the country's hero, Field Marshal Lord Kitchener. He had an eye for remarkable men. On his staff, buried at a desk job because he was undersized for the army, was a young archaeologist, an Arabic scholar, a wanderer of the lands from the Euphrates to the Nile who had just before the war done a survey of Sinai for the Palestine Exploration Fund. Perhaps it was this fact that led Kitchener to pick out T. E. Lawrence, a "desert man" like himself, and to send him to Cairo on what was vaguely called "military intelligence."

Ever since the proud days of Pasha Mehemet Ali rumbles of revolt against Ottoman rule had been heard from one corner or another of the Arab world. No one had paid much attention, but now it was suddenly to Britain's interest to mobilize what harassment of the Turk she could. The Arabs, ridden by their own rivalries, were of questionable value as allies, and their price was even more questionable; but Britain was now committed to the overthrow of the Turk and fully intended to take over his Arab dominions in some form or other. Whether by direct sovereignty, protectorate, or sphere of influence depended on how things developed; but it was necessary, or at least it would be convenient, to win the inhabitants over to her side.

Lawrence's dramatic adventures, the desert campaign, the disguises, the wooing of Hussein the old Sherif of Mecca and of his sons Feisal, the future king of Iraq, and Abdullah, the future king of Jordan, have passed into history. The promises concerning future autonomy and concerning the territory that it was to cover, made by Lawrence to the Arabs and confirmed in the correspondence between the Emir Hussein and Sir Henry MacMahon, are only tangential to this story, for they did not cover Palestine this side of the Jordan.

Before coming to them we must follow another figure in the story. Sir Mark Sykes, the one man who came the nearest to holding all the threads in his hand at any one time, and who, but for his sudden death, might have been able to bind them into a workable policy. In 1919, in the midst of the peace conference, he was stricken by influenza and died within five days at the age of forty. "Had he lived," wrote Ormsby-Gore, another veteran of the Arab Bureau, in which Sykes and Lawrence both served, "the history of the Near East would have been different. . . . The disastrous delays which followed the Armistice would never have been possible had Mark been alive, buzzing about the government offices, speaking in Parliament, interviewing everybody, compelling attention. . . ."

Sykes compelled Kitchener's attention in 1914 when, as a brilliant, erratic, adventurous foreign service officer, already widely traveled in the East, he was serving on the War Office general staff. "Sykes," said Kitchener, suddenly turning on him one day, "what are you doing in France? You must go to the East."

"What am I to do there?" Sykes asked.

"Just go there and come back," said the War Minister, whose distaste for written orders was an agony to his colleagues. But Sykes was not a man to need further instruction. He was off, he investigated, he prowled around, he interviewed, he came back. What he saw, more especially what he foresaw, shaped policy as it developed during the next four years. Like Lawrence, he exerted an influence far beyond his official position; Lawrence because he had the force that attaches to all dedicated men, Sykes because of his irresistible energy and enthusiasm. Both belonged in that long line of Englishmen possessed by the spell of the East, now fallen into neglect and decay, but once the teeming center of the world, in which the faith, the arts, the laws of nations had their birth. Upon such men the East exerted the imperative pull of a natal land. Like Lawrence, Sykes was gripped by a vision of a renaissance of the East, and both believed that the time was now at hand. With the sweeping away of the Ottoman pall the ancient Semitic peoples, Israel and Ishmael, could renew themselves and their land.

"I meant to make a new nation," wrote Lawrence in the *Seven Pillars of Wisdom*, "to restore a lost influence, to give twenty millions of Semites the foundation on which to build an inspired dream-palace of their national thoughts." The restoration of Israel he included in this dream-palace. "I back it," he said elsewhere, "not because of the Jews but because a regenerated Palestine is going to raise the whole moral and material status of its Middle Eastern neighbours."

Sykes's motive was the same. He came home determined to work for an Arab nation, and later, when he discovered the Zionists, he saw in their zeal and energy an auxiliary to the goal of Middle Eastern revival. "It might be the destiny of the Jewish race," he said, "to be the bridge between Asia and Europe, to bring the spirituality of Asia to Europe and the vitality of Europe to Asia."

At the moment what was urgent, coincidently with the

Dardanelles campaign designed to take Constantinople, relieve Russia, and annihilate the Turk, was a settlement among the Allies as to the future share of each in the Ottoman dominions. Sykes was picked to negotiate terms, and the Sykes-Picot Treaty, one of the most unpopular documents of the war, was the result. In an *ex post facto* explanation made available to Sykes's biographer, the Foreign Office described the treaty in a matchless phrase as one of "imperative expediency." One can see why. It was indeed the most delicate of problems. Each of the Allies was on tiptoe to gratify century-old ambitions and acutely sensitive to any pretensions by a fellow eagle to grab more than its share of the carcass. But how to deal out the spoils without at the same time upsetting the applecart of the Arab Bureau, which was just then slowly drawing Hussein nearer and nearer to revolt against Turkey by promises of hegemony as future king of the Arabs? Obviously secrecy was essential lest the Arabs catch a whiff and balk. Both sets of negotiations were running concurrently. While Sykes was bargaining in Petrograd and Paris, Sir Henry MacMahon was exchanging correspondence with Sherif Hussein, who had Lawrence at his elbow in Arabia. While the Sherif was being promised one form of sovereignty, his future territories were being allotted among the Allies under another form.

The Sykes-Picot Treaty, negotiated and signed in secrecy and never revealed until the Bolsheviks threw open the czarist files, was a pure imperialist bargain of the old pattern. It did allow for an Arab federation of states within Turkey's former dominions, but its terms, no matter how you stretch them, cannot be made to fit the pledge made to the Arabs. No promises having as yet been made to the Jews, their interests cannot be said to have been jeopardized. Sykes himself was not yet aware of the Zionists' existence (though he knew all about the dealings with Hussein), and anyway, if there was one thing clear in the dark maze of the Sykes-Picot terms, it was that Palestine was reserved for "special treatment" and not promised to anybody. All around it the former dominions of the Turk were most explicitly and exactly divided up, separated into Red and Blue zones, A and B areas, apportioned with regard to different levels of influence for ports, railroads, cities, districts, vilayets; this place promised to that power in return for that place to another power if the third power should not take a third place, and in the event that—Enough. But Palestine alone is designated a "Brown" zone and its fate left vague. The exact wording of the Treaty was: "Palestine, with the Holy Places, is separated from Turkish territory and subjected to a special regime to be determined by agreement between Russia, France and Great Britain."

Exactly the same exception of Palestine was made in the terms of a bargain then being committed to paper between MacMahon and the Sherif of Mecca. Britain was "prepared to recognize and support the independence of the Arabs," stated the critical letter, dated October 24, 1915, within certain limits and boundaries previously agreed on. But one area within these limits was explicitly excluded: namely, "the portions of Syria lying to the West of the districts of Damascus, Homs, Hama and Aleppo." This awkward phraseology simply means Palestine, a word that the experts could not use, because it always suffered from an unfortunate geographical inexactitude. In short, "the whole of Palestine west of the Jordan was thus excluded from Sir Henry MacMahon's pledge." The authority here speaking was Winston Churchill when, as colonial secretary in 1922, he lopped off trans-Jordan from the rest of Palestine.

No one, neither Feisal nor Lawrence nor Weizmann nor Sykes nor the Cabinet nor anyone else, thought of the promise to the Arabs as conflicting with the still inchoate plans for the Zionists, or even with the Balfour Declaration once it was issued. A huge bulk of territory was covered by the MacMahon promise to the Arabs, but not what Balfour

used to call the "small notch"* that was Palestine proper.
All the Arab claims of later years cannot conceal the fact
that both the old Sherif Hussein and Feisal, the active
leader, were cognizant of and acquiesced in the exclusion
of Palestine from the area of their promised independence,
whether or not they had any mental reservations. Even
after the British intention to make room in Palestine for
the Jews was made public they did not take exception.
When the Zionist Commission headed by Weizmann came
to Palestine in 1918, while the guns were still firing, it was
greeted by an article in the Mecca paper, published under
Sherif Hussein's name, that exhorted the Arabs to welcome the Jews as brethren and to co-operate for the common welfare. Weizmann visited Feisal at his desert headquarters in Amman, and there under the stars, with the
omnipresent Lawrence making the third of a remarkable
trio, the basis for a common understanding was reached.
Later, in Paris, it was put in the form of a written document, signed by Feisal and Weizmann, in which the Emir
agreed to "the fullest guarantees for carrying into effect
the British government's [the Balfour] Declaration of November 2, 1917," including "all necessary measures to encourage and stimulate immigration of Jews into Palestine
on a large scale." Feisal moreover addressed a letter to the
American Zionist delegates at the Peace Conference saying that the Arabs and Jews "are working together for a
reformed and revived Near East," that the Arabs wish the
Jews "a most hearty welcome home," that "there is room
in Syria for us both," and that "indeed, I think that neither
can be a real success without the other."

Only later, after the Hashimite family failed to unify all
the Arab lands and people, when they were pushed out of

*The area of Palestine under the Mandate, excluding Trans-
Jordan, was 10,434 square miles or about one per cent of the Arab
territories liberated in 1918 (now the states of Saudi Arabia,
Yemen, Jordan, Iraq, Syria, and Lebanon). The proportion in area
is about the same as that of Belgium to the whole of continental
Europe west of Russia.

Syria and lost Arabia to Ibn Saud, did a new set of Arab leaders maintain that Britain's pledge to the Jews had conflicted from the beginning with Britain's pledge to the Arabs. Only then was the MacMahon correspondence unearthed and construed as a *casus belli*. By this time the British, caught in the high tide of appeasement, were themselves engaged in a double effort to repudiate the Balfour Declaration and the terms of the Mandate and to look righteous while doing it. Government spokesmen dug Sir Henry's correspondence out of the files, shook off twenty years' dust, and declared with pained surprise that, in view of this pledge, there might indeed be some doubt of the validity of the Mandate. Nothing is more hollow than the air of sanctimony worn to cover a mean act; but there still remained participants in the original transaction willing to restate the facts. Feisal, Sykes, Lawrence, and Balfour were all dead before 1935, but Ormsby-Gore, who had served in the Arab Bureau throughout the negotiations, made it clear in Parliament that "it was never in the mind of anyone on that staff, that Palestine west of the Jordan was in the area within which the British government then undertook to further the cause of Arab independence."

Palestine west of the Jordan was the Holy Land, and it would never have done at all to leave the Holy Land under Moslem rule. Moreover the French absolutely refused to consent to Arab rule in Syria. But the chief reason why Britain left Palestine out of the pledged area was that military necessity was making her moral duty clearer than ever: Britain must occupy the place herself.

"The insistent logic of the military situation on the banks of the Suez Canal" had made this conclusion inescapable. The words were those of the *Manchester Guardian's* military correspondent, Herbert Sidebotham. On November 22, 1915 the *Guardian*, in an editorial written by Sidebotham, opened its campaign for the restoration of Israel in Palestine under a British protectorate. "There can be no satisfactory defense of Egypt or the Suez Canal so long as Palestine is in the occupation of a hostile or probably hostile Power," it stated. Arguing the case in terms of British self-interest, as Shaftesbury used to do while keeping his more pious motives to himself, the *Guardian* pointed out that in ancient times Egypt solved its defense problems through the existence of Judaea as a buffer state against the military empires of the north. "If Palestine were now a buffer state between Egypt and the North," it concluded, "inhabited as it used to be by an intensely patriotic race . . . the problem of Egypt in this war would be a very light one. It is to this condition that we ought to work. . . . On the realization of this condition depends the whole future of the British Empire as a sea Empire."

As a result of this editorial Sidebotham became acquainted with Weizmann, who urged him to expand the piece into a Memorandum for the Foreign Office. This Memorandum, presented early in 1916 to the Middle East Division of the Foreign Office, urged that the proposed buffer state be designed on an "ample plan . . . for if the second Jewish state should avoid the fate of the first, it should have room to breathe." The strategic advantage should appeal to "a rational British egoism"; but Mr. Sidebotham could not avoid mentioning the historic grandeur of the opportunity that now offered itself of restoring the Jewish state under the British crown. During the next six months Sidebotham, co-operating with the Manchester Zionists and with C. P. Scott in the background, advising, encouraging, opening channels, continued to publicize the idea through the British Palestine Committee, which he organized, and through its weekly publication, *Palestine*.

Then, fortuitously, a totally extraneous factor intervened that was to make many things coalesce. Britain had used up her timber supply, from which wood alcohol was made, from which in turn was derived acetone, an essential element in the manufacture of cordite. In the midst of war the prospect of every gun's going dead for lack of ammunition was not encouraging. Some method of producing a synthetic acetone had to be invented, and fast. Lloyd George, as minister of munitions, was "casting about for a solution," as he tells it, when he ran into C. P. Scott, "a friend in whose wisdom I had implicit faith." On being told of the search for a resourceful chemist, Scott recommended "a very remarkable professor of chemistry at Manchester" whose name was Weizmann. To employ a foreigner at such a very sore spot was risky, and Scott was uncertain of the man's birthplace—"somewhere near the Vistula," he thought. But he was sure of the professor's devotion to the Allies, because he knew that the one thing Weizmann cared about was Zionism, and he knew Weizmann to be convinced that only in an Allied victory was there hope for his people.

"I knew Mr. Scott to be one of the shrewdest judges of men I ever met . . ." says Lloyd George. "I took his word about Professor Weizmann and invited him to London to see me. I took to him at once . . . he was a very remarkable personality." Weizmann, who had long been privately at work on a fermentation process from starch, was promptly engaged to solve the government's difficulty. Within a "few weeks' time" (according to Lloyd George) he was ready with the process, although the problem of large-scale production and conversion of factories to new methods occupied him constantly up to the end of the war.

The acetone incident was crucial not so much in eliciting Lloyd George's promise of a reward for Dr. Weizmann's services as in bringing Weizmann permanently to London and, guided by the "indefatigable Mr. Scott," into contact with the makers of policy.

"Never in my life have I seen such a man as Dr. Weizmann," said Field Marshal Allenby some years later in Jerusalem. "He has the ability to convert everyone to Zionism by his infectious enthusiasm." In London in 1916–17 the hour had come, and by some unfathomable law of history the hour turns up the man. Weizmann's acetone work was under the auspices of the admiralty, where Balfour was now first lord. "You know," Balfour began when they met again, as if unconscious of any interruption since their last meeting. "I was thinking of that conversation of ours and I believe that when the guns stop firing you may get your Jerusalem."

The last stage began when Lloyd George became premier and Balfour foreign secretary in December 1916. They "talked the whole matter over," says Lloyd George, without saying more; but from then on official negotiations with the Zionists got under way. Months of furious maneuvering ensued over the claims of France in Syria, the objections of the Pope, the attitude of the United States, the effect on Russia, then swaying on the brink of revolution. The chiefest trouble was a raging controversy with the anti-Zionist English Jews, fueled in the Cabinet by the secretary for India, Edwin Montagu, and aired in the press by Alexander and Montefiore, president and secretary of the Jewish Board of Deputies. In those days the majority of respectable Jews still regarded Zionism as a mad delusion of "an army of beggars and cranks." A re-created homeland seemed to them, not the fulfillment of a dream, but the undermining of their hard-won citizenship in Western countries. Non-Jews could never understand this attitude. They ascribed it, in the words of the *Times*, to an "imaginative nervousness." On the other hand they recognized a familiar quantity in the nationalism of the Zionists, as in the nationalism of the Czechs or the Poles or the Arabs, with which they were quite accustomed to deal.

Those in the Cabinet, like Lord Curzon, who opposed the Balfour Declaration did so not because they sympathized with the anti-Zionist position, but because the Declaration committed Britain to an uncomfortable responsibility. Was not the country too far gone in decay to support a new population? Lord Curzon asked, and he warned against issuing a deliberately ambiguous statement that would allow the interpretation that a Jewish "state" was envisaged when it was questionable whether Britain was fully prepared to sponsor a state. He urged the government not to support a cause so pregnant of unresolved problems. From the point of view of practical policy he was, of course, right, as the future proved. But he was overruled.

Largely, the men in power approved the project. Lord Cromer, who had once dashed Herzl's hopes for El Arish, now astonished the Zionists by public approval of their goal in Palestine. Lord Milner, the Liberal imperialist who had succeeded to the War Office after the tragic loss of Kitchener, was one of the strongest advocates in the Cabinet. Lord Robert Cecil, whom Balfour brought in as his undersecretary, developed a personal enthusiasm for Zionism even warmer than that of his chief.

But the most dynamic of all was Mark Sykes, now strategically located as liaison officer for Middle Eastern affairs between the War Cabinet, the Foreign Office, and the War Office. In his scurrying to and fro among all the parties concerned with the Middle East he had discovered the Zionists, seen in them the engine that might turn the wheels of Middle Eastern revival, and therefore espoused their cause with all his characteristic energy and dash. He attended their meetings, laid out their strategy, arranged their appointments, told them whom to see and what to say. Up and down the corridors of Whitehall in Syke's wake "There were Zionists and rumors of Zionists," recalled Ronald Storrs, of his days in the War Office. Sykes would burst into his room bringing "a maximum of trouble and a maximum of delight"—exuberant or despondent according to the nature of some interview with Balfour or some change in the wording of the draft Declaration.

Whatever obstacle reared up to block the path—French claims or Vatican frowns or internal Zionist stresses—Sykes knew what wire to pull to clear the way. At any hour of the day or night any one of the Zionist leaders might be called by Sykes with a brain storm, a warning of some new antagonist, or a plan of new strategy. When Doctor Sokolow, representing the Continental Zionists, went on a mission to Rome in April 1917 he found that Sykes had been there shortly before, enroute to the East; he found hotel rooms reserved for him by Sykes, instructions at the Embassy for him from Sykes, at the Italian Ministry messages from Sykes, and every day telegrams arriving from Arabia from Sykes.

In that spring personal enthusiasm, for whatever reasons or from whatever source, was not of course what decided the War Cabinet to issue a public statement of Britain's intention to reopen Palestine to the Jews. Why did they do it? The motive was mixed; it differed with different individuals; and it has been endlessly disputed ever since.

They did it because they meant to take Palestine anyway for its strategic value; but they had to have a good moral case. The timing is important. When the Declaration was issued on November 2, Allenby's army had already begun its advance into Palestine in October, had taken Beersheba on the 31st, and was at the gates of Jaffa. Jerusalem would be next and was in fact taken five weeks later, on December 8. The awful moment when a British army would enter the Holy City had suddenly become a reality. The Balfour Declaration was issued to dignify that approaching moment, not only in the eyes of the world, but especially in the eyes of the British themselves. And not only the moment, but also the future. For the British meant not only to take Palestine, but likewise, by one expedient or another, to hold it. "We should so order our policy," wrote Mark Sykes in the middle of October to Lord Robert Cecil, "that, without in any way showing any desire to annex Palestine or to establish a Protectorate over it, when the time comes to choose a mandatory power for its control, by the consensus of opinion and desire of its inhabitants we shall be the most likely candidate."

To proclaim that Britain would enter Palestine as trustee for its Old Testament proprietors would fulfill this purpose admirably and above all would quiet the British conscience in advance. The gesture, far from being insincere or cynical, was essential to the British conscience. No advance in Britain's imperial career was ever taken without a moral case, even if the pretext were only the murder of a missionary or a native's insult to a representative of the Crown. How much more necessary was a good moral case when it came to the Holy Land, which of all places on earth had the most precious associations in men's minds! The conquest of Palestine would be the most delicate and unusual of imperial acquisitions, as Allenby signified when he dismounted at the Damascus gate in order to enter the Holy City on foot. It could not simply be popped into the colonial bag like Zululand or Afghanistan. More than any other people the English need to feel the assurance of rectitude. "I will explain the English to you," wrote Shaw at his most Irish. "His watchword is always duty. . . . He is never at a loss for an effective moral attitude. . . . There is nothing so bad or so good that you will not find an Englishman doing it, but you will never find an Englishman in the wrong."

Or, to put it another way, as one of Chamberlain's biographers did: "If the worst comes to the worst, England well to have a good case." And the same idea, yet again, can no doubt rely upon her good right hand; but it is also expressed with proper dignity in the magisterial tones of Lord Cromer: "In the execution of Imperialist policy . . . it is not at all desirable to eliminate entirely those considerations which appeal to the imaginative, to the exclusion of the material, side of the national character."

This was the purpose that the Balfour Declaration served: it provided the effective moral attitude, the good case. It appealed to the imaginative side of the national character. In short, it allowed Britain to acquire the Holy Land with a good conscience.

To be effective it had to be meant, and in 1917 it was meant. To regard it as half-hearted or as mere propaganda is to miss its significance entirely. The theory that it was issued to win the hearts of the Jews of the United States and of Russia is a windy product of the thirties, when the British, having become increasingly uncomfortable under the burden of living up to the terms of the Mandate, were aching to be rid of the responsibilities they had undertaken toward the Jews. The impression was allowed to take hold that the Balfour Declaration was after all nothing but a propagandist gesture flung out haphazardly in wartime.

This story falls apart at a touch. How could a Declaration favoring Zionism be expected to influence favorably the very people who would regard it with most distaste? Lloyd George says specifically in his *Memoirs* that it was hoped to secure for the Allies both the sympathy of the Jews of Russia, who "wielded considerable influence in Bolshevik circles," and "the aid of Jewish financial interests in the United States." But both these groups regarded Zionism with the most profound aversion. A child is not wheedled into friendliness by offers of castor oil. Lloyd George has tried to pretend that it was candy, but this is a fairy tale.* To capitalist Jews in America as to Bolshevik Jews in Russia, Zionism was undeniably castor oil, not candy. The influential American Jews who were in any position to render aid, moral, financial, or other, shared, with one or two exceptions like Justice Brandeis, the anti-Zionist attitude of their fellows in England. The British

---

* Lloyd George's afterthoughts on the motivation of the War Cabinet in issuing the Balfour Declaration have bewitched and bewildered all subsequent accounts of this episode. Unquestionably he doctored the picture. Why he did so is a matter of opinion. My own feeling is that he knew that his own motivation, as well as Balfour's, was in large part a sentimental (that is, a Biblical) one, but he could not admit it. He was writing his Memoirs in the 1930's, when the Palestine trouble was acute, and he could hardly confess to nostalgia for the Old Testament or to a Christian guilty conscience toward the Jews as reasons for an action that had committed Britain to the painful, expensive, and seemingly insoluble problem of the Mandate. So he made himself believe that the Declaration had been really a reward for Weizmann's acetone process or, alternatively, a propagandist gesture to influence American and Bolshevik Jews—an essentially conflicting explanation, neither so simple nor so reasonable as the truth.

government was certainly well enough acquainted with this attitude not to be in any doubt about it. They had been dealing for quite a while already with the implacable opposition of Edwin Montagu inside the Cabinet and the public protests of prominent Jews outside in the columns of the *Times*. The proposed Declaration had been debated by the Cabinet comma by comma, intermittently through the whole of 1917, to the accompaniment of anti-Zionist anguish, privately pleaded and publicly voiced. It is hardly likely, under these circumstances, that the Cabinet expected to woo the "well-connected" assimilationist Jews to America or Germany or any Western country by pronouncing what these Jews regarded as a sentence of doom upon assimilation.

The Jews of Russia were another matter. The mass was certainly pro-Zionist; but unfortunately it wielded no influence whatever. On the other hand the Jews who did wield some influence in Bolshevik circles were as anti-Zionist as the capitalist Jews abroad. As Marxists who believed that Jewishness would disappear in the international brotherhood of man, they despised Zionism as the worst kind of bourgeois nationalism. The Bolsheviks were at that moment on the very brink of power and threatening to make a separate peace with Germany, but the Balfour Declaration was hardly the right thing to lure those of them who were Jews into a pro-Allied mood sufficient to keep Russia in the war.

To assume that the British government was either so naive or so uninformed as to be ignorant of the anti-Zionism of the people they were supposedly attempting to influence is impossible. Lloyd George had a hard head and Balfour a cool one. Are we to believe that they, supported by Milner, Churchill, General Smuts, and most of the imperial War Cabinet, hardly novices in political experience, would have issued the Balfour Declaration so carelessly? "Hardly any step was taken with greater deliberation," Winston Churchill told Parliament some years later. The deliberation must have had some other objective.

Consciously or not, the objective was the British conscience, not the Jewish. As Lord Shaftesbury once wanted to restore the Jews for the sake of the Second Coming of the Christian Messiah, so now the British government repeated the experiment for the sake of imperialism's requirement of an "effective moral attitude."

On November 2, 1917, the foreign secretary, Mr. Balfour, made public the "following declaration of sympathy with Jewish Zionist aspirations which has been submitted to and approved by the Cabinet." Hammered thin to a form as innocuous as possible, it read:

"His Majesty's Government view with favour the establishment in Palestine of a national home for the Jewish people and will use their best endeavours to facilitate the achievement of this object, it being clearly understood that nothing shall be done which may prejudice the civil and religious rights of existing non-Jewish communities in Palestine, or the rights and political status enjoyed by Jews in any other country."

The wording had previously been communicated to and approved by President Wilson, although formal approval by joint resolution of Congress was not given until 1922, during the presidency of Harding. France and Italy adhered to the Declaration in February and May of 1918 respectively.

"Oh pray for the peace of Jerusalem" had once been Shaftesbury's motto. The Balfour Declaration, sounding over the roar of guns, seemed like a tocsin of peace and of a better world. Quite apart from what it meant to the Jews, it seemed to lift the spirits of others, at any rate of the editorial writers and speech-makers. It was hailed as the end of "the oldest of national tragedies," as the signal for great hopes, as the triumph of liberty, justice, and the self-determination of peoples, as the dawn of the Peace of Jerusalem for the whole world. The tyranny of the Turk would at last be crushed, Palestine would flow again with milk and honey, and, according to the Lord Mayor of Manchester, "the vision of the prophet Isaiah would be realised."

It marked not the birth of a nation, said Lord Robert Cecil, but "the rebirth of a nation. . . . I believe it will have a far-flung influence on the history of the world and consequences which none can foresee on the future history of the human race." Sykes, speaking at the same mass meeting, called by the Zionists to celebrate the Declaration, said that it opened a vision of a league of continents, of races, and of ideals. And Weizmann's cordial desert meeting with Emir Feisal a few months later almost seemed to prove him right. For a brief time an upsurge of good will and of enthusiasm was generated.

To the Jews, or to those of them who still repeated the old prayer "Next year in Jerusalem," the event was the first hope since the Fall of the Temple. Dr. Gaster, chief rabbi of the London Sephardic community, recalled the old legend that when the Temple was destroyed splinters from its stones entered the hearts of the Jewish people. "I feel the stone in my heart already loosening," he said. Later, in Jerusalem, the military governor, Ronald Storrs, watching the people waiting to greet Herbert Samuel, appointed as Palestine's first high commissioner, saw them "almost faint with happiness" and "moving as if in the glory and freshness of a dream come true."

Almost from that moment the glory began to wear off and the process of deterioration to set in, until it reached the day thirty years later when British destroyers fired on the ship named *Exodus* carrying Jewish refugees to the "National Home."

3. *In the trap of history: the mandate*

"The most important international obligation ever entrusted to a single nation" were the words used on one occasion by a British Labour peer, Lord Snell, to describe the Palestine Mandate. In reality the Mandate was not so much entrusted as it was seized, in a polite way, by Britain. British arms had made the conquest, and British arms were on the spot. The Mandate was no more than the inevitable recognition of an accomplished fact. But in assuming it the British committed themselves to an international obligation. They were, in fact, caught in a trap of their own setting.

The Mandate, not the Balfour Declaration, gave a footing in public law to the restoration of Israel in Palestine. The Balfour Declaration was simply a statement of policy that any subsequent government could have ignored, allowed to lapse, or even repudiated. But the Mandate was an international engagement, signed and ratified by the Principal Allied Powers acting through the League of Nations, and as such it raised the Balfour Declaration, which was incorporated in it, to the status of a treaty.

When the Turks capitulated on October 30, 1918 their Asiatic dominions, so long coveted by the powers of Europe, were nine tenths in British hands. Nominally Turkey, under the terms of the armistice, left her dominions at the disposal of the Allies, but practically speaking Britain was the only ally able to pick up the pieces. The Mesopotamian campaign had brought the British beyond Bagdad as far as Ramadi, near the traditional site of the Garden of Eden. The Palestine campaign left them in control of all that had been ancient Canaan. France was on the spot with only sufficient forces to claim or hold northern Syria, where her influence had always been predominant. Russia had been removed as an imperialist rival by the revolution. Germany, the latest contender, was of course, defeated. But the British were at last where they had wanted to be—from the Nile to the Euphrates, the land where it all began, Israel's Promised Land, the land that had felt the foot of every conqueror from Alexander to Napoleon, where Rome had held its sway, and then Byzantium and Islam. Now the British marched on Hadrian's roads, and their ships were anchored at Akaba on the Red Sea, where Solomon built his navy. They were in Cairo of the Pharoahs, in Nineveh and Babylon of the Assyrian kings, and they were in Jerusalem—the Jerusalem that for nearly a thousand years had appeared on medieval maps as the center of the world.

The problem that now faced the British was what to do with the inheritance; how to hold it without seeming to; how, without surrendering control, to make good the various pledges made in the course of acquiring it, to the Jews, to the Arabs, and to the French. The Sykes-Picot treaty, under which Palestine was to be left to an international administration, was now regarded as inoperative because of the disappearance of the Russian regime that had been a party to it. Some new arrangement was required. Moreover, since Sykes-Picot days a new intruder had wrought a change in the accepted European manner of dealing out colonial conquests. These things could no longer be handled in the old way. In the unaccustomed atmosphere of the Fourteen Points, diplomats had to pick their way warily. President Wilson was very insistent about the self-determination of peoples, and the would-be Mandatory was supposed to wait to be asked for by the native inhabitants.

At the Peace Conference in Paris Britain was coy about declaring herself a candidate for the Mandate. But in their own councils the British were clear as to their own intentions. Lord Curzon, who had long made the Middle East his specialty, told the Cabinet in December 1918 that Palestine was the "strategical buffer" for Egypt and the Suez Canal. The Canal must be defended from the Palestine side. The question of who was to be the "tutelar power," which the Cabinet was called to discuss prior to the departure of Lloyd George and Balfour for Paris, must be decided with this in mind. Only France, the United States, and Britain need be considered as possible candidates, and two of these Lord Curzon disposed of easily. France, he said, was not a serious candidate, because, "whatever may be her own feelings, nobody else wants her there." As for the United States, "I suggest that the Americans in Palestine might be a source not of assistance but very much the reverse to ourselves in Egypt." The answer was plain: Britain was the only possible "tutelar power," and fortunately both the Jews and the Arabs preferred her anyway. In the ensuing discussion Lord Robert Cecil, with an inkling of the future, remarked that "whoever goes there will have a poor time" and that it might be better to let the Americans have it. But the Cabinet closed with approval of Lord Curzon's recommendation.

At Paris there was a sea of words. The French wanted as much of Syria as they could enforce a claim to. The Americans, at least President Wilson, kept talking about self-determination. Number 12 of his Fourteen Points had said that in the disposition of the Turkish Empire the subject nationalities should be assured "an absolutely unmolested opportunity for autonomous development." Worse, he had included in the Covenant of the League the statement that "the wishes of the communities must be the principal consideration in the selection of the Mandatory." The Arabs had not yet even tasted the wine of independence, but its bouquet had gone to their heads. They wanted more and more autonomy over more and more territory every day. The Zionists wanted public assurance of their right to re-establish a Jewish nation in Palestine, and the anti-Zionists wanted everyone to forget the whole thing. The British wanted the "strategical buffer": Mesopotamia to protect the approach to India, Palestine to protect the Suez Canal.

Delays and difficulties in reconciling the conflicting interests dragged on for a year. Sykes, who might have made a synthesis, died. Lawrence, white-clad in flowing Arab robes, who shepherded King Feisal at the Peace Conference, eventually retired from Paris in disgust. Clemenceau grimly fought a losing battle with Lloyd George. Weiz-

mann, asked by Secretary Lansing in testimony before the
Supreme Council the crucial question, exactly what was
the meaning of "national home," gave his famous reply:
the opportunity to build up gradually in Palestine "a nationality which would be as Jewish as the French nation
was French and the English nation English."

There were public hearings in solemn and private ses-
sions in hotel rooms. There was even an American mission
to Palestine—from which the British carefully withheld
recognition—to ascertain the wishes of the local inhabitants. It might all have been spared. The governing fact
remained that while the diplomats disputed the British
army was in possession in the field. When no official agreement could be reached after a year of talk in Paris, the
existing facts took over, and it became unofficially assumed
that Britain would be the Mandatory.

The business of assigning the mandates was left to the
San Remo conference, which on April 25, 1920, to no one's
surprise, conferred the Mandates for Palestine and Mesopotamia on Britain. Palestine was a Class A Mandate: that
is, one under which the territory taken in charge was held
without provision for future independence. Actually, because of the postponement of a peace settlement with
Turkey, due to that country's foreign and domestic upheavals, it did not legally come into force until September
1923, after the peace treaty with Turkey had been finally
signed at Lausanne. By that time the seeds of trouble had
already sprouted daggers. But by that time, too, the civil
administration had already been operating for three years;
the Jewish Agency had been set up; a Zionist in spirit, Sir
Herbert Samuel, had been appointed and was governing
as the first high commissioner. It was too late to go back
to an old-fashioned colonial protectorate and too early to
repudiate pledges. Second thoughts had counseled the
British to separate Trans-Jordania under the 1922 White
Paper from the terms of the Mandate; but with that exception the Mandate was allowed to stand as drafted at

San Remo and as confirmed by the League and ratified by its members in 1922.

When the Mandate became public law the British undertook an international obligation that, in terms of *Realpolitik*, they conferred upon themselves. Only in legal fiction was the administration of Palestine a "mandate" from the League of Nations. "The League had in fact received the mandate from the Mandatory," a member of the Permanent Mandate Commission remarked wrily some years later. "We insisted upon having the mandate for Palestine assigned to us," the sober voice of the *Economist* has stated. "We, in substance, drafted the Mandate," one of the drafters, L. S. Amery, proclaimed.

There was, then, nothing unwitting or accidental about the obligation involved. It was self-assumed. It obligated the Mandatory explicitly, in the words of the preamble, to "be responsible for putting into effect the Declaration originally made on 2nd November, 1917 by the government of His Britannic Majesty and adopted by the said [Principal Allied] Powers in favor of the establishment in Palestine of a national home for the Jewish people." The next paragraph acknowledged that "thereby recognition has been given" to the grounds for "reconstituting" the Jewish home in Palestine. The fourth and fifth paragraphs "selected" Britannic Majesty as the Mandatory and recorded His Britannic Majesty's undertaking to exercise the Mandate "on behalf of the League of Nations and in conformity with the following provisions." These provisions, detailed in twenty-eight articles, start with the primary obligation. stated in Article 2, to "place the country under such political, administrative and economic conditions as will secure the establishment of the Jewish National Home."

Article 4 provides that "an appropriate Jewish agency shall be recognized as a public body for the purpose of advising and co-operating with the Administration of Palestine." Article 6 undertakes to "facilitate Jewish immigration and encourage close settlement by Jews on the land." Article 7 provides for the "acquisition of Palestinian citizenship by Jews." Thus four of the first seven articles dealt with the position of the Jews; the remaining twenty-one articles were technical. The Arabs, nowhere mentioned by name, were referred to only as "other sections of the population" or as "various peoples and communities" whose civil and religious rights and personal status were to be safeguarded. "Unquestionably," concluded the Peel Commission in 1937, "the primary purpose of the Mandate, *as expressed in its preamble and its articles,* is to promote the establishment of the Jewish National Home."

Lord Peel perhaps put the qualifying phrase in italics to indicate that there was also an unexpressed purpose of the Mandate: the imperialist purpose of the "strategical buffer." But in the Wilsonian era imperialist purposes were better left unmentioned. The logic of the sword had for over a hundred years been leading Britain physically to the Middle East. But for far longer than that the influence of the Bible had been at work, and it had established a pattern in which it became impossible to acquire the Holy Land simply as a "strategical buffer." A larger purpose and a higher aim had to be served. Thus, when Palestine came within reach Britain was trapped by her own history. In spite of uncomplicated imperialist intentions of the old school, conscience complicated matters terribly. It allowed Britain to acquire Palestine only by making room for the original owners. It put her, to her dismay, in the role of accoucheur to a new state.

For, regardless of the diplomatic egg dance in which Weizmann as well as the British government carefully stepped around any mention of the word "state," there was no question in anybody's mind that this was what was eventually contemplated. Balfour saw it clearly and said as much to the Cabinet when the final draft of the Declaration came up for decision. In explaining the phrase "National Home" he said that it did not necessarily involve the early establishment of an "independent Jewish State," but that this "was a matter of gradual development in accordance with the ordinary laws of political evolution." This was what the Cabinet understood by their own act. "There could be no doubt," the prime minister, Lloyd George, told the Peel Commission twenty years later, "as to what the Cabinet then had in mind. It was not their idea that a Jewish state should be set up immediately by the Peace Treaty.... On the other hand it was contemplated that when the time arrived for according representative institutions to Palestine, if the Jews had meanwhile responded to the opportunity afforded to them and had been a definite majority of the inhabitants, then Palestine would thus become a Jewish Commonwealth."

Other members of the War Cabinet were no less explicit. Mr. Churchill in an article for the press in 1920 foresaw "the creation in our lifetime by the banks of the Jordan of a Jewish State under the protection of the British Crown." General Smuts put it further off but foretold "in generations to come a great Jewish State rising there once more." In short, as the Peel Commission summed up the spoken and written evidence of the time, the nation's leaders and the press accepted the Mandate "in terms which could only mean that they contemplated the eventual establishment of a Jewish State."

POSTSCRIPT:

End of the Vision

Like another noble experiment the Mandate was flatly not a success. Its epitaph was spoken by Winston Churchill when the White Paper of 1939 canceled further Jewish immigration and land purchase thus ending the hope of a national home. "This," he said, "is the breach, this is the violation of the pledge, this is the abandonment of the Balfour Declaration, this is the end of the vision, of the hope, of the dream."

Yet the Mandate served a purpose. If to the British it was a perpetual headache and to the Arabs a national insult—or so they chose to regard it—to the Jews it was an opportunity, almost but not quite fatal. From the ruin of all the high hopes they wrested, by force of arms, at least the first half of that magic formula, "political independence and territorial integrity," the *sine qua non* of statehood. The tragedy did not lie in the necessity of fighting for independence (for an independence that is conferred and not fought for rarely endures) but in the enmity needlessly created which has defeated the dream of a regenerated Palestine restoring a lost influence and raising the moral and material status of the whole Middle East. Whether the political ambitions of the Jews or the intransigeance of the Arabs or the weakness of the British was chiefly responsible for the failure depends upon the individual point of view, at least while history is still smoking. Only a time-conferred objectivity can provide a final judgment.

348

Palestine was never more than a "small notch," as Balfour said, in the vast expanse of Arab lands freed by British arms after the last war. To the Arabs it represented one per cent of the area over which they were being given self-government by the British. To the Jews it represented their only hope of ever recovering home, country, and statehood. The framers of the Mandate, recognizing the relative equities involved, assumed under its terms a primary obligation toward the Jews. From the moment when the later and fatal fiction of a dual responsibility toward Arabs and Jews alike was adopted, the Mandate became unworkable.

Perhaps the fault was in the times. In another era less dominated by what Edmund Burke once called "the irresistible operation of feeble councils," the Mandate might have had a chance. Instead it became a long effort by Britain to escape the consequences that conscience had committed her to. The original pledge, which she soon found was awkward to keep, she attempted thereafter to whittle away, to invalidate, and at last, desperately weary of the entanglement, to cancel. The final years were spent in an attempt to stay on in Palestine as Mandatory after having repudiated the terms of the Mandate, until this position too became no longer tenable. "We decamp ignominiously," said Leopold Amery, another former colonial secretary, "amid carnage and confusion."

Does Israel, then, exist today because of the British or in spite of the British? As in the American colonies, England had laid the foundations of a state and then resisted the logical development of what she had begun until the original bond frayed out in bitterness and strife. The answer to the question must be neither one thing nor the other, but partly both—one of those unsatisfactory truths with which history so often defeats its interpreters.

BIBLIOGRAPHY AND NOTES

The author owes a profound debt to three sources of learning: The New York Public Library, Central Branch, without whose facilities this book could not have been written; the *Dictionary of National Biography*, edited by Sir Leslie Stephen and Sir Sidney Lee (referred to in the Notes as *DNB*); and Nahum Sokolow's *History of Zionism*, a pathfinding work of an earlier generation (now out of print), which pointed the way for this study.

The lists of Works Consulted which follow are in no sense meant as complete bibliographies of the subjects covered in the several chapters. They contain the essential sources but not general background material.

The abbreviations PPTS and EETS used in the Notes refer respectively to the Palestine Pilgrims Text Society and the Early English Text Society.

Notes to the Foreword

PAGE XIV. Curzon.—Speech opening a Palestine Exhibition at Basingstoke, 1908, reprinted in *Subjects of the Day*, Earl Curzon of Kedleston, London, 1915.

PAGE XIV. Thomas Huxley.—Quoted in *Cambridge History of English Literature*, IV, chap. II, 49.

PAGE XIV. "Insistent logic of the military situation...."—Herbert Sidebotham in the *Manchester Guardian*, November 22, 1915.

PAGES XIV.—XV. Professor Turner.—Preface to *Great Cultural Traditions*, Ralph Turner, New York, 1941.

PAGE XVI. Sir Horace Plunkett.—Quoted by D. C. Somervell in his *British Empire and Commonwealth*, London, 1954, p. 204.

Works Consulted for Chapter I

I. SEARCH FOR AN ANCESTOR

Anglo-Saxon Chronicle, ed. and translated by J. A. Giles, Bohn's Library, London, 1849.

BALE, JOHN, *The Laboryous Journey and Serche of John Leylande for Englande's Antiquities,* 1549, reprinted Manchester, 1895.

BAYLEY, HAROLD, *Archaic England,* London, 1920.

BEDE, *Ecclesiastical History of England,* ed. and translated by J. A. Giles, London, 1843–44.

BORLASE, WILLIAM, *Antiquities of Cornwall,* 1769.

CAMDEN, WILLIAM, *Britannia,* 1586, first English ed. translated by Philemon Holland, 1610, ed. Richard Gough, 4 vols., 1806.

CHADWICK, H. M., *Origin of the English Nation,* Cambridge, 1907.

CHILDE, V. GORDEN, *The Dawn of European Civilization,* 4th ed., London, 1947.

ELTON, CHARLES, *Origins of English History,* London, 1882.

GEOFFREY OF MONMOUTH, *Historia Britonum,* in J. A. Giles, *Six Old English Chronicles,* Bohn's Library, London, 1848.

GILDAS, *De Excidio Britanniae.* Also in Giles, *Six Chronicles.*

GREEN, JOHN RICHARD, *History of the English People,* 4 vols., London, 1893. *The Making of England,* London, 1881.

GUEST, EDWIN, *Origines Celticae.,* ed. W. Stubbs, 1883.

HODGKIN, T., *History of England from the Earliest Times to the Norman Conquest,* London, 1906.

KEITH, ARTHUR, *The Antiquity of Man,* 1925.

MAC CURDY, GEORGE G., *Human Origins,* Vol. II, *The New Stone Age and The Ages of Bronze and Iron,* New York, 1926.

MACKENZIE, D. A., *Ancient Man in Britain,* 1922.

MILTON, JOHN, *History of England,* 1670.

NENNIUS, *Historia Britonum,* in Giles, *Six Chronicles.*

OMAN, SIR CHARLES, *England Before the Norman Conquest,* 8th ed., London, 1938.

PALGRAVE, SIR FRANCIS, *Rise and Progress of the English Commonwealth,* 1832, rev. ed., Cambridge, 1921.

PLUMMER, CHARLES, *Introduction to Bede's Historia Ecclesiastica,* Clarendon Press, Oxford, 1896.

STUBBS, WILLIAM, *Chronicles and Memorials of Great Britain and Ireland During the Middle Ages,* London, 1876. *Historical Introductions to the Rolls Series,* ed. A. Hassall, London, 1902.

TREVELYAN, GEORGE MACAULAY, *History of England from the Earliest Times to 1919,* 2d ed., 1937.

WRIGHT, THOMAS, *The Celt, the Roman and the Saxon,* 2d ed., London, 1861.

2 . THE PHOENICIANS

COOLEY, W. D., *History of Maritime and Inland Discovery*, 3 vols., London, 1846.

CORNWALL-LEWIS, SIR GEORGE, *An Historical Survey of the Astronomy of the Ancients*, London, 1862.

HAWKINS, SIR CHRISTOPHER, *Observations on the Tin Trade of the Ancients*, London, 1811.

HENCHEN, H. O'NEILL, *Archaeology of Cornwall and Scilly*, London, 1932.

HOLMES, T. RICE, *Ancient Britain*, 1907, rev. ed., Oxford, 1936.

HUGHES, JOHN, *Horae Britannicae or Studies in Ancient British History*, London, 1818.

JACKSON, J. W., *Shells as Evidence of the Migrations of Early Culture*, Manchester, 1917.

MASSINGHAM, H. J., *Pre-Roman Britain*, London, 1927.

SAMMES, AYLETT, *Antiquities of Ancient Britain derived from the Phoenicians*, London, 1676.

SMITH, GEORGE, *The Cassiterides, An Inquiry into the Commercial Operations of the Phoenicians in Western Europe Particularly with Reference to the British Tin Trade*, London, 1863.

WADDELL, L. A., *The Phoenician Origin of Britons, Scots and Anglo-Saxons*, London, 1924.

3 . ROMAN JUDAEA AND ROMAN BRITAIN

Cambridge Ancient History, Cambridge, 1934. Vol. X, chap. XXIII by R. Syme and R. G. Collingwood and chap. XXV, "Rebellion Within The Empire," by A. Momigliano.

CHEESMAN, G. L., *The Auxilia of the Roman Imperial Army*, Oxford, 1914.

COLLINGWOOD, R. G., *Roman Britain and the English Settlements*, Oxford, 1936.

GRAETZ, HEINRICH, *History of the Jews*, ed. B. Löwy, 6 vols., Philadelphia, 1891-95.

HAVERFIELD, FRANCIS, *Roman Occupation of Britain*, ed. G. Macdonald, 1924.

JOSEPHUS, FLAVIUS, *The Wars of the Jews*, translated by William Whiston, Everyman ed., London, 1915.

MARGOLIOUTH, MOSES, *History of the Jews in Great Britain*, London, 1851.

MOMMSEN, THEODOR, *Provinces of the Roman Empire from Caesar to Diocletian*, New York, 1887.

RABIN, MAX, *The Jews Among the Greeks and the Romans*, Philadelphia, 1915.

ROTH, CECIL, *A History of the Jews in England*, Oxford, 1949.

TACITUS, CORNELIUS, *The Works*, containing the *Annals*, the *History*, *Agricola*, etc., Oxford translation, Bohn's Library, 2 vols., London, 1854.

Notes to Chapter I

PAGE 1. Remarks by Dr. Thomas, Archbishop of York.—From the *Palestine Exploration Fund Quarterly Statement for 1875*, p. 115.

PAGE 2. Sir John Morris-Jones.—Taliesin, *Y Cymmrodor*, London, 1918, XXIII, p. 23.

PAGES 3.–4. Bede on the Cymbri.—*Ecclesiastical History*, Book I, chap. XV.

PAGE 4. Gomer.—Genesis, X, 1–5. Ralph de Diceto, a chronicler contemporary with Geoffrey of Monmouth, traced the geneology of the then reigning king, Henry II, back to Noah's son Shem rather than to Japheth. *See* Stubbs, Preface to his edition of Diceto in his *Chronicles and Memorials*.

PAGE 6. Phoenicians as pilots of King Solomon's ships.—I Kings, IX, 26.

PAGE 6. Ezekiel, XXVII, 12.

PAGE 7. Herodotus and the later classical geographers.—Strabo, Posidonius, Diodorus. *See* Cornwall-Lewis and T. Rice Holmes.

PAGE 7. Evidence of the shells.—Aristotle and Pliny reported the details of the Phoenicians' method of fishing for shells in wicker baskets and of the process they used for extracting the purple dye. The finding of shell middens in Cornwall and Somerset of fossils of *Murex trunculus* and *Purpura lapillus* is given in Jackson and Massingham.

PAGE 7. Phoenicians' discovery of Britain about 1400 B.C.—*See* George Smith.

PAGES 7.–8. Date of Stonehenge.—*See* Massingham.

PAGE 11. Titus' speech on the fall of Jerusalem.—Josephus, *Wars of the Jews*, Book VI, chap. VI.

PAGE 11. The Roman legions assembled for the siege of Jerusalem are given in Tacitus, *History*, Book V, chap. I and in Josephus, *Wars of the Jews*, Book III, chap. IV. All the legions known to have been in the East at the time of the Judaean rebellion have been listed by Mommsen. He also gives the legions that held Britain in 66 A.D. Facts on the use of British auxiliaries in the legions are from Cheesman.

PAGE 12. Dispersion of the Jews after the Revolt.—*See* Theodor Reinach, article on Diaspora in the *Jewish Encyclopedia. Also* Max Rabin.

PAGE 12. The brick dug up in Mark Lane.—*See* Margoliouth. The Bar Cochba coin found in London.—*See* Cecil Roth.

Works Consulted for Chapter II

Primary sources for the various versions of the legends concerning Joseph of Arimathea, arranged in chronological order, are the following:

1. *Historia Josephi* (The Narrative of Joseph of Arimathea), a part of the Gospel of Nicodemus. English translation in Walker, *Apocryphal Gospels, Acts and Revelations,* Edinburgh, 1873.

2. WILLIAM OF MALMESBURY, *De Antiquitate Glastoniensis Ecclesiae,* 1135, in J. R. Migne, *Patrologiae Cursus Completus,* Vol. CLXXIX, Latin ed. with index, 221 vols., 1878.

3. MAP, WALTER, *Quête du Saint Graal* and *Joseph d'Arimathie,* 1170, ed. F. K. Furnivall, Roxburghe Club, London, 1864.

4. SKEAT, WALTER, ed. This volume, published by the Early English Text Society, London, 1871, contains the following:

    a. "Joseph of Arimathea or The Romance of the Saint Grall or Holy Grail, an alliterative Poem, A.D. 1350," from the unique Vernon ms. at Oxford.

    b. Wynkyn de Worde, *The Lyfe of Joseph of Armathy. A Treatyse taken out of a book whych sometime Theodosius the Emperor found in Jerusalem in the pretorye of Pylate of Joseph of Armathy,* printed by Wynkyn de Worde, 1516. This version is based on the *Nova Legendia Angliae* by John Capgrave (1393–1464) which in turn was taken from the Latin verse version *Chronica de rebus Glastoniensis* by John of Glastonbury, *ca.* 1400.

    c. *De Sancto Joseph ab Arimathea,* printed by Richard Pynson in 1516, based on John of Glastonbury.

    d. *The Lyfe of Joseph of Armathia,* printed by Richard Pynson in 1520, English translation of John of Glastonbury.

5. LONELICH, HENRY, *History of the Holy Grail,* 1450, ed F. K. Furnivall, EETS, London, 1874.

6. MALORY, SIR THOMAS, *Morte d'Arthur,* 1470, ed. Eugene Vinaver, Oxford, 1947.

Secondary sources on the combined Joseph-Grail legends:

BROWN, A. C. L., *Origin of the Grail Legend,* Harvard University Press, 1943.

Cambridge History of English Literature, Vol. I, chap. XII, "The Arthurian Legend," by W. Lewis-Jones.

Catholic Encyclopedia, articles "Acta Pilati" and "Apocrypha."

GASTER, M., "Legend of the Grail," *Folklore,* Vol. 2, London, 1892.

KENNEDY, J., "Joseph of Arimathea and the Eastern Origin of the Grail," *Imperial and Asiatic Quarterly Review,* XXVII, No. 53, 1909.

KER, W. P., *The Dark Ages,* London, 1904.

NITZE, W. A., "Glastonbury and the Holy Grail," *Modern Philology,* Chicago, October 1903.

NUTT, ALFRED, *Legends of the Holy Grail,* London, 1902.

WESTON, JESSIE L., *From Ritual to Romance,* New York, 1920.

Works on Church History and the Chroniclers:

BRIGHT, WILLIAM, *Early English History,* Oxford, 1897.

BROWNE, G. F., *The Christian Church in These Islands Before the Coming of Augustine,* London, 1899.

Cambridge History of English Literature, Vol. I, chap. IV, "Latin Chroniclers from the 11th to 13th Centuries," by W. Lewis-Jones.

CAPES, W. W., *The English Church in the 14th and 15th Centuries,* London, 1900.

DNB, articles on William of Malmesbury, Walter Map, Capgrave, John of Glastonbury, etc.

FULLER, REV. THOMAS, *Church History of Britain,* 1655, ed. James Nichols, London, 1842.

HUNT, REV. WILLIAM, *History of the English Church,* 597-1066, London, 1901.

OLLARD, S. L., and G. CROSS, *Dictionary of English Church History,* London, 1912.

OMAN, SIR CHARLES, *England Before the Norman Conquest,* London, 1938.

Notes to Chapter II

PAGE 13. Joseph in the New Testament.—Luke, XXIII, 50-51, 53; Matthew, XXVII, 57, 59-60; Mark, XIV, 64, XV, 43-46; John, II, 23, XIX, 38-42.

PAGE 14. The contemporary writers in the 3d century A.D. were Tertullian and Origen. For these and for reference to the Council of Arles, *see* Oman.

PAGE 15. The quotation from Stubbs.—A. W. Haddan and W. Stubbs, *Councils and Ecclesiastical Documents Relating to Great Britain and Ireland,* Oxford, 1869.

PAGE 15. Council of Basle.—*See* Capes, Thomas Fuller, and *Catholic Encyclopedia,* article, "Basle Council." Original Latin text of English bishops' memorial, from which the English translation given here was made, is in A. Zelfelder, *England und das Bazler Konzil,* Ebering's *Historische Studien,* Berlin, 1913.

PAGE 16. John Hardyng's *Chronicle,* 1464, ed. Sir H. Ellis, London, 1812.

PAGE 17. Joseph as ancestor of Arthur.—Pynson's 1516 Latin version of John of Glastonbury. The passage reads: "Per quod patel, quod rex Arthurus de stirpe Josephus descendit." *See also* Alfred Nutt.

PAGE 18. The sword and Solomon's ship.—Lonelich. *Also* Wynkyn de Worde.

PAGE 19. The Grail symbols, the stone and fish.—*See* Gaster and Weston.

PAGE 19. Leviathan.—Psalms, LXXIV, 14.

PAGE 20. Broughton.—Quoted by Skeat. Other seventeenth-century church historians who discuss the claims of Joseph as first apostle are: Bishop Stillingfleet, *Origines Britannicae,* 1685, and Archbishop Ussher, *Britannicarum Ecclesiarum Antiquitates,* 1639.

PAGE 21. The description of Stone Age Glastonbury.—Jacquetta Hawks, *Prehistoric Britain,* Harvard University Press, 1953.

PAGE 21. The quotation from Professor Freeman.—"Glastonbury British and English," in *Proceedings of the Somerset Archaeological Society,* XXVI (1880), reprinted in *English Towns and Districts* by E. A. Freeman, London, 1883.

Works Consulted for Chapter III

Anglo-Saxon Chronicle, ed. J. A. Giles, Bohn's Library, London, 1849.

ARCULF, *Pilgrimage of Arculfus in the Holy Land,* ed. J. R. Macpherson, PPTS, 1889. *Also* in Wright and in Giles' *Bede.*

BEAZLEY, CHARLES R., *The Dawn of Modern Geography,* 3 vols., London, 1887.

BROWNE, G. F. Listed under Chapter II.

Cambridge Medieval History, planned by J. B. Bury, 8 vols., 1911-36.

COULTON, G. G., *Life in the Middle Ages,* 4 vols., Cambridge, 1929. *Medieval Panorama,* New York, 1938. *Social Life in Britain from the Conquest to the Reformation* (contemporary documents), Cambridge, 1918.

FULLER, THOMAS, *Church History*. Listed under Chapter II.

GUYLFORDE, SIR RICHARD, *Pilgrimage of . . .*, Camden Society, n.d.

HEATH, SIDNEY, *Pilgrim Life in the Middle Ages*, New York, 1912.

HODGKIN, R. H., *History of the Anglo-Saxons*, 2 vols., Oxford, 1935.

Informacion for Pylgrymes, Wynkyn de Worde, 1498, 1515, and 1524, ed W. Gordon Duff, London, 1893.

JONES, G. HARTWELL, *Celtic Britain and the Pilgrim Movement*, Society of Cymrodorion, London, 1912.

JUSSERAND, J. A. A. J., *English Wayfaring Life in the Middle Ages*, translated by L. Toulmin Smith, London, 1892.

MANDEVILLE, SIR JOHN, *Voiage and Travaile of . . .*, ed. J. O. Halliwell, 1839. *Also* in Wright. For discussion of Mandeville's identity, *see* DNB and *Encyclopaedia Britannica*.

MIGNE, J. P., *Patrologiae Latinae Cursus Completus*, 221 vols., Paris, 1844–64.

OMAN, SIR CHARLES. Listed under Chapter I.

POWICKE, F. M., *Christian Life in the Middle Ages*, Oxford, 1935.

SAEWULF, *Travels of . . ., in 1102 and 1103*, ed. Canon Brownlow, PPTS, 1892. *Also* in Wright.

STUBBS, WILLIAM, *Lectures on Medieval and Modern History*, 3d ed., Oxford, 1900.

TORKYNGTON, SIR RICHARD, *Ye Oldest Diarie of Englysshe Travell*, ed. W. J. Loftie, London, 1883.

WAY, WILLIAM, *Itineraries of . . . to Jerusalem, 1458 and 1462*, Roxburghe Club, London, 1857.

WILLIBALD, *Travels of . . ., A.D. 721–27*, ed. Canon Brownlow, PPTS, 1891. *Also* in Wrght.

WRIGHT, THOMAS, *Early Travels in Palestine*, London, 1848.

Notes to Chapter III

PAGES 22.–23. Jerome's letters and Paula's quoted in this chapter.—Migne, Vol. XXII, Epistle XLVI, col. 489 and Epistle LXVIII, col. 581.

PAGE 23. Palladius Galata.—Browne, p. 78. Quotation from *Historia Lausiaca*, Migne, Vol. LXXIII, chap. CXVIII, col. 1200.

PAGE 25. Mahomet's dream.—Washington Irving's *Life of Mahomet*, Everyman ed., chap. XII.

PAGE 25. Omar.—Temple cleaned of filth, R. A. S. MacAlister, article "Palestine," *Encyclopaedia Britannica*, 11th ed.

PAGE 25. El-Hakim.—*Cambridge Medieval*. Vol. V, chap. VI, 254.

PAGES 26.–27. Pelagius.—Fuller, *Church History*, Vol. I, 76. *Also* Browne, Hartwell Jones, *DNB*, *Catholic Encyclopedia*.

PAGE 30. *Dicuil, De Mensura Orbis Terrae.*—Wright, Introduction, p. xiv.

PAGE 31. Margery Kempe.—*The Book of . . .*, ed. S. B. March, Early English Text Society, London, 1940.

PAGE 34. Florence of Worcester.—*Chronicle of . . .*, ed. T. Forester, Bohn's Library, London, 1854.

PAGE 34. Ealdred.—From *Anglo-Saxon Chronicle,* quoted by Beazley.

PAGES 34.–36. Sweyn.—From *Anglo-Saxon Chronicle. See also* Hodgkin, Oman, *DNB.*

PAGE 39. Medieval maps.—Beazley.

PAGES 39.–40. Godric.—Coulton, Social Life, p. 415. *See also* Baring-Gould, *Lives of the Saints,* ed. 1872, V, 322–31. *Also DNB.*

PAGE 40. Ludlow Chapel.—Hartwell Jones.

PAGE 41. *Piers Plowman,* ed. Wright, London, 1856, I, 109.

PAGE 41. Heywood's "Four Ps."—J. M. Marly, *Specimens,* I, 484.

PAGE 41. Douglas.—*Froissart's Chronicles,* Everyman ed., 1906. chap. 1, p. 16.

PAGE 41. Abbot of Ramsey.—T. Wright, *Biographica Britannica Literaria,* London, 1892.

PAGE 42. Guilds.—Jusserand, p. 380.

PAGE 44. Ships full stuffed.—*Informacion.*

PAGE 45. Henry of Bolingbroke.—Stubbs, p. 198.

PAGE 47. Archbishop Sigeric.—Beazley.

PAGE 49. Erasmus.—Jusserand, p. 353.

PAGE 49. Wyclif.—*Ibid.,* p. 351.

Works Consulted for Chapter IV

ARCHER, THOMAS, *The Crusade of Richard I, Extracts from Contemporary Accounts,* London, 1888.

ARCHER, T., and C. L. KINGSFORD, *Story of the Crusades,* New York, 1895.

BOHN, H. G., *Chronicles of the Crusades, Being Contemporary Narratives of the Crusade of Richard Coeur de Lion* by Richard of Devizes, Geoffrey de Vinsauf, and the *Crusade of Saint Louis* by Lord de Joinville, London, 1848.

Cambridge Medieval History. Listed under Chapter III.

COULTON, G. G. Listed under Chapter III.

DANSEY, JAMES C., *The English Crusaders,* London, 1849.

DAVID, C. W., *Robert Curthose,* Harvard, 1920.

DAVIS, H. W. C., *England Under the Normans and Angevins,* London, 1905.

FULLER, THOMAS, *History of the Holy Warre,* London, 1639.

GIBBON, EDWARD, *Decline and Fall of the Roman Empire,* eds. Milman, Guizot, and Smith, 6 vols.

Itinerarium Regis Ricardi (Vinsauf). English text in Bohn's *Chronicles* and excerpts in Archer. Original in *Rolls Series* 38a, ed. Stubbs.

JACOBS, J., *The Jews of Angevin England,* London, 1893.

JOINVILLE, JEAN DE, *Crusade of St. Louis,* Everyman ed. *Also* in Bohn's *Chronicles.*

LANE-POOLE, AUSTIN, *Domesday Book to Magna Carta,* Oxford, 1951.

LANE-POOLE, STANLEY, *Life of Saladin,* London, 1920.

MICHAUD, J. F., *History of the Crusades,* translated by W. Robson, 3 vols., London, 1852. *Bibliothèque des Croisades,* 4 vols.

MILLS, CHARLES, *History of the Crusades,* 2 vols., London, 1822.

NORGATE, KATE, *England Under the Angevin Kings,* 2 vols., London, 1887. *Richard the Lion Heart,* London, 1924.

OMAN, SIR CHARLES, *A History of the Art of War in the Middle Ages,* 2 vols., London, 1924.

RAMSAY, J. H., *The Angevin Empire,* Oxford, 1903.

STUBBS, WILLIAM, *Historical Introductions to the Rolls Series,* ed. A. Hassall, London, 1902. (Includes Ralph of Diceto, Benedict of Peterborough, Roger of Hoveden, *Itinerarium Regis Ricardi,* Walter of Coventry.) *Lectures on Medieval and Modern History,* Oxford, 1900.

WILLIAM OF MALMESBURY, *Chronicle of the Kings of England,* ed. Giles, Bohn's Library, London, 1883.

Notes to Chapter IV

PAGES 50.–51. Bernard of Clairvaux.—Gibbon, VI, chap. LIX, 109.

PAGE 51. Effigies.—Richard Gough, *Sepulchral Monuments of Great Britain,* London, 1876.

PAGE 51. Saracen's Head.—C. W. Bardsley, *English Surnames, Their Source and Significations,* London, 1889.

PAGE 51. Foolish metrical romances.—*See* Appendix to Scott's *Talisman.*

PAGE 52. Richard's height.—According to Ramsey, p. 367, Richard was 6′ 2″.

PAGE 53. First Crusade, 30 vessels.—David, *Robert Curthose.*

PAGE 54. William of Malmesbury.—Quoted Gibbon, VI, chap. LVIII, note 77.

PAGE 54. English ships.—David, *Robert Curthose.*

PAGES 54.–55. Robert's Crusade.—*Ibid. Also* Dansey.

PAGE 55. Robert's weeping.—*DNB.*

PAGES 55.–56. Edgar Atheling.–*DNB*, David, Dansey.

PAGE 56. Heywood's *Four Prentices*.–*Ancient British Drama*, 3 vols., London, 1810.

PAGE 57. Urban's speech.–William of Malmesbury, Book IV, chap. II. *Also* Michaud's *History*, Book I, p. 49.

PAGE 57. Jews.–Gibbon, VI, chap. LVIII. *Also Cambridge Medieval*, Vol. II, chap. VII.

PAGE 58. Usury.–W. E. H. Lecky, *History of Rationalism*, New York, 1883, II, 266. *Also* H. W. C. Davis.

PAGE 58. Ritual murder.–Michaud's *History*, Book VI. *Also* H. W. C. Davis.

PAGE 58. Jews attacked in England in Third Crusade.–Contemporary authorities are Ralph of Diceto and William of Newburgh. *See* Stubbs, *Introductions*. *Also* Jacobs and Ramsay.

PAGE 59. Nine Worthies.–Caxton's Preface to *Morte d'Arthur*.

PAGE 59. Second Crusade, peopled heaven with martyrs.–Geoffrey of Clairvaux, quoted Dansey.

PAGES 59.–60. Alms-boxes.–Austin Lane-Poole.

PAGE 60. Henry's vow after Becket's murder.–Roger of Hoveden, Stubbs, *Introductions*.

PAGE 60. Pope Urban II died of grief.–Roger of Hoveden, quoted Mills II, 10.

PAGE 61. Saladin tithe.–Austin Lane-Poole.

PAGE 61. All things were for sale.–*Ibid.*, p. 350, quoting Richard of Devizes.

PAGE 62. "I would sell London. . . ."–*Ibid. Also* Norgate's *Richard*, Book II, chap. I.

PAGE 63. Henry of Cornhill.–*Pipe Roll 2 Richard I* in Archer.

PAGE 64. Two palfreys.–*Ibid.*

PAGES 64.–65. Richard's fleet.–Contemporary authorities are Roger of Hoveden, Ralph of Diceto, Richard of Devizes, and *Pipe Roll 2 Richard I*. *See* Stubbs' *Introductions*. *Also* Norgate's *Richard*, Book II, chap. II.

PAGE 65. Population of England *ca.* 1200, at the time of *Domesday Book*.–*See* S. R. Maitland, *Domesday Book and Beyond*, Cambridge, 1897, p. 437. At the time of the 1377 poll tax.–*See* David MacPherson, *Annals of Commerce*, 1805, I, 548. *See also* M. Postan, "Population in the Later Middle Ages," *Economic History Review*, 2d series, II, No. 3, London, 1950. Josiah Cox Russell, *British Medieval Population*, University of New Mexico Press, 1948.

PAGE 65. Owlde Roule.–Dansey.

PAGE 66. Bohadin.–Michaud's *Bibliothèque*, Vol. IV, passim. *Also* excerpts in Archer.

PAGES 66.–67. Siege of Acre and massacre of prisoners.—*IRR*, Bohadin, Roger of Hoveden in Archer.

PAGE 68. Melec Ric.—Stanley Lane-Poole, p. 357.

PAGE 68. Richard hindered by the King of France.—Richard of Devizes, quoted *Historians' History of the World*, VIII, 389, note 1.

PAGE 70. March to Arsuf.—*IRR* in Archer.

PAGES 71.–72. Johanna's proposed marriage.—Bohadin, *IRR*, etc., in Archer.

PAGE 72. Saladin's gifts.—Book I, chap. III in Bohn's *Chronicles*.

PAGE 72. Richard's remark on Jerusalem.—Joinville, chap. CVIII.

PAGE 74. Spirit of Melec Ric.—These stories all come from Joinville who was in Palestine 50 years after Richard. Gibbon, VI, chap. LIX; Michaud's *Bibliothèque*, IV, 304; Norgate's *Richard*, p. 262.

PAGES 74.–75. John de Camoys and Andrew Astley.—Dansey.

PAGES 75.–76. Osborne Gifford, Roger de Mowbray, Hugh de Hatton, Fulk.—Dansey.

PAGE 76. William de Pratelles.—*IRR* in Archer, etc.

PAGE 76. John took the cross.—Stubbs, *Constitutional History*, chap. XII, quoting Walter of Coventry.

PAGES 76.–77. Richard of Cornwall.—Joinville, Matthew Paris, Continuers of William of Tyre, Mills, Vol. II, chap. V. *Also DNB*.

PAGE 77. William Longsword.—*Ibid*.

PAGE 78. Simon de Montfort called Joshua.—In the "Song of Lewes," in *Political Songs of England from the Reign of John to that of Edward II*, ed. Thomas Wright, Camden Society, London, 1839.

PAGE 78. "A drum filled with wind." The Moslem poet was Essahib Giémal-Edden Ben-Matroub who composed verses on the departure of the French king.—Bohn's *Chronicles*, Appendix, p. 554.

PAGE 78. Edward's crusade.—Archer and Kingsford, chap. XXV; Mills, Vol. II, chap. VI; Fuller, *Holy Warre*, Book 4, chap. 29.

PAGE 78. Sir Joseph de Cancy.—*A Crusader's Letter from the Holy Land*, PPTS, 1890.

PAGE 79. Grand Master of the Templars.—*Historians' History of the World*, published by Encyclopaedia Britannica, 26 vols. and index, Vol. VIII, chap. VI.

Works Consulted for Chapter V

BROOKE, STOPFORD A., *History of Early English Literature*, London, 1892.

Cambridge History of English Literature, Vol. I, chap. VII, "From Alfred to the Conquest," Vol. IV, chap. II, "The Authorized Version and Its Influence."

COULTON, G. G., *Chaucer and His England*, London, 1937.

CRAWFORD, S. J., *The Old English Version of the Heptateuch, Aelfric's Treatise on the Old and New Testaments and His Preface to Genesis*, EETS, London, 1922.

DAICHES, DAVID, *The King James Version of the Bible*, Chicago, 1941.

FOXE, JOHN, *Actes and Monuments*, ed. Townsend and Cattley, 8 vols., London, 1839.

FULLER, THOMAS, *Church History of Britain*, ed. J. S. Brewer, 6 vols., Oxford, 1845.

GAIRDNER, JAMES, *Lollardy and the Reformation*, 2 vols., London, 1908. *The English Church in the 16th Century*, London, 1902.

HALL, EDWARD, *Chronicle Containing the History of England*, 1548, printed for J. Johnson, 4 vols., London, 1809.

HENSON, HERBERT H., "Bible, English" in *Encyclopaedia Britannica*, 11th ed.

HOARE, H. W., *Evolution of the English Bible*, London, 1901.

PENNIMAN, JOSIAH H., *A Book About the English Bible*, New York, 1919.

POLLARD, A. W., *Records of the English Bible*, Oxford, 1911.

SKEAT, REV. WALTER, *Aelfric's Lives of the Saints*, EETS, London, 1900.

STRYPE, JOHN, *Memorials of Thomas Cranmer, Archbishop of Canterbury*, 1694, Oxford, 1848–54.

TREVELYAN, GEORGE MACAULEY, *England in the Age of Wycliffe*, London, 1899.

WESTCOTT, B. F., *History of the English Bible*, rev. ed., New York, 1916.

WHITE, CAROLINE L., *Aelfric, A New Study of his Life and Writings*, Yale, 1898.

Notes to Chapter V

PAGE 80. Henry's Proclamation.—Foxe, V, 167.

PAGE 80. Arnold.—"Hebraism and Hellenism," chap. IV of *Culture and Anarchy*, 1869.

PAGE 81. Huxley.—Quoted *Cambridge Lit.*, IV, 48–49.

PAGE 82. Powys.—*Enjoyment of Literature*, New York, 1938.

PAGE 82. Anglo-Israel movement.—First formulated in 1794 by Richard Brothers, the Anglo-Israel movement attracted to itself over the next hundred years nearly two million followers in England and the United States dedicated to the proposition that the Anglo-Saxon people were in reality the Ten Lost Tribes of Israel (as distinct from the Jews representing the remaining tribe of Judah). Starting from the assumption that Jeremiah meant Britain when he referred to the "isles afar off," the theory was stuck together from bits and pieces of Biblical phrases, twisted out of context and mixed with scraps of pseudophilology based on the similarity of words and sounds. 'British' is derived from the Hebrew 'Berit' meaning 'covenant' and 'ish' meaning 'man'—ergo, 'man of the Covenant'; the Saxons were said to be 'Isaac's sons.' Brothers, who claimed he was a direct descendant of David and should replace George III on the throne, was arrested for treason but judged insane. Notable expressions of the theory are: Richard Brothers, *A Correct Account of the Invasion of England by the Saxons, Showing the English Nation to be the Ten Lost Tribes*, London, 1822; J. Wilson, *Our Israelitish Origin*, 1845; Edward Hine, *Identification of the British Nation with Lost Israel*, 1871. *Also* the following periodicals, *The Nation's Glory Leader, weekly* (irregular), 1875–80; *Our Race*, quarterly, 1890–1900; *The Watchman of Israel*, monthly, 1918–.

PAGE 82. Gladstone.—Introduction to *Sheppard's Pictorial Bible*.

PAGE 83. Lloyd George.—Weizmann, *Trial and Error*, New York, 1949, p. 152.

PAGE 83. Ruskin.—*Praeterita*, London, 1885, p. 1.

PAGE 85. Wyclif Bible, 170 mss.—Penniman.

PAGE 85. "Our bishops damn and burn. . . ."—Trevelyan's *Age of Wycliffe*.

PAGE 85. Archbishop Arundel.—*Ibid*.

PAGES 85.–86. *De Heretico Comburendo.*—*Ibid*.

PAGE 86. John de Trevisa.—Fuller, II, 381.

PAGE 86. Cost of Wyclif Bibles.—Coulton, p. 99.

PAGE 86. Load of Hay.—Foxe, IV, 218.

PAGE 87. Translations in Saxon times.—Penniman.

PAGES 87.–88. Bede on Caedmon.—*Cambridge Lit.*, Vol. 1, chap. VII. *Also* Penniman.

PAGES 88.–89. Abraham and Exodus. — Translated by Stopford Brooke.

PAGES 89.–90. Aelfric.—Caroline White, S. J. Crawford. *Also Cambridge Lit.*, I, chap. VII, 136 ff.

PAGE 89. Esther and Maccabees.—Skeat.

PAGE 91. Judith.—Brooke. *Also Cambridge Lit.*, I, chap. VII.

PAGE 92. "Boy that dryveth ye plough."—Foxe, V, 117.

PAGE 93. Roger Bacon on Hebrew.—Daiches.

PAGE 94. Constantine's dialogue with More.—Hall's *Chronicle*, pp. 762–63.

PAGE 94. Anthony Marler.—Westcott, p. 78.

PAGE 95. Burning of Tyndale's translation.—Foxe, V, 114–34.

PAGE 95. Clergy's petition of 1534.–Penniman.

PAGE 97. William Maldon's story.–Quoted by Pollard.

PAGE 97. Henry burns three Lutherans and three papists.–Gairdner's *Lollardy*, II, 289.

PAGE 97. Luther on Squire Harry.–*Letters and Papers of the Reign of Henry VIII*, XV, 737.

PAGE 98. ". . . in your open Tavernes."–Pollard.

PAGE 98. Porter's preaching and death.–Foxe, V, 451.

PAGE 98. Act of Parliament forbidding Bible to be read aloud.–Gairdner's *Lollardy*.

PAGE 99. Dr. Taylor's death at the stake.–Foxe, VI, 677.

PAGE 99. Latimer's last words.–Foxe, VII, 550.

PAGE 99. Caution to editors of Bishops' Bible.–Pollard.

PAGES 100.–101. Revisers of the King James Version.–Westcott, Pollard, Henson.

Works Consulted for Chapter VI

BENT, J. T., *Early Voyages and Travels in the Levant*, Hakluyt Society, 1893.

CHEW, SAMUEL C., *The Crescent and the Rose; Islam and England During the Renaissance*, Oxford University Press, New York, 1937.

CUNNINGHAM, WILLIAM, *Growth of English Industry and Commerce*, 3 vols., Cambridge, 1892.

FOSTER, SIR WILLIAM, *English Quest of Eastern Trade*, London, 1933.

HAKLUYT, RICHARD, *The Principal Navigations, Voyages, Traffiques and Discoveries of the English Nation*, 12 vols., ed. MacLehose, Glasgow, 1903. Vol. V, 167–328, contains "The Renuing and Increasing of An Ancient and Commodious Trade into Diverse Places in the Levant" which includes many of the letters and transactions between the Queen and the Company as well as Harborne's reports and other documents covering the history of the Company from 1579 to 1585. Vol. VI, 73–104, covers the Second Levant Charter and Sir Edward Barton's first mission.

HOLINSHED, RAPHAEL, *Chronicles of England and Scotland*, 1577, 6 vols., London, 1807–8.

LITHGOW, WILLIAM, *Relation of the Travels of . . . in Candy, Greece, the Holy Land, Egypt and other parts of the East. In Purchas, His Pilgrimes (q.v.)* X, 447–92.

MORISON, FYNES, *An Itinerary Containing his ten Yeeres travel*, 1617, ed. MacLehose, 4 vols., Glasgow, 1907.

PURCHAS, SAMUEL, *Hakluytus Posthumous* or *Purchas, His Pilgrimes, Contayning a History of the World in Sea Voyages and Lande Travells by Englishmen and Others*, 1625, ed. MacLehose, 20 vols., Glasgow, 1905–7.

ROSEDALE, H. G., *Queen Elizabeth and the Levant Company*, London, 1904.

ROWLAND, ALBERT L., *England and Turkey; the Rise of Diplomatic and Commercial Relations*, University of Pennsylvania, 1924.

ROWSE, A. L., *The England of Elizabeth*, London, 1950.

SANDERSON, JOHN, *Travels of . . . in the Levant, 1584–1602*, ed. Sir William Foster, Hakluyt Society, 2d series, Vol. LXVII, London, 1931.

SANDYS, GEORGE, *A Relation of a Journey begun an. dom. 1610 containing a description of the Turkish Empire, Aegypt, the Holy Land . . . 1615*. In Purchas, His Pilgrimes (q.v.) VIII, 89–248.

TIMBERLAKE, HENRY, *A True and Strange Discourse of the Travailes of two English Pilgrims*, 1603, in *Two Journeys to Jerusalem*, printed for Nathaniel Crouch, London, 1704.

UNWIN, GEORGE, *Studies in Economic History*, Royal Economic Society, 1927, chap. V, "The Merchant Adventurers' Company in the Reign of Elizabeth."

WILLIAMSON, JAMES A., *Maritime Enterprise, 1485–1558*, Oxford. 1913. *The Age of Drake*, London, 1938.

WOOD, ALFRED C., *A History of the Levant Company*, Oxford University, 1935.

Notes to Chapter VI

PAGE 102. "Stirrers abroad."—*Epistle Dedicatorie*, Hakluyt, I, xviii.

PAGE 104. Purchas on pilgrimages.—Purchas, IX, 478.

PAGE 104. Ascribing sanctity to a place is Jewish.—Purchas, VIII, 19.

PAGE 106. "Divers tall ships of London. . . ."—Hakluyt's "The Antiquitie of the trade with English ships into the Levant," from *Voyages and Travels*, ed. C. R. Beazley, 2 vols., II, 181.

PAGE 106. Knolles on Lepanto.—*Generall Historie of the Turkes*, 1604, ed. Sir Paul Rycaut, 1700.

PAGE 106. Lafuente.—Quoted in *Historians' History of the World*, IX, 475.

PAGE 106. Bonfires burned on news of Lepanto victory.—Holinshed, IV, 262.

PAGE 107. Lecky on defeat of the Armada.—*History of Rationalism*, II, 320.

PAGE 107. "Inquisition dogs."—Tennyson's "The Revenge."

PAGE 107. Staper's tombstone.—Rosedale.

PAGE 108. Walsingham.—*State Papers Domestic*, Elizabeth, Vol. CXLIV, No. 7.

PAGES 108.–109. Charter of 1581.—Hakluyt, V, 192.

PAGE 109. Three mastifs and other gifts for the Sultan.—*Ibid*, 243.

PAGE 110. Nash on Harborne.—Wood.

PAGES 110.–111. Levant Company's earnings.—Hakluyt, V, 167–328, passim.

PAGE 110. Consulate opened at Aleppo.—*Ibid.*

PAGE 110. Cargo of "rawe silks."—Rosedale.

PAGE 111. Cotton weaving in Lancashire.—Rowse, p. 147.

PAGE 111. Coffee drinking among the Turks.—Sandys in Purchas, VIII, 89–248.

PAGE 112. Venetian ambassador on Elizabeth.—*Calendar State Papers*, Vol. VIII, No. 994.

PAGE 112. Snowball hits the French ambassador.—Rowland.

PAGE 113. "Stipendiary of merchants."—Wood.

PAGE 113. Barton's whores.—Sanderson.

PAGE 113. "A most wicked people."—Letter from Staper, *State Papers Domestic*, James I, Vol. XV, No. 4.

PAGE 113. "This happy Porte."—Quoted in Rowland.

PAGES 114.–115. Bacon's Holy War.—*Works*, III, 477, eds. Spedding, Ellis, and Heath, 7 vols., London, 1857–74.

PAGE 115. Biddulph.—Purchas, VIII, 248.

PAGE 116. Heywood's *English Traveller.*—Act I, Scene 1, *Dramatic Works*, 6 vols., London, 1879.

PAGE 117. Fynes Morison.—*Itinerary*, II, 1.

PAGE 117. Hakluyt on Jews.—Hakluyt, V, 271.

Works Consulted for Chapter VII

ARNOLD, MATTHEW, *Culture and Anarchy*, chap. IV, "Hebraism and Hellenism," London, 1869.

BARDSLEY, CHARLES W., *Curiosities of Puritan Nomenclature*, London, 1888.

Cambridge History of English Literature, Vol. VII, chap. VIII, "Scholars and Scholarship, 1600–60," by Professor Foster Watson.

CARLYLE, THOMAS, *Oliver Cromwell's Letters and Speeches*, 3 vols., 1884, Boston.

CROUCH, NATHANIEL (alias of Robert Burton), *Two Journeys to Jerusalem* and *Memorable Remarks Upon the Ancient and Modern State of the Jewish Nation*, etc., London, 1704, (first published 1683).

FIRTH, SIR CHARLES, *Cromwell's Army*, London, 1902. *Oliver Cromwell and the Rule of the Puritans in England*, London, 1900.

GARDINER, SAMUEL RAWSON, *History of England, 1603–42*, 10 vols., 1885–1900. *History of the Great Civil War, 1642–49*, 4 vols., 1901. *History of the Commonwealth and Protectorate, 1649–60*, 3 vols., 3d ed., 1901.

GRAETZ, HEINRICH, *History of the Jews*, Vol. V, chap. II, "Settlement of the Jews in England and Manasseh ben Israel."

MACAULAY, T. B., *History of England*, 5 vols., Philadelphia, 1861.

MARSDEN, J. B., *History of the Early Puritans to 1642*, London, 1850.

MASSON, D., *Life of John Milton*, 6 vols., Cambridge, 1859–80, index vol., 1894.

MORLEY, JOHN, *Life of Oliver Cromwell*, 1900.

NEAL, DANIEL, *History of the Puritans, or the Rise, Principles and Sufferings of the Protestant Dissenters*, 5 vols., new ed., London, 1822.

OSTERMAN, NATHAN, *The Controversy Over the Proposed Readmission of the Jews to England*, Jewish Social Studies, July 1941.

PATENKIN, DON, *Mercantilism and the Readmission of the Jews to England*, Jewish Social Studies, July 1946.

PRYNNE, WILLIAM, *A Short Demurrer to the Jewes Long Discontinued Barred Remitter into England*, 1656.

ROTH, CECIL, *A History of the Marranos*, Jewish Publishing Society of America, Philadelphia, 1947, chaps. IX and X, "The Dutch Jerusalem" and "Resettlement in England." *Life of Manasseh ben Israel*, Philadelphia, 1934.

SELBIE, W. B., "The Influence of the Old Testament on Puritanism" in *The Legacy of Israel*, eds. E. A. Bevan and C. Singer, 1927.

TREVELYAN, GEORGE MACAULAY, *England Under the Stuarts*, rev. ed., London, 1938.

WILLIAMS, ROGER, *The Bloudy Tenent of Persecution . . .*, 1644, ed. E. B. Underhill, Hansard Knollys Society, London, 1848.

WOLF, LUCIEN, *Manasseh ben Israel's Mission to Oliver Cromwell*, Jewish Historical Society, London, 1901. Contains full text of *The Hope of Israel, the Humble Address*, and the *Vindiciae Judaeorum*.

Notes to Chapter VII

PAGE 121. Cartwrights, *The Petition of the Jews for the Repealing of the Act of Parliament for their Banishment Out of England*, London, 1649.–Text in Patenkin, from a facsimile of the original in the Sutro Branch of the California State Library, San Francisco.

PAGE 123. Henry Jessey.—From *A Narrative of the late proceedings at Whitehall concerning the Jews*, 1655. Quoted by Osterman.

PAGE 123. Carlyle on "awful devout Puritanism."—*Cromwell's Letters and Speeches*, I, 32.

PAGE 123. Cromwell ". . . with his Bible and his sword."—From Macaulay's poem, "The Battle of Naseby."

PAGE 124. Bishop Sandys' Indictment.—Marsden.

PAGE 124. "We fight the Lord's battles."—From a letter to Major-General Fortescue quoted by Firth in *Oliver Cromwell*.

PAGES 125.–126. Macaulay on the Puritans.—*History of England*, I, chap. I, 71.

PAGES 126.–127. Charles receives the threat, "To thy tents, O Israel!"—Gardiner, *History of England*, X, 142. This incident occurred on January 5, 1642, after the King's frustrated attempt to arrest the five Members when he went to Parliament and found "the birds flown." That was January 4. The next day he went to the City to procure an order for the surrender of the Members from the Common Council while the streets filled with rumors and crowds. On his return to Whitehall, after failing to obtain the order, multitudes surrounded his carriage shouting, "Privileges of Parliament!" and one bold man with red hair thrust into his coach the pamphlet with the inflammatory title, "To thy tents, O Israel!" As Gardiner says, "The allusion to Rehoboam's deposition was one which Charles could not fail to understand." According to some accounts the bold man was the journalist Henry Walker who had sat up with his printer the whole of the previous night writing the pamphlet, handing the sheets of the copy to the printer to be set up in type as fast as he finished them. No copy of the tract, however, survives. *See* J. G. Muddiman, *Trial of King Charles the First*, Edinburgh and London, n.d., pp. 15–16.

PAGE 127. Psalm to celebrate Naseby. Firth, *Cromwell's Army*.

PAGE 127. Cunningham.—Listed under Chapter VI.

PAGE 128. Millenary Petition to James I.—Marsden, p. 252.

PAGE 128. Carlyle on the "last of all our heroisms."—*Cromwell's Letters and Speeches*, I, chap. I, 1.

PAGE 130. Extremist sects practiced Judaism.—Wolf, Introduction, p. xxi.

PAGE 130. £500 for Rabbi's Library.—Osterman.

PAGE 130. Leonard Busher.—Masson, III, 102.

PAGE 130. Bishop Hall on the fanatic sects.—Marsden.

PAGE 130. Council of Mechanics.—Wolf, Introduction, p. xix.

PAGE 131. Cromwell, "I would rather Mahometanism . . ."—Morley, p. 367.

PAGE 131. Sir Henry Finch.—Wolf, Introduction, p. xxi. *Also DNB*.

PAGE 131. Fuller on Finch.—*A Pisgah—sight of Palestine*, Book V, p. 194.

PAGE 132. Old Testament names.—Bardsley.

PAGE 132. Cowley's play, *Cutter of Coleman Street.* — Cited by Bardsley.

PAGES 132.–133. Ordinance on Hebrew and Greek.—Watson in *Cambridge Lit.*

PAGE 133. "Knit in Chaldee."—*The City Match*, Mayne, 1639.

PAGE 133. Pools, Ussher, Seldon, Leigh.—Watson in *Cambridge Lit.*

PAGE 133. John Aubrey on Milton.—Masson.

PAGES 133.–134. Pococke.—Watson in *Cambridge Lit. Also DNB.*

PAGE 136. Brett's account.—*Relation of the Great Council of the Jews in the Plains of Hungaria in 1650 to examine the Scriptures Concerning Christ*, by S.B., an Englishman there present. In Crouch.

PAGES 136.–140. Basic source material for Manasseh's mission and the resettlement was collected by Lucien Wolf. *See also* Roth's two books, and articles by Patenkin and Osterman.

PAGE 140. Cromwell's motives.—Wolf, Introduction, p. xxx, Patenkin, Roth. Bishop Burnet in *A History of His Own Times* (1724) says that when Cromwell understood the Jews' position in international trade, "he more upon that account, than in compliance with the principles of toleration, brought a company of them over to England and gave them leave to build a synagogue."

PAGES 140.–141. Oliver's speech to the Barebone Parliament.—Carlyle, II, 322.

PAGES 141.–142. Manasseh's *Humble Address.*—Wolf.

PAGE 143. Reaction to petition.—Prynne. *Also* Edward Nicholas, *An Apology for the Honorable Nation of the Jews and All the Sons of Israel*, 1648. *Israel's Condition and Cause Pleaded; or some Arguments for the Jews Admission into England*, by D.L., 1656. Quoted by Osterman. *See also* Wolf, pp. xli–xlvi.

PAGES 143.–144. Whitehall Council.—Henry Jessey's "A Narrative of the late Proceedings at Whitehall Concerning the Jews," *Harleian Miscellany*, VII, 623. *Also* "The Proceedings about the Jews in England in the year 1655" in Crouch. Other sources for the membership and debates of the Council are the *Thurloe State Papers*, IV, 321 ff., and *State Papers Domestic*, 1, 76 (1655), passim. *See* Wolf, pp. xlvii–lv. *Also* Gardiner, *History of the Commonwealth and Protectorate*, III, pp. 216–24.

PAGE 144. Cromwell's speech.—The person who commented that this was the best speech Cromwell ever made was Sir Paul Rycaut, a former diplomatic agent of the Levant Company and editor of Knolles' *History of the Turks. See* Wolf, p. liii, note 2.

PAGE 145. Readmission by "connivancy."—The author of the phrase was a certain Robinson, in a letter contained in the *State Papers Domestic* which is quoted by Gardiner, *History of the Commonwealth and Protectorate*, III, 221, note 3. William Godwin, while preparing his *History of the Commonwealth*, 1828, searched the records of the Bevis Marks Synagogue and found a cemetery lease dated 1656–57 indicating that the right of residence as practicing Jews, not as Marranos, was already acknowledged within a year of the Whitehall Council. *See also* Graetz, V, 49.

PAGES 145.–146. Charles II and the Jews.—Roth, Wolf.

Works Consulted for Chapter VIII

BENN, A. W., *History of English Rationalism in the 19th Century*, 2 vols., 1906, Vol. I, chap. III, "The English Deists" and chap. IV, "The 18th Century."

BUNYAN, JOHN, *The Pilgrim's Progress.*

CROUCH, NATHANIEL. Listed under Chapter VII.

FULLER, THOMAS, *A Pisgah-sight of Palestine and the Confines thereof with a Historie of the Old and New Testaments acted thereon*, London, 1650.

GIBBON, EDWARD, *Memoirs of My Life and Writings*, 1795. Included in Vol. I of *Decline and Fall*, eds. Milman, Guizot, and Smith.

LECKY, W. E. H., *A History of England in the 18th Century*, New York, 1883.

MACAULAY, T. B., article "Bunyan," *Encyclopaedia Britannica*, 11th ed.

MAUNDRELL, HENRY, *A Journey from Aleppo to Jerusalem at Easter, a.d. 1697*, Oxford, 1697.

POCOCKE, RICHARD, *Description of the East*, 3 vols., folio, 1743–45.

SHAW, THOMAS, *Travels and Observations Relating to Several Parts of Barbary and the Levant*, 1738.

STEPHEN, SIR LESLIE, *English Thought in the 18th Century*, 2 vols., 1876.

TREVELYAN, G. M., *English Social History, A Survey of Six Centuries*, illus. ed., 4 vols., London and New York, 1949–52.

TYRON, RICHARD, *Travels from Aleppo to the City of Jerusalem*, Glasgow, 1790.

Notes to Chapter VIII

PAGE 147. Trevelyan, "age of aristocracy and liberty. . . ."—*Social History*, III, chap. II, 47.

PAGE 149. Gibbon, "fat slumbers."—From his *Autobiography*.

PAGE 149. Macaulay on Bunyan.—From Macaulay's article, "Bunyan," in *Encyclopaedia Britannica*, 11th ed., p. 806, b.

Works Consulted for Chapter IX

ALLISON, ARCHIBALD, *History of Europe During the French Revolution, 1789–1815*, 10 vols., Edinburgh and London, 1839, Vol. III, chap. XXV.

BOURIENNE, *Mémoires*, 10 vols., Paris, 1829–32.

BULWER, SIR HENRY LYTTON (later Lord Dalling), *Life of Viscount Palmerston*, 3 vols., 1870–74. Covers only the period up to 1846.

BURCKHARDT, JOHN LEWIS, *Travels in Syria and the Holy Land*, London, 1822.

Cambridge History of British Foreign Policy, eds. Ward and Gooch, 3 vols., 1922–23.

CHATEAUBRIAND, RENE DE, *Itinéraire de Paris à Jérusalem*, Paris, 1811. English translation also 1811.

GREVILLE, CHARLES C. F., *The Greville Memoirs, 1814–60*, 7 vols., plus index vol., eds. Lytton Strachey and Roger Fulford, London, 1938.

GUEDALLA, PHILIP, *Napoleon and Palestine* (reprint of a lecture, 63 pp.), Jewish Historical Society, London, 1925. *Palmerston*, London, 1926.

IRBY, CHARLES LEONARD, and JAMES MANGLES, *Travels in Egypt, Nubia, Syria and the Holy Land, including a journey around the Dead Sea and through the country east of the Jordan*, London, 1844.

KINGLAKE, A. W., *Eothen*, London, 1844.

KOBLER, FRANZ, "Napoleon and the Restoration of the Jews to Palestine" in *New Judaea*, August, October, November, and December 1940 and February 1941.

LAMARTINE, ALPHONSE M. L., de *Voyage en Orient*, Vols. VI–VII of *Oeuvres Complètes*, 8 vols., Paris, 1842, in English translation, *Pilgrimage to the Holy Land*, 1832–33.

LECKY, W. E. H., *History of England in the 18th Century*, London, 1887.

MARRIOTT, JAMES A. R., *The Eastern Question, An Historical Study*, 4th ed., Oxford, 1940.

ROSE, J. HOLLAND, *Life of William Pitt*, 1923. *Life of Napoleon I*, 11th ed., London, 1934, chap. IX, "Egypt" and chap. X, "Syria."

ROSEBERY, EARL OF, *Life of Pitt*, London, 1898.

SEETZEN, ULRICH, *A Brief Account of the Countries Adjoining Lake Tiberias, the Jordan and the Dead Sea*, London, 1813.

TEMPERLEY, HAROLD W. V., *England and the Near East: The Crimea,* London, 1936. The subtitle is misleading. The book covers in minute detail the diplomatic history of the Eastern Question from 1830–54.

TREVELYAN, GEORGE M., *British History in the 19th Century, 1782–1901,* London, 1922.

Notes to Chapter IX

PAGES 161.–162. Pitt and Catherine and Turkey.—Rose's *Pitt,* chap. XXVI, pp. 585–606; Marriott, pp. 153–58; Temperley, pp. 43–46. *See also Cambridge BFP,* Vol. I, chap. I, "Pitt's First Decade."

PAGE 162. Burke, "disgusting empire."—*Parl. Hist.* XXIX, March 1791, 75–79. Quoted in Temperley, p. 44.

PAGE 161. "Wheresoever this carcase is. . . ."—Matthew, xxiv, 28.

PAGE 162. Earl of Chatham, "I am quite a Russ. . . ."—Quoted in Lecky.

PAGE 163. Proclamation to the Jews.—Text in Kobler. *See also* Guedalla's *Napoleon and Palestine.*

PAGE 163. Napoleon's Eastern expedition.—Allison; Rose's *Napoleon,* chap. IX, "Egypt" and chap. X, "Syria"; Bourienne, Vol. II; Marriott, pp. 164–92.

PAGE 164. Leibnitz.—A. L. Thiers, *Histoire de la Revolution Française,* 10 vols., Paris, 1828, IX, 63.

PAGE 165. Napoleon on glory in the East.—Bourienne, II, 82.

PAGE 165. Napoleon on Acre.—*Ibid.,* II, 243.

PAGE 166. Napoleon on Sidney Smith.—Allison, III, 486.

PAGE 167. Manqué à ma fortune.—Lucien Bonaparte, *Mémoires,* II, chap. XIV.

PAGES 167.–168. Lady Hester.—Some account of her may be found in every diary of Eastern travel of the period for no visit to Syria was considered complete without a glimpse of the famous recluse. Lamartine's account is the fullest.

PAGE 169. William Bankes.—*DNB.*

PAGE 170. "Occupier of the road to India."—Letter to Sir William Temple, Bulwer, II, 145.

PAGE 171. "Active Arabian sovereign."—*Ibid.*

PAGES 170.–172. Mehemet's career and the Syrian Crisis. Temperley, pp. 87–156; Marriott, pp. 225–49; *Cambridge BFP,* Vol. II, chap. IV, "The Near East and France" (covers the period 1829–47).

PAGE 172. Ponsonby, "Porte as vassal."—Foreign Office, Turkey, July 12, 1833, quoted *Cambridge BFP,* II, 166.

PAGE 172. Ponsonby, rising at 6 A.M.—Bulwer, II, 257. Bulwer, who was secretary of embassy of Constantinople at the time, was writing as an eyewitness.

PAGE 172. Ponsonby, "wholly erroneous."—F.O. 78/274, No. 52 of April 24, 1836, quoted Temperley, p. 75.

PAGE 173. Palmerston "very merry."—Greville, diary for October 7, 1840, IV, 308.

Works Consulted for Chapter X

BALLEINE, G. R., *A History of the Evangelical Party*, London, 1908.

BUNSEN, FRANCES, BARONESS, *A Memoir of Baron Bunsen*, 2 vols., London, 1868.

DALLING, LORD (Sir Henry Lytton Bulwer), and EVELYN ASHLEY, *Life of Lord Palmerston*, Vol. III, 1874, Vols. IV and V, 1876. This is a completion of the earlier life by Bulwer.

FINN, MRS., *Reminiscences*, London, 1929.

GIDNEY, REV. W. T., *The History of the London Society for the Propagation of Christianity Among the Jews from 1809 to 1908* (centenary vol.), London, 1908.

GOODMAN, PAUL, *Moses Montefiore*, Jewish Publication Society of America, Philadelphia, 1925.

HALEVY, ELIE, *A History of the English People in 1815*, (this is Vol. I of what was to become Halévy's *History of the English People in the 19th Century*), translated by Watkin and Barker, London, n.d., Book III, chap. I, "Religion."

HAMMOND, J. L. and B., *Lord Shaftesbury*, London, 1923.

HODDER, EDWIN, *Life and Works of the Seventh Earl of Shaftesbury*, 3 vols., London, 1886. (Invaluable and indispensable, not only for the subject of this chapter but for its information on the religious core of the Victorian age: Evangelicalism and the war between faith and science.)

HOLLAND, T. E., *The European Concert in the Eastern Question 1826–1885; A Collection of Treaties and other Public Acts*, Oxford, 1885.

HYAMSON, ALBERT M., *The British Consulate in Jerusalem, 1839–1914*, 2 vols., London, 1939. *British Projects for the Restoration of the Jews*, British Palestine Commission, London, 1917.

LONDON SOCIETY FOR THE PROPAGATION OF CHRISTIANITY AMONG THE JEWS, *Annual Reports*, 1809, passim. *Historical Notice*, London, 1850.

MONTEFIORE, *Diaries of Sir Moses and Lady Montefiore, 1812–1883*, 2 vols., ed. L. Löewe, London, 1890.

RODKEY, FREDERICK S., "Lord Palmerston and the Rejuvenation of Turkey," *Journal of Modern History*, June 1930.

TEMPERLEY, H. V. W. Listed under Chapter IX.

VICTORIA, *Letters of Queen Victoria, 1837–61*, 1st series, ed. A. C. Benson and Viscount Esher, 3 vols., 1907.

WARBURTON, ELIOT, *The Crescent and the Cross*, New York, 1845.

WOLF, LUCIEN, *Sir Moses Montefiore*, London, 1884.

Notes to Chapter X

PAGE 175. Palmerston's letter of August 11, 1840 (to Ponsonby).—F.O. 78/390, No. 134, in Rodkey. *Also* Temperley, p. 186 and note 275.

PAGE 176. Ashley, in diary of August 29.—This, and all subsequent quotations from Ashley's diary, letters, and speeches are from Hodder's *Life*, viz. Vol. I, chap. VI, 1838–39, VIII, 1840, IX, 1841, X, 1842 and Vol. III, chap. XXIII, "The Inner Life."

PAGE 177. Ashley "purest, palest. . . ."—A word portrait written in 1838, quoted by Hodder, I, 228.

PAGE 178. Dickens.—Hammond.

PAGE 180. 1798 Annual Register.—Trevelyan's *Social History*, IV, 29.

PAGE 182. Charles Simon.—Balleine.

PAGES 183.–184. Facts on Jews Society.—*Annual Reports, Historical Notice*, and Gidney, passim.

PAGE 183. Basil Woodd.—Balleine.

PAGE 183. "God of the Jews only?"—*Ibid.*

PAGE 185. Facts about Lewis Way.—Gidney and Society's *Annual Reports* and *Historical Notice*.

PAGES 185.–186. Facts about Rev. MacCaul.—*Ibid. Also* Mrs. Finn.

PAGE 186. "Knew little—cared less."—Mrs. Finn, *Reminiscences*.

PAGE 186. "Lawful owners."—*Ibid.*

PAGE 187. Lunacy Commission.—Hodder, Ill., 139

PAGE 188. "Errors and absurdities."—Gidney.

PAGE 188. Paul.—Romans, iv, 4.

PAGE 188. Simeon's sermon.—Delivered May 8, 1818, Society's *Annual Report* for 1818.

PAGE 189. Macaulay's speech.—April 17, 1833, in the House of Commons, reprinted in the *Works*, 12 vols., ed. Albany, London, 1898, XI, 540. Macaulay made his maiden speech on April 5, 1830, on the subject of the Jewish Disabilities Bill and a third speech on the same subject on March 3, 1841. He also contributed an essay on the Bill to the *Edinburgh Review*, January 1831.

PAGE 190. Consul's instructions.—F.O. 78/368, No. 2, January 31, 1839, Hyamson's *Consulate*.

PAGE 191. Young's census of the Jews.—Rodkey.

PAGE 191. Complaint about Young.—Hyamson's *Consulate*.

PAGE 191. Young upheld.—*Ibid.*; F.O. 78/368, No. 8, November 23, 1839.

PAGE 191. 40 books a year.—Compiled from Edward Robinson, *Biblical Researches in Palestine*, 3 vols., Boston, 1841, Vol. III, Appendix A is a chronological list of works on Palestine and Mount Sinai.

PAGE 193. Montefiore on Rosh Hashanah.—Goodman.

PAGE 193. "Palestine in the seat of the Jewish Empire."—Wolf, p. 276.

PAGE 194. "Begin . . . building in Jerusalem."—Wolf, p. 267.

PAGE 195. Damascus Incident.—Graetz, Vol. V, chap. XVII, "The Year 1840 and the Damascus Blood Accusation."

PAGE 195. Mehemet Ali's promise to Montefiore.—Montefiore, *Diaries*.

PAGES 195.–196. Memorials, etc. about the Jews.—Hyamson's *Projects*.

PAGE 196. Montefiore and Louis Philippe.—Wolf, pp. 109–10.

PAGE 196. Queen Victoria and Montefiore.—*Ibid.*, p. 62.

PAGES 200.–201. Palmerston's dispatches to Ponsonby.—F.O. Papers 78/427, No. 33 of February 17, 1841. The letter of February 17 is marked in the margin, "Appd. Victoria R."—Hyamson.

PAGE 201. Straits Convention.—*British and Foreign State Papers, 1840–41*, Vol. XXIV, London, 1857.

PAGE 201. "Antiquated imbecility."—Guedalla's *Palmerston*, p. 295.

PAGE 201. Aberdeen to Young.—Hyamson's *Consulate*.

PAGE 203. Gladstone to Bunsen.—Bunsen.

PAGE 203. Bunsen's call on Gladstone.—*Ibid.*

PAGE 203. Bunsen, "this is a great day. . . ."—Hodder, I, chap VIII.

PAGE 204. Palmerston, "I wrote to Ponsonby."—Ashley's diary, October 16, 1841 in Hodder, I, 377.

PAGE 204. Melbourne's grumble.—Bunsen.

PAGES 204.–205. Bunsen "moved to tears."—Letter to Ashley, August 13, 1841 in Hodder, I, 373.

PAGE 206. Aberdeen to Young.—F.O. 78/501, No. I, May 3, 1842, Hyamson's *Consulate*.

Works Consulted for Chapter XI

CHURCHILL, CHARLES HENRY, *Mount Lebanon*, 3 vols. London, 1853.

COHEN, ISRAEL, *The Zionist Movement*, rev. ed., Zionist Organization of America, New York, 1946.

DISRAELI, BENJAMIN, *Alroy, Coningsby, Contarini Fleming, Life of Lord George Bentinck, Tancred*.

EGERTON, LADY FRANCIS, *Journal of a Tour in the Holy Land*, London, 1841.

FINN, JAMES, *Stirring Times or Records from Jerusalem Consular Chronicles*, 2 vols., London, 1878.

FINN, MRS. Listed under Chapter X.

HYAMSON, ALBERT M. Listed under Chapter X.

KOBLER, FRANZ, "Charles Henry Churchill, A Zionist Pioneer. Centenary of the Damascus Episode," *New Judaea*, June-July 1941.

LINDSAY, ALEXANDER, LORD, *Letters from Egypt, Edom and the Holy Land*, London, 1838.

MARTIN, SIR THEODORE, *Life of H.R.H. the Prince Consort*, 5 vols., 1875–80.

MONYPENNY, W. F., and G. E. BUCKLE, *The Life of Benjamin Disraeli, Earl of Beaconsfield*, 6 vols., London, 1910–20. (Referred to in Notes as M and B.)

ROTH, CECIL, *Benjamin Disraeli, Earl of Beaconsfield*, New York, 1952.

SOKOLOW, NAHUM, *History of Zionism, 1600–1918*, 2 vols., London, 1919.

WARBURTON, ELIOT. Listed under Chapter X.

Notes to Chapter XI

PAGES 209.–210. Churchill's letter to Montefiore.—Cohen, p. 51.

PAGES 209.–210. Board of Deputies.—Kobler.

PAGE 210. Churchill's reply.—*Ibid.*

PAGE 213. Bunsen on Egerton's book.—Letter to his wife, July 13, 1841, Baroness Bunsen's *Memoirs*.

PAGE 214. Dr. Thomas Clarke.—Hyamson's *British Projects*.

PAGE 214. Samuel Bradshaw.—*Ibid.*

PAGES 214.–215. Rev. Crybbace.—*Ibid.*

PAGE 216. E. L. Mitford.—Cohen, p. 52.

PAGES 216.–217. Col. Gawler.—Hyamson's *Projects. See also* Cohen, p. 52.

PAGE 217. Prince Alfred.—Mrs. Finn's *Reminiscences*.

PAGES 217.–219. The Finns' work in Jerusalem.—*Ibid.*

PAGE 219. Consul Finns' correspondence with Foreign Office. F.O. 78 11274, Pd. No. 36, Hyamson's *Consulate*.

PAGE 220. Disraeli's speech on Emancipation, December 1847.—M and B, III, 69.

PAGE 221. "Gazed on Jerusalem."—From *Contarini Fleming* (his novel written while on the tour), part VI, chap. 4.

PAGE 222. Alroy as Disraeli's "ideal ambition."—M and B, I, 196.

Works Consulted for Chapter XII

AHAD HA'AM, *Essays, Letters and Memoirs (on Judaism and Zionism)*, ed. and translated by Leon Simon, Oxford, 1946.

BYRON, GEORGE GORDON, LORD, *Hebrew Melodies*, 1815.

COHEN, ISRAEL, *Zionism*. Listed under Chapter XI.

CROCE, BENEDETTO, *History of Europe in the 19th Century*, translated by Henry Furst, New York, 1933.

CROSS, J. W., *George Eliot's Life as Related in her Letters and Journals*, 3 vols., New York, 1885.

DUBNOW, S. M., *History of the Jews in Russia and Poland, from the Earliest Times to the Present Day*, translated by I. Friedlander, 3 vols., Philadelphia, 1916.

ELBOGEN, ISMAR, *A Century of Jewish Life*, Philadelphia, 1944. (Planned as a continuation of Graetz' History).

ELIOT, GEORGE, *Daniel Deronda*. "The Modern Hep Hep," (Essay XVIII in *The Impressions of Theophrastus Such*, 1879).

GOTTHEIL, RICHARD, *Zionism*, Philadelphia, 1914.

HALDANE, ELIZABETH S., *George Eliot and Her Times*, New York, 1927.

HESS, MOSES, *Rome and Jerusalem*, translated by M. Waxman, 2d ed., New York, 1945.

Jewish Encyclopedia. Articles on individuals mentioned.

KING, BOLTON, *Life of Mazzini*, Everyman ed.

LAZARUS, EMMA, *An Epistle to the Hebrews, from the American Hebrew*, 1882–83, republished Federation of American Zionists, 1900.

PINSKER, LEON, *Auto-Emancipation*, translated by D. S. Blondheim, New York, 1935.

SIMON, LEON, *Studies in Jewish Nationalism*, London, 1920.

SOKOLOW, NAHUM. Listed under Chapter XI.

STEIN, LEONARD, *Zionism*, 2d ed., London, 1934.

STEPHEN, SIR LESLIE, *George Eliot*, London, 1902.

Notes to Chapter XII

PAGE 224. "If I am not for myself, who will be for me."—A saying of Hillel the Great, Doctor of the Law at Jerusalem in the time of King Herod, chief theological authority of Palestinian Judaism until 500 A.D. *Jewish Encyclopedia*, VI, 398.

PAGE 225. Mazzini, *Duties of Man and Other Essays*, Everyman ed., 1915, p. 53.

PAGE 225. Graetz, "The Rejuvenescence of the Jewish Race."—Quoted Gottheil, p. 38.

PAGE 228. Hess.—For the early Zionists before Herzl *see* Sokolow, Vol. I. *Also* Cohen, Part I, chap. II, "The Advocacy of Restoration," and Part II, chap. III, " 'The Love of Zion' Movement"; Elbogen, Book 3, chap. I, "The Lovers of Zion," Gottheil, chaps. I, II, III.

PAGES 229.–230. Rabbi Kalischer.—Sokolow, I, 202 and II, 262.

PAGE 231. Smolenskin.—Cohen, p. 59 ff.

PAGES 231.–232. Lucien Wolf on Easter pogroms.—*Encyclopaedia Britannica*, 14th ed., article, "Anti-Semitism."

PAGE 233. Kattowitz Conference.—Sokolow, I, 188, 216.

PAGE 234. Jellinek.—*Ibid.*, I, 188.

PAGE 234. Weizmann on Rothschild.—*Trial and Error*, p. 162.

PAGE 237. George Lewes and Moses Hess.—*Universal Jewish Encyclopedia*, IV, 78.

PAGE 237. Leslie Stephen on *Daniel Deronda*.—Stephen's *George Eliot*, p. 189.

PAGES 237.–238. George Eliot's letter to Mrs. Stowe.—Cross, III, 212.

Works Consulted for Chapter XIII

ARNOLD, MATTHEW, *Culture and Anarchy*, 1869. *St. Paul and Protestanism*, 1870. *Literature and Dogma; An Essay Towards a Better Understanding of the Bible*, 1873. *God and the Bible*, 1875.

BESANT, SIR WALTER, *Thirty Years Work*, 1865–1895, London, 1895. (A history of the Palestine Exploration Fund.)

BENN, A. W., *History of English Rationalism in the 19th Century*, 2 vols., 1906.

Cambridge History of English Literature, "The Oxford Movement" by Rev. W. H. Hutton, Vol. XII, chap. XII, and "The Growth of Liberal Theology" by Rev. F. E. Hutchinson, Vol. XII, chap. XIII.

CARPENTER, J. E., *The Bible in the Nineteenth Century*, 1919.

CHEYNE, THOMAS K., *The Founders of Old Testament Criticism*, 1893.

COLERIDGE, SAMUEL TAYLOR, *Confessions of an Enquiring Spirit*, ed. H. N. Coleridge, 3d ed., 1853.

CONDER, CLAUDE REGNIER, *Tent Work in Palestine, A Record of Discovery and Adventure*, 2 vols., Palestine Exploration Fund, New York, 1878. *Memoirs of the Survey of Western Palestine*, 7 vols., Palestine Exploration Fund, 1883.

Essays and Reviews, Benjamin Jowett, Mark Pattison, Frederick Temple, *et al.,* 1860.

HALEVY, ELIE, *A History of the English People in the 19th Century,* Vol. III, 1830–41, Part I, chap. III, "Revolt of the Established Church and the Sects"; "Victory of the Church," translated by Watkin, New York, 1930.

Hasting's Encyclopedia, article "Criticism, O.T.," IV, 314.

LOWDERMILK, WALTER CLAY, *Palestine, Land of Promise,* New York, 1944.

MILMAN, HENRY HART, *The History of the Jews,* 3 vols., 3d ed., 1863.

MORLEY, JOHN, *Life of W. E. Gladstone,* 3 vols., 1903.

PALESTINE EXPLORATION FUND, *Quarterly Reports.* (Referred to in Notes as P.E.F.)

PROTHERO, ROWLAND, E., *Life and Correspondence of Arthur Penrhyn Stanley,* 2 vols., New York, 1894.

SMITH, WILLIAM ROBERTSON, article "Bible," in *Encyclopaedia Britannica,* 9th ed.

STRACHEY, LYTTON, *Eminent Victorians,* London, 1918.

TREVELYAN, G. M., *19th Century.* Listed under Chapter IX.

YOUNG, G. M., *Victorian England, Portrait of an Age,* Oxford, 1936.

Notes to Chapter XIII

PAGE 239. Prince of Wales' Tour of the Holy Land.—P.E.F., *Quarterly Reports. Also* Prothero's *Stanley.*

PAGE 239. Conder's contribution greatest since Tyndale.—Besant.

PAGE 240. Conder, "iron chain of Talmudic law."—*Tent Work.*

PAGE 242. Keble's Assize Sermon.—*Sermons, Academical and Occasional,* Oxford, p. 127.

PAGE 242. Pusey, 9 lectures a week.—*Cambridge Lit.,* XII, chap. XII.

PAGES 242.–243. Heresy trial of 1860.—*Ibid.,* chap. XIII.

PAGE 246. Donors to P.E.F.—Besant.

PAGE 246. Finn's Jerusalem Literary Society.—*Ibid.*

PAGE 246. Sir Charles Wilson.—*Report on the Survey of Sinai,* P.E.F., 1869.

PAGE 248. Conder, "not a mile of road."—*Tent Work.*

PAGES 249.–250. Shaftesbury's address to P.E.F.—P.E.F., *Quarterly Report,* 1875, p. 115.

PAGES 250.–251. Shaftesbury's article of 1876.—Sokolow, Vol. II, Appendix.

Works Consulted for Chapter XIV

ASHLEY, EVELYN, *Life of Henry George Temple, Viscount Palmerston*, 2 vols., 1879. A re-editing of the five-volume *Life* by Dalling and Ashley listed under Chapter X.

CECIL, LADY GWENDOLYN, *Life of Robert, Marquis of Salisbury*, 4 vols., London, 1929–31, Vol. II, chaps. IV–IX on the Eastern Question and the Congress of Berlin.

Cambridge BFP., Vol. II, chap. IV, "The Near East and France" (covers 1829–47), Vol. II, chap. VII, "Prelude to the Crimean War" (covers 1853–54), Vol. II, chap. VIII, "The Crimean War."

FITZGERALD, PERCY, *The Great Canal at Suez*, 2 vols.

FOREIGN OFFICE, *Syria and Palestine*, F.O. Historical Section, H.M. Stationery Office, London, 1920.

GLADSTONE, W. E., *The Bulgarian Horrors and the Question of the East*, London, 1876.

HEADLAM-MORLEY, SIR JAMES, *Studies in Diplomatic History*, New York, 1930.

HOLLAND, T. E., *Treaties*. Listed under Chapter X.

HOSKINS, H. L., *Routes to India*, New York, 1928.

MARRIOTT, J. A. R., *Eastern Question*. Listed under Chapter IX.

MARTIN, THEODORE, *Prince Consort*. Listed under Chapter XI.

MONYPENNY AND BUCKLE, *Disraeli*. Listed under Chapter XI.

Punch, Mr. Punch's History of Modern England, 1841, 1919, ed. Charles Graves, 4 vols., London, n.d.

SEELEY, JOHN R., *The Expansion of England*, London, 1898.

SETON-WATSON, R. W., *Britain in Europe, 1789–1914*, Cambridge, 1937.

TEMPERLEY, H. W. V., *Near East*. Listed Chapter IX. "Disraeli and Cyprus," *English Historical Review*, XLVI, (April 1931).

TEMPERLEY, H. W. V., and L. M. PENSON, *Foundations of British Foreign Policy, 1792–1902*, Cambridge, 1938.

VICTORIA, *Letters and Journal of Queen Victoria, 1862–1901*, 2d series, ed. G. E. Buckle, 5 vols.

WALPOLE, SPENCER, *Life of Lord John Russell*, 2 vols., London, 1889.

Notes to Chapter XIV

PAGE 252. Cromer, "imperious necessity. . . ."—Cromer's *Ancient and Modern Imperialism*, p. 20.

PAGES 252.–253. Million and quarter square miles.—*Ibid.*, p. 20.

PAGE 253. Chamberlain, "greatest of governing races."—S. H. Jeyes, *Joseph Chamberlain*, London, 1896, p. 245.

PAGE 253. Rosebery, "finger of the Divine."—*Question of Empire*, London, 1900.

PAGE 253. W. T. Stead, *Review of Reviews*, January 15, 1891.

PAGE 253. "Mania for grabbing," Labouchère in debate on the Sudan.—Hansard, 4, 38, 1030.

PAGE 253. "Fatal lust for empire."—From *Liberalism and Empire*, London, 1890. (Three anti-imperialist essays.)

PAGE 254. Nicholas' proposal to partition Turkey.—Martin's *Prince Consort*, I, 215; Temperley's *Near East*, pp. 255–57.

PAGE 255. Seeley, "We seem, as it were, to have conquered the people of half the world in a fit of absence of mind."—*Expansion of England*, p. 10.

PAGE 255. Quarrel over the Holy Places.—Temperley's *Near East*, chap. XI. For Crimean War, *see also Cambridge BFP*, Vol. II, chap. VIII and Marriott, pp. 249–85.

PAGE 255. Princess Lieven, remark to Lord Henry Lennox.—Quoted M and B, III, 524.

PAGE 256. Palmerston's reply to the Queen.—Guedalla's *Palmerston*.

PAGE 256. Treaty of Paris.—Text in Holland.

PAGES 256.–257. Lebanon incident.—*Cambridge BFP*. Also Seton-Watson.

PAGE 257. Text of the Lebanon protocol.—Holland.

PAGE 257. Russell on France in Lebanon.—Seton-Watson, p. 420.

PAGE 257. Gifford Palgrave.—*DNB*.

PAGE 258. Palmerston to de Lesseps.—Fitzgerald, I, 53.

PAGE 258. Mr. Disraeli's "large ideas."—*Letters of Queen Victoria*, II, 428.

PAGE 259. Salisbury, "zeal for the greatness of England."—M and B, VI, 624.

PAGE 259. Corry's account of Rothschild loan.—M and B, V, 447.

PAGE 259. Willy's letter.—M and B, V, 452.

PAGE 260. Disraeli, "dare I say to settle?"—Letter to Lady Bradford, M and B, VI, 14.

PAGES 260.–261. Queen's anxiety about Constantinople.—Letter to Disraeli, July 15, 1877, *Queen's Letters*, 2d series, II, 548.

PAGE 261. Jingo song.—*Disraeli* by D. L. Murray, Boston, 1927, p. 268.

PAGE 262. *Punch* cartoon.—*Mr. Punch's History*, Vol. III.

PAGE 262. *Times* correspondence on annexing Cyprus.—Headlam-Morley.

PAGE 262. Disraeli, "times for action."—M and B, VI, 381.

PAGE 263. Salisbury, letter to Layard, May 9, 1878.—Temperley and Penson.

PAGE 263. Salisbury, "taking the country for ourselves."—Letter to Layard, May 10, 1878, Temperley in *English Historical Review*.

PAGE 263. Salisbury, "nearer than Malta . . ." and proposed terms of alliance.—Quotations are from the two letters to Layard noted above.

PAGES 263.–264. Cyprus Convention.—Text in Holland.

PAGE 264. Bismarck on Disraeli.—M and B, VI, 311.

PAGE 264. Disraeli on Bismarck.—Letter to Tenterden, July 2, 1878, Temperley and Penson.

PAGE 264. King Leopold.—Letter to the Queen, July, 1878, M and B, VI, 344.

PAGE 264. Gortschakoff.—Letter from Crown Princess Frederick of Prussia (Queen Victoria's daughter) to the Queen, July 16, 1878, *Ibid.*

PAGE 265. "Sophisticated rhetorician."—M and B, VI, 356.

PAGE 265. Buckle's comment.—*Ibid.*, VI, 367.

Works Consulted for Chapter XV

CECIL, LADY GWENDOLYN, *Life of Salisbury*. Listed under Chapter XIV.

DRUCK, DAVID, *Baron Edmond de Rothschild,* New York, 1928.

FOREIGN OFFICE, *Syria and Palestine*. Listed under Chapter XIV.

HOGARTH, D. G., *The Nearer East*, London, 1902.

NAIDITCH, ISAAC, *Edmond de Rothschild*, translated by M. Z. Frank, Zionist Organization of America, Washington, D.C., 1945.

OLIPHANT, LAURENCE, *Land of Gilead*, London, 1881. *Haifa, or Life in Modern Palestine*, London, 1885. "The Jews and the Eastern Question," article in the *Nineteenth Century*, August 1882, 242–55.

OLIPHANT, MARGARET, *Memoirs of the Life of Laurence Oliphant*, 2 vols., New York, 1891.

REVISKY, ABRAHAM, *Jews in Palestine*, New York, 1935.

Notes to Chapter XV

PAGE 269. Deutsche Palästina Bank, railroad concessions, etc.—Foreign Office, *op. cit.*

PAGES 270.–271. Oliphant.—In addition to works listed, *see DNB*, article by Sir Leslie Stephen and notices of Oliphant in memoirs of the period.

PAGE 270. Henry Adams on Laurence Oliphant.—*The Education of Henry Adams,* Boston and New York, 1918, p. 139.

PAGE 275. Salisbury, "They have thrown it away into the sea. . . ."—Cecil, II, 326.

PAGE 275. Salisbury, "this sickly . . . Sultan. . . ."—*Ibid.,* letter to Sir William White, August 10, 1887.

PAGE 276. Salisbury explains Sultan's hate of England.—*Ibid.,* letter to Sir William White, September 14, 1891.

PAGE 277. Sultan's edicts on Jerusalem and Jewish colonies.—Foreign Office, *op. cit.*

PAGES 277.–278. Early Jewish colonizers.—Druck, Revisky.

PAGE 277. Figures on Jewish colonies.—Revisky.

PAGE 279. Rothschild, "only salvation of the Jewish people."—Speech at opening of the Hebrew University, 1925, quoted in Druck.

Works Consulted for Chapter XVI

See works on Zionism listed under Chapter XII, with the addition of the following:

AMERY, JULIAN, *The Life of Joseph Chamberlain,* Vol. IV, London, 1951. (This is the final volume of the *Life* of which the first 3 volumes were written by J. L. Garvin.)

BEIN, ALEX, *Theodor Herzl,* translated by Maurice Samuel, Philadelphia, 1940.

DE HAAS, JACOB, *Theodor Herzl,* 2 vols., New York, 1927.

HERZL, THEODOR, *Altneuland,* translated by J. de Haas, New York, 1902. *Der Judenstaat,* translated by J. de Haas, New York, 1904. *Diaries; Excerpts from the Tagebüche,* translated into English, New York, 1941.

Jewish Chronicle, London, files.

RABINOWICZ, OSKAR K., "New Light on the East Africa Scheme," a chapter in *The Rebirth of Israel; a Memorial Tribute to Paul Goodman,* various authors, London, 1952.

WEISGAL, MEYER, (ed.). *New Palestine: Herzl Memorial Issue,* New York, 1929 (a collection of memoirs by various writers).

WEIZMANN, CHAIM, *Trial and Error,* New York, 1949.

The pamphlet and periodical literature on Zionism is so voluminous that no attempt has been made here to list anything but the essential works.

Notes to Chapter XVI

PAGE 283. Ussishkin, "his eyes must not be opened."—Quoted by Dr. Julian Sternberg in Weisgal, *Herzl Memorial.*

PAGE 284. Herzl on France.—Bein, p. 116.

PAGES 284.–285. Herzl, "going out of my mind. . . ."—*Diaries,* June 16, 1895.

PAGE 287. Herzl's phrase, "a basis of recognized right and not of sufferance," achieved immortality under other auspices when Colonial Secretary Winston Churchill said in the White Paper of July 1922 that the Jews were in Palestine "as of right and not on sufferance."

PAGE 287. Herzl, "publicly recognized, legal guarantee."—Bein, p. 234.

PAGE 287. Rabbi Isaac M. Wise.—Central Conference of American Rabbis, *Yearbook for 1897–98.*

PAGE 287. Rabbi Güdeman.—Herzl's *Diaries,* January 6, 1897.

PAGES 287.–288. Harzl had not read *Auto-Emancipation.*—Gottheil, p. 89.

PAGE 288. Herzl refused to kiss Pope's hand.—Weisgal, *Herzl Memorial.*

PAGE 288. Herzl decrees frock coats.—Bein. p. 230.

PAGE 288. Basle Congress: "everyone sat breathless."—Observer was Ben Ami, Hebrew writer, quoted Bein, p. 232.

PAGE 289. Basle Program.—Cohen, p. 77.

PAGE 289. I.C.A.—Jewish Colonization Association.

PAGES 290.–291. Negotiations with the Kaiser.—Bein, chap. IX.

PAGE 292. Herzl, "England will understand us. . . ."—Bein, p. 346.

PAGE 293. Herzl, "the Archimedean point."—Message to Zionist Conference in London, February 28, 1898, quoted Cohen, p. 79.

PAGE 293. Herzl's interview with Rothschild.—Bein, p. 390.

PAGE 294. Chamberlain, on extending the Empire.—Speech, June 2, 1892.

PAGE 295. Salisbury, "most intelligent Englishman." — John Raymond reviewing A. L. Kennedy's *Life of Salisbury, New Statesman and Nation,* April 1, 1953.

PAGE 296. Baron Sonnino episode.—Wickham Steed, *Through Thirty Years,* New York, 1924, I, 163.

PAGE 297. Chamberlain's thesis, Jews as a "useful instrument."—Julian Amery.

PAGE 297. Balfour, "It was not Zionism."—From the Introduction to Sokolow.

PAGES 297.–298. Herzl's interview with King Victor Emmanuel.—Herzl's *Diaries,* quoted in Amery.

PAGE 298. Herzl's letter to Rothschild on El Arish. Bein, p. 390.

PAGES 298.–306. Herzl's interview with Chamberlain.—This, and the following account of the negotiations with Chamberlain, Lansdowne, Cromer, *et al*, is taken from Amery whose account is based on his own translation of Herzl's *Tagebüche*. *See also* Bein, chap. XIII, and Rabinowicz.

PAGES 303.–304. Kishinev pogroms.—Elbogen, pp. 376–89; Dubnow, III, 78.

PAGE 305. Greenberg on British offer involving "political recognition."—Rabinowicz.

PAGE 305. Text of the Draft Agreement with marginal comments by Lansdowne and Hurst.—F.O. 2 (785) Africa (East) Jewish Settlement, 1903, and is reprinted in full by Rabinowicz.

PAGE 307. Sixth Congress reception of the Uganda proposal.—Weizmann, pp. 83–88; Bein, chap. XIV.

PAGE 308. Herzl, "Don't do anything foolish when I am dead."—Letter to Wolffsohn, May 6, Bein, p. 500.

Works Consulted for Chapter XVII

ANTONIUS, GEORGE, *The Arab Awakening*, New York, 1939.

ASQUITH, H. H., *Memories and Reflections*, 2 vols., London, 1928.

BAKER, RAY STANNARD, *Woodrow Wilson and World Settlement*, 3 vols., New York, 1923.

BALFOUR, ARTHUR JAMES, *Opinions and Arguments*, New York, 1928. Preface to Sokolow's *Zionism*, 1919. *Retrospect, An Unfinished Autobiography*, 1930. *Speeches on Zionism*, ed. Israel Cohen, London, 1928.

BATTERSEA, LADY CONSTANCE, *Reminiscences*, London, 1922.

CHURCHILL, WINSTON, *Great Contemporaries*, New York, 1937.

DUGDALE, BLANCHE E. C., *Arthur James Balfour, first Earl Balfour*, 2 vols., New York, 1937.

GRAVES, PHILIP, *Palestine: the Land of Three Faiths*, London, 1922.

GREY OF FALLODON, *Twenty-five Years*, 2 vols., London, 1926.

HANSARD, *Parliamentary Debates*.

HUNTER-MILLER, DAVID, *My Diary at the Peace Conference*, printed for the author, New York, 1924.

LAWRENCE, T. E., *Seven Pillars of Wisdom*, New York, 1935.

LEAGUE OF NATIONS, *Minutes of the Permanent Mandates Commission*.

LESLIE, SHANE, *Mark Sykes: His Life and Letters*, New York, 1923.

LLOYD GEORGE, DAVID, *War Memoirs*, 3 vols., New York, 1933. *Memoirs of the Peace Conference*, 2 vols., Yale University, 1939 (published in England under the title, *The Truth About the Peace Treaties*).

MAC MAHON CORRESPONDENCE, *Parl. Papers, Great Britain*, 1938–39, *Command 5957*, London, 1939. *Also Command 5964 and 5974* covering British policy vis-a-vis the Arabs in the years 1915–18.

MANDATE, THE PALESTINE, Text, *Parl. Papers, Great Britain, Command 1785*, London, 1922.

MONTEFIORE, CLAUDE, *Liberal Judaism and Jewish Nationalism*, London, 1917. (One of many studies representing the Anti-Zionist point of view.)

PEEL, EARL, *Report of the Palestine Royal Commission, Command 5479*, July 1937.

RONALDSHAY, EARL OF, *Life of Lord Curzon*, 3 vols., London, 1928.

SAMUEL, HERBERT, VISCOUNT, *Grooves of Change*, New York, 1946.

SIDEBOTHAM, HERBERT, *Great Britain and Palestine*, London, 1937.

SOKOLOW, NAHUM. Listed under Chapter XI.

STORRS, SIR RONALD, *Memoirs*, New York, 1937.

SYKES, CHRISTOPHER, *Two Studies in Virtue*, New York, 1953.

SYKES, SIR MARK, *Dar ul-Islam, Record of a Journey through the Asiatic Provinces of Turkey*, London, 1904.

SYKES-PICOT TREATY, *The Secret Treaty of London, Command 671*, 1920.

WEIZMANN, CHAIM. Listed under Chapter XVI.

Notes to Chapter XVII

PAGE 311. Balfour, "quite fearless."—Churchill, p. 205.

PAGE 311. Dugdale, Balfour's life-long interest.—*Life of Balfour*, I, 324. All subsequent quotations from Mrs. Dugdale are from this book, chiefly Vol. I, chap. XIX, and Vol. II, chap. XI.

PAGES 311.–312. Lady Constance, "talked about the Jews."—Diary for September 6 and 7, 1895.

PAGE 312. Balfour, "why Palestine?"—Introduction to Sokolow.

PAGE 312. Meeting of Balfour and Weizmann.—Dugdale, I, chap. XIX.

PAGE 313. Weizmann's boyhood.—*Trial and Error*, p. 26.

PAGE 313. Storrs on Weizmann.—*Memoirs*, p. 439. All subsequent quotations from Storrs are from this book.

PAGES 314.–315. Weizmann's interview with Balfour.—*Trial and Error*, chap. VIII.

PAGE 315. Balfour's deathbed.—Dugdale, II, 303.

PAGES 315.–316. Balfour, Zionists as a conservative force.–Quoted Dugdale, II, 158.

PAGE 316. Balfour, speech in the Lords, June 21, 1922.–*Opinions and Arguments.*

PAGES 316.–317. Lady Constance, A. J. B. "hugely interested."–Letter to Mrs. Yorke, October 17.

PAGE 317. Another book of memoirs about the Rothschilds.–*Lady de Rothschild and Her Daughters, 1821–1931,* Lucy Cohen, London, 1935.

PAGE 317. Anti-Zionist position.–*See* Claude Montefiore. *Also* correspondence in the *Times* beginning with the Alexander–Montefiore letter of May 24, 1917 and replies from Lord Rothschild, Rabbi Hertz, Weizmann, *et al.*

PAGE 317. Balfour, "ancient antipathies."–Introduction to Sokolow.

PAGE 318. Lloyd George, reward for Weizmann.–*War Memoirs,* II, 50.

PAGES 321.–322. Samuel, Grey, and Lloyd George discussions.–Samuel, p. 174.

PAGE 322. Grey on "Jewish state."–*Ibid.*

PAGE 322. Grey inquiry at Petrograd.–Memorandum of British Embassy to Foreign Minister Sazonov, Stein, p. 138.

PAGE 322. Weizmann meeting with Lloyd George.–*Trial and Error,* p. 150.

PAGE 323. Asquith finds Samuel's memorandum "distasteful."–*Memories,* II, 59–60.

PAGE 323. Lord Bertie.–*Trial and Error,* p. 151.

PAGE 323. Asquith believes Lloyd George "does not give a damn." –*Memories,* II, 65–66.

PAGE 323. Lloyd George on Palestine place names.–*Trial and Error,* p. 152.

PAGE 325. Ormsby-Gore on Sykes.–Leslie, pp. 285–90.

PAGES 325.–326. Kitchener to Sykes.–Sokolow, II, xxvi.

PAGE 326. Lawrence, "I back it. . . ."–*Manchester Guardian,* May 20, 1935.

PAGE 326. Sykes, "destiny of the Jewish race. . . ."–Speech at the London Opera House meeting in celebration of the Balfour Declaration, December 2, 1917, quoted in Leslie.

PAGE 327. Foreign Office, "imperative expediency."–Leslie, p. 250.

PAGE 327. Arab Bureau promises.–MacMahon correspondence.

PAGES 327.–328. Sykes-Picot text.–*Command 671,* 1920.

PAGE 328. Churchill on MacMahon pledge.–Quoted *Peel Report,* p. 20.

PAGE 328. Balfour, "small notch."–Speech at Albert Hall, July 12, 1920, *Opinions and Arguments.*

PAGE 329. Hussein and Feisal acquiesced.—Hunter-Miller, XIV, 230.

PAGE 329. Mecca newspaper.—*Al Qibla*, March 23, 1918.

PAGE 329. Weizmann meeting with Feisal.—*Trial and Error*, chap. 21.

PAGE 329. Feisal–Weizmann agreement. — Text published in the *Times* (London), June 10, 1936.

PAGE 329. Feisal letter to Americans.—*Trial and Error*, p. 246.

PAGE 330. Ormsby-Gore in Parliament, speaking as colonial secretary.—Commons debate on Partition, July 21, 1937.

PAGES 331.–332. Lloyd George and C. P. Scott.—*War Memoirs*, II, 48.

PAGE 332. Allenby on Weizmann.—Speech at dedication of Hebrew University, reported in *New Palestine*, April 8, 1925.

PAGE 333. Balfour, "You may get your Jerusalem. . . ."—*Trial and Error*, p. 152.

PAGE 333. *Times*, "imaginative nervousness."—Article May 29, 1917 on controversy provoked by Alexander–Montefiore letter.

PAGE 333. Curzon's position.—Ronaldshay, III, 156–61.

PAGE 335. Sykes to Lord Robert Cecil.—Leslie.

PAGE 336. Shaw explains the English.—From his play, *The Man of Destiny*.

PAGE 336. One of Chamberlain's biographers.—S. H. Jeyes, *Life of Chamberlain*, p. 256.

PAGE 336. Lord Cromer.—*Modern Egypt*, New York, 1908, II, 109.

PAGE 337. Lloyd George's reasons.—*Memoirs of the Peace Conference*, II, 726 and chap. XXIII, passim.

PAGE 338. Churchill, "Hardly any step. . . ."—Commons debate on the MacDonald White Paper, May 23, 1939.

PAGE 339. Lord Mayor of Manchester, Cecil, Sykes, and Dr. Gaster. —All quotations are from speeches made at the London Opera House celebration of the Balfour Declaration on December 2, 1917.

PAGE 340. Lord Snell.—Debate in Lords on White Paper, 1939.

PAGES 342.–343. Cabinet meeting on "tutelar power."—Ronaldshay, III, 262–65. *Also* Lloyd George, *Memoirs of the Peace Conference*, II, 739–43.

PAGES 343.–344. Weizmann testimony at Supreme Council.—*Trial and Error*, p. 244. Lloyd George, *Ibid.*, II, 748.

PAGE 344. American mission.—The King–Crane mission, Hunter-Miller, XVI, 461.

PAGE 345. Permanent Mandates Commission member quoted.— *Minutes of the 17th Session*, June 3–21, 1930. Official No. C 355, M 147, 1930, VI.

PAGE 345. *Economist.*—March 1936.

PAGE 345. Leopold Amery.—Letter to the *Times,* May 14, 1948.

PAGES 346.–347. Balfour, Lloyd George, and Smuts on meaning of National Home.—*Peel Report,* pp. 24–25.

PAGE 347. Churchill in press article.—*Illustrated Sunday Herald,* February 8, 1920.

NOTES TO THE POSTSCRIPT

PAGE 348. Churchill, "This is the end of the vision. . . ."—Commons debate on the MacDonald White Paper, May 23, 1939.

PAGE 349. Leopold Amery, "We decamp ignominiously. . . ."—Letter to the *Times,* May 14, 1948.

INDEX

398 / BIBLE AND SWORD

France: and Crusades, xv, 51, 62, 64 (*see also* Philip Augustus); in Levant trade, 119–120, 164–165; Revolution, 147–148, 180, 225, 255; and Eastern Question, 170–174, 195–197; Commune, 225–226; anti-Semitism, 227, 284; in Syria, 229, 260, 330, 333, 341; in Crimean War, 255–256; in Lebanon, 256–257, 274; builds Suez Canal, 257–258; in World War I, 319–320; Sykes-Picot Treaty, 328, 342; as possible Mandatory, 342; at Peace Conference, 343

Francis I, 255

Franco-Prussian War, 258

Franks, xiii, 69; truce with Moslems, 77

Frederick, Crown Prince of Prussia, 267

Frederick William, King of Prussia, 203, 205–206

Freeman, E. A., 21, 51

Froude, James Anthony, 51

Fulk, Fitzwarin, 75–76

Fuller, Rev. Thomas: on Joseph of Arimathea, 20; on Crusades, 50; on Wyclif Bible, 86; on Sir Henry Finch, 131; on Palestine, 151–153

Galahad, 18, 19

Garibaldi, 271

Garstyne, Sir William, 303, 304

Gaster, Moses, Chief Rabbi, 340

Gawler, Col. George, 216–217

Genoese, in Crusades, 54

Geoffrey of Monmouth, 4

George V, 247

Germany, xv; anti-Semitism, 226–227; 231; Nürnberg laws, 232; Biblical scholarship in, 241–242; imperial rival in East, 254, 258, 265–266, 267–269 (*see also* William II)

Gibbon, Edward, 149

Gidney, Rev. W. T., 188

Gifford, Osborne, 75

Gildas, 3, 87

Gladstone, William Ewart: on Christianity's debt to Hebrews, 82; Evangelical beginnings, 181; on Jerusalem Bishopric, 203, 205; anti-imperialist, 253, 259, 274; on Turkish atrocities, 261; calls Cyprus Convention "insane," 264–266

Glastonbury Abbey, 13, 15–16, 17, 20, 21

Glyn, Justice, 143

Gobineau, Joseph, 283

Godfrey of Bouillon, 56

Godric, 39–40

Godwin, Earl, 35

Goethe, 226

Goldsmith, Col., 304

Gomer, 2–6

Gordon, General Charles George, 181, 247, 274

Gortchakoff, Prince, 264

About the Author

BARBARA W. TUCHMAN achieved prominence as a historian with *The Zimmermann Telegram* and international fame with *The Guns of August*, a huge best-seller and winner of the Pulitzer Prize. There followed five more books: *The Proud Tower*, *Stilwell and the American Experience in China* (also awarded the Pulitzer Prize), *A Distant Mirror*, *Practicing History*, a collection of essays, and, most recently, *The March of Folly*. *The First Salute* was Mrs. Tuchman's last book before her death in February 1989.